THE BIGOD EARLS OF NORFOLK
IN THE THIRTEENTH CENTURY

Framlingham Castle

THE BIGOD EARLS OF NORFOLK
IN THE THIRTEENTH CENTURY

Marc Morris

THE BOYDELL PRESS

First published 2005
The Boydell Press, Woodbridge
Paperback edition 2015

ISBN 978 1 84383 164 8 hardback
ISBN 978 1 78327 009 5 paperback

The Boydell Press is an imprint of Boydell & Brewer Ltd
PO Box 9, Woodbridge, Suffolk IP12 3DF, UK
and of Boydell & Brewer Inc.
668 Mt Hope Avenue, Rochester, NY 14620–2731, USA
website: www.boydellandbrewer.com

A CIP catalogue record for this book is available
from the British Library

Contents

List of Illustrations

To Cie, with love

Preface

This book is a biography of two men, an uncle and his nephew, who were consecutive earls of Norfolk during the thirteenth century. Both were called Roger Bigod, and were respectively the third and fourth heads of their family to bear that name, so I have distinguished them by calling them Roger III and Roger IV (see below, p. xviii). Like most medieval magnates, they are remembered, if only dimly, for their walk-on parts in the great drama of England's constitutional history. It was Roger III who led the march on Westminster Hall in 1258 and demanded that King Henry III expel his alien kinsmen and reform his realm, thereby launching the revolutionary programme which lasted until 1265. In similar fashion, Roger IV was the man who confronted Edward I in 1297, first by refusing the king's demand to fight in Gascony, and later by storming the exchequer to prevent the collection of an 'unconstitutional' tax.

On both these occasions the Bigods were to some extent maintaining a family tradition. Their namesake ancestor, Roger II, had taken a similar stand in 1215 against King John, and had been one of the twenty-five individuals charged with the enforcement of Magna Carta. His career lies outside the scope of the present study, but the problems he faced – the imperfections of 'Angevin' kingship and the inadequacies of the charter as a remedy – continued to be problems for his descendants. Only to a limited extent, however, can the motives of the Bigods in 1258 and 1297 be regarded as dependent upon the events of 1215; the very fact these crises were separated in each case by four decades should make us wary of ascribing individual involvement to a longstanding family position on constitutional matters. While the structure of this book, with its two largest chapters focused on 1258 and 1297, reflects the importance of these turbulent years in the careers of Roger III and Roger IV respectively, the aim in general has been to chart their careers from beginning to end. From this detailed analysis, other factors emerge which can be shown to have determined the earls' political agenda: their personal relationships with Henry III and Edward I, their grievances and ambitions, and even (to some degree at least) their personalities.

As earls, the Bigods were members of an extremely elite group: at the start of the thirteenth century there were never more than eighteen men in England who could claim the use of the title, and their number fell to as few as ten towards the century's close. The word 'earl' itself was a survival from the Anglo-Saxon period, and had originally been understood to mean something like 'provincial governor'. By the thirteenth century, however, although all earls continued to be styled toponymically (earl of Norfolk, earl of Pembroke, and so on), the days when they held unchallenged sway over a particular province were long gone. Royal government had expanded dramatically under the Angevin kings, and the

Crown now had agents – sheriffs, justices, coroners – it could appoint and remove at will to carry out its orders. To this extent, to be an earl was to be an anachronism, since the title itself conferred almost no territorial rights or special benefits. Yet it remained a highly prestigious distinction. In the thirteenth century, English lay society was much less strictly stratified than it would become in the later Middle Ages. Unless you were born a villein – an unfree peasant – the possibilities for advancement were almost limitless. Those who acquired sufficient wherewithal to maintain themselves in an appropriate style, for example, might take up arms as a knight. Knighthood, however, remained an accolade that could be bestowed by anyone; only a king, by contrast, could make a man into an earl. It was, therefore, still a much-prized and jealously guarded designation.[1]

Whether he was an earl or a knight (or, for that matter, a bishop or a priest) the amount of real power an individual exercised depended for the most part on crude material measures: how much money he had and, especially, how much land he controlled. Here the Bigods again outclassed almost all of their contemporaries. Even among the earls they were middle- to high-earners, a ranking which improved as the thirteenth century progressed thanks to the workings of inheritance and marriage. Their position in the rich-list is one aspect of their careers that this study establishes for the first time. Chapter Two provides an overview of their estate as it existed at the time of Roger III's accession and attempts to place a precise value on his landed income; Chapter Four explores how the estate developed during the career of Roger IV, and gives closer attention to the new lands which the Bigods acquired outside of East Anglia, in Wales and Ireland.

As well as owning a vast amount of private property (the manors and lordships they held 'in demesne'), the earls were also overlords to scores of lesser landowners. In some cases this tenurial relationship provided little more than an occasional windfall of additional revenue; in other instances, however, it could have (or be developed to have) a deeper political dimension. To dominate and control their localities, the Bigods sought to bind such lesser men to their side, while lesser men for their part sought to raise themselves by entering the earls' service. Precisely how this system worked, and especially how it evolved, have been in recent years the subjects of intense debate. The term 'bastard feudalism' is now generally used to describe it, while another term from the later Middle Ages, the 'affinity', has been imported to indicate the circle or circles of men who would surround a particular magnate. Sometimes these men were tenants of the magnate in question; more often, in the thirteenth

---

[1] In general, see D. Crouch, *The Image of Aristocracy in Britain, 1000-1300* (London, 1992), pp. 41-75. One special perquisite that earls did continue to enjoy in the thirteenth century was the 'third penny' of their county. Ibid., and below, p. 6n.

century, they were not. In Chapters Three and Five of this book I have tried to shed as much light as possible on the affinities of the earls of Norfolk: their size, their origins, and their quality. In both cases, the amount of suitable evidence for such an undertaking is very limited, and the conclusions therefore remain at best highly tentative. For this reason I have not offered a general rehearsal of the debates on 'the decline of the honor', the switch 'from tenure to contract', or the transition from feudalism to bastard feudalism, nor have I dared to launch an assault on any existing positions when my own seems so insecure. Instead, I have dealt with the Bigods as I found them, and drawn what I believe are credible interpretations of how they maintained – or failed to maintain – their power.[2]

At one stage I attempted to deal with the affinities of both earls in a single chapter. This made it easier to relate my findings to the existing debates, but had the disadvantage of rendering the findings themselves almost impossible to comprehend. The followings of Roger III and Roger IV are therefore treated separately (although I have sought to compare them where this is genuinely appropriate and when the evidence allows). Similarly, it would have been possible to corral the Bigods' financial affairs into a single section, but not one that I could imagine many readers negotiating from start to finish. The story of the family's debts to the Crown, for example, is a tortuous saga that extends across at least 140 years, from 1166 to 1306. Rather than attempting to recite it at a single sitting, I opted instead to discuss financial issues as and when they arose during the earls' careers, in the hope that the story would be more readily comprehensible and digestible. For those who would have preferred to take the debts undiluted, or wish to effect comparisons of their own between the earls' affinities, I hope that the index will prove an adequate guide. There is also at the end of the book a calendar of the charters issued by the Bigod family between 1177 and 1305. Those given by Roger III and Roger IV are described in detail, with lists of witnesses where these are known and further comment where it seemed appropriate. Grants by earlier generations of the family are described only briefly, and are included for comparative purposes and because in some instances they are mentioned in the main text. The majority of these charters (about 90 per cent) were transcribed by David Crouch, whom I would like to thank for his generosity and his permission to use them.

---

[2] For these debates, see P.R. Coss, 'Bastard Feudalism Revised', *Past & Present*, 125 (1989), pp. 27-64, and the subsequent exchanges between Coss, Carpenter and Crouch in *Past and Present*, 131 (1991), pp. 165-203. See also D. Crouch, 'From Stenton to McFarlane: models of society of the twelfth and thirteenth centuries', *TRHS*, 6th ser., 5 (1995), pp. 179-200; D.A. Carpenter, 'The Second Century of English Feudalism', *Past & Present*, 168 (2000), pp. 30-71; S.L.Waugh, 'From Tenure to Contract: lordship and clientage in thirteenth-century England', *EHR*, 111 (1986), pp. 811-39.

The following pages, therefore, shed new light on the last two Bigod earls of Norfolk, their lands, their affinities, their financial affairs and their politics. This, coupled with the book's somewhat idiosyncratic structure, give it some claim to originality. It will be readily apparent, however, that in its general approach this study seeks to emulate the work of others: John Maddicott's biography of Simon de Montfort and David Crouch's study of William Marshal have been especially inspirational. It is also indebted to earlier studies of comital families, such as those dealing with the earls of Gloucester and the earls of Huntingdon.[3] To a large extent the book is based on my doctoral thesis, submitted in 2003, and in the course of researching and writing it I incurred many large personal debts. My thanks go to the Arts and Humanities Research Board of the British Academy for the financial support which enabled the first three years of research from 1998 to 2001; also to the Institute of Historical Research for a Scouloudi Fellowship which paid for a further six months in 2002. Merton College made generous grants which enabled me to make regular trips to the then Public Record Office (now the National Archives) at Kew, to attend several important conferences, and to visit many of the sites connected with the Bigod family. I would also like to thank a number of individuals for their assistance and support. Paul Brand fielded several thorny legal questions; David Crouch, in addition to providing the charters, responded helpfully to email inquiries on a number of other subjects; Robert Stacey generously allowed me to consult his unpublished master's thesis on Roger II Bigod (1177-1221), and Nigel James of the Bodleian Library provided much-needed last-minute assistance with the map of East Anglia. More generally, I would like to thank David Carpenter, Rees Davies, Steve Gunn and Richard Huscroft for their support and advice. My biggest debt in this regard, however, is to my former supervisor, John Maddicott, both for the great care he took in nurturing the thesis to completion, and also for allowing its author time off to pursue other projects. Lastly, thanks (as always) to Catherine.

---

[3] J.R. Maddicott, *Simon de Montfort* (Cambridge, 1994); D. Crouch, *William Marshal: Knighthood, War and Chivalry, 1147-1219* (Harlow, 2002); M. Altschul, *A Baronial Family in England: The Clares, 1217-1314* (Baltimore, 1965); K.J. Stringer, *Earl David of Huntingdon 1152-1219 : A Study in Anglo-Scottish History* (Edinburgh, 1985).

Abbreviations

AM	*Annales Monastici*, ed. H.R. Luard (5 vols., Rolls Ser., 1864-69).
ANS	*Anglo-Norman Studies.*
Baronial Plan	Treharne, R.F., *The Baronial Plan of Reform, 1258-63* (2nd edn, Manchester, 1971).
BIHR	*Bulletin of the Institute of Historical Research*
BL	British Library.
Blomefield	Blomefield, F., *An Essay towards a Topographical History of the County of Norfolk* (11 vols., London, 1805-10).
Bury	*The Chronicle of Bury St Edmunds, 1212-1301*, ed. A. Gransden (London, 1964).
CACWales	*Calendar of Ancient Correspondence Concerning Wales*, ed. J.G. Edwards (Cardiff, 1935).
CChR	*Calendar of Charter Rolls* (HMSO, 1903-27).
CChW	*Calendar of Chancery Warrants, 1244-1326* (HMSO, 1927).
CCR	*Calendar of Close Rolls* (HMSO, 1892–).
CDI	*Calendar of Documents Relating to Ireland*, ed. H.S. Sweetman (5 vols., 1875-86).
CDS	*Calendar of Documents Relating to Scotland*, ed. J. Bain et al. (5 vols., Edinburgh, 1881-1988).
CFR	*Calendar of Fine Rolls* (HMSO, 1911-62).
CIM	*Calendar of Inquisitions Miscellaneous* (HMSO, 1916-68).
CIPM	*Calendar of Inquisitions Post Mortem* (HMSO, 1904–).
CLR	*Calendar of Liberate Rolls* (HMSO, 1916-64).
CM	*Matthaei Parisiensis, Monachi Sancti Albani, Chronica Majora*, ed. H.R. Luard (7 vols., Rolls Ser., 1872-83).
Cotton	*Bartholomaei de Cotton, Historia Anglicana (A.D. 449-1298)*, ed. H.R. Luard (Rolls Ser., 1859).
Councils and Synods	*Councils and Synods, II, 1205-1313*, ed. F.M. Powicke and C.R. Cheney (Oxford, 1964).
CPL	*Calendar of Papal Registers: Papal Letters, 1198-1342*, ed. W.H. Bliss (2 vols., HMSO, 1893-95).
CPR	*Calendar of Patent Rolls* (HMSO, 1906–).
CR	*Close Rolls, Henry III* (HMSO, 1902-38)
Cron. Maior.	*De Antiquis Legibus Liber. Cronica Maiorum et Vicecomitum Londoniarum*, ed. T. Stapleton (Camden Soc., 1846).
CRR	*Curia Regis Rolls* (HMSO, 1922–).
CRsup	*Close Rolls (Supplementary) of the Reign of Henry III, 1244-66* (HMSO, 1975).
CRV	*Calendar of Various Chancery Rolls, 1277-1326* (HMSO, 1912).

CSM	*Chartularies of St Mary's Abbey, Dublin with the register of its house at Dunbrody and Annals of Ireland, 1162-1370*, ed. J.T. Gilbert (2 vols., Rolls Ser., 1884-86).
DBM	*Documents of the Baronial Movement of Reform and Rebellion, 1258-1267*, ed. R.F. Treharne and I.J. Sanders (Oxford, 1973).
Denholm-Young, *SAIE*	Denholm-Young, N., *Seignorial Administration in England* (Oxford, 1937).
DKPR Ireland	*Reports of the Deputy Keeper of the Public Records in Ireland* (HMSO, Dublin, 1869-1922).
Documents 1297	*Documents Illustrating the Crisis of 1297-98 in England*, ed. M. Prestwich (Camden Soc., 4th ser., xxiv, 1980).
EHD	*English Historical Documents 1189-1327*, ed. H. Rothwell (London, 1975).
EHR	*English Historical Review*.
Excerpta	*Excerpta e Rotulis Finium in Turri Londinensi. Asservatis...1216-1272*, ed. C. Roberts (2 vols., Record Comm., 1835-36).
EYC	*Early Yorkshire Charters*, i–iii, ed. W. Farrer (3 vols., Edinburgh, 1914-16), iv–x, ed. C.T. Clay (7 vols., Yorkshire Archaeological Soc., Record Ser., extra ser., 1935-55).
Farrer, *Honors*	Farrer, W., *Honors and Knights' Fees* (3 vols., London and Manchester, 1923-25).
Flores	*Flores Historiarum*, ed. H.R. Luard (3 vols., Rolls Ser., 1890).
Foedera	*Foedera, Conventiones, Litterae et Acta Publica*, ed. T. Rymer, amended edn by A. Clarke and F. Holbrooke (4 vols. in 7, Record Comm., 1816-69).
Gervase	*The Historical Works of Gervase of Canterbury*, ed. W. Stubbs (2 vols., Rolls Ser., 1879-80).
Great Cause	*Edward I and the Throne of Scotland, 1290-1296. An Edition of the Record Sources for the Great Cause*, ed. E.L.G. Stones and G.G. Simpson (2 vols., Oxford, 1978).
Guisborough	*The Chronicle of Walter of Guisborough*, ed. H. Rothwell (Camden Soc., lxxxix, 1957).
HMSO	Her Majesty's Stationery Office.
Jacob, *Studies*	Jacob, E.F., *Studies in the Period of Baronial Reform and Rebellion* (Oxford, 1925).
Langtoft	*The Chronicle of Pierre de Langtoft*, ed. T. Wright, ii (Rolls Ser., 1868).
McFarlane, 'Policy'	McFarlane, K.B., 'Had Edward I a "Policy" towards the Earls?', *The Nobility of Later Medieval England* (Oxford, 1973).
Maddicott, *Montfort*	Maddicott, J.R., *Simon de Montfort* (Cambridge, 1994).

Morris, 'Murder'	Morris, M., 'The "Murder" of an English Earldom? Roger IV Bigod and Edward I', *TCE*, ix (2003).
PA	*Placitorum in Domo Capituluri Westmonasteriensi Asservatorum Abbreviatio* (Record Comm., 1811).
Parl. Writs.	*Parliamentary Writs and Writs of Military Summons*, ed. F. Palgrave (2 vols. in 4, Record Comm., 1827-34).
PatR	*Patent Rolls of the Reign of Henry III, 1216-32* (2 vols., HMSO, 1901-3).
Peerage	Cockayne, G.E., *Complete Peerage of England, Scotland, Ireland, Great Britain and the United Kingdom*, ed. V. Gibbs et al. (12 vols. in 13, 1912-59).
PQW	*Placita de Quo Warranto*, ed. W. Illington (2 vols., Record Comm., 1818).
PR	*Pipe Roll.*
RBE	*Red Book of the Exchequer*, ed. H. Hall (3 vols., Rolls Ser., 1896).
RCWL Ed I	*The Royal Charter Witness Lists of Edward I*, ed. R. Huscroft (List and Index Soc., 2000).
RCWL HIII	*The Royal Charter Witness Lists of Henry III*, ed. M. Morris (2 vols., List and Index Soc., 2001).
Reg. Giffard	*The Register of Walter Giffard, Lord Archbishop of York, 1266-1279*, ed. W. Brown (Surtees Soc., cix, 1904).
Ridgard	*Medieval Framlingham*, ed. J. Ridgard (Suffolk Records Soc., 1985).
Rishanger, *C&A*	*Willelmi Rishanger, Chronica et Annales*, ed. H.T. Riley (Rolls Ser., 1865).
Rishanger, *De Bellis*	*The Chronicle of William de Rishanger of the Barons' Wars*, ed. J.O. Halliwell (Camden Soc., 1840).
RLC	*Rotuli Litterarum Clausarum in Turri Londonensi Asservati*, ed. T.D. Hardy (2 vols., Record Comm., 1833-34).
RLP	*Rotuli Litterarum Patentium in Turri Londonensi Asservati*, ed. T.D. Hardy (Record Comm., 1835).
Rot. Hund.	*Rotuli Hundredorum* (2 vols., Record Comm., 1812-18).
Rot. Parl.	*Rotuli Parliamentorum*, i (Record Comm., 1783).
Select Cases KB	*Select Cases in the Court of King's Bench*, ed. G.O. Sayles (7 vols., Selden Soc., lv, lvii, lviii, lxxiv, lxxvi, lxxxii, lxxxviii, 1936-71).
Sibton	*Sibton Abbey Cartularies*, ed. P. Brown (4 vols., Suffolk Charters, vii–x, Woodbridge, 1985-88).
SR	*The Statutes of the Realm*, ed. A. Luders, T.E. Tomlins, J. France, W.E. Taunton and J. Raithby, i (Record Comm., 1810).
Stacey, *Politics*	Stacey, R., *Politics, Policy and Finance under Henry III, 1216-1245* (Oxford, 1987).

TCE	*Thirteenth Century England.*
TRHS	*Transactions of the Royal Historical Society.*
VCH	*Victoria County History.*
Vincent,	Vincent, N., *Peter des Roches: An alien in English politics,*
des Roches	*1205-1238* (Cambridge, 1996).
Yorks. Fines	*Feet of Fines for the County of York,* ed. W.P. Baildon, J. Parker, F.H. Slingsby and M. Roper (5 vols., Yorkshire Archaeological Soc. Record Ser., lxii, lxvii, lxxxii, cxxi, cxxvii, 1910-65).
Yorks. Inq.	*Yorkshire Inquisitions,* ed. W. Brown (4 vols., Yorkshire Archaeological Soc., Record Ser., xii, xxiii, xxxi, xxxvii, 1892-1906).

EDITORIAL NOTE

All sums of money given in the main text have been rounded to the nearest pound or mark: precise figures are given in the footnotes where required. References such as 'RBIII 2', 'MAUD 5' and 'RBIV 17' are to the charters calendared in Appendix E.

The Bigod Family: Selective Family Tree

Heads of the family are shown in bold

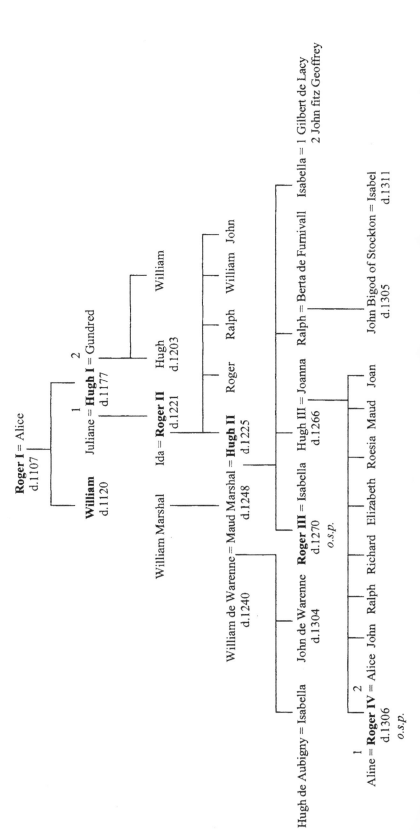

CHAPTER 1

The Outsider: Roger III Bigod, 1209-45

ACQUIRING AN EARLDOM

Roger III and Roger IV Bigod could rightly regard themselves as coming from a family whose history was not only long but also distinguished. Respectively the fourth and fifth earls of Norfolk since the Norman Conquest, from 1246 they also successively gloried in the additional title 'marshal of England'. With such honours firmly in mind, both men may have been able to view their surname with the same mild amusement it habitually provoked in others. 'By God!' appears to have been such a common pun in the thirteenth century that some people – perhaps the earls themselves – believed that it was as a profanity that the name had originated. Others may have understood *bigot* or *bigote* to mean something not dissimilar to the modern word which derives from it: a person who, if not necessarily prejudiced, was at least boorish and uncouth. It was, therefore, laughably inappropriate for men who moved in the topmost tiers of aristocratic society.[1]

Nevertheless, it was precisely what the Bigods had once been. The first of the earls' ancestors whom we can identify is Robert Bigod, a Norman knight whose poverty in 1055 was reportedly so acute that emigration in search of a better life seemed to be his only viable option. His luck turned, however, when he was able to reveal a rebellion plot to William the Conqueror; the grateful duke rewarded him with land in western Normandy – albeit not very much. The family's real fortune was made in England, and its founder was Roger I Bigod. Roger, certainly a relation of Robert's, possibly his son, established himself in East Anglia in the decade after the Conquest. By serving the Crown, first as sheriff of Norfolk and later as a royal councillor, he amassed sufficient land, wealth and power to build a massive castle at Framlingham in Suffolk and found a major priory at Thetford in Norfolk. By the time of his death in 1107, the Bigods had become barons of the first rank.[2]

---

[1] Guisborough, p. 290; *The Political Songs of England*, ed. T. Wright (Camden Soc., vi, 1839), 68; *CM*, i, 450; C. Moor, 'The Bygods, Earls of Norfolk', *Yorkshire Archaeological Journal*, 32 (1935), pp. 172-3; *The Oxford English Dictionary*, ed. J.A. Simpson and E.S.C. Weiner (20 vols., 2nd edn, Oxford, 1989), ii, 185.

[2] A. Wareham, 'The Motives and Politics of the Bigod Family, c. 1066-1177', *ANS*, xvii (Woodbridge, 1994), 224-9; L.C. Loyd, *The Origins of Some Anglo-Norman Families*, ed. C.T. Clay and D.C. Douglas (Harleian Soc., ciii, 1951), 14-15; *Peerage*, ix, 575-9; F.J. Raby and P. Reynolds, *Framlingham Castle* (London, 1959), p. 3; *idem, Thetford Priory* (London, 1979), p. 11.

Setbacks caused by the minority and early death of Roger's eldest son, William (1107-20), were soon overcome by his second son, Hugh I (1120-77). Like his father, Hugh also rose in royal service, but later in life he found it more advantageous to act independently. During the reign of King Stephen his exertions earned him the town and castle of Bungay (where he built an impressive stone tower, now vanished, in the 1160s), and also a string of new manors in the same area. Most importantly, in 1141 Hugh obtained the title 'earl of Norfolk' (either from Stephen, or from his rival, Matilda). By 1166, thanks to the earl's vigorous efforts, the Bigods had risen to become the fifth richest family in England.[3]

Only at the very end of his career did Hugh miscalculate; rebellion against Henry II in 1174 cost him and his dynasty dearly.[4] Many of the earl's manors were confiscated and his title was denied to his heirs.[5] The work of rebuilding was left to Roger II (1177-1221), who gradually bought back his father's acquisitions and added new properties to the ancestral estate.[6] In 1189, he was permitted to buy back the lost earldom, and Framlingham Castle, razed to the ground by Henry II's engineers, was rebuilt on a grand scale and in the latest curtain-wall style.[7] By the start of the thirteenth century, the Bigods were once again a force to be reckoned with.

They were also a family worth marrying into. Around Christmas 1181, at the start of his long road to recovery, Roger had married Ida de Tosny, a royal ward.[8] In the years that followed, the couple had at least eight children – a resource which they used to good effect. The earl found good husbands for his three daughters: Mary Bigod was married to the Yorkshire baron Ranulf fitz Robert, Margaret to the royal steward William de Hastings, and Alice to Aubrey de Vere, earl of Oxford.[9] The greatest match, however, Roger secured for his eldest son. Late in 1206 or early in 1207, Hugh II Bigod was married to Maud, eldest daughter of William

---

[3] Wareham, 'Motives and Politics', pp. 223, 229-42; *Peerage*, ix, 579-86; D. Crouch, *The Reign of King Stephen, 1135-1154* (Harlow, 2000), pp. 118-20, 156-7; H. Braun, *Bungay Castle: Historical Notes and an Account of the Excavations* (new edn, Bungay, 1991), pp. 12, 25, 49.

[4] Cf. the different emphasis in Wareham, 'Motives and Politics', pp. 240-42.

[5] *PR 34 Henry II*, pp. 65, 83 gives a good indication of the scale of the family's losses.

[6] *Cartae Antiquae Rolls*, ii, 158-9; *PR 6 Richard I*, p. 63.

[7] *Peerage*, ix, 587; R.A. Brown, 'Framlingham Castle and Bigod, 1154-1216', *Castles, Conquest and Charters: Collected Papers* (Woodbridge, 1989), pp. 194-201.

[8] In 1275, jurors in Norfolk stated that when Henry II gave Ida to Roger, he also gave him the manors of Acle, Halvergate and South Walsham. The king had confiscated these manors after the death of Hugh I Bigod. At Michaelmas 1182, however, Roger had been holding them for three-quarters of the year. *Rot. Hund.*, i, 504, 537; *PR 23 Henry II*, pp. 125, 137; *PR 24 Henry II*, pp. 26-7; *PR 28 Henry II*, p. 64.

[9] *Rot. Hund.*, i, 467; *EYC*, v, 303; I.J. Sanders, *English Baronies* (Oxford, 1960), p. 52; T. Milles, *The Catalogue of Honor* (London, 1610), p. 503.

Marshal, earl of Pembroke.[10] With the possible exception of the earl of Chester, the Marshal was the greatest of the Anglo-Norman magnates, and there were strong similarities between his career and that of Roger II Bigod. Both men had been born in Stephen's reign, schooled at the Angevin court, married to royal wards and promoted to comital rank. Both had outlasted the turbulent dynasty that made them, and ended their lives as respected elder statesmen.[11] When Roger died in the late summer of 1221, it is possible to picture a scene similar to the one which attended William's death two years before: an old man, surrounded by a large, lamenting family, making good his end. A sad occasion, but an expected one. The earl was a man of great age, and his passing can have come as no great surprise.[12]

The surprise came four years later, shortly before 18 February 1225, when Hugh II Bigod unexpectedly followed his father to the grave.[13] He was only in his early forties, and his death looks to have been sudden; less than a week beforehand he had been present in a great council at Westminster.[14] The earl was survived by his wife, their daughter (Isabella) and three young sons (Roger, Hugh and Ralph).[15] Faced with her family's reduced circumstances, Maud moved swiftly to make alternative arrangements. Within a few months she had remarried, taking as her second husband the next most important man in East Anglia – William de Warenne, earl of Surrey.[16] For the countess and her younger children, life would now revolve around Castle Acre and Conisbrough rather than Framlingham and Bungay.

The same was not true, however, for Roger III, the eldest of the Bigod boys, whose story begins at this juncture.[17] Roger had probably been born in or around the year 1209, and thus at the time of his father's death he

---

[10] *L'Histoire de Guillaume le Maréchal*, ed. P. Meyer (3 vols., Société de l'Histoire de France, 1891-1901), lines 13,335-48, 14,917-32. Roger had four other sons. William died in infancy (RBII 23). For Ralph, Roger and John, see Appendix C.

[11] For the Marshal's career, see D. Crouch, *William Marshal* (2nd edn, Harlow, 2002).

[12] *L'Histoire*, ed. Meyer, lines 18119-978 (*EHD*, iii, 98-101).

[13] *PatR*, 1216-25, p. 508. Hugh must have been one of the first four of the eight Bigod children, and was therefore probably born in the early 1180s.

[14] *SR*, i, 25 (*EHD*, iii, 346).

[15] *CSM*, ii, 313. This genealogy is the only evidence for the existence and marriages of Isabella. While garbled and inaccurate in places, it accords with other more certain sources for Hugh and Maud's three sons.

[16] *AM*, iii, 94. Their marriage took place between early May and early October 1225. Maud 1; *RLC*, ii, 82.

[17] There is one possible reference to Roger before 1225 – he may have been 'the son of Hugh Bigod' who was held hostage by King John during the civil war of 1215-17, and whose capture perhaps occurred when Framlingham was surrendered to royalist forces in March 1216. The unnamed boy was subsequently held in Norwich Castle, before being transferred to the king at Sandwich. *RLP*, p. 179; *RLC*, i, 254-5.

was about sixteen years old – too young to inherit the earldom.[18] As an under-age heir to an estate held by feudal tenure, his lands and person were at the disposal of his overlord, and, since the Bigods were tenants-in-chief, the overlord in question was the king. The guardianship (or 'wardship') of an heir and his estate was a valuable windfall which a lord was entitled to use to his best advantage.[19] When Roger became a royal ward, however, his situation was complicated by another factor: the king himself was under age. Just as Roger's lands and person were being managed by others, so too the estate and affairs of Henry III were in the hands of trustees. In seeking to understand the complicated series of transactions involving Roger and his lands that occurred during the 1220s, we therefore have to bear in mind the agenda of those conducting government in the king's name during his minority.[20]

A third of Hugh Bigod's lands was automatically set aside after his death to provide for his widow; as was customary, Maud would keep these properties for the rest of her life. In addition, some of the goods on the estate were seized by the sheriff of Norfolk in order to clear the debts which Hugh had owed at the exchequer. What remained of the earldom, however – still very much the lion's share – was assigned in February 1225 to one of the leading figures in the regency government.[21] William Longespee, earl of Salisbury, was a bastard son of Henry II and thus an uncle to the young Henry III. Earlier in the same month he had been chosen to lead a military expedition to Gascony (recently lost by the English Crown), and the revenue from the Bigod lands was evidently intended to defray his costs.[22] Salisbury, however, was given no say in the fate of the ward himself. Before sailing for Gascony, the earl agreed with the king's regents that, should Roger be married during his absence, £100 of the Bigod estate would be set aside to sustain him.[23] Roger's person and his marriage were themselves valuable assets, and the regency government wasted no time in capitalizing on them. A plan was soon hatched to have Roger married to Isabella, sister of Alexander, king of Scots, and it was rapidly put into effect. By mid-May, the groom was being

---

[18] Roger cannot have been born earlier than May 1207 because he was not of age in April 1228. Equally he cannot have been born later than December 1209 because he was litigating from January 1231. *PatR, 1225-32*, pp. 183-4; *CRR*, xiv, *1230-32*, p. 326. A birthday in 1209 is likely for reasons discussed below, n. 32. The incorrect date of 1212/13 given in *Peerage*, ix, 590 is probably assumed from his investiture as earl in 1233.

[19] For wardship in the thirteenth century, see S.L. Waugh, *The Lordship of England: Royal Wardships and Marriages in English Society and Politics, 1217-1327* (Princeton, 1988) and N.J. Menuge, *Medieval English Wardship in Romance and Law* (Cambridge, 2002).

[20] In general, see D.A. Carpenter, *The Minority of Henry III* (London, 1990).

[21] *PatR, 1216-25*, p. 508; *Excerpta*, i, 125.

[22] Carpenter, *Minority*, pp. 30, 376. Compare Salisbury's intentions for the Bigod estate as expressed in his will with the actions of the earl's executors after his death. *RLC*, ii, 71; below, p. 6.

[23] *RLC*, ii, 58.

escorted northwards, and his bride-to-be had been assigned a dower from his estate. On 1 June, the young couple were married at Alnwick.[24]

Up to a point, Roger's marriage to a Scottish princess was preordained. Ever since 1209, Isabella and her elder sister Margaret had been preparing themselves for the likelihood that their husbands would be English. Under the terms of the Treaty of Norham, they were to be married to Henry III and his younger brother Richard; their joint nuptials would be the means by which a lasting Anglo–Scottish peace was established. This scheme, however, was later modified. In 1221 Alexander II married Henry III's sister, Joanna, and it was agreed that Isabella and Margaret would be found husbands of appropriate rank among the English aristocracy. At a superficial level, therefore, Roger's marriage to Isabella in 1225 can be regarded simply as the English government fulfilling a longstanding diplomatic obligation to the Scottish Crown. On the other hand, the English had demonstrated no urgent desire to honour the agreement up until this point. All three Anglo–Scottish royal weddings were supposed to have taken place before October 1221, but in the event only two were actually celebrated: no groom was found for Isabella. In 1223, she had been returned unmarried to Scotland.[25]

So why the urgent, belated effort to provide the young lady with a husband some two years later? It may have had less to do with cross-border diplomacy, and more to do with the position of the English justiciar, Hubert de Burgh. Hubert, although he was by no means a great magnate, had been selected in 1221 as a suitable candidate for the hand of Isabella's sister, Margaret. An important figure in Henry's minority government from its inception, he had emerged by the mid-1220s as its single most important minister. This supremacy had not been achieved without a fight; at the end of 1223 the justiciar had led a coalition of earls and bishops to drive out of court a rival faction headed by Peter des Roches, bishop of Winchester and former tutor to the young king. While this was a success, Hubert found himself somewhat isolated in the wake of his victory. To survive he needed to build his own power-base, and the Bigod wardship thus presented him with a perfect opportunity. There can be little doubt that Roger's marriage to Isabella was carried out with the justiciar's approval, not to say at his instigation. The princess may have finally gained a suitably aristocratic husband; more important (one suspects) was the fact that Hubert de Burgh had acquired a rich and powerful brother-in-law.[26]

For the time being, however, there was little opportunity for the justiciar to cultivate this potentially useful relationship. After his marriage, Roger continued to reside at Alexander's court, and probably remained

---

[24] *PatR, 1216-25*, pp. 525, 527; *Excerpta*, i, 128.
[25] A.A.M. Duncan, *Scotland: The Making of the Kingdom* (Edinburgh, 1975), pp. 244-8, 525-7.
[26] Carpenter, *Minority*, pp. 245-6, 314-42. Vincent, *des Roches*, pp. 259-61.

there for the next three years.[27] Whether or not this domestic arrangement was intended from the outset is impossible to say; but Alexander's right to act as guardian was immeasurably strengthened when he stepped in and purchased the wardship of the Bigod estate after Salisbury's death in March 1226.[28] By the summer of that year, the earl's executors had agreed to transfer custody of the lands in return for a payment of 4,000 marks, plus an undertaking from the Scottish king that he would clear whatever debts Salisbury had owed at the exchequer. These had yet to be determined, but were evidently considered to be large enough to merit an immediate down-payment of £1,000.[29] As far as can be judged, the subsequent transactions were carried out with the minimum of fuss. There was evidently some degree of disputation during early autumn between Alexander and William de Warenne over the precise extent of Maud's dower, just as there had been between the Warennes and the English government on the same issue. In October, however, the regents acted to stop such controversies by ordering a series of local inquisitions, and these appear to have been successful.[30] In 1227 a hush descends upon the affairs of the Bigod family: not a single reference to them appears in the chancery rolls.

In 1228, however, Roger entered into his inheritance. He was still under age, probably by a couple of years, but the English government evidently considered that he was sufficiently mature to take responsibility for his own affairs. Alexander II also accepted his brother-in-law's precocious desire for independence, but at the same time charged him for the privilege. An early accession stood to leave the Scottish king out of pocket, so he simply transferred his outstanding financial responsibilities for the wardship to the ward himself. The complicated arrangements that this transaction entailed are partially revealed by four charters enrolled at Westminster in April 1228.[31] All told, his early inheritance cost Roger 3,150 marks (£2,100).[32] This sum, to be raised over a period of six years (from

[27] *PatR, 1225-1232*, pp. 7-8.
[28] *RLC*, ii, 103, 105. Note that Framlingham Castle and £50 of land for its upkeep were reserved by the government in this transfer. In October the castle was nominally returned to Roger, but in practice it was kept for him until his majority by Hubert de Burgh. *PatR, 1225-32*, p. 66.
[29] *PatR, 1225-32*, p. 54; *RLC*, ii, 128.
[30] *CDS, 1108-1272*, p. 179; *CRR*, xii, *1225-26*, pp. 442-3, 521-2. At this time, Alexander paid £500 to have custody of the escheats, wardships and advowsons from the estate, plus the third penny of the earldom. These had been reserved by the Crown at the time of Salisbury's death. *PatR, 1225-32*, pp. 68, 113; *RLC*, ii, 144.
[31] See *CChR, 1226-57*, pp. 72-3 (RBIII 1-3) for all the information in the next two paragraphs unless indicated otherwise.
[32] This figure permits some interesting incidental conclusions. Alexander had contracted to pay 4,000m for the custody of Roger's lands, plus 500m for the feudal incidents and at least £1,000 to clear Salisbury's exchequer debts. In total, therefore, he had pledged to pay £4,000. That Roger had to pay around half this sum to acquit himself is quite revealing. For Alexander not to have lost money from the deal, he would have had to have

certain named manors), was reckoned to be sufficient to buy out all the parties who had acquired an interest in the Bigod estate since it had first come on the market. A sum of 550 marks would satisfy the demands of the English exchequer, and by extension Salisbury's executors; 600 marks were earmarked for Alexander, presumably to compensate him for the revenue he was forgoing. The Scottish king's actual losses from surrendering the wardship were far greater, but at the same time he still owed his sister a marriage portion. Thus a further 2,000 marks were to be raised from the estate and used to purchase additional lands in England for Roger and Isabella.[33]

So, in the spring of 1228, we have to imagine Roger Bigod, nineteen years old, heading south from Scotland to England, and taking up residence at Framlingham.[34] The privilege was going to cost him a considerable sum, but there is no reason to think that he was anything less than happy about the change in his circumstances. His early inheritance had been approved by the leading men of the kingdom, including some of his closest relatives.[35] The mechanisms for raising the money were securely in place, their sound operation entrusted to a dependable council of his father's former servants.[36] Although a great deal of his disposable wealth would be siphoned off for several years to come, a large portion of it would eventually be used to buy new lands and thereby increase his estate. In the meantime, he and Isabella had no children to support, and little in the way of a political following to reward. To make matters easier for the young couple, the king had generously permitted them to raise an aid from their tenants.[37] All in all, the bargain Roger had struck was by no means a bad one.

---

recouped at least £2,000 from the Bigod estate in the two years between 1226 and 1228. This in turn suggests that the estate, less Maud's dower, was worth around £1,000 per annum. Using this as an approximate figure, it suggests that when the value of the wardship was calculated in 1226, both Salisbury's executors and Alexander's representatives assumed that the Scottish king would enjoy custody for about four more years, i.e. that Roger would come of age in 1230, and was therefore born around 1209. See above, pp. 3-4; below, pp. 40-41.

[33] However, the only identifiable acquisition made with this money is Peasenhall in Suffolk, purchased in 1232 by Roger and Isabella for 650m. In 1235, Alexander formally granted the manor to Roger for his homage and service. CP25/1/213/9, no. 29; below, nn. 69, 78.

[34] For other evidence which suggests that Roger was back in England by this date, see *CR, 1227-31*, pp. 59-60, 129; *CChR, 1226-57*, p. 84; *CRR*, xiii, 1227-30, p. 305.

[35] i.e. his brother-in-law, Hubert de Burgh, his uncle, William Marshal, and his step-father, William de Warenne.

[36] Below, p. 61.

[37] *PatR, 1225-32*, p. 194.

COMING OF AGE: THE MARSHAL REBELLION

Soon after Roger Bigod entered into his inheritance, the minority of Henry III officially came to an end: on 1 October 1228, the king turned twenty-one.[38] Despite being of full age, however, Henry remained very much under the tutelage of his ministers, and in particular of Hubert de Burgh. Since 1225, the justiciar had continued as the driving force in government, and had accumulated great rewards, including the earldom of Kent and extensive lordships in South Wales. From the end of the 1220s, however, Hubert found himself increasingly at odds with the majority of the English baronage, partly because of his parvenu posturing, but mainly because of his disastrous foreign policy initiatives.[39] Whereas the effort to recover Gascony in 1225 had been a great success (albeit a costly one), a similar attempt to win back the other parts of the Angevin empire in 1230 was an unmitigated disaster (and no less expensive).[40] Roger, like his stepfather, William de Warenne, voted with his feet and chose not to participate in the expedition;[41] evidently the prospect of regaining the £240 of land once held by his grandfather in Normandy was not a sufficiently tempting inducement.[42] It proved a wise move. Any nobles who might have crossed the Channel entertaining such hopes had them quickly dashed; the campaign, which began in Brittany, was soon directed southwards to Poitou. The result was not only a military fiasco and a financial disaster, but a political faux pas of the first order for Hubert de Burgh.

It was in Wales, however, that the justiciar's fate was sealed. The armies sent there in 1228 and 1231 were, if anything, even less successful, and even more damaging for Hubert personally, since their objectives were clearly identified with his own ambitions in the region. As such they drove a wedge between the justiciar and his erstwhile supporters, the Marshal earls of Pembroke. Without the backing of Earl Richard Marshal

[38] Carpenter, *Minority*, pp. 124, 389.
[39] Vincent, *des Roches*, pp. 259-73.
[40] Stacey, *Politics*, pp. 160-72.
[41] For Warenne's non-participation, see D.A. Carpenter, *The Struggle for Mastery: Britain 1066-1284* (London, 2003), p. 311. Roger's absence is chiefly adduced from his fine *pro passagio* and his payment of scutage (*PR 14 Henry III*, pp. 351-2; below, p. 16). Moreover, he does not feature in the muster roll of 1229 (I.J. Sanders, *Feudal Military Service in England* (Oxford, 1956), pp. 121-9). While there are two Roger Bigods issued with letters of protection in 1230 (*PatR, 1225-32*, pp. 358, 362), at least one of them was probably Roger's namesake uncle, for whom see Appendix C.
[42] F.M. Powicke, *The Loss of Normandy, 1189-1204* (2nd edn, Manchester, 1961), p. 264n. In 1227 a burgess of Caen reported a rumour that the regent of France, Blanche of Castile, was planning a conquest of England, and looking for the support of those English nobles who had held lands in Normandy before the Capetian conquest of 1204. 'The earl Bigod' was among the names he mentioned. This, however, can only have been idle and ill-informed chatter; Roger was not even in possession of his English estates at this point. *Diplomatic Documents*, ed. P. Chaplais (HMSO, 1964), i, 139-40; J.C. Holt, 'The End of the Anglo-Norman Realm', *Magna Carta and Medieval Government* (London, 1985), pp. 64-5. Cf. Carpenter, *Struggle for Mastery*, pp. 310-11.

(1231-34), Hubert was left dangerously exposed, and in 1231 his enemies seized their chance. In August that year, just as the full extent of the justiciar's folly in Wales was becoming apparent, Peter des Roches nonchalantly walked back into Henry's court and restored himself to the king's good graces; within a year Hubert had been hounded from office by the bishop and his party. From July 1232, the balance of power lay between des Roches and his Tourangeaux companions, and Richard Marshal and his English allies.[43]

On which side of this political divide did Roger Bigod stand? He had responded to the justiciar's call to arms in Wales on both occasions, but thereafter his movements and sympathies are difficult to determine.[44] According to Nicholas Vincent, Roger was a member of the Marshal party from as early as 1231, but this seems to be an assumption based on later evidence.[45] Peter des Roches appears to have regarded Roger's allegiance as undecided and therefore winnable in the spring of 1233. On 22 May that year, the bishop arranged a grand ceremony at Gloucester to celebrate the investiture of three young earls: Hugh de Vere and Thomas de Newburgh were respectively recognized in their titles as Oxford and Warwick, and Roger himself was belted with the earldom of Norfolk.[46] In the cases of both Roger and de Vere, it is hard to see why this had not happened earlier. Both men were two to three years past their majorities, and must since the start of the decade have been eager to assume their ancestral honours.[47] Whatever the reason for the delay, des Roches must have hoped that, by satisfying their ambitions, he could attract this new generation of magnates to his and Henry's side.

It was, however, an unsuccessful overture. Grand though the gesture at Gloucester may have been, it was not nearly large enough to offset the massive amount of ill-will which the bishop and his associates had provoked in the short time since their return. Des Roches was very much a creature of King John: a man who believed ardently in the plenitude of royal power, and a keen advocate of arbitrary methods of government. By the spring of 1233, he had succeeded in alienating both the baronage and his fellow bishops. Under des Roches's influence, Henry III had readopted the old Angevin practice, prohibited by Magna Carta, of countering dissent with disseisin *per voluntatem regis*. A particularly egregious example had occurred in February 1233, when Gilbert Basset, a leading

---

[43] Vincent, *des Roches*, pp. 265-309.
[44] *CDS, 1108-1272*, p. 188; *CR, 1227-31*, p. 539.
[45] Vincent, *des Roches*, pp. 263, 311. While other magnates who sided with Pembroke against des Roches (including the earls of Chester, Hereford, Surrey, Derby and Cornwall) made regular appearances at court in 1231 and 1232, Roger is invisible. Cf. Appendix A.
[46] *AM*, i, 90; iii, 132. For the history and significance of comital investiture, see Crouch, *Image of Aristocracy*, pp. 72-5.
[47] *Handbook of British Chronology*, ed. E.B. Fryde, D.E. Greenway, S. Porter and I. Roy (3rd edn, London, 1986), p. 476.

familiaris of Richard Marshal, was deprived of his Wiltshire manor of Upavon. This was the final straw for the earl and his supporters – it drove them out of court and into rebellion.[48]

The Marshal and his sympathizers arranged to meet on the first day of August at High Wycombe (another Basset manor, and conveniently close to London). It was probably the earl's intention to muster a large armed force and drive des Roches and his cronies from power. On the day itself, however, the expected army of malcontents failed to materialize. The earls of Cornwall, Derby and Warenne, all of whom had backed the Marshal in recent months, stayed away. In fact, besides the earl himself and Gilbert Basset, the only attendee of any consequence – and at this stage in his career, that phrase can only be loosely employed – was Roger Bigod. The new earl of Norfolk arrived from East Anglia, ready to support his uncle, but accompanied by only a handful of men.[49]

The would-be rebels made a swift assessment of their collective strength and decided to abandon their plan. The Wycombe gathering had been so small and insignificant that no chronicler noticed it, or considered it worth recording. But the armed assembly did not escape the attention of the king, who summoned local levies in the surrounding counties, and quit the capital in order to confront his opponents. By the time he reached Windsor, however, Henry was minded to be merciful. On 3 August, safe conducts were issued for both the Marshal and his nephew. Those who had bothered to turn up at Wycombe were allowed to make a promise of good behaviour, and return to their own parts unmolested.[50]

But the settlement, such as it was, quickly collapsed. Instead of heading east, Roger followed his uncle westwards, and further in the direction of rebellion. From Wycombe the confederates rode to the Welsh Marches, where they besieged and captured the castles of Hay-on-Wye and Ewyas Lacy. These were not royal properties, but the respective possessions of Richard of Cornwall and Walter de Lacy. Both men had until recently been aligned with the opposition to des Roches, but in the course of the summer they had returned to the king's camp. No doubt still chafing from his failure at the start of the month, the Marshal seems to have decided to take revenge on these fair-weather friends. Moreover, as Vincent has observed, the new earl of Norfolk may have had his own reasons for joining in – or perhaps even suggesting – the attack on Ewyas. Until quite recently the castle had belonged to de Lacy's son, Gilbert, who had once been the husband of Roger's sister, Isabella. But Gilbert had died in 1230, and thereafter Ewyas had been restored to his father: Isabella, who was

---

[48] Vincent, *des Roches*, pp. 334-9, 395-6.

[49] R.F. Walker, 'The Supporters of Richard Marshal, Earl of Pembroke, in the Rebellion of 1233-1234', *Welsh History Review*, 17 (1994), pp. 42, 44; Vincent, *des Roches*, p. 311. Roger was accompanied by his uncle Ralph Bigod, and also two members of his affinity, William Lenveise and Roger fitz Osbert. Below, pp. 62-3.

[50] Vincent, *des Roches*, p. 386; *CPR, 1232-47*, p. 22; *CR, 1231-34*, p. 321.

entitled to a dower, had received nothing. By attacking and capturing the castle therefore, the earl may well have considered that he was seizing property that rightly belonged to the Bigod family, or taking justifiable retribution for his sister's losses.[51]

When news of these attacks reached the king, the court moved westwards, and whilst it was en route to Wales the confiscation of the rebels' lands began. On 23 August Henry arrived at Hereford, and ordered the seizure of both the Marshal and Bigod estates.[52] From there he proceeded to reverse the effects of their recent attacks. In the two weeks that followed, Hay and Ewyas were recaptured, and the king went on to besiege the Marshal's own castle at Usk. It was there, around 7 September, that a truce was agreed, and it was probably at this juncture that Roger finally abandoned his uncle's camp and sought terms from the king.[53] The following day, at Abergavenny, his estates were restored; on 10 September at Hereford the earl witnessed his first royal charter. The price of disobedience, however, was made plain. Framlingham Castle was not returned, but committed to the Norfolk baron Oliver de Vaux to be kept at the king's pleasure. Meanwhile, the right of Roger's sister to Ewyas Lacy was implicitly recognized, but only in a writ that transferred custody of the castle to Peter de Rivallis, the most powerful and despised of des Roches's Tourangeaux henchmen.[54]

Having made his peace, Roger appears to have remained with the king for at least a few more days – long enough to intercede for the *familiares* who had joined him in rebellion, and to seek respite for a plea moved against him in Norfolk.[55] At this point, however, the precise composition of the court becomes mysterious, and consequently the earl's movements are impossible to trace.[56] Henry returned to Westminster in October, and Roger may have travelled to East Anglia to oversee the safe return of his estates. It appears, however, that the earl rejoined the court before the end of the year. In November Henry was back in Wales, and by the middle of the month his army was stopped at Grosmont. According to Roger of Wendover, the castle there was insufficiently large to accommodate the whole host, and the royalists were thus obliged to leave their baggage train outside the walls. This proved too good an opportunity for the Marshal's men to miss; during the night they swept down and made off with their enemy's equipage. Among those who 'lost everything' as a result of the raid, says Wendover, was the earl of Norfolk.[57] This was pure bad luck, but nevertheless deeply ironic. Prior to abandoning his uncle's

---

[51] Vincent, *des Roches*, pp. 390-91; above, p. 3.
[52] C60/32, m. 3.
[53] Vincent, *des Roches*, pp. 400-401.
[54] *RCWL HIII*, i, 137; *CR, 1231-34*, pp. 258, 265-6.
[55] *CR, 1231-34*, pp. 267, 269.
[56] No charter roll survives for 18 Henry III.
[57] Vincent, *des Roches*, pp. 408-19; *CM*, iii, 253.

cause, just two months before his arrival at Grosmont, Roger had been all in favour of such attacks on the property of deserters.

The open conflict that started in the summer of 1233 was over by the spring of 1234, but neither Richard Marshal nor Bishop Peter emerged as the victor. Both men faced the same fundamental problem, which was that they lacked the support of a sufficiently wide cross-section of the political community. From the farcical start of his rebellion at Wycombe, through the successive splits within his own affinity, the reality of this point was eventually brought home to the Marshal after his withdrawal to Ireland at the start of the new year. In a battle fought at the Curragh on 1 April, the earl was deserted for a final time, on this occasion by his own retainers; a few days later he died from his injuries. Before the news reached England, des Roches had received a similar vote of no-confidence from his peers which, in political terms at least, was no less deadly. At a council in February, the bishop's episcopal colleagues had voiced a damning criticism of his rule, and by Easter the king had also abandoned him.[58]

In these dramatic developments, Roger Bigod finds no place. While evidence of his contact with the court is lacking, it was probably not very full in the first place. Framlingham was restored to him at the start of February, a move which suggests either that the scions of the old regime were casting around desperately for allies, or that new and saner voices were already starting to dominate the king's counsels.[59] The earl's first certain appearance at court occurs at the end of June, by which time the malign effects of the bishop of Winchester's rule had been all but overturned.[60] Hubert de Burgh, having been humiliated, imprisoned and dramatically rescued, was now restored to royal favour. Gilbert Marshal, younger brother of the late Earl Richard, had also been reconciled with Henry and permitted to take up the earldom vacated by Richard's death.[61] On 2 July, Roger stood beside the new Marshal in the king's presence at Westminster, and in the company of others who had until recently been estranged or exiled.[62] The same day, he was given his first official duty by the new government. Peter de Rivallis, the chief agent and principal beneficiary of des Roches's regime, had fled the court; the earl of Norfolk, along with Richard Siward and William Longespee, was charged with his pursuit and arrest.[63] This posse was no doubt selected on the basis of its members' vigorous reputations.[64] Yet all three men had also suffered as a

---

[58] Vincent, *des Roches*, pp. 429-40.

[59] *CPR, 1232-47*, p. 39. Cf. *Excerpta*, i, 255 and also RBIII 4.

[60] Appendix A. It was not until June that Roger recovered the goods that had been seized from his manor of Settrington the previous year. *CR, 1231-34*, p. 450.

[61] Vincent, *des Roches*, pp. 415-16, 440-42.

[62] *CChR, 1257-1300*, p. 434. The other exiles included Walter Mauclerc and Godfrey de Crowcombe. Cf. Vincent, *des Roches*, pp. 319-20, 329-30.

[63] *CPR, 1232-47*, p. 58.

[64] For Roger's reputation, see below, pp. 18, 25. For Siward's, see D. Crouch, 'The Last Adventure of Richard Siward', *Morgannwg*, 35 (1991), p. 18.

result of de Rivallis's rise. Most recently, Roger had been forced to stand and watch while the former royal favourite had been granted custody of his sister's dower lands.[65] We might therefore allow ourselves to imagine the earl and his companions reflecting on such personal losses as they mounted their horses, and setting out to get their man with considerable gusto.

HENRY III'S PERSONAL RULE: THE FIRST TEN YEARS

For both Roger Bigod and Henry III, 1233-34 was in many respects a more important turning point in their careers than 1228. For the earl, it was a time in which he inherited his comital title and became drawn into the world of politics. For the king, it was the moment when he finally emerged from the tutelage of his father's ministers and, for better or worse, embarked upon a long period of personal rule that lasted until 1258.[66] Both men had properly come of age, and both had learned valuable lessons. At the outset of the Marshal rebellion, Roger had clearly believed it was important to defend the rights of his friends and family by force of arms. A year later, however, his uncle's example and his own experiences had taught him that force alone could achieve only limited results. The victory that was finally won in 1234 was obtained not by the barons, but by the bishops, relying on persuasion and argument rather than raids and sieges. Henry, meanwhile, having been briefly encouraged to believe that he was free to rule unfettered, now understood that this was not an appropriate way to govern. If his subjects were to recognize his authority, he would have to remember his responsibilities as their ruler.[67] In the immediate aftermath of des Roches's fall, therefore, a new co-operative spirit prevailed in the conduct of royal government. Important matters of state, such as the king's marriage and the reform of the law, were discussed in great councils at Westminster in June 1235 and Merton in January 1236.[68] Roger Bigod attended both these meetings, and he and his friends were often at court. In 1235 Gilbert Marshal was the most frequent witness to royal charters by a considerable margin, and Gilbert Basset (now reseized of Upavon) witnessed as many grants as any of the high-ranking earls.[69]

---

[65] Vincent, *des Roches*, pp. 383-4, 387-8, 406.
[66] For which, in general, see D.A. Carpenter, 'King, Magnates and Society: The Personal Rule of King Henry III, 1234-1258', in his *The Reign of Henry III* (London, 1996), pp. 75-106.
[67] Vincent, *des Roches*, pp. 462-3; F.M. Powicke, *King Henry III and the Lord Edward* (Oxford, 1947), pp. 123-55.
[68] *Handbook of British Chronology*, ed. Fryde et al., p. 536; Powicke, *Henry III*, pp. 148-51
[69] Appendix A; *RCWL HIII*, i, 140-53. The Marshal witnessed 41 charters, Bigod 11 and Basset 10. This contradicts the analysis given in Stacey, *Politics*, pp. 93-4, where certain men said to be important in fact witnessed far less frequently. The trio's high scores are all the more notable in view of their trip to Scotland in August 1235, where they celebrated the Marshal's marriage to Marjorie, sister of Alexander II (and thus sister-in-

This amicable *modus operandi*, however, did not last long. After his marriage in January 1236, Henry's honeymoon with his magnates came to a sudden end. The new queen, Eleanor of Provence, arrived in England accompanied by her uncles from Savoy, and by Easter the king's council had been reconstituted under the direction of one of these men, William of Savoy, bishop-elect of Valence. Individuals such as Marshal, Basset and Bigod were no longer invited to contribute their views on the running of the realm. In Roger's case, the arrival of the Savoyards marked the start of a period of absence from court which lasted, virtually unbroken, for over five years. Having been closely involved in the direction of royal policy in 1235, the earl and his friends found themselves once more out in the cold.[70]

A traditional reading of this period, based exclusively on the comments of chroniclers, would attribute Henry's political difficulties to his decision to surround himself for a second time with unpopular foreign councillors. Reacting against this, Robert Stacey has suggested that disquiet among the magnates in the late 1230s was grounded not so much on their personal animosities with members of the government, but rather their alarm at the policies pursued by these men. Up to a point, this is correct. William of Savoy was determined to set the king's financial affairs in order, and his money-raising schemes caused considerable resentment; an attempt to recover lost Crown rights resulted in several arbitrary disseisins of the des Roches variety, and was therefore regarded with suspicion and alarm. Moreover, there is good reason to believe that another of the council's policies – namely an attempt to ascertain the true number of knights' fees in England – would have been particularly alarming to Roger Bigod.[71]

Since 1066, the knight's fee had been the fundamental unit of taxation in England: soon after the Conquest, William I had imposed service quotas on his tenants-in-chief based on the number of fees they had created. As time wore on, however, and more knights were enfeoffed, the Conqueror's quotas bore increasingly less resemblance to reality. In 1166, a reassessment was attempted by Henry II, who asked his barons how many 'old' (*de veteri*) fees they had held in 1135 and how many 'new' (*de novo*) ones they had created in the meantime – the results of the king's inquiry are preserved in the *Cartae Baronum*. In the event, however, Henry found it difficult to persuade his subjects to accept the revised figures, and a

law to Roger). Their old comrade-in-arms Richard Siward was also at the Scottish court at this time, and Roger received a formal grant of Peasenhall from the Scottish king. *Peerage*, x, 373; Crouch, 'Last Adventure', p. 18; Queen's College, Oxford, MS 166, f. 28.
[70] Stacey, *Politics*, p. 96; Appendix A. After February 1236, Basset witnessed only two charters (23 and 24 July), the Marshal only one (possibly October). *RCWL HIII*, i, 157, 159.
[71] Stacey, *Politics*, pp. 97–102.

compromise was reached. When future aids and scutages were assessed, most barons would pay on their old fees, but not on their new ones.[72]

Like others who had done well for themselves in the twelfth century, the Bigod family found that there was a considerable discrepancy between their original post-Conquest quota of sixty knights and the figures as recorded in the *Cartae*: by 1135 they had amassed 125¼ old fees, and by 1166 they had created 37½ new ones.[73] Unlike the majority of other tenants-in-chief, however, the Bigods never arrived at a compromise settlement with Henry II.[74] Throughout his entire career, Roger II Bigod remained convinced that he was only obliged to pay scutage on his family's ancient quota of sixty fees. Anything charged to him beyond this, he would repeatedly claim, was *superdemanda*. The barons of the exchequer, naturally, were unconvinced; on each occasion the earl refused to pay the extra, they simply made a note of this unacknowledged amount.[75] By the time of Roger's death in 1221, the issue had still not been permanently resolved. In 1211 King John had intervened and, in return for a punitive fine of 2,000 marks, allowed the earl to pay on sixty fees for the rest of his life. As to the rate at which subsequent generations of the Bigod family would have to pay scutage, the question was left unanswered.[76]

This, then, was the financial situation faced by Roger III Bigod. The debts he had inherited from his ancestors were not large; all told they had amounted to £286, and had been cleared during his minority by the government's sale of his father's goods.[77] By contrast, the sums he had agreed to pay for having his inheritance before his majority were more substantial, but at the same time (as we have seen) not unreasonable. Given the guarantees the earl had made and the mechanisms that had been put in place, there is no reason to believe that there was any difficulty in raising this money, or that any of it remained unpaid by 1235.[78] If Roger had a financial problem at this point, it arose not because of either of the above factors, but as a result of the longstanding

---

[72] S. Painter, *Studies in the History of the English Feudal Barony* (Baltimore, 1943), pp. 34-6. Cf. the revisions to this argument made by T.K. Keefe, *Feudal Assessments and the Political Community under Henry II and His Sons* (Berkeley, 1983), pp. 41-89.

[73] *RBE*, i, 38, 395-7.

[74] Speculatively, this may have been because Roger's comital title was withheld by the Crown until 1189. Cf. Keefe, *Feudal Assessments*, p. 42.

[75] e.g. *PR 5 Richard I*, p. 20; *PR 9 Richard I*, p. 232; *PR 6 John*, p. 235; *PR 12 John*, p. 44.

[76] *PR 13 John*, p. 2. As its terms are so unfavourable, one suspects that the deal was forced on him, and that it probably fuelled his opposition in 1215-16. Above, p. ?; cf. Carpenter, 'King, Magnates and Society', pp. 90-91.

[77] E372/69, m. 2d; *RLC*, ii, 143. The £286 was made up from Roger II's scutage arrears, a 10m fine, and a 100m forest fine incurred by Hugh II in Yorkshire. *PR 6 Henry III*, p. 178.

[78] Most of this money (2,600m of 3,150m) was owed to Alexander II, so full proof of payment is lacking. However, we know that Roger paid the remaining 550m to the English exchequer as required, and spent 650m of the 2,000m earmarked for his wife's dower on the manor of Peasenhall. *CDS, 1108-1272*, p. 188; *PR 14 HIII*, p. 343; above, nn. 33, 69.

controversy over the scale of the Bigods' tax assessment. Ever since the earl had refused to cross the Channel with the king in 1230, the exchequer had been trying to charge him for the so-called 'Poitevin' scutage, which had been set at £2 per knight's fee. However, the sum being demanded in Roger's case – a hefty £338 – indicated that the barons had based their assessment not only on his *de veteri* fees, but also on his *de novo* ones. The earl, for his part, maintained the equally extreme position first adopted by his grandfather. When he finally rendered account in 1235, he acknowledged liability for only £120 – i.e. the money due from just sixty fees.[79] At that point he paid in £43, and over the next five years he paid off the remaining £87 (as well as clearing certain smaller debts he had incurred in the way of prests and fines). By 1240, therefore, Roger was declared quit on all counts – except, of course, for the small matter of £218 which the exchequer insisted was outstanding for the Poitevin scutage, but which the earl himself squarely refused to recognize.[80]

More than most people, therefore, Roger would not have welcomed an attempt by the government to establish the true number of knights' fees he held in chief.[81] At the same time, however, his argument with the exchequer was an ancient one which long pre-dated the creation of Henry III's new 'Savoyard' council. Moreover, while the barons continued to regard the earl as £218 underpaid on the Poitevin scutage, there is no evidence to suggest that he was pursued for this debt (he does not, for example, appear to have been distrained). None of this denies the truth of Stacey's basic point; many landowners must have viewed the measures introduced in 1236 with dismay, and Roger was doubtless among them. In a parliament which met at the start of the following year, the council was persuaded to abandon some of its more controversial policies, and Henry was obliged to reissue Magna Carta before the assembly would agree to vote him further financial aid. The magnates also demanded a greater say in royal government, and succeeded in forcing onto the council three nominees from their own ranks. One of these men was John fitz Geoffrey, a victim of the recent disseisins, and also a brother-in-law to the earl of Norfolk. Again, Roger probably approved of this appointment. The fact remains, however, that the earl himself had not suffered from such abuses, nor does he seem to have attended the parliament which sought to check them. While the Marshal and Basset were there to witness the reissue of the Charters, Roger was notably absent.[82]

---

[79] E372/79, m. 13. The precise figure of £337 16s 8d was calculated on the basis of 162¾ fees (i.e. 125¼ + 37½) and the 6⅙ fees which Roger II had acquired in Essex from Richard de Reimes (cf. *PR 3 HIII*, p. 111).

[80] E372/79, m. 13d; E372/80, m. 3d; E372/84, mm. 8, 8d. The precise outstanding sum was £217 16s 8d.

[81] Cf. Stacey, *Politics*, p. 98n.

[82] Stacey, *Politics*, pp. 114-15; *RCWL HIII*, i, 161. John fitz Geoffrey married Roger's sister Isabella, the widow of Gilbert de Lacy. *CSM*, ii, 313.

The earl and his allies may not have approved of the government's policies, but their decision to boycott the court had far more to do with the personalities who surrounded Henry III from the start of 1236. The arrival of the Savoyards, an unwelcome eventuality in itself, also gave support and encouragement to a raft of other undesirables. Simon de Montfort, for instance, a young Frenchman with a claim to the earldom of Leicester, had done much since his arrival in England in 1231 to ingratiate himself with the king, but little to impress the likes of Roger Bigod. On the very day of Henry's wedding, the two men had a very public quarrel.[83] It was customary on such occasions for members of the aristocracy to perform ceremonial roles. In this instance, for example, the earl of Chester bore the sword of St Edward before the royal bride and groom, and the earl of Lincoln, in his capacity of constable of Chester, cleared the way for their procession. Several of Roger's friends and relatives had similar duties: William de Warenne, the earl's stepfather, acted as butler at the banquet; Uncle Gilbert, as marshal, brandished his wand of office; even Richard Siward, a man who had done little to endear himself to the king in recent years, was allowed to carry one of the royal sceptres.[84] Roger himself, however, had no place in the proceedings; his ancestors had at one time been hereditary stewards of the royal household, but following a dispute in 1199, and in exchange for a grant of ten knights' fees, his grandfather had relinquished the role to a rival claimant – the earl of Leicester. This formed the background to the earl's row with Montfort. The Bigods, it transpired, had only received seven-and-a-half of the promised ten fees from Simon's family. This was hardly enough, however, for Roger to claim – as he did – the greater right to act as steward, and accordingly his case was thrown out.[85] No doubt his protest was partially provoked by pique; Montfort, after all, was as yet not even belted with his earldom. Nevertheless, the earl was obliged to defer to the upstart, and this cannot have gratified him. His self-imposed exile from court began four days later.[86]

Roger was not alone in finding Montfort objectionable; there was a general suspicion about the Frenchman and his motives, not least because he had flirted with the government of Peter des Roches. As such, his continued rise was symptomatic of a wider trend, for several of the bishop's creatures found they were able to return to a court controlled by the Savoyards. Stephen de Seagrave, justiciar under the old regime, had been sent into exile as recently as 2 January 1236. So too had Peter de Rivallis, perhaps the most detested of des Roches's cronies, and the object of the Bigod/Siward manhunt in 1234. But by May 1236 both men were

---

[83] Maddicott, *Montfort*, pp. 7-9, 13-14, 20.
[84] *CM*, iii, 336-9; M. Howell, *Eleanor of Provence* (Oxford, 1998), pp. 16-20; Crouch, 'Last Adventure', p. 18.
[85] L.W.V. Harcourt, *His Grace the Steward* (London, 1907), pp. 72-83.
[86] Appendix A.

back at court, exerting an influence over the king to settle old scores. In May, for example, Siward was arrested on the joint orders of Montfort and de Rivallis. At the same time, respected and stalwart members of Henry's government were being excluded or sidelined. The royal steward Ralph fitz Nicholas was gone by March. Attempts were made to deprive Ralph Neville, the conscientious chancellor, of the king's seal. Such changes of personnel and such personal clashes pre-dated the shifts in government policy, and were crucial in driving the likes of Bigod, Basset and Marshal away from the council table.[87]

The resentments engendered by these changes were played out on the tournament field. On 8 March 1237, the 'ins' and 'outs' at court faced each other at Blyth in Nottinghamshire. Roger Bigod, Gilbert Basset and Richard Siward arrayed themselves against the likes of des Roches and Seagrave. The outcome was not recorded – we only know from Matthew Paris that Roger in particular distinguished himself (he was, after all, a grandson of William Marshal). As to the overall spirit of the occasion, however, Paris thought it more like a battle than a sporting event. Indeed, such was the degree of hostility it engendered that only the subsequent intervention of Cardinal Otto, the papal legate who arrived in England during the summer, could reconcile the warring parties.[88] Signs of any genuine *rapprochement*, however, are lacking. Bigod, Basset and Marshal continued to stay away from court, while the likes of Montfort and William of Savoy continued to dominate the king's councils.[89]

This, broadly speaking, was the pattern maintained for the rest of the decade, though we may make some minor qualifications. The evidence for the period 1237-39 is not as full as one could wish: in particular, no patent rolls survive for 23 and 24 Henry III. One or two scraps of information may perhaps be taken to indicate that Roger had some dealings with the court. In July 1238 the earl received an unexplained gift of deer from the king. More significantly, in the summer of 1240 he accompanied Richard of Cornwall to France in order to negotiate a new Anglo–French truce.[90] It is also worth noting that in the last years of the 1230s Henry's kaleidoscopic council received fresh shakes. William of Savoy died in 1238 and Montfort was exiled in 1239; by 1240 the king's government had contracted to little more than the men of his own household.[91] Nevertheless, despite these changes, the diplomacy and the deer, the

---

[87] Maddicott, *Montfort*, pp. 13-14, 20; Stacey, *Politics*, pp. 95-6; D.A. Carpenter, 'Chancellor Ralph de Neville and Plans of Political Reform', *Reign of Henry III*, p. 62.

[88] *CM*, iii, 403-4.

[89] Compare the virtual absence of Marshal, Bigod and Basset from the witness lists to royal charters in 1237 and 1238 with the dominance of Montfort and Savoy. *RCWL HIII*, i, 161-7.

[90] *CR, 1237-42*, p. 73; N. Denholm-Young, *Richard of Cornwall* (Oxford, 1947), p. 41; below, p. 21.

[91] Stacey, *Politics*, pp. 124, 140-42.

overwhelming impression is that Roger continued to remain aloof from the court. The charter rolls for these years are quite complete, and show that the earl witnessed no royal charters. Instead, he continued to associate with his friends and family, the Bassets and the Marshals. On the eve of his departure for France in June 1240, we catch him (by means of the witness list to a private charter) in the company of Gilbert Marshal, Philip and Gilbert Basset, and also Ralph fitz Nicholas.[92] These men, like Roger, were absentees from court, and disgruntled ones at that. In 1238 Earl Gilbert had briefly rebelled in protest at Montfort's clandestine marriage to Eleanor (sister to the king, but also sister-in-law to the Marshal himself), and suffered as a result. Later in the same year, at Christmas, he was deliberately excluded from court, and in 1240 the king would openly accuse him of treason.[93] Ralph fitz Nicholas had not recovered from his fall in 1236 when the Savoyards had driven him from office. Both Basset brothers, like Bigod, had rebelled against the king in 1233. These men may also have sympathized with the plight of Roger's aged brother-in-law, Hubert de Burgh, who, having suffered greatly in the period in 1232–33, was once again persecuted by the king in 1238 at the behest of his enemies on the council. If not Roger himself, then his friends and relatives continued to be treated by Henry and his ministers in ways which were perceived to be unjust. This, we must suppose, was the principal reason behind the earl's prolonged absence.[94]

If there was a time before 1245 when Roger's relations with the court showed signs of improvement, it was the year 1241. At the start of the year, admittedly, the prospects for the earl enjoying a greater role in government seemed unlikely; politically speaking, it was business as usual. Another of the queen's uncles, Peter of Savoy, had arrived in England that winter, and his coming generated fresh waves of anti-Savoyard suspicion; by Easter, tensions were once again ready to be played out on the tournament field, when the new councillor organized a match at Northampton (*'quasi hostile'*, according to Paris) to test his mettle against that of the English (and, in particular, the earl of Norfolk). The meeting, however, brought the first of the year's major surprises. When Roger, the Marshal and the other, unnamed Englishmen assembled in arms, they were angered to discover that many of their number, succumbing to royal threats and bribes, had sided with the Savoyards; it must have been particularly galling to find that, of all people, Gilbert Basset had taken the king's shilling and lined up with the deserters.[95] But worse was to come. At a second tournament two months later, the Marshal was knocked from his horse and killed. A short time afterwards

---

[92] *Sir Christopher Hatton's Book of Seals*, ed. L.C. Loyd and D.M. Stenton (Oxford, 1950), p. 59.
[93] *CM*, iii, 476, 522-4; iv, 3-4.
[94] Vincent, *des Roches*, pp. 397, 461.
[95] Howell, *Eleanor of Provence*, pp. 30-32; *CM*, iv, 88.

Basset also fell from his mount (in this case while hunting) and died from the injuries he sustained.[96] Suddenly, Roger found that the circle of friends who had supported him since the start of his career was fast diminishing. Moreover, the passing of the two Gilberts took place against a backdrop of similar departures. The earl of Lincoln, one of the leading lights in government during the 1230s, also died in 1241; William de Warenne, Roger's stepfather, had died the previous year. Richard of Cornwall and Simon de Montfort, meanwhile, were temporarily absent on crusade.[97] Almost for want of competitors, therefore, Roger began to appear more prominent. When, in the autumn of 1241, Henry summoned a parliament to Westminster, the earl was one of a number of notable new faces (others included his new brother-in-law, Hugh de Aubigny, earl of Arundel, and also Hugh de Vere, the rarely seen earl of Oxford).[98] The assembly had been summoned to deal with the aftermath of the king's 'bloodless' campaign in Wales which had taken place during the summer – an unexciting adventure, but nevertheless one in which Roger had clearly played his part.[99] Like the thinning of the upper ranks of the aristocracy, the king's need for military support also explains why the earl appears more prominently in the period 1241-45 than in the years beforehand.

At the same time, Roger's participation in government during these years only increased in relation to his total non-involvement up to this point. His hostility towards members of the king's inner circle, and especially towards Peter of Savoy, continued unabated. In May 1241, Savoy was granted the honour of Richmond, and in September he received the wardship of John de Warenne (son of the late William and half-brother to Roger).[100] Together these grants made him a major landowner in East Anglia and thus a rival to the earl of Norfolk. The initial hostility the two men displayed on the tournament field appears to have been prolonged and sharpened down to 1245 by a series of disputes between their bailiffs. Matters were eventually brought to arbitration by a jury, and a transcript of the jurors' returns has survived. Unfortunately, the answers given are too short and allusive to permit a full reconstruction

---

[96] *CM*, iv, 89, 135-6.

[97] Powicke, *Henry III*, p. 142; Maddicott, *Montfort*, pp. 29-30.

[98] *RCWL HIII*, i, 182. Aubigny was married to Isabella, daughter of Warenne and Roger's mother Maud, and had previously been Warenne's ward. He made few public appearances before his premature death in 1243, but those which we know about suggest quite a close relationship with his Bigod brothers-in-law. Ibid., 187; *CM*, iv, 243; *The Making of King's Lynn*, ed. D.M. Owen (Records of Social and Economic History, new ser., 9, London, 1984), pp. 96-9; *Report on the Hastings Manuscripts*, ed. F. Bickley and J. Harley (4 vols., Historical Manuscripts Comm., 78, 1928-47), i, 23. For more on his widow, Roger's half-sister, see below, p. 51.

[99] J.E. Lloyd, *A History of Wales* (London, 1911), pp. 697-8; Appendix A.

[100] Howell, *Eleanor of Provence*, p. 31. John de Warenne was later earl of Surrey and an important political figure throughout the rest of the thirteenth century. In spite of his blood-ties with the Bigods, however, there is little to suggest that their relationship was especially close. See below, pp. 31, 37, 87, 104n, 115n.

of the issues at stake ('they say that the beasts were Brian's' is one typically enigmatic response), but nevertheless they allow us to glimpse a jurisdictional dispute of some considerable bitterness, fuelled on both sides by distraints and violence. The document, dry as it is, even testifies to Roger's bellicose personality; asked, finally, whether either magnate had encouraged the rivalry of their bailiffs, the jurors testified that the earl was well aware (*bene cognoscit*) of his men's activities; indeed, they said, he had ordered them *ex ira*.[101]

In the same way, while Henry's demands for military service in the early 1240s meant that the incidence of Roger's witnessings increased, the campaigns themselves did little to improve the relationship between the king and his magnates. While the low-key expeditions to Wales in 1241 and 1245 proved uncontroversial, and the muster against the Scots in 1244 abortive, Henry's main ambition at this time was the reconquest of his ancestral lands on the Continent, and this remained as divisive and unpopular as ever. In January 1242 the king summoned a parliament in the hope of raising money from his subjects to fund a campaign, but the assembly refused outright to vote any funds. Having given little thought or attention to parliament in its infancy, the Crown now found itself faced with an awkward, obstreperous child. Consecutive assemblies voiced criticism not only of Henry's foreign ambitions but also of the increasingly heavy financial burden his government placed on the shires.[102] Moreover, while the assembly's lesser members complained of costs, magnates found fault with royal policy on strategic grounds. In 1242, according to Matthew Paris, they questioned the wisdom of breaking the truce, negotiated just two years before by 'those outstanding men', Richard of Cornwall and Roger Bigod – a comment borne out by the king's promise to both earls in early March not to violate the truce 'without just cause'. Neither *minores* nor *maiores* shared Henry's enthusiasm for the coming campaign.[103]

The lack of money, consensus and resolve meant that the expedition to Poitou was an another disaster: a fiasco which confirmed that the English Crown's earlier loss of the province was indeed to be permanent. The turnout at Winchester in April, in response to a feudal summons in February, was extremely poor.[104] The army arrived in France later than expected, and wasted more time waiting for Henry's Poitevin allies, who in the event never materialized. Such delays gave the French king Louis IX ample time to ready his forces in response, and very soon the English were

---

[101] E163/1/20. Since Roger is not styled 'earl marshal', the inquest almost certainly dates to 1241 x 1246.

[102] J.R. Maddicott, '"An Infinite Multitude of Nobles": Quality, Quantity and Politics in the Pre-Reform Parliaments of Henry III', *TCE*, vii (1997), pp. 17-46.

[103] *CM*, iv, 182-4; *CPR, 1232-47*, p. 274; Maddicott, *Montfort*, pp. 34-5.

[104] Stacey, *Politics*, p. 191. Only two of the men granted protections can be positively identified as members of Roger's affinity. Below, pp. 64n, 65n.

on the retreat. As they withdrew southwards along the Garonne, a skirmish took place at Saintes; the earl of Norfolk was among those whom Paris singles out for praise. But by the end of July they were holed up in Bordeaux, the campaign effectively over. Henry was determined to remain in France, but the magnates, including Roger, had had enough. Together they approached the king and sought leave to return home, taking the opportunity (according to Paris) to spell out the reasons for his military failure.[105]

Failure in Poitou further widened the rift between Henry and his nobility. Initially this was because the king chose to linger in Gascony until the end of 1243; Roger's first opportunity for contact with the court came at Christmas that year, when he and the other magnates turned out *en masse* to celebrate Richard of Cornwall's second marriage. But thereafter, with Henry back in England, the earl continued to keep his distance. In 1244 he attended the muster against the Scots at Newcastle, but otherwise stayed away.[106] Poor Crown–magnate relations were due only in part to the loss of prestige the campaign had entailed; another factor was money. During his time in France the king had spent heavily – first on troops, then on gifts. Back in England, the same was true – money poured from his treasury to pay for royal building works, almsgiving and a second war in Wales. Henry's failure to husband his resources compelled his ministers to return to the fiscal policies that had so alarmed landowners in 1236; the inquests into royal rights, abandoned due to popular pressure in 1237, were now revived (and, on this occasion, the earl of Norfolk looks to have been adversely affected). As a result, when the king summoned a parliament for November 1244 in search of further financial aid, he found himself facing fresh demands to reform his government.[107]

The Westminster parliament of 1244 has conventionally been seen as an important staging post on the road to the revolution of 1258: an occasion, as in January 1237, when the community of the realm attempted to limit Henry's extravagances and overturn his unjust policies. The assembly saw the production of the so-called 'Paper Constitution', a document which envisaged quite radical reforms (in particular, the election of four 'conservators of liberties' as permanent members of the king's council, with the power to regulate royal expenditure). This, however, was evidently only a draft; the actual proposals put forward in parliament were considerably less extreme. Twelve men – four bishops, four earls and four others – were elected to consider Henry's request for money, and this committee echoed the Paper Constitution only in its demand for a

---

[105] *CM*, iv, 212-13, 228; *AM*, i, 127. For a full account of the campaign, see Stacey, *Politics*, pp. 192-200.
[106] Appendix A. Denholm-Young, *Richard of Cornwall*, p. 51.
[107] Stacey, *Politics*, pp. 237-51; *CR, 1242-47*, p. 318; *CIM*, i, 6.

chancellor and a justiciar to be chosen with their consent. Rather than requiring the total purview of royal finances, the Twelve asked only that any aid which parliament might grant should be subject to their own supervision. Orthodox opinion on the committee is therefore that it was not a radical body, but composed largely of men sympathetic to the king. According to Stacey, only two of its members (the bishops of Lincoln and Norwich) can be regarded as royal opponents.[108]

This analysis, however, is open to question. Of the four earls on the committee, Leicester and Cornwall were indeed close to Henry III. Both had benefited for example, from the extravagant spate of royal gift-giving at court the previous Christmas.[109] Their counterparts, however, were Norfolk and Pembroke, and neither man had been nearly so well favoured. Roger Bigod, as has been seen, was by no means a curialist: in the nine years between 1235 and 1244 he had witnessed only twenty royal charters.[110] Walter Marshal, meanwhile, enjoyed a relationship with the king no better than that of any of his deceased brothers; Henry had maintained the frosty tone in 1241 by attempting to prevent the earl from inheriting his estate.[111] The sympathies of the four remaining members (two barons and two abbots) are more difficult to divine, but that should not allow us to write them off as irrelevant. With two of the four bishops openly critical, and two of the four earls at the very least disgruntled, it would be more accurate to see the Twelve as composed of both critics and supporters of the Crown, their representation probably evenly matched, perhaps (as in 1258) deliberately so.[112] The final outcome of the king's quest for money certainly suggests that the earl of Norfolk may have voiced real opposition to royal policies. In spite of the moderation of the committee's proposals, Henry rejected them outright and dissolved the parliament. When it reconvened after Christmas, he sought to circumvent his critics by demanding a feudal rather than a gracious aid (20s per knight's fee for the marriage of his infant daughter). Significantly, parliament would only consent to this money being levied on the customary service quotas – an indication that the king had been forced to abandon attempts to re-evaluate England's knight service. Since his accession, Roger had been privately resisting such reassessment, and defending his ancient quota. It therefore seems very likely that the earl was among those who forced the permanent abandonment of one of Henry's more ambitious money-raising schemes.[113]

---

[108] *CM*, iv, 362-3, 366-8 (*EHD*, iii, 359-60); Stacey, *Politics*, pp. 247-50.
[109] Stacey, *Politics*, p. 238; Maddicott, *Montfort*, pp. 32-3.
[110] Appendix A. Stacey's belief that Roger was a royalist appears to be based on the erroneous assumption that the earl had grown up at Henry's court. Stacey, *Politics*, p. 255.
[111] *CM*, iv, 157-8.
[112] Below, p. 74.
[113] Stacey, *Politics*, pp. 248, 250.

This is not to claim, of course, that Roger was a radical or a reformer; such terms are more easily applied to Henry's ministers between 1236 and 1244 than to his opponents. The earl's objections to royal government, when they moved beyond the personal, were essentially reactionary. The measures he wanted were traditional ones: a chancellor and a justiciar, and no questions asked about his tax assessment.[114] Such demonstrably conservative tendencies may have made Roger a popular figure (they evidently endeared him to Matthew Paris, who is always quick to praise the earl and to forgive his failings).[115] This may in turn explain why, when parliament assembled the following year, he was among those chosen to represent 'the whole community of the barons in England' on an embassy to the pope. In 1245, the laity and the clergy drew together to resist the papal demands for taxation, and to complain about the provision of foreign clerics to English benefices.[116] With an international Church council set to meet in the French city of Lyon that summer, Roger was selected to head the English delegation. His companions were curialists, but men with outstanding credentials. John fitz Geoffrey, his brother-in-law, had been the man intruded by popular demand into the king's council in 1237. Philip Basset, just beginning a career at court, was an old associate and a friend of the Marshal family. Ralph fitz Nicholas, restored to his stewardship in 1242, had also once belonged to the same party of 'outs'.[117] While these men achieved little as a result of their mission (the pope refused to answer their demands, and the earl and his colleagues left in high dudgeon), their initial selection by parliament is a mark of the esteem in which they were held at home. Roger's theatrical performance at Lyon in 1245 can only have cemented his reputation as a force for good among the wider political community.[118]

At the same time, there were also signs that by this date the earl's frosty relationship with the Crown was finally starting to thaw. Having isolated himself from his greater subjects since 1239, Henry III was now trying to build bridges.[119] Roger attended court at Norwich in March, and again at Woodstock on 20 May.[120] Two days later, he received a gift of deer from the king – the first specific sign of royal favour for almost seven years.[121] When the earl returned from Lyon in the autumn (a journey that was not

---

[114] This is assuming, of course, that he agreed with the committee's requests. In the light of his demands in 1258, there seems to be no reason to doubt this.

[115] e.g. *CM*, iii, 404; iv, 183-4, 213; v, 269, 382-3, 423-5.

[116] Powicke, *Henry III*, pp. 356-8.

[117] *CPR, 1232-47*, pp. 454, 463; *CLR, 1240-45*, p. 308; *CM*, iv, 419-20, 431; Stacey, *Politics*, pp. 114, 141.

[118] *CM*, iv, 478-9. Roger and the other delegates left Lyon, says Paris, 'giving vent to terrible threats, and swearing a terrible oath that they would never satisfy the detestable avarice of Rome...'.

[119] Stacey, *Politics*, pp. 254-5.

[120] Appendix A.

[121] *CR, 1242-47*, p. 310.

entirely trouble-free), he joined Henry in North Wales as the king set out for a second time against Dafydd ap Llywelyn. When the court celebrated Christmas at Westminster that year, Roger was among those present for the festivities.[122]

All this was a marked change from his position in the previous decade. For most of this time, the earl had stayed away from court, preferring to keep company with other outsiders – most notably his mother's kinsmen. More than anything else, his connection with the Marshal family seems to have shaped Roger's outlook in the opening years of his career. During the 1230s the earl can often be identified in the company of Gilbert Marshal, and in 1233 he was the only other magnate to join Richard Marshal in rebellion. It is tempting to wonder how many times as a boy Roger had heard the tales of William Marshal, either in the newly composed *Histoire*, or straight from the old man himself. A desire to emulate his illustrious ancestor could well explain the earl's excellence on the tournament field, as well as his readiness to pick fights with Frenchmen.[123] By 1245, however, Roger was apparently willing to put the clashes of the past decade behind him. At the Christmas court, he mixed with both Simon de Montfort and Peter of Savoy. Perhaps, like Henry, the earl sensed it was time to move on. Death had been busy in the past five years. Roger had lost not only old friends and relatives like Gilbert Marshal, Hubert de Burgh, William de Warenne and Gilbert Basset; new members of his circle, such as Hugh de Aubigny, had also been cut down in their prime. It was, moreover, not just the earl's allies who had departed. Old adversaries like Peter des Roches and Stephen de Seagrave had also passed on. As Powicke observed, the stage had gradually cleared.[124]

At the end of 1245, there were two further dramatic exits, the consequences of which were profound. On 27 November, Walter Marshal died at Goodrich Castle. A month later, just days before Christmas, his younger brother Anselm also gave up the ghost.[125] Roger's restoration to Henry's good graces had come not a moment too soon. All five sons of William Marshal were now dead, and all five had died without heirs. The greatest private estate in the British Isles was thus set to be carved up among a plethora of competing claimants. The earl of Norfolk would need all the favour he could muster if he was to lay claim to his fair share, and obtain the ancestral honour that he now regarded as his unquestionable right.

---

[122] Appendix A. For Roger's adventures on his way home from Lyon, see *CM*, v, 85-6.
[123] For francophobia in the *Histoire*, see Crouch, *William Marshal*, pp. 2, 123, 151-2.
[124] Powicke, *King Henry III*, pp. 141-2; *CM*, iv, 491-2.
[125] *William Worcestre, Itineraries*, ed. J.H. Harvey (Oxford, 1969), pp. 62-3; *CM*, iv, 491.

CHAPTER 2

The Making of a Magnate: Roger III Bigod, 1245-58

BECOMING EARL MARSHAL

The deaths of Walter and Anselm Marshal heralded the end of a dynasty, but the effects of their passing continued to be felt long after the brothers themselves were gone. As well as his five sons, William Marshal senior had also been blessed with five daughters, each of whom had married into the English aristocracy, and each of whom had produced several children. As a result, the Marshal estate in 1245 was set to be divided among an assortment of heirs, with political consequences that would reverberate throughout the rest of Henry III's reign and beyond.[1]

Roger Bigod was set to become a major beneficiary of this division – he was the eldest son of the eldest Marshal sister, and therefore stood to inherit a fifth share of the estate. For the moment, however, his mother still lived. In the immediate term, it was Maud Marshal, now a double dowager, who was enriched by the recent deaths in her family. The earl's main concern from the end of 1245 was more narrow: who was going to inherit the role of marshal? There was clearly some controversy between the various heirs as to which of them had the greater right to this important honour, as well (perhaps) as some reluctance on the king's part to grant it to any of them. By the summer of 1246, however, Henry had arrived at a decision. On 22 July he accepted that Maud, as the senior heir, had the strongest case; a few weeks later, the countess was allowed to transmit the marshalship to her son.[2]

What did it mean to be marshal? Although Roger liked to call himself 'marshal of England', contemporaries would normally refer to the Bigods, like the Marshals before them, as 'earls marshal'.[3] This, however, was merely a convenient shorthand. In reality there was no connection between the comital status of either family and the office that they held. In fact, like the name 'Bigod', the word 'marshal' was an indication of very humble origins. The Old French word *marescalcus* had meant 'horse-slave', and suggested that the first marshals had been servile stable-hands in royal and aristocratic households; assistants to the more important *comites*

---

[1] For the descent of the Marshal lands, see Sanders, *English Baronies*, pp. 63-4.

[2] *CR, 1242-47*, pp. 443, 454-5; *CM*, iv, 548; *CSM*, ii, 143. Roger was styled with his new title when he witnessed royal charters from November 1246. It was, however, inconsistently applied by the chancery clerks down to 1248 – an indication, perhaps, that some degree of controversy remained. As late as 1249, some of the other heirs were still insisting that the marshalship should be partitioned. *RCWL HIII*, i, vi–vii; ii, 17; *CPR, 1364-67*, p. 269.

[3] Crouch, *William Marshal*, p. 228.

stabuli, or constables.[4] By the early twelfth century, however, the marshal of the king's household in England had risen considerably. His improved fortunes can be gauged from a document drawn up around the time of the death of Henry I, now known as the *Constitutio Domus Regis*. Here the marshal, although still quite lowly in comparison with certain other royal officers (such as the chancellor and the steward), is styled 'master-marshal', and assisted in his work by four deputies. The nature of their work, however, remains somewhat obscure. The *Constitutio* reveals only that they were responsible for billeting arrangements, and that the master-marshal exercised some kind of supervision of financial matters (he was, for example, to keep the tallies for gifts and allowances made by the treasury and chamber).[5] From later evidence, however, it can be adduced that the marshal and his assistants were responsible for policing the area around the king ('the verge'), as well as disciplining the personnel of the household.[6] As regards their financial duties, these are more fully set out in the *Dialogus de Scaccario*, a tract that dates to the 1170s. Here the marshal is not only said to be responsible for keeping the tallies of debtors; in addition, he is responsible for the custody of non-payers, and also for paying the wages of household knights.[7]

The office of marshal was a hereditary one. From the time of our earliest records, it was held by the Marshal family – the position, of course, had given the family their surname. By the time the *Constitutio* was compiled, the role was being filled by John fitz Gilbert (or John the Marshal as he was commonly known), and he was succeeded by his namesake son. But the second John Marshal died without heirs, and the office therefore passed to his younger brother, William, who went on to become earl of Pembroke, regent of England, and hero of legend.[8] Clearly, at some stage, the marshal would have performed all his various duties in person. But it is equally clear that, even by the time the *Constitutio* was drafted, John Marshal senior had deputies to take care of his more menial tasks. Furthermore, as Sidney Painter pointed out, John was frequently far removed from the king's side for long periods. By the middle of the twelfth century, therefore, delegation must have been normal practice. In the next generation, the meteoric rise of William Marshal can only have served to widen the gulf between the marshal's duties as set down in the *Constitutio* and the reality of the situation within the royal household.

---

[4] Crouch, *William Marshal*, p. 226. In the mid-eleventh century *marescal* was equated with *equorum domitor* (tamer or trainer of horses). *Peerage*, x, 92n.

[5] *RBE*, iii, 812-13 (*EHD*, ii, 426-7).

[6] Below, p. 29.

[7] *Dialogus de Scaccario*, ed. C. Johnson, F.E.L. Carter and D. Greenway (Oxford, 1983), pp. 20-21 (*EHD*, ii, 502-3). Cf. J.O. Prestwich, 'The Military Household of the Norman Kings', *EHR*, 96 (1981), p. 7.

[8] *Peerage*, x, 92-7.

Painter was surely right to conclude that, by Henry II's reign, the office was an honorary one, and that the Marshal family would only carry out their duties in person on ceremonial occasions. As we have already seen, when Eleanor of Provence was crowned in 1236, Gilbert Marshal, for all that he was earl of Pembroke, took great pride in keeping back the crowds with his rod of office, 'quelling the tumult' in the king's hall, and organizing the seating arrangements for the wedding banquet.[9]

However, this still leaves certain important questions unanswered. Who performed the marshal's duties on a day-to-day basis, and what was their relationship with the earls marshal? It is sometimes assumed that there was no strong link between the men who actually acted as marshals at the king's court, and the earls who periodically turned up to wave their wands of office on state occasions.[10] The evidence for such a connection is indeed quite hard to come by; nevertheless, such scraps as we have are sufficient to show that both the Marshals and the Bigods did indeed control the appointment of their own deputies, and jealously guarded their right to do so.

To carry out their financial duties, the earls marshal nominated a deputy known as 'the marshal of the exchequer'. Maud Marshal was permitted to do this in the summer of 1246, and the following year we find Roger putting forward one of his clerks to fill the position.[11] Similarly, it is clear that the earls appointed deputies in the king's household. The most clear-cut example is Fulk de Vaux, who performed the office for Roger IV Bigod; he was described as the earl's deputy marshal in a law case of 1293, and styled 'marshal of the household' in the following year.[12] Other individuals, less well documented, appear to have been Bigod nominees to the same position.[13] The earl marshal also appointed a deputy to the court

---

[9] S. Painter, *William Marshal* (Baltimore, 1933), pp. 103-4; *RBE*, ii, 759. *CM*, iii, 338; above, p. 17.

[10] Cf. M. Prestwich, *Edward I* (London, 1988), p. 147.

[11] *Dialogus de Scaccario*, ed. C. Johnson et al., p. 20 (*EHD*, ii, 502); *CR*, 1242-47, p. 443; T. Madox, *The History and Antiquities of the Exchequer of England, 1066-1327* (2 vols., London, 1711), ii, 285. Roger similarly appointed Master Roger de Gosbeck in 1251. At Michaelmas 1264, the earl was notified because his deputy was absent (E368/26, m. 1d; E368/39, m. 1). His successor was upbraided by the barons of the exchequer for identical reasons in 1275 (E159/49, m. 9d). For deputies appointed by Roger IV, see E159/55, m. 1d; E159/56, m. 1; E159/64, m. 12 (this last contains a copy of the earl's letters patent requesting the admission of his deputy).

[12] *Select Cases KB*, ii, 149-51 (also *PA*, p. 232); *CPR*, 1292-1301, pp. 70, 75. Fulk witnessed two of Roger IV's charters and campaigned with the earl in 1294. RBIV 19, 20; *CRV*, p. 357. For more on the lawsuit of 1293, see below, pp. 157, 160.

[13] Walter de Fanacourt held the place of Roger IV Bigod in the *curia regis* during 1288-89. *Records of the Wardrobe and Household, 1286-1289*, ed. B.F. and C.R. Byerly (HMSO, 1986), pp. 228-32, 234, 240-41, 245, 248-52. For his other appearances in connection with the earl, see SC6/873/11 and *CR, 1279-88*, p. 190. He witnessed royal charters on 10 May 1286 and 16 July 1290 (*RCWL Ed I*, pp. 81, 95). Philip de Buckland, a long-serving member of Roger IV's affinity (below, pp. 67-72, 97, 121, 137, 142-3, 145-6, 149-51), first occurs as 'the

of King's Bench (*coram rege*); this may have been the same individual who acted as marshal of the household, but such limited evidence as exists suggests otherwise.[14] Certainly all of the marshal's deputies had judicial functions, and this in turn explains why the earls themselves were keen to ensure that their right to appoint was respected: money as well as pride was at stake. In the exchequer, individuals who were committed to the custody of the marshal for non-payment of debts were further burdened by a fine payable to their gaoler.[15] The marshal of the household discharged his responsibility of keeping order around the king by holding a regular court with the steward.[16] Again, any fines that were levied there accrued to the marshal himself. Similarly, the marshal in King's Bench was entitled to fees exacted from all prisoners.

Something of the scale of the profit these exactions could generate is provided by a memorandum drawn up in 1307, soon after the death of Roger IV Bigod in connection with the dower entitlement of his widow.[17] The marshal of the exchequer, we learn, charged sheriffs and bailiffs half a mark for every night they were in his custody, and the marshal of the household likewise expected half a mark from any knights, clerks, king's bailiffs or 'renters' of the church committed to his care.[18] Only prostitutes, charged at fourpence a night, escaped these extortionate rates. Since the deputy marshals were salaried (we know, for example, that Fulk de Vaux received £10 a year from Roger IV Bigod whilst in office), it seems very likely that their masters expected these profits to be returned to the comital coffers.[19] This was certainly the case for the monies collected whenever a tenant-in-chief did homage to the king. According to the same memorandum, the marshal of England took £10 from an earl or

king's marshal' in 1257. Bartholomew Bigod, whose kinship to the earls of Norfolk cannot be proved, was marshal of the household in 1255. *CPR, 1247-58*, pp. 423, 578.

[14] See *Select Cases KB*, i, lxxxix–xc, and in particular xc, n. 1. The earl marshal did not, however, control the marshalsy of the eyre, which seems to have devolved to the ushers of the hall, and was claimed in hereditary right by a particular family from the mid-thirteenth century. In 1259, Roger III Bigod asserted his right to the fines imposed by the special eyre of the justiciar, but his claim was disputed. Below, pp. 79-80; H.M. Cam, 'The Marshalsy of the Eyre', *Cambridge Historical Journal*, 1 (1923), pp. 126-37.

[15] *Dialogus de Scaccario*, ed. Johnson et al., pp. 20-21 (*EHD*, ii, 503). In 1253, Roger III Bigod complained to Henry III that this right was not being respected, and that debtors who should have been committed to the marshal of the exchequer were being sent straight to the Fleet prison. In 1260, the earl had a similar complaint about prisoners at the exchequer of the Jews. *CR, 1253-54*, p. 196; *Baronial Plan*, p. 211; Jacob, *Studies*, pp. 13-14.

[16] *Select Cases on the Law Merchant*, ed. C. Gross and H. Hall (3 vols., Selden Soc., xxiii, xlvi, xlix, 1908-32), ii, cix–cxii. For specific instances, see *CPR, 1292-1301*, pp. 70, 75.

[17] E175/1/23, m. 3, printed in *Select Cases KB*, i, cxlix–cl. Unfortunately, this document says nothing about the marshalsy of the bench, despite ending with a subheading that indicates a similar list of fees for that branch of the marshalsy was also intended.

[18] In the case of the marshal of the household, it is not stipulated whether or not the fee of half a mark is a one-off payment or a daily rate. Cf. *CR, 1349-54*, p. 292.

[19] SC6/1000/21 (cf. SC6/1000/18).

archbishop performing homage, and five-and-a-half marks from each baron or bishop, prior or prioress, abbot or abbess doing the same. Lesser tenants-in-chief were also tapped for money, their contribution determined by the size of their tenancy. In similar fashion, every time the king bestowed the honour of knighthood, the earl marshal expected to receive gifts from the newly dubbed individual. Tenants-in-chief were obliged to pay five-and-a-half marks, or, alternatively, to produce a palfrey; others paid only half a mark, or a saddle.[20] The option to offer horses or saddlery suggest that these privileges were ancient ones, enjoyed by the marshal since his early days in the royal stables. When Roger III Bigod demanded a palfrey from young Alexander III of Scotland on the occasion of his knighting by Henry III, Paris commented that the earl was concerned 'lest the ancient custom in similar cases should die away through his neglect'. He was not, the chronicler added, motivated by considerations of the animal's value, or by greed. However, even if we accept this typically charitable assessment of Roger's motives, we should not allow it to disguise the substantial financial benefits that the earl marshal obtained by virtue of defending his heritage.[21]

Finally, to all these peacetime functions, the marshal had additional duties and privileges during wartime.[22] In the first place, he was responsible, along with the constable, for drawing up the lists of those present at a muster of the royal host.[23] While on campaign, the marshal was responsible for discipline in the army, a jurisdiction which presumably arose as an extension of his normal responsibility for discipline in the royal household. This jurisdiction was once again wide-ranging and lucrative, as a surviving plea roll from the Scottish campaign of 1296 reveals.[24] As well as the profits he made from justice, the marshal also claimed certain ancient rights, such as parti-coloured beasts taken as booty, wine, cloth and wax from a captured town, and the arms and money of a surrendered captain.[25] His right to take 2d in the pound for all wages paid to foot-soldiers, if rigorously applied, would have been extremely lucrative.[26]

---

[20] *Select Cases KB*, i, cxlix. Cf. *SR*, i, 92 and *RBE*, ii, 759.

[21] *CM*, v, 269. For other possible motives specific to 1251, see Duncan, *Making of a Kingdom*, p. 560.

[22] Cf. M.C. Prestwich, *War, Politics and Finance under Edward I* (London, 1972), p. 263n.

[23] e.g. *CM*, vi, 373; *CCR, 1272-79*, p. 484; *CACWales*, p. 114. For Roger IV's refusal to do this in 1297, see below, p. 165.

[24] Below, p. 161.

[25] *Select Cases KB*, i, cl; C47/2/21/23; F. Grose, *Military Antiquities Respecting a History of the English Army* (2 vols., London, 1801), i, 193.

[26] *Select Cases KB*, i, cl. Applied to infantry wages of £15,746 in 1301, his entitlement would have been £131, but on this occasion we know that Roger IV accepted less. Prestwich, *War, Politics and Finance*, pp. 175, 267.

The rights that belonged to the earl marshal were an intermittent source of tension between the earls of Norfolk and the Crown. This tension ran high during the reign of Edward I, and was a contributing factor to the stand Roger IV took against the king in 1297. There is less evidence for such major strains during the reign of Henry III, although there were clearly disagreements from time to time, as Roger III's complaints about his rights at the exchequer show.[27] In all these disputes, it is often impossible to establish which party is more in the right. The earls no doubt seized every opportunity to expand their ancestral claims, just as the Crown clearly took steps to limit, undermine and deny these claims wherever it could. Part of the problem, of course, was that the rights of the marshal were customary and therefore by nature ill-defined. As in other cases where their subjects asserted liberties as their ancient right, both Henry III and Edward I tended to suspect innovation and invention, and demanded written evidence as proof of entitlement. For the marshalship, this was sadly lacking; on those occasions when a king ordered a search of the rolls, all it produced was the venerable text of the *Constitutio Domus Regis*.[28] There was no hard and fast statement of the marshal's rights, and thus even contemporaries were sometimes faced with uncertainty.[29] On the whole, Henry III was disposed to accept the assertions of the Bigod family; Edward I was inclined to challenge them.[30]

LANDS AND FINANCES

On 29 March 1248, Maud Marshal died.[31] The last of the Marshals, she had outlived not only all of her five brothers, but also each of her four younger sisters. She had likewise outlasted two husbands, Hugh II Bigod and William de Warenne. Her career as a wife and a mother had shaped the destinies of two of the greatest families in England (and, incidentally, the two greatest families in East Anglia). When her funeral was held at Tintern Abbey in Monmouthshire, her eldest son, Roger, was naturally present among the mourners. Also in attendance were his younger brothers, Hugh and Ralph, along with Maud's son by her second marriage, the teenaged John de Warenne. Together the four of them acted as pallbearers that day, carrying their mother's body through the great abbey church and into the choir, where Maud was finally laid to rest.[32]

---

[27] For a possible dispute over the earl's military rights in 1254, see below, p. 48.

[28] e.g. *CCR, 1296-1302*, pp. 179-80; SC1/30/1; *CDS, 1108-1516*, p. 156.

[29] Cf. the referral to parliament of a question concerning the marshal's rights, below, pp. 79-80.

[30] For Henry's acceptance, see *CDI, 1177-1251*, p. 448. For Edward's challenges, see below, pp. 156-7, 160, 169, 171.

[31] Worcestre, *Itineraries*, ed. Harvey, p. 55.

[32] *CSM*, ii, 143.

The transformation of Roger Bigod, begun by the deaths of his uncles, was completed by that of his mother. In the first place, it meant that the earl regained control of the third portion of his father's estate which had been assigned to Maud in dower. At the time of his death in 1225, Hugh II Bigod held some twenty-three manors, all of which lay in East Anglia.[33] Ten were in Norfolk (Acle, Ditchingham, Earsham (with its half-hundred), Forncett, Framingham Earl, Halvergate, Hanworth, Lopham, Suffield and South Walsham), and a further eleven lay in Suffolk (Bungay, Dunningworth, Earl Soham, Earl Stonham, Framlingham, Hacheston, Hollesley, Hoo, Kelsale, Staverton and Walton). In addition, Hugh held manors at Dovercourt and Great Chesterford in Essex, and he also held some woodland at Romford in the same county.[34]

It is difficult to say precisely what this estate was worth. Although we have several hundred manorial accounts from the late thirteenth century for many of these properties, they form an incomplete series, and the figures they provide are not a reliable indication of the actual values of the manors themselves.[35] We also have some valuations of the entire Bigod estate, but these date from the fourteenth century, by which time its composition had changed considerably.[36]

---

[33] Only the Bigods' demesne manors are considered here. The earls were, of course, overlords for many other properties: as we have seen, by 1166 they had created 162¾ knights' fees in East Anglia (above, pp. 15-16). A full picture of these under-tenancies does not emerge until the death of Roger IV in 1306 (*CIPM*, iv, 297-303). For the importance of tenurial ties to the Bigod affinity, see below, pp. 61-2, 64-5, 71. For their continued importance in general to overlords during the thirteenth century, see D.A. Carpenter, 'The Second Century of English Feudalism', *Past and Present*, 168 (2000), pp. 30-71.

[34] There is insufficient space here to give a full history of how and when these manors were acquired (or reacquired in the case of those which were confiscated by Henry II). The following references are intended only as proof of tenure before 1225 (and, in the case of properties recovered from the Crown, after 1189). *Domesday Book*, ed. J. Morris (35 vols. in 40, Chichester, 1975-86), 33, ff. 178b, 180b, 181a, 183b, 184b, 189a+b (Forncett, Lopham and Suffield, held uninterruptedly since 1086); *PatR, 1216-25*, p. 508 (Framlingham); *CChR, 1226-57*, pp. 72-3 (Acle, Bungay, Ditchingham, Dunningworth, Earl Soham, Earsham and its half hundred, Framingham Earl, Halvergate, Hollesley, Kelsale, South Walsham, Staverton and Walton); *RLC*, i, 523 (Dovercourt); *RBE*, ii, 478, 569, 590 (Earl Stonham); *Rotuli Chartarum in Turris Londinensi Asservati*, ed. T.D. Hardy (Record Comm., 1837), pp. 52, 112 (Hanworth and Romford); *CPR, 1364-67*, p. 269 (Great Chesterford, Maud's *maritagium*). Hacheston seems to have been a dependent manor of Framlingham (*CIPM*, iv, 293), and since Roger II Bigod granted the chapel there to Hickling Priory, it was almost certainly acquired before 1221 (RBII 22). Hoo is first explicitly identified as a Bigod property in 1270 (*CIPM*, i, 241), but since its tenure was connected with Notley in Essex, held by Roger II Bigod in the early thirteenth century (RBII 6), it was very likely acquired at the same time.

[35] Below, pp. 101-2; R.R. Davies, 'Baronial Accounts, Incomes, and Arrears in the Later Middle Ages', *Economic History Review*, 2nd ser., 21 (1968), pp. 214-15.

[36] *CPR, 1301-1307*, p. 460; Denholm-Young, *SAIE*, p. 22. These figures are considered below.

By far the most useful piece of information we have is a list of figures drawn up in 1307, and evidently used to calculate the dower of Roger IV Bigod's widow, Alice de Hainault. This document provides the following values for those manors held by Hugh II Bigod in 1225:[37]

Table 1. The Bigod Inheritance

Place	Value (to the nearest pound)
Acle	–
Bungay	60
Ditchingham	39
Dovercourt	–
Dunningworth	23
Earl Soham	38
Earl Stonham	43
Earsham	38
Earsham Half Hundred	42
Forncett	56
Framingham Earl	42
Framlingham	105
Great Chesterford	43
Hacheston	(member of Framlingham)
Halvergate	48
Hanworth	–
Hollesley	33
Hoo	28
Kelsale	57
Lopham	40
Romford	8
South Walsham	37
Staverton	39
Suffield	–
Walton	65

Encouragingly, there are very few gaps: the total of the above figures – £884 – is well on the way to being a complete one. We lack a value for Acle because it was alienated by Roger IV before his death, and for Dovercourt and Suffield because Alice continued to hold them in her own right (she and Roger had been jointly re-enfeoffed by Edward I).[38] There is also a mysterious blank for the manor of Hanworth, which was held by the

[37] SC12/22/13. The values given correspond exactly with those in the final dower assignment. *CFR, 1272-1307*, pp. 551-2; *CCR, 1302-1307*, p. 509.
[38] Below, pp. 138, 172n.

earl at the time of his death, but apparently overlooked when the dower was calculated.[39]

In some instances, these gaps can be filled by using other evidence. From a memorandum of rents and customs drawn up in 1302, it seems that Acle might have had a gross value of £90.[40] Its net value was probably considerably lower, but not as low as £22, the rate at which the manor was let to farm by the Crown in the late twelfth century.[41] As a crude rule of thumb, those manors seized from the Bigods by Henry II were farmed at roughly half their value as recorded in 1307.[42] Applying this rule to Acle suggests that it was probably worth around £45.

By rather more devious means, it is possible to suggest a combined value for Dovercourt, Suffield and Hanworth. Unfortunately, there is no record of which manors were assigned to Maud Bigod as dower in 1225. However, from the financial arrangements that Roger III made with the king of Scots in 1228, it seems that his mother's dower cannot have included the manors of Acle, Bungay, Ditchingham, Dunningworth, Earl Soham, Earsham (or its half hundred), Framingham Earl, Halvergate, Hollesley, Kelsale, South Walsham, Staverton or Walton, nor can it have included Framlingham.[43] Only nine of the manors that had belonged to Hugh II Bigod were not involved in his son's fund-raising scheme to purchase an early inheritance – Chesterford, Dovercourt, Earl Stonham, Forncett, Hacheston, Hanworth, Hoo, Lopham and Suffield. It seems therefore very likely that these properties were the ones that formed Maud's dower.[44]

By lucky chance, we have values for all of the properties in the first group of manors (the ones Roger III retained after his mother had been dowered). Together, they give a total of £711. The second group (the putative dower manors) contains the three manors for which we do not have values (Dovercourt, Hanworth and Suffield). If this second group was indeed Maud's dower, it should have been equal to half of Roger's share (i.e. half of £711, viz. £356). The other five manors in the second group (Chesterford, Earl Stonham, Forncett, Hoo and Lopham, plus the £8 of woodland in Romford) combine to produce £218. Therefore, the three manors for which we have no values (Dovercourt, Hanworth and Suffield)

---

[39] Cf. *CIPM*, iv, 297.

[40] Worcestre, *Itineraries*, ed. Harvey, pp. 56-9. The total of the figures given is £89 12s 11d.

[41] *PR 26 Henry II*, p. 14.

[42] Compare the values of the farmed manors in 1188 with the 1307 figures. Halvergate (£22 10s: £48); South Walsham (£20: £37); Staverton (£20: £39); Dunningworth (£10: £23). *PR 34 Henry II*, pp. 53, 65.

[43] *CChR, 1226-57*, pp. 72-3; above, pp. 6-7.

[44] I have also, for the sake of argument, assumed that the fairly negligible £8 of woodland in Romford was also part of Maud's dower.

Map: The Bigod Estate in East Anglia, c. 1248

should together make up the difference between £356 and £218, i.e. they should be worth around £138.

Thus, with only minimal sleight of hand, it is possible to reach an approximate figure for the whole of Hugh II Bigod's estate based on the dower assessment of 1307. Taking the known value of £884, and the estimated values for Acle (£45), Hanworth, Suffield and Dovercourt (£138), we reach a grand total of £1,067.

While his mother lived, Roger had to make do with only two-thirds of this sum – a diminished estate worth some £711. To this, however, the earl made several significant additions. In 1232 he purchased the Suffolk manor of Peasenhall from his neighbour, Ralph de Peasenhall, using 650 marks from the money that had been raised to buy his wife's marriage portion.[45] It was worth around £22 a year.[46] Around the same time, Roger acquired the manors of Theberton in Suffolk, and half of the manor of Settrington in Yorkshire. These, however, he appears to have granted to his younger brothers.[47] In 1240 the Suffolk manor of Cratfield was added to the Bigod estate. The previous year Roger had revived an ancient dispute with William de Aubigny, the roots of which stretched back to the early twelfth century. The earl laid claim to the honour of Belvoir in Leicestershire, but was eventually persuaded to drop his claim in return for the compensatory grant of Cratfield.[48] The property was valued in 1307 at £12 per annum.[49]

Roger's inquisition post mortem of 1270 reveals one or two other properties that appear to have been acquired by the earl himself rather than inherited from his ancestors. He held some property in the town of Ipswich, worth only 10s per annum in 1307, and also twelve acres of land

---

[45] Above, pp. 7n, 14n, 15n.

[46] Roger IV Bigod granted £20 of land in Peasenhall to Nicholas de Seagrave. In 1302, the residue of the manor beyond this amount was assessed at 54s. The purchase price of 650m was therefore very close to the customary twenty times the annual value (£22 x 20 = £440 = 660m). *CIM*, i, 511; *CPR, 1301-1307*, p. 64.

[47] For Settrington, see Appendix C. For Theberton, see below, n. 56.

[48] *CRR*, xvi, 1237-42, pp. 176, 184; *Lincolnshire Records: Abstracts of Final Concords*, vol. 1, ed. W.O. Massingberd (London, 1896), p. 357; *PQW*, p. 736. As a consequence of the marriage of Roger I Bigod to Alice, daughter of Robert de Tosny, the Bigods inherited a large portion of the Tosny inheritance, including manors in Yorkshire that had once belonged to Robert de Lisle, husband of Aubrey de Tosny. These Yorkshire manors descended to Hugh I Bigod, but part of the Tosny inheritance – the honour of Belvoir – descended to the de Aubigny family through the agency of Hugh's sister, Cecily, who had been given in marriage to William de Aubigny by Henry I. For the tortuous descent of the Tosny lands, see K.S.B. Keats-Rohan, 'Belvoir: The Heirs of Robert and Berengar de Tosny', *Prosopon*, 9 (1998); J.A. Green, 'The Descent of Belvoir', *Prosopon*, 10 (1999). Cf. Wareham, 'Motives and Politics', p. 231. The Bigods had attempted to challenge this settlement before. Hugh II Bigod had been attempting much the same in the weeks before his death, and perhaps so had Roger II Bigod in 1197. *CRR*, xii, 1225-26, p. 1; *Feet of Fines 10 Richard I… and a Roll of the King's Court* (Pipe Roll Soc., 24, 1900), p. 236.

[49] SC12/22/13.

at Alby in Norfolk (never assessed, but also negligible).[50] The only property of note that is mentioned in 1270 for the first time is Banham in Norfolk; Roger reportedly held the manor from the earl Warenne for the service of one knight.[51] Precisely how or when it was obtained is not known, but no doubt the kinship between the Bigods and the Warennes created by the second marriage of Roger's mother played its part. Here, alas, the search for financial evidence draws a blank. Banham was no longer held in demesne in 1307, and no document has been unearthed which might indicate its value.

Our estimate of the value of Roger's estate between 1228 and 1248 must therefore remain somewhat rough. To his diminished inheritance of £711 the earl had added a further £34 (Peasenhall and Cratfield), and perhaps the mysterious manor of Banham, which could have been acquired at any point down to 1270. Assuming he obtained it in the first half of his career, and that it ranked among his more valuable properties, Banham might push the annual value of Roger's estate to somewhere in the vicinity of £800.

When his mother died in March 1248, Roger took possession of the lands she had held in dower for the previous twenty-three years. This immediately boosted his income to around £1,150 (c. £800 plus £356). But Maud's death also brought Roger extra lands – the huge tenurial windfall she had received in 1246 when her brothers' earldom was broken up. The Marshals had been earls of Pembroke, and as such they controlled a large amount of territory in South Wales. They had also held lands in many southern English counties. In England, Maud had inherited new demesne manors at Bosham in Sussex, Weston in Hertfordshire, Kemsing in Kent, Toddington in Bedfordshire and Hamstead Marshall in Berkshire. In Wales, she had acquired the lordship of Chepstow, in which her own property included the town and castle of Chepstow itself, and the very large manor of Tidenham over the Gloucestershire border.[52]

The most valuable part of the Marshal inheritance, however, lay across the Irish Sea. As the heirs of 'Strongbow', William Marshal and his sons had acquired the whole of the former kingdom of Leinster.[53] Even a fifth share of this territory constituted a large amount of land. Maud's portion comprised the county of Carlow, in which her demesne holdings included the town and castle of Carlow itself, the borough and manor of Fothered,

---

[50] *CIPM*, i, 240. Roger I Bigod held some property in Ipswich at the time of Domesday, but this was apparently unconnected to Roger III's holdings, which were said to be held from the earl of Aumale. *Domesday Book*, ed. Morris, 34, f. 378b.

[51] *CIPM*, ii, 241.

[52] *CPR, 1364-67*, pp. 266, 269, 274. Hamstead Marshall included the properties at Speen and Newbury.

[53] Crouch, *William Marshal*, pp. 70, 87-9.

and other properties at Ballycrinnigan and St Mullins. She also inherited several properties outside of the county. To the north, in County Kildare, she acquired the manor of Ballysax. To the south, downstream from Carlow along the River Barrow, she held important properties in County Wexford, including the very large manor of Old Ross, the burgeoning port of New Ross, and the area now known as Great Island.[54]

The values for these properties, as assessed between the years 1247 and 1249, are given in the table below:[55]

Table 2. The Marshal Inheritance

Place	*Value (to the nearest pound)*
Ballycrinnigan	12
Ballysax	28
Bosham	97
Carlow (town and county)	49
Chepstow	76
Fothered	53
Great Island	43
Hamstead Marshall	35
Kemsing	26
New Ross	53
Newbury	5
Old Ross	73
Speen	29
St Mullins (Tamolyn)	39
Tidenham	68
Toddington	18
Weston	50

In the short period between acquiring these properties in 1246 and her own death in 1248, Maud alienated some of them to her younger sons. The valuable manor of Bosham she gave to Hugh III Bigod, while the barony of St Mullins in Ireland she bestowed upon her third son, Ralph Bigod of Stockton.[56] The manor of Ballycrinnigan was granted to the abbey of

---

[54] *CPR, 1364-67*, p. 271 (Katherlac = Carlow; Ballydunegan = Ballycrinnigan; Sotherec = Fothered; Camulin = Tamolyn = St Mullins).

[55] *CPR, 1364-67*, pp. 266, 269, 271, 274.

[56] For Hugh's acquisitions and career, see below, pp. 54-5, 102-3. Ralph's son and heir, John Bigod of Stockton, is found holding St Mullins in the 1280s (*CDI, 1285-92*, pp. 110, 201). Ralph also acquired the manors of Stockton in Norfolk and Theberton in Suffolk. Both had belonged to the Bigods since the twelfth century. Theberton was seized by Henry II after 1177 but restored to Roger II Bigod before 1200, when the earl granted it to a certain William fitz Alan for a term of life. When fitz Alan died around 1233, the manor reverted to Roger III Bigod. At some point thereafter Roger granted it to Ralph (there is

Tintern Parva. The first occasion on which we learn of this alienation is in 1301, and therefore it could have been a gift of either Maud, Roger III or Roger IV.[57] Maud, however, is the most likely benefactor. Apart from the fact that the abbey had been founded by her father, the countess also visited Ireland in the period 1246 x 1248, accompanied by her two younger sons. The grant of St Mullins to Ralph and the gift of Ballycrinnigan to Tintern were probably made during this visit.[58]

Maud, then, used Bosham and St Mullins to provide for her sons, and perhaps Ballycrinnigan to provide for her soul. Beyond this she made no other alienations from her share of the Marshal estate, and the remainder therefore descended to Roger in 1248. His inheritance, however, was complicated by more dowers: specifically, those created for the widows of the Marshal brothers. Several properties were earmarked for Margaret de Lacy, widow of Walter Marshal, including Bosham and Hamstead Marshall. However, it is by no means certain that the dowager countess ever enjoyed seisin of either manor. When challenged over Hamstead in 1249, Roger argued that it belonged to him as a sergeantry indivisible from the marshalship, and it would appear that he won his point. He is found in possession of the manor during the 1250s, and his brother Hugh had likewise established himself at Bosham in the same period.[59]

Roger had less success in denying the dower claims of Eleanor de Montfort, once the wife of William Marshal the younger, and since 1238 the wife of the celebrated Earl Simon. Her settlement, drawn up at Easter 1249, included the lands in Kemsing, Newbury, Weston and Toddington, and she appears to have had possession of the first three of these manors down to her death in 1275, when they were finally obtained by Roger IV Bigod.[60] With regard to Toddington, however, Eleanor appears to have

no mention of the manor in the earl's inquisition post mortem). In 1305 it was held by Ralph's son, John (*PR 34 Henry II*, p. 65; *Feet of Fines for the County of Norfolk*, ed. B. Dodwell (2 vols., Pipe Roll Soc., new ser., 27, 32, 1952-58), ii, 149-50; *CRR*, xv, 1233-37, p. 77; *CIPM*, iv, 216). Stockton was reportedly granted to Roger II Bigod by Henry II (*Rot. Hund.*, i, 467), but the first time the manor was allowed in the farm of Norfolk was 1191, so it was perhaps more likely to have been a gift of Richard I made in connection with the restoration of the earldom (*PR 2 Richard I*, p. 91; cf. *Cartae Antiquae Rolls*, i, 158-9). Roger II proceeded to give a third of the manor in marriage with his daughter Mary to Ranulf fitz Robert. At some point during his brief comital career, Hugh II Bigod granted the remaining two-thirds of Stockton to one of his leading *familiares*, Hamo Lenveise. However, soon after Hugh's death in February 1225, Maud bought back this part of the manor from Hamo and bestowed it on Ralph (*Rot. Hund.*, i, 467; *CIPM*, i, 239; HBII 2; Maud 1, 3).
[57] In 1301, the abbot of Tintern Parva held Ballycrinnigan from Roger IV Bigod in free alms. *CDI, 1293-1301*, p. 362.
[58] Maud 4.
[59] *CR, 1256-59*, pp. 99-100. Intriguingly, however, Margaret de Lacy was resident at Hamstead when she died in 1266, suggesting some form of accommodation had been reached. *AM*, ii, 104, 373.
[60] *CPR, 1364-67*, p. 266; below, p. 116.

lost out; Roger III seems to have obtained the manor, and thereafter alienated it to royal servant Paul Peyvre.[61] Exactly how the earl achieved or justified this appropriation is unknown. The only clue is that Peyvre was one of the two individuals responsible for arranging the partition of the Marshal estate. It appears that Roger had been willing to sacrifice a small part of his entitlement in order to guarantee that the overall outcome would be weighted in his favour.[62]

Bearing in mind these alienations and assignments, we can work out the value of the lands inherited by Roger Bigod in 1248. From the figures in the table above, his family's share of the Marshal estate was £754. Less the values of the lands alienated by his mother (Bosham, Ballycrinnigan and St Mullins), the properties that had gone in dower to Eleanor de Montfort (Weston, Kemsing and Newbury) and the manor of Toddington (which the earl himself had alienated), Roger had acquired new lands worth £507. When this figure is added to his paternal inheritance in East Anglia (worth about £1,150), it raises his overall income after 1248 to around £1,650.

Because this figure is based on dower calculations, it is probably considerably lower than Roger's real income. To illustrate the gulf between an estate's gross revenue and the values used when assessing a dower, we need turn no further than the arrangements made after the death of Roger IV Bigod in 1306 for his widow, Alice. The total value of the lands allotted to Alice in England and Wales comes to £454. The total of her Irish dower is £114. Altogether, therefore, the countess's dower was reckoned at £568.[63] If this did indeed represent a third of the Bigod estate, then the estate as a whole had been valued at around £1,700. Yet when Crown officials had assessed exactly the same estate just three years beforehand, they had come up with the substantially larger figure of £4,000.[64] Clearly, Roger IV's real income must have lain somewhere between these two extremes. By the same token, Roger III's real income must have exceeded the £1,650 suggested by using dower values. For instance, as we saw above, these figures suggest that in 1228 the earl's estate was worth only a little over £700. Yet, as we noted in the previous chapter, the sums involved in the negotiations for Roger's wardship suggest that his guardians hoped to extract at least £1,000 a year from

---

[61] *PQW*, p. 10; *Rot. Hund.*, i, 7; *CChR, 1226-57*, p. 349; *CM*, v, 242-3. Cf. Maddicott, *Montfort*, p. 50. M.M. Wade has nothing particular to say on Toddington, but she observes that 'the discrepancy between what was granted to Eleanor on paper and what she actually held is very obvious'. M.M. Wade, 'The Personal Quarrels of Simon de Montfort and his Wife with Henry III of England' (B.Litt. thesis, Oxford Univ., 1939), p. 46.

[62] *CPR, 1364-67*, p. 266. Cf. RBIII 4, a similar *douceur*.

[63] *CFR, 1272-1307*, pp. 551-2; *CCR, 1302-1307*, p. 509.

[64] *CPR, 1301-1307*, p. 460.

these same lands. In other words, they anticipated profits that were at least 40 per cent bigger than the dower values.[65]

The fact that it is impossible to obtain an exact value for Roger's income is regrettable, but it does not render the above calculations irrelevant. On the contrary, they are very useful in helping to place the Bigods in the pecking order of contemporary comital families. In the first place, the figure of £1,650 was arrived at using dower figures from 1306 and 1247. On the basis of the same information, the income of the Marshal family has been assessed as £3,500. Roger, in other words, was worth only half what his uncles had been – the new earl marshal was not a patch on the old ones.[66] Nor were the Bigods in the same league as the de Clares. In 1304, the earldom of Norfolk was valued at £4,000; a decade later, the earldom of Gloucester was valued at £6,000. Whatever their real incomes may have been, these nearly contemporary assessments suggest that their assets were in the ratio 2:3 – Gloucester was 50 per cent better off than Norfolk. Furthermore, we are entitled to project this ratio back into the reign of Henry III: one of the striking things that emerges from the above analysis is that, despite undergoing several changes and contortions, the estate of Roger III Bigod in 1248 (£1,650) was almost identical in value to the estate of his nephew in 1307 (£1,700). Gloucester's real income in Henry's reign has been estimated as £3,700. Accordingly, we should perhaps expect Roger III's real income to be around £2,500.[67]

The Bigods thus emerge in a new light in relation to their peers. Clearly they were very wealthy men. Yet they did not belong in the top rank of super-earls, where they have sometimes been placed. Whichever method of reckoning is used, Rogers III and IV do not measure up to the likes of William Marshal, Gilbert de Clare or Richard of Cornwall. They were, in fact, closer in wealth to the likes of William de Valence (£2,500) and Simon de Montfort (£2,000).[68]

The most important (and incontrovertible) fact to emerge from this analysis is how dramatically Roger's position had been changed by the death of his mother. Of the £1,650 the earl enjoyed after 1248, more than half had come to him as a direct result of Maud's death (£356 from her dower, and £507 from the Marshal inheritance). Overnight, Roger's income had been doubled.

---

[65] Above, pp. 6-7n. Cf. F.G. Davenport, *The Economic Development of a Norfolk Manor, 1086-1565* (London, 1906), pp. 37-44, where figures extracted from the whole run of accounts for Forncett suggest an average net profit of £90 per annum – 60 per cent more than the £56 given in the dower calculations.

[66] M. Altschul, *A Baronial Family in England: The Clares, 1217-1314* (Baltimore, 1965), p. 205.

[67] Altschul, *The Clares*, p. 205; J.R. Maddicott, *Thomas of Lancaster* (Oxford, 1970), p. 23.

[68] Maddicott, *Montfort*, p. 55; H. Ridgeway, 'William de Valence and his *Familiares*, 1247-72', *Historical Research*, 65 (1992), p. 242.

Thus the deaths of his uncles and his mother transformed the life and career of Roger III Bigod. Twenty-three years after it was broken by the premature death of his father, his family's estate had been made whole; once again, the Bigods were the most powerful force in East Anglia. But they were also now much more than this. The deaths of his relatives in the period 1245 to 1248 had effectively redefined Roger as a political figure. He had been promoted from an aristocrat with exclusively regional concerns to a magnate with interests in many southern counties. He had simultaneously become a marcher lord and an Irish colonist. In terms of material wealth, he was twice the man he had been before. He had also successfully asserted his right to the marshalship of England, the ancient dignity borne by his mother's family since time immemorial. It was an office that not only magnified the earl's personal prestige and further enhanced his fortune; it also carried unique privileges and responsibilities that would cast his relations with the Crown in a new light. Up to 1248, Roger had been 'comital small-fry'. From now on, he was a big fish.[69]

POLITICS, 1246-58

The second half of this chapter considers Roger's career from the time he became earl marshal in 1246 down as far as the year 1258, when he was one of the leading participants in a revolutionary movement that effectively deprived Henry III of executive power. If there is a dominant theme to the politics of this period, it is provided by the king's Lusignan half-brothers, who arrived in England in the spring of 1247 and were banished as a direct consequence of the 1258 revolution. The four brothers – Guy and Geoffrey de Lusignan, and especially William and Aymer de Valence – were shown indiscriminate favour by Henry, a bias which bred resentment among the established English baronage, and created tension between the newcomers and the Savoyard circle around the queen.[70] At the same time, there was a rising chorus of discontent with the king's rule as a result of more deep-seated grievances – in particular, the fiscal exploitation practised by justices in eyre and sheriffs. Protest was expressed conventionally in the shire courts, and novelly in the developing institution of parliament.[71] This situation was exacerbated from 1253-54 as a result of fresh financial strains created

[69] Maddicott, *Montfort*, p. 55.
[70] Howell, *Eleanor of Provence*, pp. 49-70, 128-51; H. Ridgeway, 'Foreign favourites and Henry III's problems of patronage, 1247-58', *EHR*, 104 (1989), pp. 590-610; *idem*, 'King Henry III and the "Aliens"', *TCE*, ii (1988), 81-92; *idem*, 'The Lord Edward and the Provisions of Oxford (1258): A Study in Faction', *TCE*, i, (1986), 89-99.
[71] Carpenter, 'King, Magnates and Society', pp. 75-106; J.R. Maddicott, 'Magna Carta and the Local Community, 1215-1259', *Past and Present*, 102 (1984), pp. 25-65; *idem*, 'Pre-Reform Parliaments', pp. 17-46.

by Henry's successful but costly military campaign in Gascony and by the king's ill-conceived scheme to put his younger son Edmund on the throne of Sicily.[72]

Where does the earl of Norfolk figure against this general political background? Roger's witnessing of royal charters shows that he was more frequently at court after 1245 than before.[73] From the mid-1240s, the earl benefited from Henry's conscious decision to improve his hitherto fractious relationship with the great men of his realm.[74] Like other magnates, Roger was wooed with royal gifts of timber and deer.[75] He was never so isolated from the king as he appears to have been in the late 1230s. Yet while the earl was occasionally seen at court, he was not quite the paid-up curialist that has sometimes been suggested.[76] While his witnessing is more frequent after 1245, it nevertheless falls into a pattern which suggests he turned up largely for special occasions: parliaments and occasionally the festivities at Christmas. Significantly, his attendance is most frequent during the years 1246 and 1247, the exciting but uncertain period when the Marshal estate was being carved up, and very much a time to maintain good relations with the Crown.[77] Thus, when his mother fell ill in March 1248, Roger did not rush to her bedside, but continued to shadow and entertain Henry, taking care to make sure that Chepstow Castle would not slip through his fingers.[78] Even during these exceptional years, however, there were long periods when the earl was apparently absent from court. He witnessed no charters in the first half of 1246, and none in the last five months of 1247. After his mother's death, once Roger was securely possessed of her lands, his attendance dropped dramatically.[79] No doubt he spent much of his time visiting his new lordships and investigating their potential.[80]

The earl also had to attend to other private matters which may have taken him away from the king's side for weeks or months at a time. From 1245, for example, he embarked upon a long quest to have his marriage

---

[72] Maddicott, *Montfort*, pp. 124-9.

[73] Appendix A.

[74] Stacey, *Politics*, pp. 254-5.

[75] Carpenter, *King, Magnates and Society*, p. 95. For gifts of deer, see *CR, 1242-47*, p. 310; *CR, 1247-51*, p. 309; *CR, 1254-56*, pp. 120, 126. In 1256 and 1257 Roger received gifts of timber to help with building works at Hamstead Marshall. *CR, 1254-56*, pp. 294, 297; *CR, 1256-59*, pp. 99-100.

[76] Stacey, *Politics*, pp. 249, 255; Maddicott, *Montfort*, pp. 35-6. Cf. Howell, *Eleanor of Provence*, p. 141; D.A. Carpenter, 'What Happened in 1258?', *Reign of Henry III*, p. 194.

[77] Cf. Maddicott, *Montfort*, p. 36.

[78] *CR, 1247-51*, p. 110; *CACWales*, p. 29 (translated in *Letters of Medieval Women*, ed. A. Crawford (Stroud, 2002), pp. 217-18). Maud died on 29 March, even as Roger was preparing to receive Henry at Framlingham the next day. News of the countess's death had reached the court by 7 April. Above, p. 31; Appendix A; *Excerpta*, ii, 31.

[79] *CPR, 1247-58*, pp. 15, 19; *Excerpta*, ii, 33.

[80] For example, he was evidently at Chepstow in the summer of 1250. *CR, 1247-51*, p. 309.

annulled.[81] Three years later the case was revoked to Rome, which raises the distinct possibility that his visit to the pope in 1249 was personal rather than diplomatic.[82] Roger's argument, which rested on consanguinity, was evidently weak; his real reason for dissatisfaction in 1245 was more likely to have been that, after twenty years of marriage, he and Isabella had produced no heirs. The mortality of his Marshal uncles that year had emphasized how quickly events could overtake and destroy a powerful family, and may have caused the earl to fear that the Bigods might be similarly extinguished. In this respect, the final verdict was highly unfavourable. In 1253, he was told (again, possibly in person) that his marriage to Isabella was above suspicion. According to Paris, however, Roger reacted with good grace, even satisfaction, upon hearing the news. The general family situation, perhaps, allowed the chivalrous re-acceptance of his countess. In the years after 1245, his brother Hugh had fathered several children (at least one of whom was male); the Bigod dynasty, if not the earl's own line, now seemed secure.[83]

Relations with the court, therefore, were improved but remained occasional. Roger was now too powerful a figure to ignore completely, but he was still far from being a leading light in Henry III's government. From around Christmas 1245, he seems to have buried the hatchet to some extent with Peter of Savoy and, by extension, the Savoyard circle around the queen.[84] But the earl of Norfolk was neither a queen's man or a king's man; he cannot be positively aligned with any particular set of interests at an increasingly polarized court.

Because of his lack of regular involvement with royal government, and his aloofness from the factional squabbles at court, Roger is sometimes portrayed as a man more in touch with the sensibilities of the provinces; the type of individual who might have recognized the resentments which were accumulating in the shires and sought to represent them in parliament.[85] This may have been the case; but as with other earls (most obviously Leicester), there is precious little evidence that Roger harboured any reformist tendencies prior to the revolution of 1258.[86] His reputation in this regard appears to be assumed in light of his behaviour after that point, and the belief he was a force for good undoubtedly owes much to the praise that contemporary chroniclers bestowed on his brother Hugh. The earl's credentials as a reformer (as well as those of his brother) are

---

[81] *CPL, 1198-1304*, p. 253.

[82] Cf. Stacey, *Politics*, p. 255.

[83] *CPR, 1247-58*, pp. 52, 185; *CM*, v, 382-3; below, pp. 102, 187, 189.

[84] Above, p. 25; *CPR, 1232-47*, p. 472. Roger held his Suffolk manor of Earl Soham from the Savoy's honour of Richmond. *CIPM*, i, 240.

[85] Howell, *Eleanor of Provence*, p. 141.

[86] Maddicott, *Montfort*, p. 137.

examined in the next chapter, with particular reference to the quality of his lordship and the extent of his connections with gentry society.[87] For now, we shall confine ourselves to his actions before the revolution.

As we saw in the previous chapter, it is quite possible that Roger voiced real concerns about the king's government in the parliaments of 1244 and 1245, and his combative behaviour at the Council of Lyon may have enhanced his public standing.[88] It comes as no surprise, therefore, to find the earl prominent among the signatories in a letter to the pope in 1246, complaining about Rome's ongoing exactions and requesting redress.[89] This, however, does not prove he was an implacable critic of the Crown; opposition to papal demands, like distrust of the king's foreign favourites, united Englishmen of all degrees, from the lowliest freeholder to the greatest native earl. While both were issues in 1258, more important was the demand for reform in local government, and here we can be much less certain that Henry's critics spoke with a single voice; maladministration in the provinces was principally the concern of the lesser baronage and gentry rather than the great magnates.[90] Certainly, no earl emerges during the 1250s as a champion of the lay opposition to the Crown in the way that the bishop of Lincoln, down to 1253, spearheaded the clergy's resistance to the king's policies.[91]

Criticism of royal government was particularly fierce during the years 1253-54, a period when Henry III embarked upon another military expedition to southern France, where English rule was on the brink of collapse. To finance the campaign, the king turned to parliament in search of an aid, but opposition to his request was stiff. Unable to persuade the assembly to vote him the money freely, he was obliged to resort to the same device that had paid for his previous Continental adventure. In 1245 it had been a feudal aid for the marriage of his infant daughter; Henry now wanted a similar levy for the knighting of his eldest son. Even this, however, was not conceded lightly. The king's humiliation was further compounded by parliament's insistence that this money (to which he should have been entitled without question) would only be granted in return for a confirmation of Magna Carta.[92]

It is now appreciated that this intransigence in the face of royal demands was not led (as once supposed) by the greatest magnates, but born of a groundswell of protest from the lower laity in parliament, who were unable to escape the burden of the king's increasingly extortionate government. The latter group could only benefit from a stricter

[87] Below, pp. 73-80.
[88] Above, pp. 22-4.
[89] *CM*, iv, 533-4.
[90] *DBM*, pp. 81, 99; *AM*, i, 164; Maddicott, 'Magna Carta', pp. 51-4.
[91] F.M. Powicke, *The Thirteenth Century, 1216-1307* (2nd edn, Oxford, 1962), pp. 453-6.
[92] Maddicott, 'Pre-Reform Parliaments', pp. 34-5; above, p. 23.

observation of Magna Carta. Men of Roger Bigod's degree, on the other hand, apparently took a more neutral view of events. While they may have doubted the wisdom of military action in Gascony (after their humiliation in Poitou in 1242, the native aristocracy could hardly be expected to endorse wholeheartedly another expedition which would benefit only Henry and his half-brothers), their position on the Charter is seen as more ambivalent. While they cherished certain clauses, others – particularly those which called on magnates to observe the same conditions to their tenants as the king did to his – threatened to curb their own ability to extort money. Henry was alive to this ambivalence of attitude among his greater critics, and may even have deliberately exploited it in order to divide his opponents in the years before 1258, driving wedges between men of Roger's rank from those beneath them.[93]

Two documents from 1253 show the earl giving his support to the confirmation of both Magna Carta and the Charter of the Forest. The first is a sentence of excommunication published by the English bishops against those violating the charters, to which Roger, along with three of his peers, gave assent. The second is a set of royal letters patent, in which Henry himself, three named earls (Norfolk, Hereford and Warwick) and Peter of Savoy endorsed the bishops' sentence, and to which they applied their seals 'at the instance of the other magnates and the people'. The king evidently conceded these confirmations grudgingly, hedging his endorsement around with a final clause saving the rights of the Crown.[94] Was the assent of Roger and his peers demanded because they too were perceived to have failed to uphold the Charter? Or was it required because, as men with greater reputations for probity, these earls could bolster Henry's promise?[95] Unfortunately, the documents themselves are too prosaic and uncommunicative for us to reach a decisive verdict. Certainly, Hereford, Warwick and Norfolk are never identified as major offenders against the charters (in contrast, say, to the likes of Gloucester and Cornwall).[96] By the same token, it requires a large leap of faith to conclude that Roger and his colleagues had the full confidence of the 'other magnates and people', and that the earl heartily endorsed the charters as a remedial draught for the ailing body politic.

The balance might perhaps be tipped in favour of the latter view, however, by an episode which occurred once the Gascony campaign was underway. Having obtained his money, Henry embarked for the Continent on 6 August 1253.[97] Roger was among the earls who crossed

---

[93] Maddicott, 'Magna Carta', pp. 51-4.

[94] *Councils and Synods*, i, 474, 477-9.

[95] Cf. Henry's bid for popularity in 1262. Below, p. 89.

[96] Maddicott, 'Magna Carta', pp. 54-61.

[97] Powicke, *Thirteenth Century*, p. 116.

with the king (as earl marshal, he must have played an important role in the fighting, but what we know of his conduct is undistinguished).[98] To the surprise of many, the expedition was a success, and secured the English Crown's hold on the province. Victory, however, came at an enormous cost, not least because Henry was obliged to purchase the support of the earl of Leicester, whose services came at a high premium. By Christmas, the royal war chest was empty, and the king was forced to turn to parliament in search of more money. Unable to put his request in person, he sent an embassy back to England to make the case, and for this task he selected the earl marshal.[99] This proved to be a long and therefore fruitless voyage for Roger. Delayed by almost a fortnight by contrary winds, he arrived in Westminster to find the parliament (an assembly celebrated as the first to which knights were summoned) had already debated and refused the request for an aid. Worse still, when he put the king's case, which not only stressed dire need but also the imminent danger of an attack from Castile, the baronage suspected they were being misled and refused the request.[100]

On first inspection, the episode seems to reflect poorly on Roger, who appears as an unsuccessful diplomat and a royal dogsbody. Was this, however, how he was actually perceived by the laity in parliament? Matthew Paris, who was very likely present in the assembly, whilst quick to condemn Henry for being disingenuous, was anxious to exonerate the earl marshal, whom he thought had probably been imposed upon to represent the king.[101] His comments might be taken to suggest that there were some in parliament who viewed the earl with sympathetic eyes. This body of opinion, moreover, may have been quite substantial. Why, after all, should Henry, given the wide choice of potential ambassadors among his entourage, choose Roger Bigod – a figure with whom he had little regular contact, and who was not normally counted among his intimate advisers? The answer, plausibly, is that the earl was selected precisely because of this distance, and because he was a popular figure in parliament. The best candidate for the job of persuading the lower laity to vote an aid would have been an individual with a reputation for probity and independence of action. Henry's decision to send Roger home to negotiate suggests that, far from being a royalist stooge, the earl was a figure of whom the wider political community approved. It increases

---

[98] For his activities, see Appendix A; *CR, 1251-53*, p. 484; *CR, 1253-54*, pp. 166, 190; *CPR, 1247-58*, p. 244.
[99] Maddicott, *Montfort*, pp. 122-4; Howell, *Eleanor of Provence*, p. 121. The earl was accompanied on his mission by John Balliol, and possibly Gilbert de Seagrave. *Royal and Other Historical Letters Illustrative of the Reign of King Henry III*, ed. W.W. Shirley (2 vols., Record Comm., 1862-6), ii, 101; *CM*, v, 423-5; vi, 282-4.
[100] Howell, *Eleanor of Provence*, p. 121.
[101] *CM*, v, 423.

rather than diminishes the likelihood that he had actively backed the confirmation of the Charters in 1253.

Exactly how long Roger remained in Gascony after his empty-handed return is unclear.[102] He was still in Henry's company on 19 March, but had definitely departed before 4 June; a writ directed to him on 20 May might be taken to indicate that he was back in England before this date.[103] The reason for the earl's departure is hardly more certain, but Matthew Paris nevertheless suggests a plausible cause. At some point in the spring, he tells us, there was dissension among the Welsh troops in the royal army, and the king's Poitevin half-brothers took it upon themselves to hand out the punishments. This incensed Humphrey de Bohun, earl of Hereford, since it ignored his rights as constable, and he complained to Henry. When the king responded by doing nothing, his English nobles were reportedly scandalized. Although Henry corrected his error, the damage was irreversible; soon afterwards many of the magnates, including Roger, sought licence to withdraw, and returned to England.[104] On the one hand, this is just another example of Henry's seemingly innate ability to irritate people through his inability to do justice. There is good reason, however, to suppose that Roger Bigod, like Humphrey de Bohun, took personal offence at the king's behaviour. To overlook the rights of the constable was surely to overlook the rights of the marshal: both figures were responsible for discipline in the royal host.[105] In the course of the campaign, Roger had already had cause to complain that his rights as marshal were not being respected.[106] Now, it seems, they had been flagrantly violated. This episode in the spring of 1254 is arguably the precursor of later, more celebrated clashes over the same issue.[107]

A more explosive and better-documented row between Roger and the king occurred in the following year, in the wake of Henry's decision to intervene in Scottish politics. Four years beforehand, the king had given his daughter, Margaret, in marriage to Alexander III, the new king of Scots. Alexander had been a minor at the time of the wedding, and was still under age in 1255, when Henry received reports from his daughter complaining that she and her husband were being ill-treated by their guardians. In the summer, therefore, the English king moved his court northwards, and summoned the men in question, John Balliol and Robert de Ros, to meet him near the Scottish border. When they appeared

---

[102] Cf. Appendix A.
[103] *CPR, 1247-58*, p. 278; *CR, 1254-56*, pp. 134-5, 304.
[104] *CM*, v, 442-3.
[105] Above, p. 30.
[106] *CR, 1253-54*, p. 196.
[107] Below, pp. 135-6, 156-7, 163-4, 165, 169, 171.

at court, both were deprived of their lands and had enormous fines imposed upon them.[108]

Roger accompanied Henry on this mission. En route, he hunted in Yorkshire to provide the royal household with deer, and he played a leading role in the negotiations that took place once the English court had arrived in the Borders.[109] After their return south, however, the earl and the king argued violently over the fate of de Ros. Roger was loosely related to the accused man, and it is not impossible that as youngsters they had spent time in each other's company at the Scottish court.[110] According to Paris, such was the seriousness of de Ros's crime that his life was in danger.[111] This seems implausible; the prospect of an execution would surely have generated more widespread consternation among the English aristocracy. The likeliest explanation for Roger's intervention is simply that he believed that de Ros was not guilty. Four years later – after Henry had been forcibly persuaded to listen to the opinions of the earl and his fellow reformers – the judgement against the Scottish baron was reversed. 'By the advice of the magnates of his council', the king declared that it had all been a mistake: de Ros was in fact innocent. His fine was lifted, and attempts to seize his estate were abandoned.[112]

In 1255, however, Roger was seemingly alone in calling for clemency, and Henry was in no mood to brook such criticism. The earl's intervention enraged the king, who publicly called Roger a traitor. It prompted a famous exchange:

'You lie,' the earl replied. 'I have never been a traitor, nor shall I ever be. If you are just, how can you harm me?'

'I can seize your corn, and thresh it, and sell it,' retorted the king.

'Do so,' said Roger, 'and I will send back your threshers without their heads.'[113]

Henry was undeterred. The official record not only bears out Paris's dramatic reportage, but also shows that the king moved quickly to call Roger's bluff.[114] For over a decade, he had deigned to ignore the earl's debts to the Crown, which had increased substantially owing to the old argument over the Bigod service quota. In the early 1240s, as we have

---

[108] Duncan, *Making of a Kingdom*, pp. 560-68.

[109] *CR, 1254-56*, pp. 124-6; *CPR, 1247-58*, pp. 424, 441; *Anglo-Scottish Relations, 1174-1328*, ed. E.L.G. Stones (London, 1965), pp. 68-9.

[110] Roger's countess and de Ros's mother were both daughters of King William the Lion. *Dictionary of National Biography* (63 vols., London, 1885-1900), xlix, 218.

[111] *CM*, v, 530.

[112] *CDS, 1108-1272*, p. 425.

[113] *CM*, v, 530 (translation from Powicke, *Henry III*, p. 342).

[114] The following should be compared with the account given in Carpenter, 'King, Magnates and Society', pp. 89-91.

seen, the exchequer contended that Roger had an outstanding liability of £218 for the Poitevin scutage of 1231. The earl, on the other hand, having paid £120 – a sum suggested by his family's ancient quota of sixty knights' fees – was adamant that he was quit.[115] By 1255, this pattern had been repeated on two further occasions. The exchequer had anticipated £163 from Roger for the aid of 1245 (set at £1 per fee and granted for the marriage of Henry's daughter), and had been hoping to receive £356 for the aid of 1253 (£2 per fee, granted on the occasion of Edward's knighthood). The earl, however, paid on just sixty fees in each case (£60 and £120 respectively).[116] By 1257, therefore, there was a considerable difference of opinion: the exchequer regarded him as being in arrears to the tune of £576, but Roger considered he had paid in full.[117] The earl also owed other, less debatable sums. Chief among these were the arrears he had allowed to accumulate for his share of an annual payment made by the Crown to Eleanor de Montfort – the countess's compensation for her inadequate dower from the Marshal estate.[118] Roger's contribution had been fixed at 80 marks a year, but since 1248 he had paid nothing, and consequently in 1255 he had a liability of 640 marks.[119]

Since 1242, the exchequer had been attempting to compel the earl to settle up by ordering distraint on his plough-beasts, but the king, in line with his general policy of appeasing his magnates, had repeatedly intervened and granted respite. After their row in 1255, however, Henry abandoned his indulgent stance. He personally ordered the exchequer to distrain Roger, thereby making good on his reported threat to humble the earl by seizing his agricultural assets.[120]

It would be very convenient to be able to present Roger's row with Henry in 1255 as the beginning of a slide towards the more dramatic confrontation of 1258. Unfortunately, however, plenty of evidence flies in the face of Paris's opinion that 'anger and hatred resulted from the quarrel'.[121] The argument over de Ros shows every sign of being a flash in

---

[115] Above, p. 16.

[116] E368/20, m. 15d; E368/32, mm. 26d, 27d. Bigod's outstanding debt for the 'marriage' aid was £102 15s, indicating that he had paid £60. His assessment of £355 16s 8d for the 'knighthood' aid was based on 162¾ fees *de veteri* and *de novo* in East Anglia, the 6⅙ fees he held in Essex, and an additional 9 fees for his Marshal lands. The account for 1257 states that he owed £223 10s and £12 ½m for the Essex fees, which meant that he had paid £120.

[117] E372/102, m. 1. Precisely, £575 11s 8d; this being the sum of £217 16s 8d (for the Poitevin scutage), £338 11s 8d (for the feudal two aids) and £19 3s 4d (the 1245 aid charged to his Essex fees).

[118] Maddicott, *Montfort*, pp. 50, 130.

[119] E159/34, m. 1; Carpenter, 'King, Magnates and Society', p. 90.

[120] Carpenter, 'King Magnates and Society', pp. 89-91.

[121] *CM*, v, 530.

the pan between two men with notoriously short tempers. Quickly, their anger appears to have cooled. Within a month the king had called off the distraint, and granted the earl terms on which to pay off his debts.[122] Roger, for his part, showed that there were no hard feelings the following year when he entertained Henry at Framlingham, and participated in one of the few officially sanctioned tournaments of the reign.[123]

But the argument in 1255, if not the start of a critical slide, nevertheless resonates with other heated exchanges between the king on the one hand, and Roger, his family and friends on the other. Most obviously perhaps, it parallels the angry exchanges and name-calling (which had also included accusations of treason) that took place between Henry and the Marshal brothers in the 1230s. Roger had inherited not just his uncles' title and rod of office, but also the association of the Marshal name with opposition and rebellion. The fact that the earl was moved to deny not merely being a traitor in the present circumstances of 1255, but that he had never been one, suggests that both he and Henry had long memories, and that neither had succeeded in putting the conflicts of the 1230s behind them.[124]

The argument of October 1255 also echoes a dispute that had taken place three years beforehand between the king and Roger's sister, Isabella. The widowed countess of Hugh de Aubigny, earl of Arundel, Isabella had been deprived by Henry of a wardship that pertained to her dower, and angrily remonstrated with him for denying her justice. 'One cannot now obtain what is just at your court', she allegedly told the king, before going on to outline the faults of his government in general, not least his failure to abide by Magna Carta. This was much the same theme taken up by Roger, albeit more succinctly, when he demanded of Henry in 1255, 'if you are just, how can you harm me?'. Despite the restoration of cordial relations in the wake of the de Ros incident, it is difficult to shake the belief that the earl and his family regarded the king and his government as fundamentally inequitable.[125]

In the 1250s, Roger watched as injustices which touched him directly, if not personally, began to pile up. Soon after his sister's complaint, there had been the denial of Humphrey de Bohun's rights as constable during the Gascon campaign. The following year came the perceived injustice shown to de Ros. In the same year (1255), Roger may have had additional cause to doubt the value of Henry's justice. That summer, the king ordered both him and the earl of Gloucester to arrest certain of their own

---

[122] *CR, 1254-56*, p. 238; Carpenter, 'King, Magnates and Society', pp. 89-90.
[123] Appendix A. Over-exertion at the tournament (held at Blyth, the scene of his youthful triumphs) left Roger dangerously unwell at Christmas. *CM*, v, 557, 609. Cf. N. Denholm-Young, 'The Tournament in the Thirteenth Century', *Studies in Medieval History presented to F.M. Powicke*, ed. R.W. Hunt, W.A. Pantin and R.W. Southern (Oxford, 1948), p. 256.
[124] Above, pp. 8-12, 19, 23.
[125] *CM*, v, 336-7. Cf. Carpenter, 'King, Magnates and Society', p. 80.

men in their Welsh lordships. The crimes these individuals had committed are not specified in any great detail – we only learn that they had been indicted before the king's justices for robbery and the reception of robbers.[126] It is tempting, however, to imagine that their accuser might have been the other magnate with substantial interests in South Wales, William de Valence. As the parvenu lord of Pembroke, Valence had recently asserted his judicial rights in the region over the men of both Bigod and Clare.[127] In addition, at some point Valence seems to have illegally seized the seven knights' fees in Pembroke that had been assigned to Roger from the Marshal inheritance.[128] Furthermore, on the eve of the storm in 1258, Valence alleged that the success in the marches of the Welsh leader Llywelyn ap Gruffudd was due to the connivance of certain English nobles, among them the earl of Gloucester.[129] None of this proves Valence was behind Henry's demand that Roger should imprison his own men in 1255. But whoever was the sponsor of the request, it can only have bolstered the earl's belief that royal justice appeared to be working against his own interests.

This belief was further reinforced the following year, when Roger had a grievance against Valence's younger brother, Aymer, bishop-elect of Winchester. The earl accused the elect of deforcing him of a wardship, and brought the matter before the justices in eyre. Although the outcome of the case is not known, it seems likely that, after enduring several months of needless delay, Roger was awarded compensation of 100 marks. His victory, however, was immediately stymied. Rather than pay the earl directly, Aymer persuaded his brother the king to deduct an identical sum from Roger's Crown debts. This, it has been observed, may not have been an outcome that the earl himself welcomed.[130]

Unable to gain satisfactory redress against the king's relatives, Roger also found he could not obtain justice against the charmed circle who surrounded the queen. Since the early 1250s the earl had been trying to recover the Norfolk manor of Redenhall against the Kentish knight Nicholas de Lenham. Once again, his initial success at law was undone by his opponent's court connections. In 1257 Lenham leased Redenhall to Queen Eleanor, and then, after protests from Roger, granted the manor to Peter of Savoy. The earl reacted furiously, but neither direct action (at one point he simply seized the manor) nor further litigation could avail him when his opponents stood so close to the king. In Roger's own opinion, Lenham had acted 'maliciously' to thwart him, and aspects of the case had

---

126 *CR, 1254-56*, p. 201.
127 *CACWales*, p. 212.
128 *CPR, 1364-67*, p. 263; *PA*, p. 217. Having recovered these fees in 1289, Roger IV Bigod immediately granted them to Edward I and Eleanor of Castile. RBIV 17.
129 Maddicott, *Montfort*, p. 154.
130 JUST/1/778, mm. 10, 13; *CLR, 1251-60*, p. 292; Carpenter, '1258', p. 192.

proceeded 'less than rightly'. Regardless of the merits of his claim to the manor, which were far from strong, the earl was once again left with the feeling that justice had been denied to him.[131]

By 1258, therefore, Roger had been left in little doubt as to the realities of his position. Although Henry III might try to soothe his feelings with gifts and favours, the fact of the matter was that the earl had been unable to obtain satisfactory judgements on a number of issues. From the time of his elevation as earl marshal, justice had become increasingly skewed in favour of a select circle of magnates who surrounded the king. Matthew Paris famously defined this group in 1256 when he alleged that Henry had forbidden the issue of any writ which might damage the interests of his Lusignan half-brothers, the earls of Cornwall and Gloucester, and Peter of Savoy. The earl of Norfolk found himself on the outside of this circle: denied the opportunity to exercise the same dubious privileges and, more frustratingly, unable to obtain redress against its untouchable members.[132]

To this extent, Roger resembled that other earl who flitted in and out of court in the 1250s, Simon de Montfort. Occasionally seen on the fringes of government, but rarely at its centre, he suffered not from outright lack of royal favour, but from its insufficiency.[133] His deprivation, however, was in some respects more acute than that experienced by Montfort. For all that the earl of Leicester had grievances against Henry which were broader and deeper than Roger's own, he also had a good degree of success in gaining redress. In return for his support in Gascony, for example, Montfort had wrung from the king an astonishing series of financial agreements, culminating in an arrangement which allowed him to take money at source from the sheriffs of half a dozen English counties.[134] By contrast, Roger had been rewarded for his service in the same campaign with a single tun of wine and some meagre favours to a few of his followers.[135] Montfort, like Roger, had run up large debts to the Crown, but had managed to persuade Henry to write some of them off.[136] The most Roger could manage in this period was to have his debts – a large portion of which he evidently did not regard as legitimate – postponed or attermined. Montfort, by virtue of his wife, had an entrée

[131] KB26/145, m. 6d; KB26/147B, m. 13; KB26/148, m. 8; KB26/154, m. 15; KB26/158, m. 14d; JUST/1/567, m. 13; CP25/1/158/84, no. 1269; CP25/1/283/15, no. 351; *CR, 1256-59*, p. 145. For a full account of this episode, see D.A. Carpenter, 'Justice and Jurisdiction under King John and Henry III', *Reign of Henry III*, pp. 30-32. Cf. *idem*, 'King, Magnates and Society', p. 83, which uses the same evidence to support a rather different argument.

[132] *CM*, v, 594.

[133] Maddicott, *Montfort*, p. 59.

[134] Ibid., pp. 122-3, 137, 151

[135] *CPR, 1247-58*, pp. 256, 278. *CR, 1251-53*, pp. 395-6. For more on Bigod *familiaris* Richard de Holbrook, see below, pp. 67-70, 72, 97, 112-13, 143.

[136] Maddicott, *Montfort*, p. 33.

into court circles, and in particular enjoyed a close relationship with the queen and her Savoyard faction.[137] Roger's marriage, arranged in his minority, had produced for him neither heirs nor political advantage.

By 1258, however, the earl of Norfolk did have a contact at court in the form of his younger brother. While Roger's destiny had been mapped out for him in his teens by others, Hugh Bigod had enjoyed the younger son's advantage of being allowed to make his own way in the world. Indeed, Hugh is an almost stereotypical example of the medieval self-made man. Free to chose his own bride, he waited patiently through his twenties until a suitable candidate presented herself.[138] In 1243 he married Joanna de Stuteville, a lady recently bereaved but enormously enriched by the loss of her husband and her cousin in the Holy Land.[139] The match transformed him from a minor landowner surviving on handouts from his relatives to a major baron in the north of England.[140] In the 1250s, Hugh's talents marked him out for royal preferment.[141] In Yorkshire, he was made hereditary forester of Farndale, and licensed to hunt throughout the entire county; in the middle of the decade, the royal castle of Pickering and its wapentake were committed to his custody.[142] With these responsibilities came rewards; grants of deer, free warren, markets, and fairs were all forthcoming.[143] The royal gift-giving peaked in 1256 when he was granted the manor of Levisham and several other parcels of land in Yorkshire.[144]

As far as can be judged, Hugh had an amicable relationship with his elder brother. Roger appears to have granted Hugh land at Settrington in

---

[137] Howell, *Eleanor of Provence*, p. 142.

[138] Hugh was born at some point in the decade between 1210 and 1220, i.e. after Roger's birth in 1209 and 21 years before his first recorded grant of land. *Yorks. Fines*, ii, 108.

[139] *EYC*, ix, 18-23. Hugh married Joanna between May 1243 and February 1244. *CR, 1242-47*, pp. 129, 154. There is no contemporary evidence to support the oft-repeated assertion that Hugh had been married at an earlier date to Joanna, daughter of Robert Burnell. It appears to originate from the occasionally useful but usually unreliable Milles, *Catalogue of Honor*, pp. 504-5. Cf. *Dictionary of National Biography*, v, 24.

[140] In addition to the lands he received from his brother and mother (above, p. 38; Appendix C), Hugh also obtained the manor of Stoughton in Sussex from his brother-in-law Hugh de Aubigny (*CRR*, xviii, 1243-45, p. 247; cf. *CIPM*, iv, 292). Joanna was sole heir to the Stuteville estate, which included the barony of Liddel in Cumbria and several manors in Yorkshire. In 1242, in return for a 10,000 mark fine, she obtained custody of all the lands of her former husband, Hugh Wake, as well as custody of their infant son, Baldwin, and the right to marry where she chose. The Wake estates were in Lincolnshire. *EYC*, ix, 18-23.

[141] He first witnesses a royal charter on 19 October 1252. *RCWL HIII*, ii, 72.

[142] *CR, 1251-53*, pp. 368-9; *CR, 1254-56*, pp. 84, 307; *CChR, 1226-57*, p. 445-6; *CPR, 1247-58*, pp. 408, 447.

[143] *CR, 1251-53*, pp. 124, 385; *CR, 1253-54*, p. 263; *CR, 1254-56*, pp. 125, 232, 309; *CChR, 1226-57*, p. 375.

[144] *CR, 1302-1307*, pp. 132, 140-41. There is no original of this grant: the royal charter roll for 1256 (C53/46B) is fragmentary.

Yorkshire, probably in the 1230s.[145] We find them in each other's company at times of special significance, such as Roger's endowment of the hospital of St Giles in Norwich, or their half-sister's foundation of a nunnery at Marham.[146] Memorably, both brothers appear together in mourning on the occasion of their mother's funeral.[147] More tellingly, perhaps, we catch up with Roger and Hugh in 1255, again in Yorkshire, mixing business and pleasure. That summer, as Henry III made his way towards Scotland, the brothers teamed up with their cousins, the fitz Ranulfs, in order to supply the royal household with deer. To judge from the number of animals they caught between them, the hunt was an activity at which the Bigods excelled.[148]

Around the middle of 1257, Hugh graduated from being a provincial royal agent to a fully-fledged courtier. In June he was employed as an envoy to France and Spain.[149] On his return to England, he joined his brother and the king on campaign against Llywelyn ap Gruffudd in North Wales in September.[150] When the fighting was over, Roger, as was his wont, disappeared from Henry's side. Hugh, however, remained deep in the king's counsels throughout the autumn and into the new year.[151]

Finally, both Roger and Hugh had a further point of contact with the court in the shape of their brother-in-law, John fitz Geoffrey. Ever since his appointment to the council by popular demand in 1237, fitz Geoffrey had been a leading member of the circle around Queen Eleanor.[152] The closeness of his relationship to the Bigod brothers is almost impossible to gauge, but again there is a suggestive episode involving the chase: in August 1251 we catch John hunting with Roger in the earl's Welsh lordship of Chepstow.[153]

Such family connections are easy to overlook precisely because they are so badly documented; yet they were often the principal spurs to political action. In 1233, Roger had made his political debut by rebelling in support of his uncle Richard Marshal. Subsequently he participated in the attacks on the castles of the de Lacy family, probably in protest at the violation of the dower rights of his sister. Now, twenty-five years after these youthful adventures, the kinship ties that bound the earl to his wider family were

---

[145] Appendix C.
[146] RBIII 11; W. Dugdale, *Monasticon Anglicanum* (6 vols. in 8, London, 1817-30), v, 743-4.
[147] Above, p. 31.
[148] *CR, 1254-56*, pp. 124-6, 130, 138, 415. For the relationship with the fitz Ranulfs, see above, pp. 2, 39n.
[149] *CPR, 1247-58*, pp. 561, 594.
[150] For Roger's involvement in this campaign, we only have his movements as given in Appendix A, and the brief comments in *CM*, vi, 373-4. For the campaign itself, see R.R. Davies, *Conquest, Coexistence and Change: Wales, 1063-1415* (Oxford, 1987), p. 310.
[151] Appendix A; *RCWL HIII*, ii, 110-19; *CR, 1261-64*, p. 57.
[152] Howell, *Eleanor of Provence*, pp. 56, 115, 142.
[153] E32/28, m. 4.

once again set to pull him into rebellion, and would require him to become involved in politics to an unprecedented degree. In early April 1258, the servants of John fitz Geoffrey were assaulted by the armed retainers of Aymer de Valence. It was an attack which resulted in murder, yet when fitz Geoffrey appealed to Henry III, the king refused to hear him.[154] It was the last and most flagrant denial of justice that the monarch was allowed to make. After stoically enduring more than a decade of such provocative royal behaviour, Roger Bigod was once again ready to confront his king.

[154] Carpenter, '1258', pp. 192-3.

CHAPTER 3

The Bigods and the Reform Movement, 1258-70

A REVOLUTIONARY LEADER

In the spring of 1258, the misdeeds of Henry III's Lusignan half-brothers galvanized their enemies into action. The assault on the servants of John fitz Geoffrey by the bishop-elect of Winchester, and the king's subsequent refusal to do justice, provided the spark for the flame. For Roger Bigod and his brother Hugh, it was not only an unpunished attack on a close kinsman; it was also indicative of the general offensiveness of Henry III's personal rule – the most recent in a long line of gratuitous abuses of royal power.

At the same time, a more immediate and potentially greater danger had arisen: the Lusignans had captivated the king's eldest son. This was a threat sufficient to alarm even those privileged courtiers who stood around the queen. Edward, who was eighteen at the start of 1258, had been raised under the tutelage of his mother and her Savoyard circle. Now, as the prince stood on the cusp of adulthood, their patient labours looked set to be undone. It was therefore imperative to deal with the Lusignans: the spell they had cast over the heir to the throne would have to be broken, if necessary by force.[1]

In this atmosphere of heightened danger and shared threat, the Lusignans' chief opponents forged a secret alliance. On 12 April 1258, while attending a parliament at Westminster, Roger and Hugh, the earls of Gloucester and Leicester, Peter of Savoy, John fitz Geoffrey and Peter de Montfort swore to assist and support each other against 'all people': a coded reference to the Lusignans.[2] At the end of the month, when the parliament was set to conclude, the confederates confronted the king. According to the Tewkesbury Annalist, they armed themselves in splendid fashion and, accompanied by a host of other barons and knights, marched on Westminster Hall. Although they left their swords at the entrance, the threat of force was all too evident to Henry III:

'What is it, my lords?' asked the shaking and stammering king. 'Am I, wretched fellow, your captive?'

'No, my lord,' said Roger Bigod. 'No. But let the wretched and intolerable Poitevins and all aliens flee from your face and ours as from the face of a lion, and there will be "glory to God in the heavens, and in your land peace to men of goodwill".'

---

[1] Ridgeway, 'The Lord Edward', pp. 89-99.
[2] Maddicott, *Montfort*, p. 153; Carpenter, '1258', p. 194. For the sworn agreement, see C. Bémont, *Simon de Montfort* (Paris, 1884), pp. 327-8 (*EHD*, iii, 361).

Roger proceeded to demand that Henry and Edward should swear to follow the counsels of the baronage, and outlined a scheme the magnates had devised 'for the dignity, honour and profit of the kingdom'. Henceforth, the king's actions would require the approval of an elected council of twenty-four prudent men, who in turn would appoint a discreet man to act as chancellor. Having listened to the terms, Henry, seeing that he had no choice in the matter, duly consented. Edward, who was even less willing than his father, was also induced to comply.[3]

And so the revolution of 1258 began. Tewkesbury's account is not without its problems; Henry's opening line contains a Latin pun, and Roger's response ends with a paraphrase of St Luke. Neither man, in short, seems to be acting entirely within character.[4] Nevertheless, the high level of circumstantial detail suggests that in the main the annalist's account is accurate, and may have been based on a newsletter from an eye-witness.[5] There is certainly no reason to doubt that, when the barons entered the hall and challenged Henry, it was Roger Bigod who took the lead.

Why was the earl of Norfolk chosen to be the baronial spokesman? He was one of the most important magnates, but he was hardly pre-eminent. In the witness lists to Henry III's charters, Roger typically took second or third place among the laity, depending on who else was present; the king's brother, Richard of Cornwall, always took precedence over the other earls, and in most circumstances Roger was outranked by Richard de Clare.[6] This was in part a reflection of their material wealth; both Cornwall and Gloucester were considerably better off than Norfolk.[7] Similarly, at almost fifty years old, Roger was a senior figure among the baronage, but most of his allies were veterans too. Peter of Savoy, Simon de Montfort and John fitz Geoffrey were all fifty or thereabouts, and Hugh Bigod was unlikely to have been more than a few years younger than his brother. Gloucester, who was thirty-seven, was the most junior member of the group.[8] '1258' was in some respects a generational struggle between a set of established courtiers and the disruptive magnates of a younger generation; thus, distinguished in years as he was, Roger could claim no

---

[3] *AM*, i, 163-4; Carpenter, '1258', pp. 187-8.

[4] For Henry's lack of wit, see D.A. Carpenter, 'An Unknown Obituary of King Henry III from the Year 1263', *Reign of Henry III*, p. 253. For Roger's religious sensibilities, see below, pp. 99-100.

[5] Carpenter, '1258', pp. 188-9. The same account seems to be echoed in a later piece of doggerel, which includes the lines *Totam turbat terra modica terram turba canum / Exeat aut pereat genus tam prophanum!*. Rishanger copied it into his chronicle under the year 1264, but it may have originated earlier. Rishanger, *De Bellis*, p. 19; J.H. Ramsey, *The Dawn of the Constitution* (London, 1908), p. 180. The poem's chief value comes in the first line of this stanza, where Roger is described as a *miles strenuus*.

[6] e.g. *RCWL HIII*, ii, 8, 14, 63, 72, 95-6.

[7] Above, p. 41; below, p. 70.

[8] *Handbook of British Chronology*, ed. Fryde *et al.*, pp. 463, 479; Maddicott, *Montfort*, p. 4; *The Dictionary of National Biography: Missing Persons*, ed. C.S. Nicholls (Oxford, 1993), p. 224.

special distinction on this occasion.[9] In terms of his personal antagonism towards Henry, Roger was again equalled or outclassed by others. John fitz Geoffrey had been the most recent victim of royal caprice; Simon de Montfort had been nursing major grievances for over a decade. And Montfort, of course, was blessed with a silver tongue; Norfolk's speciality, by contrast, seems to have been the angry exchange.

R.F. Treharne suggested that Roger took the lead in 1258 because, as earl marshal, he was 'the natural spokesperson for the baronage on such an occasion'.[10] There is little, however, to support this supposition. Historically, the Marshal family had often been opposed to the king's policies during Henry's reign. It was an opposition, however, born of personal grievances rather than any peculiar representative or constitutional role.[11] The knights who came in arms to the king's hall may have fallen in, as if for battle, under Roger's supervision, as they had done the previous year in Wales.[12] But there is no reason to think that the earl marshal was a natural conduit for baronial grievances, or that the baronage as a whole looked to him as their 'natural' leader on what was, after all, a most unusual occasion.

If it was not by virtue of being earl marshal, then perhaps it was because of his own standing. Of all the magnates who stood against the king in 1258, Roger's connections with the court were the weakest. Indeed, it is arguable that he was only drawn into what was largely a court confederacy because of the attack on his brother-in-law, and through the agency of his courtier younger brother. For most of his career, the earl had operated on the fringes of the court, something of a political outsider, even a backwoodsman. Did this make him the natural spokesman for the barons and knights who also marched on the king's hall? Might he have participated in '1258' because of pressure from below, as much as provocation from above? The relationship between the palace revolution and the demand for grass-roots reform is indeed 'a vexed question'.[13] It is time to consider it in the case of Roger Bigod, and examine the ties that bound the earl to local society.

THE ROOTS OF POWER: THE AFFINITY OF ROGER III BIGOD

Like all men (and women) of consequence in the Middle Ages, Roger Bigod surrounded himself with a number of lesser individuals, both to help him in the management of his widespread estates, and to accompany him from time to time when he travelled, magnifying his presence and

[9] Ridgeway, 'The Lord Edward', p. 97.
[10] R.F. Treharne, 'Why the Battle of Lewes Matters in English History', in his *Simon de Montfort and Baronial Reform* (London, 1986), p. 96.
[11] Vincent, *des Roches*, pp. 327-31.
[12] *Paris*, vi, 373-4.
[13] Howell, *Eleanor of Provence*, pp. 140-41.

enhancing his political standing. In Roger's own case, we are fortunate in possessing four lists of names which illuminate this entourage. Importantly, these are not military lists of the kind we encounter with increasing frequency during the reign of Edward I, and are all the more valuable because they are not inflated with temporary associates.[14] In 1245, when Roger travelled to the Council of Lyon, twenty-three individuals received letters of protection for travelling with him.[15] A decade later, the earl took some of his *familiares* to hunt with him in Yorkshire on Henry III's orders, and the king subsequently instructed his justices not to prosecute these men for forest offences.[16] Shortly afterwards, in 1257, Henry again wrote to his justices, this time ordering them to respite any pleas against eighteen individuals whom Roger had with him in London for the Michaelmas parliament that year.[17] Finally, the names of those individuals who had quittance of common summons in Norfolk were listed on the 1268 close roll. Among them is an isolated group of ten men who appear to have been grouped together because they were Roger's *familiares*.[18]

In addition to these lists, we have the witness lists to Roger's *acta*. A total of thirteen charters have been discovered; a disappointingly small number for man of such great standing with a forty-five-year career.[19] Moreover, the value of this tiny corpus is further reduced by a number of other factors. The three earliest charters (RBIII 1-3) were drawn up at Westminster in April 1228, and their witness lists therefore reflect the composition of the king's court rather than Roger's own circle. Of the remaining ten charters, one (RBIII 8) is badly mutilated, and not all of its terms or witnesses can be recovered. Another (RBIII 5) has been curtailed by the scribe who copied it, and consequently we have the name of only the first witness. Furthermore, only one of these ten deeds (RBIII 7) is dated; for the remainder we have to rely on internal evidence to work out their possible date ranges.

By way of small compensation, we do possess a copy of the earl's will (RBIII 14), drawn up in the anxious atmosphere of early June 1258, when it looked as if civil war was inevitable.[20] This provides us with the names of Roger's intended executors. Besides Simon de Montfort and Richard de Clare (his allies at the time), these included three members of the earl's own entourage. We also know the names of the men who actually acted as

---

[14] It is, however, regrettable that we have no information about Roger's entourage during any of the military campaigns of Henry III's reign. For Roger IV Bigod's household during the wars of Edward's reign, see below, pp. 149-53.

[15] *CPR, 1232-47*, p. 454.

[16] *CR, 1254-56*, p. 415.

[17] *CR, 1256-59*, pp. 151-2. The men in this list are explicitly identified as Roger's 'familiares'.

[18] *CR, 1264-68*, p. 500.

[19] RBIII 1-13: see Appendix E.

[20] Below, pp. 73-4.

executors after Roger's death, thanks to scattered references in exchequer, chancery and court rolls.[21] Occasionally, we can identify other individuals as members of Roger's circle from the same sources. However, because of the small amount of data, and in particular the paucity of charter evidence, what follows is impressionistic rather than rigidly statistical. In general, any individual who can be connected to the Bigod family on more than one occasion has been investigated as a potential member of his affinity.

We have some indication of the important individuals who surrounded Roger at the very start of his career. In 1228, the knights Oliver de Vaux, Roger fitz Osbert and Hamo Lenveise, together with Richard, prior of Thetford, stood as sureties for the financial arrangements by which Roger purchased his early inheritance from Alexander, king of Scots.[22] Possibly these men were the executors of the will of Hugh II Bigod, and therefore had an ongoing interest in seeing to the proper administration of the late earl's estate.[23] Three years earlier, the same three laymen had been charged with extending £100 of land to support Roger during his minority. They were joined in this task by two other East Anglian knights, William Lenveise and William de Hingham.[24]

All these men had strong connections with the earls of Norfolk stretching back over many years. The priors of Thetford had enjoyed a close relationship with the Bigod family since Roger I Bigod had founded their house in 1106.[25] The five knights ordered to make the extent were identified with the affinity in the most literal sense; they undertook the assignment 'so that the friends of Roger should be content'.[26] William and Hamo Lenveise, Roger fitz Osbert and Oliver de Vaux belonged to families that had held lands from the earls of Norfolk since before 1166, while William de Hingham had been granted land by Roger II Bigod.[27] In most cases, their records of service were equally distinguished. William Lenveise had been seneschal to Roger II Bigod, and William de Hingham had performed the same office for Hugh II.[28] Both men had been among the garrison at Framlingham (in Lenveise's case, as constable) during King John's siege of the castle in 1216.[29] Likewise, Hamo Lenveise had been

---

[21] E368/44, m. 4d; *Select Cases in the Exchequer of Pleas*, ed. H. Jenkinson (Selden Soc., xlviii, 1932), 89; *CPR, 1266-72*, p. 491.

[22] *CChR, 1226-57*, pp. 72-3. For the context, see above, pp. 6-7

[23] Cf. the executors of Roger III's will in 1270, who included the prior of Thetford. Below, p. 112-13.

[24] *RLC*, ii, 58.

[25] Above, p. 1; below, pp. 99-100.

[26] *RLC*, ii, 58. Hamo Lenveise was ordered to assist in making the extent, but does not appear to have turned up on the day itself. *CPR, 1225-32*, pp. 7-8.

[27] *RBE*, i, 395-7; *Blythburgh Priory Cartulary*, ed. C. Harper-Bill (2 vols., Suffolk Charters, ii–iii, 1980-81), i, 10; *Sibton*, i, 51, 106-8; *CR, 1247-51*, p. 184.

[28] RBII 23; HBII 2.

[29] *RLP*, p. 169; *RLC*, i, 254.

rewarded for his services to Hugh II Bigod with a grant of the Norfolk manor of Stockton.[30]

Relics of the affinities of his father and grandfather, these men were important members of Roger III's entourage during the initial stages of his comital career. All but one of them appear as witnesses to at least one of his early charters.[31] William Lenveise reprised his role as seneschal in the early 1230s, and he and Roger were among those accused of homicide by an appellant around the same time.[32] He also joined the earl in supporting the rebellion of Richard Marshal in 1233, as did Roger fitz Osbert; like their young master, both men suffered temporary loss of their lands as a result.[33] The same episode, however, casts Oliver de Vaux's attachment to Roger in a rather more ambiguous light. By far the most powerful man among the earl's circle, the evidence suggests that he may have been closer to its fringes than the others.[34] An important baron in his own right and the greatest of the Bigod subtenants (he answered to the Bigods for 31¾ fees), in 1233 he stayed loyal to the Crown.[35] His independence was further underlined by subsequent events; while the earl and his close adherents lost control of their lands, de Vaux was entrusted with the custody of Framlingham Castle.[36]

Other important individuals during Roger's early years are indicated to some extent by the witness lists of his charters. Again, there is evidence of continuity from the time of Roger's forefathers. William de Verdun, William de Burnaville and Reginald de Pirnhow were all scions of families whose connection with the Bigods had been established before 1166; each of them witnesses one of Roger's early charters.[37]

---

[30] HBII 2. After her husband's death, Maud Bigod bought the manor back from Hamo and bestowed it on her youngest son, Ralph (above, p. 39n). Hamo also witnesses charters HBII 1, 3 and Maud 1. For more on him, see *Sibton*, ii, 285n.

[31] RBIII 7 (fitz Osbert); RBIII 6 (Hingham); RBIII 4 (William Lenveise and Vaux) and RBIII 5 (Vaux again). The exception is Hamo Lenveise, who died before Roger was invested with his earldom.

[32] RBIII 4; *CR, 1231-34*, p. 267. Sadly there are no other references to the murder case.

[33] *CR, 1231-34*, p. 269.

[34] He witnesses none of the many charters of Roger II Bigod, and only one charter of Hugh II (HBII 2). For more on his career, see *Sibton*, i, 106-7; J.C. Holt, *The Northerners* (Oxford, 1961), p. 62; Sanders, *English Baronies*, p. 47.

[35] His ancestor William de Vaux held 30 fees in 1166, but cf. the inquisition post mortem of his son John de Vaux in 1287, which gives 31¾. *RBE*, i, 395; *CIPM*, ii, 402.

[36] *CR, 1231-34*, p. 258.

[37] In 1166, the Verduns held six fees from Hugh I Bigod, the Burnavilles held three fees and the Pirnhows held one fee (*RBE*, i, 395-6). William de Burnaville witnessed HBII 2 and 3 and campaigned in Wales with Roger III in 1231 (*CR, 1227-31*, p. 539). William de Verdun was present at Framlingham in 1216 (*RLC*, i, 255) and witnesses RBII 15 and16 and HBII 2 and 3. For more on his family, see *Sibton*, i, 108-9 and M. Hagger, *The Fortunes of a Norman Family: the de Verduns in England, Ireland and Wales, 1066-1316* (Dublin, 2001), pp. 243-5. Reginald de Pirnhow was also at Framlingham (*RLC*, i, 254) and witnesses RBII 11, 15 and 16 and HBII 2. For more on his family, see *Sibton*, i, 84-6. All three men witness RBIII 6 (1233 x 1246).

Far more important, however, were two of Roger's relatives. Ralph Bigod, the earl's uncle, appears in four of his charters, often as the first-named witness.[38] Thomas Bigod, who cannot be precisely placed in the family tree, also witnesses on four occasions. The fact that he was not quite so prominent may have been due to his clerical status; in 1242 he was styled 'parson of Framlingham'.[39] In 1233, Ralph joined his nephew in rebellion, and it looks very much as if Thomas was also involved.[40] Both men remained involved in Roger's affairs until the 1250s.[41]

Only one man could match – indeed, possibly outmatch – the influence of Roger's relatives. Like Ralph (and perhaps Thomas), Herbert de Alencon belonged to the same generation as the earl's father.[42] There is, however, no indication of any contact between Herbert and earlier generations of the Bigod family, and nor was he a Bigod tenant. Whereas Ralph and Thomas illustrate the importance of ties of kinship to Roger's affinity, Herbert underlines the importance of neighbourhood, for he held a string of manors a few miles to the north of Framlingham.[43] Onetime sheriff of Norfolk and Suffolk, Herbert was clearly an important individual in his own right, but in Bigod circles he is something of an *éminence grise*; despite his prominent position among the witnesses to Roger's charters, it is never possible to associate Herbert directly with any of the earl's political activities, and he finds no place in any of the household lists. (By the time the first of these was compiled in 1245, however, he was fairly senior, and he was probably dead before the later lists of *familiares* were drawn up.) His value was doubtless due to his considerable local weight and his frequent employment as a royal agent in East Anglia.[44] The one occasion when we appear to catch him acting on Bigod's behalf occurs in a case recorded in the Suffolk eyre roll for 1240. When twenty-five young and low-born men were convicted of disseising William de Caston and his wife of twenty acres of land in Peasenhall and eight acres of land in Bruisyard, Herbert acted as one of the sureties for the gang's fine. Another surety was Ralph Bigod, identified on the roll as the uncle of Roger III. The episode is obscure, but since the disseisors are described as being 'of the honour of Earl R[oger] Bigod', it seems that this

[38] RBIII 6, 8, 10, 12.

[39] RBIII 4, 7, 10, 11.

[40] Ralph's lands in Yorkshire (see Appendix C) were seized in retaliation. On the same day that they were restored, Ralph and Thomas stood surety for the loyalty of another East Anglian rebel, William de Wiggenhall. *CR, 1231-34*, pp. 268-9.

[41] RBIII 11, 12.

[42] As his parents were married at Christmas 1181 (above, p. 2), Ralph was probably born in the late 1180s or early 1190s. Herbert was born between October 1181 and January 1182. *Eye Priory Cartulary and Charters*, ed. V. Brown (2 vols., Suffolk Charters, xii–xiii, 1992-94), ii, 68n.

[43] He held land at Badingham, Colston, Dennington, Brundish and Tannington, although some of these he later alienated. *Sibton*, i, 28-9; *Eye Priory Cartulary*, ed. Brown, ii, 57-8, 64, 67-8.

[44] *Sibton*, i, 28-9.

was a case of the earl being brought to book for indulging in strong-arm tactics, and sending two senior members of his entourage to make the necessary amends in court.[45]

All the men described above were the old guard, and at least a generation older than their new overlord. Accordingly, their numbers started to thin as Roger's career progressed. Hamo Lenveise died before 1232, and the same year William de Verdun made his last datable appearance.[46] William de Burnaville occurs for the last time in 1238, Reginald de Pirnhow in 1240 and Roger fitz Osbert in 1242.[47] Oliver de Vaux was definitely dead by 1242, and by 1245 so was William Lenveise.[48] William de Hingham is last heard of in 1249.[49] Only Herbert de Alencon and Ralph Bigod soldiered on into the 1250s, by which time they were both elderly men.[50]

Thus by the time we reach the mid-1240s, the personnel of Roger's household had changed considerably. The older men who had served his father and grandfather are conspicuous by their absence from the list of men who accompanied him to Lyon. In their place, a new generation of bachelors has appeared. Notably prominent is Hubert de Bavent, who witnessed four charters in the period 1246 x 1257 and appears in two of the household lists (1245 and 1255).[51] Somewhat less outstanding but of equal status are three more knights: Bartholomew de Creake, Matthew de Mautby and Gervase de Bradfield (who for a time was seneschal of Roger's estate).[52] Robert Hovel, with no witnessings to his credit, is a good example of a man whose importance might be discounted were it not for his appearance in three of the four of the household lists.

Few of these new men, however, were newcomers in the strictest sense. Possibly Robert Hovel had enjoyed no previous connection with the Bigods; the tenurial link that existed between him and Roger III by 1263 may well have been established as a result of their political relationship, rather than vice versa.[53] Similarly, there is nothing to indicate that Gervase

---

[45] JUST/1/818, m. 8d.

[46] *CRR*, xiv, 1230-32, p. 530; *CR, 1234-37*, p. 232. Verdun was definitely dead by 1246. W. Rye, *A Short Calendar of the Feet of Fines for Norfolk* (2 vols., Norwich, 1885-86), i, 70.

[47] *CPR, 1232-47*, p. 234; *Sibton*, ii, 266; *CPR, 1232-47*, p. 304.

[48] Sanders, *English Baronies*, p. 47; *Sibton*, i, 51.

[49] *CR, 1247-51*, p. 184.

[50] Ralph was dead by 1253 (*Excerpta*, ii, 333). Herbert makes his final appearance in 1255. W. Rye, *Calendar of the Feet of Fines for Suffolk* (Ipswich, 1900), p. 56.

[51] RBIII 8, 9, 11, 12.

[52] Bartholomew de Creake witnesses Maud 1 and 3, RBIII 10 and 12, and occurs in connection with Roger III in 1233 (*CRR*, xv, 1233-37, pp. 33-4). For more on him, see Farrer, *Honors*, iii, 428-30. Matthew de Mautby witnesses RBIII 11 and 12. He accompanied Bigod to Lyon in 1245 and perhaps also to Poitou in 1242 (*CPR, 1232-47*, p. 295). Gervase de Bradfield witnesses RBIII 7, 9 and 10, and was seneschal between 1245 and 1249 (see Appendix D).

[53] The Hovel family had been lords of Wyverstone in Suffolk since the eleventh century, and by 1263 had acquired lands in the same county at Istead, Risby, Chediston and

de Bradfield, whose first datable appearance in Roger's entourage comes in 1242, held any lands from him (although he had clearly been in the service of the earl's mother and father).[54] But in many cases, the new knights that Roger III recruited in the middle of his career were drawn from among his established tenantry. Hubert de Bavent, for example, hailed from a family who had held 2½ fees from the Bigods since before 1166; his namesake grandfather had been witness to one of the early charters of Roger II Bigod.[55] Bartholomew de Creake also came from a family of tenants established in the twelfth century,[56] and Matthew de Mautby, whose ancestry and landholdings have proved untraceable, may also have had a tenurial connection to the Bigods.[57] Moreover, there were other individuals among the earl's entourage, less distinguished and important than the foregoing, who nevertheless represented families of long-established tenants. The shadowy Robert de Pirnhow, the obscure William de Beaumont, and the undistinguished Hugh de Vaux did not add much lustre to the earl's household, but their surnames alone suggest that strong traditions of service were still being maintained.[58]

The real 'new men' who appeared in Roger's household during the 1240s were not knights but individuals who had risen from further down the social spectrum. One such was John Algar, who accompanied the earl to Lyon in 1245, and clearly enjoyed the position of a leading *familiaris* despite his non-knightly status.[59] Having already acquired some property in Loddon, Norfolk, apparently by virtue of his marriage, Algar's fortunes

---

Market Weston. This last manor was held from the Bigods, but it is not clear when the relationship was established. Weston was not part of the Bigods' Domesday fee, so it could have been acquired and alienated at any point in the period 1086-1263. There is no evidence to suggest that any earlier members of the Hovel family had served the Bigods, so the tenurial link may well have been established by Roger III. J.J. Muskett, *Suffolk Manorial Families* (3 vols., Exeter, 1902-8), ii, 54-76; *CIPM*, iv, 301; *CChR, 1257-1300*, p. 46.

[54] HBII 2; Maud 1, 3. Cf. *Sibton*, i, 35-6.

[55] *RBE*, i, 400; RBII 9; Easton Bavents and Chediston in Suffolk were held for one fee; Cookley perhaps accounted for the remaining one-and-a-half fees (*CCR, 1301-1307*, p. 512; *CIPM*, iv, 301). The connection between the Bavents and the Bigods had been little cultivated by Hubert's father. Michael de Bavent appears frequently in the Crown records in Suffolk down to 1241 (C66/49, m. 9d is his last appearance), but he witnessed no Bigod charters, and cannot be placed with his overlords on any occasion other than the siege of Framlingham in 1216. Cf. *Sibton*, i, 30-31.

[56] *RBE*, i, 395.

[57] The Bigods had held the Norfolk manor of Mautby in 1086, and at the time of his death in 1270, Roger III held 12 acres of arable in Alby from a Walter de Mautby. *Domesday Book*, ed. Morris, 33, f. 180a; *CIPM*, i, 240. Cf. Blomefield, xi, 226.

[58] Cf. *Sibton*, i, 84-6, where Robert finds no place in the Pirnhow family tree. The only other certain reference to him comes in 1238, when he was a guardian of the two sons of Bartholomew de Creake (*CRR*, xvi, 1237-42, p. 76). He may have been the Robert de Pirrow who crossed to Gascony in 1242 (*CPR, 1232-47*, p. 295). William de Beaumont was probably a descendant of Godfrey de Beaumont, who witnesses four of the early charters of Roger II Bigod. RBII 3, 6, 8 and 14. Hugh de Vaux witnesses HBII 2 and 3; RBIII 7, 9 and 10.

[59] He witnesses charters RBIII 10, 11 and 13, and appears in the 1257 list of *familiares*.

were further improved in 1253 by the life grant of the manor of Brockley (Suffolk) from Roger III.[60] The true rising star, however, was Thomas Lenebaud. Born the son of Roger Lenebaud, huntsman to Roger II Bigod, Thomas laboured to become perhaps the single most important member of Roger III's household.[61] He had trained as a clerk, and had also spent some time as a scholar (after his own death, he was styled 'Master Thomas').[62] His involvement in Roger III's affairs had begun as early as 1240, when he was among the band of disseisors noted above in Suffolk, after which he acted (with Herbert de Alencon and Ralph Bigod) as a surety for the other accused.[63] Thereafter he witnessed five of Roger III's charters (the earliest in 1242, the latest after 1257) and was the only individual to feature in both sets of the earl's executors.[64] He appears in at least three, possibly all four of the household lists, and his pre-eminent status is further emphasized by his having a private chamber at the Bigod manor of Kelsale.[65] His promotion to the rank of archdeacon, which occurred before 1274, may have been down to his employer's influence; it seems certain that it was Roger III and not his successor who appointed Thomas as parson of Framlingham.[66] He must also have acquired a considerable fortune during his time in the earl's service. A number of final concords between 1258 and 1276 and an undated charter indicate that Thomas was purchasing property in and around Ipswich, and he was also able to follow his master's lead in making a benefaction to the hospital of St Giles, Norwich.[67] Of all Roger III's men, Master Thomas was clearly the most indispensable.

The list of *familiares* drawn up in 1257 provides us with a glimpse of Roger's household towards the end of his career, on the eve of his confrontation with the king. By this date, the grand old men of the earl's affinity, Herbert de Alencon and Ralph Bigod, were both dead, as was Bartholomew de Creake and probably also Gervase de Bradfield.[68] Survivors from the 1240s included Hubert de Bavent, John Algar and the

---

[60] *CR, 1253-54*, p. 21; Blomefield, x, 155; CP25/1/214/23, no. 201.

[61] Norwich Record Office, Great Hospital Deeds, no. 1246 ('Thomas, son of Roger Lenebaud of Framlingham'); *RLP*, p. 171.

[62] E159/57, m. 2.

[63] JUST/1/818, m. 8d.

[64] RBIII 7, 10-14; *Select Cases in the Exchequer of Pleas*, ed. Jenkinson, p. 89.

[65] He may be 'Master Thomas the Physician' in the 1245 list. For the reroofing of his chamber in 1268, see SC6/1000/8.

[66] He is styled 'archdeacon of Suffolk' in CP25/1/215/32, no. 15, and 'parson of the church of Framlingham' in C66/97, m. 23d. For the argument between Roger IV Bigod and Master Thomas over the goods and chattels of Roger III, see below, pp. 115n, 143.

[67] CP25/1/214/25, no. 13; CP25/1/214/27, no. 42; CP25/1/215/32, no. 15; CP25/1/215/33, no. 2. Suffolk Record Office, HD1047/1/20. For his grant to St Giles, see above, n. 61.

[68] For Herbert de Alencon and Ralph Bigod, see above, n. 50. Gervase de Bradfield makes his last appearances in the 1250 Suffolk eyre (JUST/1/560, mm. 22, 61d; JUST/1/561, m. 6d). Bartholomew de Creake died in 1252 (Farrer, *Honors*, iii, 429).

redoubtable Thomas Lenebaud.[69] To these old stalwarts the earl added new young bloods. Among the significant additions, Philip de Buckland was a young knight with several manors in the east of Suffolk, as well as some property in Hertfordshire (probably including Buckland itself); it was not long before Roger nominated him to act as marshal of the king's household.[70] Richard de Holbrook was also a substantial Suffolk landowner, with manors that stretched along both sides of the Orwell estuary.[71] Two further newcomers to the affinity, Henry de Rushall (who was definitely a knight) and Thomas de Shotford (who may not have been) were also close neighbours. Neither man held land from Roger, but both may have been drawn into his circle around this time by the earl's aggressive expansion of his interests along the River Waveney.[72] Less visible but still noteworthy, Sir William Malherbe first appears in connection with the earl as his seneschal of Carlow in Ireland in 1257.[73] (This was a convenient posting, because his absence excused him – temporarily at least – from explaining before the justices on eyre in Suffolk precisely what part he had played in the death of certain men in the county.)[74] After his return to England, which took place before June 1258, he was for a time seneschal of the Bigod estate in East Anglia, and named as an executor of the earl's will.[75] Two further knights, William de Burgh and Robert de Vaux, witnessed charters datable to the later part of Roger's career, and appear in the 1255 and 1257 lists.[76] Of the non-knightly newcomers, Robert Blund (seneschal in East Anglia, 1252-53), Richard de Cransford and Hugh de Tuddenham were the most significant.[77]

---

[69] Bavent was not in the 1257 list but hunted with Bigod in 1255. He is last heard of in 1281 (*Sibton*, i, 31). Algar witnesses RBIII 13 (1257 x 1270). W.A. Copinger, *The Manors of Suffolk* (7 vols., London, 1905-11), vii, 13 asserts that he was alive in 1286, but cites no evidence. Lenebaud died in 1282 (*Bury*, p. 77).

[70] *CPR, 1247-58*, p. 578. His youth is adduced from his long career in the service of Roger IV Bigod, which lasted until his death in 1294. Below, pp. 121, 137, 142-3, 145-6, 149-51.

[71] He held lands in Suffolk at Bentley, Bucklesham, Foxhall, Freston, Holbrook, Nacton, 'Rushaugh', 'Slich', Sproughton, 'Stubover', Tattingstone and Wherstead. He also had property in Seething, Norfolk. *CPR, 1247-58*, p. 256; *CChR, 1257-1300*, pp. 76, 330.

[72] Below, n. 120. Henry de Rushall, who witnesses RBIII 8, 10, 12 and 13, held lands in Rushall and Semer (*CChR, 1257-1300*, p. 50). Thomas de Shotford, a witness to RBIII 9, 10 and 11, had property in Thickbroom, Mendham, and probably Shotford itself (*Sibton*, i, 99). In 1251 he was Roger III's seneschal in East Anglia (Appendix D). The first witness to his grant to Sibton Abbey was Stephen de Brockdish, who for a time resisted the earl's expansionist schemes in their neighbourhood (*Sibton*, iv, 91-2; below, pp. 76, 78).

[73] *Calendar of Ormond Deeds*, i, 1172-1350 (HMSO, 1932), p. 28 (cf. pp. 27, 30, 32); *CDI, 1285-92*, p. 294.

[74] JUST/1/567, m. 1. For his other violent and illegal acts, see *CR, 1242-47*, pp. 76-7; *CR, 1247-51*, pp. 355-6; *CR, 1251-53*, p. 63.

[75] RBIII 13 and 14.

[76] RBIII 12 and 13; C. Moor, *Knights of Edward I* (5 vols., Harleian Soc., 1929-32), i, 162.

[77] Blund witnesses RBIII 8, 9 and 10, and appeared as seneschal at the exchequer in 1252 and 1253 (Appendix D); Cransford witnesses RBIII 10 and 11, and may have crossed to Gascony with Roger in 1253 (*CPR, 1247-58*, pp. 219, 235). Tuddenham witnesses RBIII 13 and was an executor of Roger's will in 1258 (RBIII 14).

Among this last generation of affinity members, considerably fewer were Bigod tenants. There is no evidence to suggest that William Malherbe, Philip de Buckland, Henry de Rushall, Thomas de Shotford, Richard de Cransford, Robert Blund or William de Burgh held any lands from Roger III. Robert de Vaux is an obscure figure whose landholdings are untraceable; if he was, as seems likely, a minor scion of the great East Anglian family of the same surname then he had a landed link of sorts. Similarly, it is possible that Hugh de Tuddenham found his way into the earl's entourage because of a pre-existing tenurial bond.[78] Only in the case of Richard de Holbrook, however, can we say with absolute certainty that Roger was still recruiting from among his tenants.[79]

It is difficult to say how many of these men were in Roger's service at one time. The two longer lists of 1245 and 1257 suggest that, excluding all but the most menial types (carters, grooms and porters), Roger III typically travelled with around twenty people. Even this number, however, included people of no great significance. Roger the Butler, Reginald the Marshal and William the Cook, all of whom feature in both lists, had long careers in the earl's service, but in political terms they were inconsequential figures.[80]

One way of determining importance is to count the number of knights in Roger's entourage. Of the twenty-nine individuals discussed above, twenty can be definitely shown to have been of knightly status. A further five men, by contrast, were almost certainly not knights (in two cases, because the men in question were high-ranking clerics). In the case of the remaining four men, it has not been possible to determine their status, but their toponymic surnames and familiar-sounding pedigrees strongly suggest that they were also knights.

It is clear from the foregoing that not all of these men were in the earl's service at the same time. The table overleaf shows all the men who can be identified as important members of Roger's affinity across his entire forty-

---

[78] In the late twelfth or early thirteenth century, Roger II Bigod was recognized as the lord of 6⅙ fees which had once been of Richard de Reimes (above, pp. 16n, 50n). These included lands in Newton and 'Easton' held by one Edmund de Tuddenham. In 1306 an Oliver de Tuddenham held lands in Newton and Wherstead from Roger IV Bigod. Although no relationship can be proved, it seems very likely that Hugh de Tuddenham was the missing dynastic link who held these lands from Roger III Bigod in the middle of the century. *The Book of Fees, Commonly Called Testa de Nevill* (3 vols., HMSO, 1920-31), i, 136, 233; *CIPM*, iv, 301.

[79] The Holbrooks held Friston and Holbrook from the Bigods. *CIPM*, iv, 301.

[80] Reginald the Marshal and William the Cook appear in both the 1245 and 1257 household lists. Roger the Butler, or Roger Plantyn, appears in the 1245, 1257 and 1268 lists. In 1254 he and two other of the earl's men attacked a Gascon merchant in Ipswich, and in 1258 he was granted a wardship by Henry III. *CR, 1253-54*, pp. 134-5; *CPR, 1247-58*, p. 633.

Table 3. The Familiares *of Roger III Bigod*

Name	Status	No. of witnessings
Herbert de Alencon	knight	6
John Algar	not a knight	3
Hubert de Bavent	knight	4
Ralph Bigod	knight	5
Thomas Bigod	clerk	4
Robert Blund	not a knight	3
Gervase de Bradfield	knight	3
Philip de Buckland	knight	1
William de Burgh	knight	2
William de Burnaville	uncertain	1
Richard de Cransford	uncertain	2
Bartholomew de Creake	knight	2
Roger fitz Osbert	knight	1
William de Hingham	knight	1
Richard de Holbrook	knight	0
Robert Hovel	knight	0
Thomas Lenebaud	clerk	5
William Lenveise	knight	1
William Malherbe	knight	1
Matthew de Mautby	knight	2
Reginald de Pirnhow	uncertain	1
Robert de Pirnhow	knight	1
Henry de Rushall	knight	4
Thomas de Shotford	uncertain	3
Hugh de Tuddenham	not a knight	2
Hugh de Vaux	knight	3
Oliver de Vaux	knight	2
Robert de Vaux	knight	0
William de Verdun	knight	1

five-year career.[81] The best indications of the size of the earl's entourage at any one point come not from manipulation of the figures but from the evidence we already have to hand. The three Bigod charters which distinguish between the status of witnesses show Roger keeping company with five, six and eight knights on each separate occasion.[82] In 1255, while hunting with his cousins in Yorkshire, the earl had with him six knights, plus his leading clerk Thomas Lenebaud and the non-knightly Hugh de Tuddenham. Similarly, of the eighteen men whom the earl had with him

---

[81] Cf. G.G. Simpson's estimate for the size of Roger de Quincy's *familia*, below, p. 70.
[82] RBIII 8, 12 and 13. Note that Henry de Rushall appears in all three charters, but is only included with the knights in two of them.

in 1257, six were definitely knights (Buckland, Vaux, Hovel, Burgh, Rushall and Holbrook), four were non-knights (definitely in the case of Thomas Lenebaud and John Algar, very probably in the case of Richard de Cransford and Roger le Gras) and a further four appear to have been regular but menial members of the household.[83] The remaining four individuals cannot be linked to Roger on any occasion, and appear in most cases to be men of little importance.[84] When travelling to Lyon in 1245, Roger had at least eight knights in his company, and possibly as many as eleven. However, only five of them appear with him on other occasions; the remaining names may have been travelling companions selected especially for the purpose of an important overseas trip.[85]

It seems, therefore, that Roger Bigod may typically have travelled with around six knights in attendance, while on special occasions (such as his trip to Lyon) he might have scraped together around double this number. A retinue of this size sounds about right for a man of his stature and income, as the table below shows:[86]

Table 4. Magnate Incomes and Affinities

Magnate	Income	No. of knights
Roger de Quincy	£400+	up to 15
Simon de Montfort	£2,000	6 to 12
Roger III Bigod	£2,500	6 to 12
William de Valence	£2,500	6 to 12
William Marshal	£3,500	up to 18
Gilbert de Clare	£3,700	20 or more
Richard of Cornwall	£5,000-£6,000	up to 30

[83] Cransford and le Gras witness charter RBIII 11, after the non-knightly John Algar. Roger the Bastard may be the same man as Robert the Bastard in the 1245 list. For the other three menials, see above, n. 80.

[84] They were Walter de Fakenham, Roger de Framlingham, Walter de Brundish and Ralph de Ardern. The first three men, all East Anglian by their surnames, leave no trace in Crown records. Ralph de Ardern was a man of some importance, having acted as sheriff of Essex between 1254 and 1256 (*List of Sheriffs for England and Wales* (HMSO, 1898), p. 43). However, he and Brundish appear to have been added to the roll after the other names, and were probably only temporary members of the earl's circle.

[85] The definite knights were Ernulf de Munteny, William de Munchensi, Robert de Pirnhow, Matthew de Mautby, Hugh Peche, William de Beaumont, Robert Hovel and Hubert de Bavent. Lewis de Gerardville, Robert de Charneles and John de Wattisham may also have been from knightly families. Cf. *Sibton*, i, 44; *Eye Priory Cartulary*, ed. Brown, ii, 49-50.

[86] G.G. Simpson, 'The *Familia* of Roger de Quincy, Earl of Winchester and Constable of Scotland', *Essays on the Nobility of Medieval Scotland*, ed. K.J. Stringer (Edinburgh, 1985), pp. 107, 123n; Maddicott, *Montfort*, pp. 55, 69; Ridgeway, 'William de Valence', pp. 242, 244-5; Crouch, *William Marshal*, p. 148; Jacob, *Studies*, p. 129; Denholm-Young, *Richard of Cornwall*, pp. 90-91. Roger de Quincy is the only figure who does not fit the pattern. However, there are grounds for doubting whether Quincy really had such a large number of knights. Simpson's calculations are based solely on charter evidence, and his method of reckoning does not allow for changes in the affinity across time.

If Roger's affinity was similar in size to those of his contemporaries, in other ways it may have been considerably different. As the foregoing analysis shows, at least a third of the earl's *familiares* were drawn from among his tenantry. This, again, would seem to make him normal.[87] It is quite likely, however, that the number of tenants in Roger's entourage was higher than average. Several of the individuals discussed above leave no traces in the records of royal government, and cannot be biographized in any great detail. Their surnames, however, indicate that they were probably younger sons of prominent Bigod tenants. If we include these men in our reckoning, the number of tenants in Roger's household rises to around half of the total.[88]

Another striking feature of the Bigod affinity is its geographical cohesion. All of Roger's *familiares* were East Anglian men, the majority of them hailing from Suffolk. This appears to be as true for the period after Roger had obtained a share of the Marshal inheritance as it was during the years beforehand. Despite the earl's acquisition of new lands in England, Wales and Ireland in 1248, the greater part of his income was still raised from his eastern estates; the majority of his property, including the castles at Framlingham and Bungay, lay south of the River Waveney. Like many of his followers, therefore, Roger regarded Suffolk as home.

On first inspection, the predominant characteristic of the Bigod affinity appears to be its mediocrity. None of the men we can identify in the earl's 'charmed circle' was important in national politics. Only Philip de Buckland got to spend any time in the king's company, and this was because the earl had nominated him to a position at court.[89] As a result, Roger's *familiares* appear lacklustre when compared to the high-achievers who accompanied Simon de Montfort. Similarly, they seem superficially less interesting than the courtier knights who trotted after William de Valence.[90]

Roger, however, had an affinity that was not 'court' but firmly 'country'. Of the older generation of the earl's household knights, all were deeply involved in East Anglian government. Men like William de Burnaville, William de Hingham, William Lenveise and Roger fitz Osbert served frequently as assize judges, tax-collectors and wardens of important local fairs.[91] Herbert de Alencon, perhaps the most important

---

[87] Cf. Crouch, *William Marshal*, p. 148; Maddicott, *Montfort*, p. 62

[88] There are, in fact, only a few of Roger III's *familiares* of whom we can say with total confidence that there was no tenurial connection with the earl, e.g. Philip de Buckland and Henry de Rushall.

[89] *RCWL HIII*, ii, 97-9, 101-2, 106, 108, 117, 136. See also *EHD*, iii, 164.

[90] Maddicott, *Montfort*, p. 70; Ridgeway, 'William de Valence', p. 255.

[91] William de Burnaville: *CPR, 1225-32*, p. 295; *CPR, 1232-47*, p. 234; C66/46, m. 7d, C66/47, m. 10d, C66/48, m. 10d. William de Hingham: *CR, 1231-34*, p. 159; *CR, 1234-37*, p. 547; *CPR, 1232-47*, pp. 68, 119; many judicial commissions between *PatR, 1216-25*, p. 312 and C66/53, m. 8d. William Lenveise: *PatR, 1216-25*, pp. 559; *CRR*, xiii, 1227-30, pp. 519, 523; *CPR, 1225-32*, pp. 155, 294-5, 312, 349, 352; Roger fitz Osbert: *CR, 1231-34*, p. 129; *PatR,*

member of Roger's affinity during the early part of his career, served as sheriff of Norfolk and Suffolk in the period 1227-32.[92] During this time he appears to have run up sizeable debts, and his experience may well have discouraged later generations of Bigod men from taking up the office.[93] Certainly, this was the general pattern: as the reign of Henry III progressed, there was an increasing reluctance among the landowning class to participate in local government.[94] Accordingly, the later members of Roger's *familia* sought exemption from office-holding, and probably sought their patron's assistance in this regard. The earl marshal rarely had the king's ear, but Henry III found it difficult to refuse him favours when on campaign. In 1253, on the eve of departing for Gascony, Bigod man Richard de Cransford was exempted from being put on assizes or being made sheriff.[95] At Chester in 1257, when Roger was deep in the king's counsels, his *familiares* Hubert de Bavent, Richard de Holbrook and Robert de Vaux all secured similar grants.[96] During the parliament at Oxford in June 1258, when Roger was also in a position to speak for his men, Philip de Buckland received the same royal dispensation.[97]

The men who made up Roger's household in his later years therefore do not feature frequently in the records of royal government. Nevertheless, there is good reason to believe that men like Henry de Rushall, Richard de Holbrook and Philip de Buckland were influential local figures. Rushall, for example, was one of the two men charged with making inquisitions in East Anglia after the battle of Evesham.[98] Buckland, who owned five manors in eastern Suffolk, was made warden of Dunwich in 1272.[99] Holbrook, who owned a dozen manors in the south of the county, was constable of Orford Castle in 1276.[100] He was also one of the three new 'stewards' appointed by Edward I in 1275, part of a reform process predicated on the need to address the concerns of local society.[101]

Such individuals, at first glance mediocre, were in fact the bedrock of county society: the very kind of men who had suffered during the personal rule of Henry III. As far as the thirteenth century is concerned, East Anglia is an under-investigated region; little or no work has been

---

1216-25, pp. 559, 576; *RLC*, ii, 78, 139, 141; *CPR, 1225-32*, pp. 62, 143, 154-5, 312, 354, 524; *CPR, 1232-47*, pp. 159, 304.

[92] *List of Sheriffs for England and Wales*, p. 86.

[93] *Sibton*, i, 28-9; *CR, 1231-34*, pp. 110, 378. Cf. Vincent, *des Roches*, pp. 296-7.

[94] H. Cam, *The Hundred and the Hundred Rolls* (New York, 1930), p. 8.

[95] *CPR, 1247-58*, pp. 219, 235. During the same campaign one of the earl's clerks secured a similar grant for his father. *CPR, 1247-58*, p. 278.

[96] *RCWL HIII*, ii, 110-13; *CPR, 1247-58*, pp. 577-8.

[97] *CPR, 1247-58*, p. 635.

[98] *CIM*, i, 187.

[99] *CR, 1268-72*, p. 487.

[100] *CIM*, i, 327.

[101] J.R. Maddicott, 'Edward I and the Lessons of Baronial Reform: Local Government, 1258-80', *TCE*, i (Woodbridge, 1986), 21-2.

done on the experiences and political sympathies of its inhabitants.[102] It is clear, however, that the region as a whole had been one of those hit hardest by the increasing burdens of royal government: between 1230 and 1257, increments above the county farm of Norfolk and Suffolk had risen by over 400 per cent.[103] Rises on this scale probably meant that the Bigod affinity was politicized to a greater degree than the non-curial careers of its members might lead us to imagine.[104] They may not have wanted to serve on assizes, but the record shows that Roger's men were quick to litigate and therefore knew the law.[105] Many of them, like the earl himself, came from families which had been established in the region for several generations. Combined with recent hardships, this may well have made for an affinity which was stronger and more resolute than its apparent 'mediocrity' now suggests – one which did a good job in maintaining Roger's local power. As we shall see, it was certainly a network which both Henry III and Simon de Montfort were obliged to acknowledge, and eager to exploit, in the years after 1258.

THE BIGODS AND THE PROVISIONS OF OXFORD:
IDEALISM OR SELF-INTEREST?

Following their confrontation with the king at the end of April, the confederates remained at Westminster for at least another week. Shortly after 8 May, however, they disappeared from court. It had been agreed that a new parliament would meet at Oxford the following month. In the meantime, while Henry made his way to Winchester, the magnates prepared for what they assumed would be the coming fight.[106] Roger Bigod probably headed for East Anglia, there to marshal his strength. On 5 June we catch him en route to Oxford, paused at his manor of Great Chesterford on the Essex–Cambridgeshire border. There, in the company of his household, the earl composed his will. An affirmation of his recent political alliance with the earls of Leicester and Gloucester, it also

---

[102] No modern county histories have been prepared for Norfolk or Suffolk. While useful information about Norfolk can be found in Blomefield, it can only rarely be verified. Copinger's *Manors of Suffolk* is more narrow in its focus and in many respects even less reliable.

[103] D.A. Carpenter, 'The Decline of the Curial Sheriff in England, 1194-1258', *Reign of Henry III*, p. 172.

[104] However, only one member of Roger's affinity – Robert Hovel – ran up substantial Jewish debts (£50), the first record of which comes in 1268. *Calendar of Plea Rolls of the Exchequer of the Jews*, ed. J.M. Rigg and others (5 vols., Jewish Historical Soc. of England, 1905-72), i, 174, 222-3, 296.

[105] For cases in 1250 and 1257 involving Herbert de Alencon, Hubert de Bavent, Gervase de Bradfield, Philip de Buckland and Thomas de Shotford, see JUST/1/560, mm. 4, 46d, 61, 61d; JUST/1/561, m. 5d; JUST/1/820, m. 14.

[106] *RCWL HIII*, ii, 119-20. Hugh Bigod was still in Henry's company on 14 May.

underlined the uncertain future the confederates now faced, and the fear that the coming days could be bloody ones.[107]

In the event, the expected violence never materialized. Instead, the Oxford parliament saw the process of reform demanded in April by Roger and the baronage being put into effect. The wide and miscellaneous nature of the issues that were debated by the assembly as a whole is reflected in the so-called Petition of the Barons. The equally broad concerns of the council of twenty-four, now constituted from twelve of the barons and twelve of the king's supporters, are reflected in their famous memoranda, the Provisions of Oxford.[108]

Roger and Hugh Bigod were central to these deliberations. Both were members of the baronial committee of twelve, and Roger also sat on the committee that was nominated to negotiate an aid with the parliament. More importantly, when the council of twenty-four proved unworkable (probably due to the obstruction of the Lusignans, who were numbered among the king's councillors), the Bigods were intimately involved with the creation of a replacement. A new council of fifteen was proposed, its membership to be determined by four electors – two from the king's twelve, chosen by the barons, and two from the baronial twelve, picked by the king's men. In the event, the royalists nominated Roger and Hugh. Presumably, there was more to this choice than the hope that the Bigods would prove to be royalist sympathizers: by this stage, Hugh's commitment to reform can have been no great secret. Likewise, after his performance in April, there could not have been much doubt as to Roger's feelings on the subject, or the strength of his opposition to the Lusignans. It is arguable, therefore, that the king and his advisers picked the Bigods because, of all their opponents, the brothers were the most likely to act with probity and fairness when creating the new council.[109]

Roger, naturally, was a member of the council of fifteen. His younger brother, on paper at least, was not. For him a more important role had been reserved. After twenty-five years of dormancy, the office of justiciar was resurrected and vested in Hugh. The significance of his appointment was immediately and widely recognized.[110] Unlike his predecessors, Hugh had a clearly defined mission. He was charged with touring the country to bring justice to all. In this task, he would be assisted by four knights from every shire, who would inquire into abuses by officials of all kinds, royal and seigniorial.[111]

Having restructured the machinery of government in their favour, the reformers were concerned to secure physical guarantees of their position. Both the Petition and the Provisions had emphasized the undesirability of

---

[107] RBIII 14. For the general situation, see Carpenter, '1258', pp. 195-6.
[108] *DBM*, pp. 76-91, 96-113.
[109] Ibid., pp. 100-101, 104-5; Maddicott, *Montfort*, p. 158.
[110] *DBM*, pp. 90-91; *Flores*, ii, 426; Paris, v, 698.
[111] *DBM*, pp. 112-15.

having royal castles in the custody of aliens and, accordingly, a grand sweep of replacements was carried through by the council. Surprisingly, the king's castles in East Anglia, which were later committed to Roger Bigod, were left alone at this stage. Hugh Bigod, however, was given custody of the Tower.[112] The control of castles, in the event, proved to be the decisive issue for the Lusignans, and prompted a celebrated exchange between William de Valence and the intemperate earl of Leicester. Forced into a corner by their opponents, the Lusignans chose to run. The Oxford parliament broke up as the barons gave chase, and the pursuit ended at Winchester, where all four of Henry's half-brothers were sent into exile.[113]

Between the break-up of the Oxford parliament and the start of November there is no record of royal charters, and thus the movements of the Bigod brothers are harder to trace. Hugh's itinerary has been recovered from his eyre rolls, and can be further enhanced by his occasional endorsement of royal writs. As this suggests, his itinerary was quite similar to that of the king, saving the occasional rapid excursion to clean up a particularly abusive local regime.[114] Roger, meanwhile, continued to play a central role on the baronial council between the king's departure from Winchester and the October parliament. The earl's activities and movements are less well documented, but it is clear that he took a leading role in the council's business. On 23 July, for example, Roger went to the Guildhall in the company of Simon de Montfort and John fitz Geoffrey, and there all three magnates obliged the mayor and aldermen of London to take the oath to the Provisions.[115] On 4 August, a great many orders were enrolled on the council's authority. Roger was appointed as keeper of the seashore for Norfolk and Suffolk, and charged with taking the oath from the men of the major ports in the region.[116]

How committed were the Bigods to the success of the reform movement? The question of the magnates' sincerity was first raised at the Michaelmas parliament of 1258, when two issues dominated the council's agenda: the demand for better-behaved sheriffs, and the complaint against landowners who made novel or unreasonable demands for suit of court.[117] None of the magnates – even conservatives like Gloucester – could have objected to the first demand; the kind of men wanted in the counties were local sheriffs, who would be easier to overawe, suborn and exclude than

---

[112] *DBM*, pp. 80-83 (clauses 4, 5 and 15), 90-91, 112-13. The castles at Colchester and Orford were committed to Roger in October. *CPR, 1247-58*, p. 655; *CR, 1256-59*, p. 341.
[113] *Baronial Plan*, pp. 76-9.
[114] A.H. Hershey, 'Success or Failure? Hugh Bigod and Judicial Reform during the Baronial Movement, June 1258–February 1259', *TCE*, v (1993), 66, 83-4.
[115] *Cron. Maior*, pp. 38-9. For his other appearances in London, see Appendix A.
[116] *CR, 1256-59*, p. 324; *CPR, 1247-58*, pp. 645, 649.
[117] *DBM*, pp. 118-31

the more powerful outsiders appointed by the king.[118] What, however, did the magnates make of complaints about suit of court? The legislation drafted in October 1258 went some way to safeguarding the existing rights of great landowners, but in overall terms it 'struck a heavy blow at their feudal courts'.[119] Roger Bigod would certainly have had strong views on the subject, for he had expended considerable time and effort in recent years enforcing such suits to his private hundred court at Earsham on the Norfolk–Suffolk border. In 1249 the earl had successfully sued a local man, Stephen de Brockdish, for withholding suit from the hundred, and in 1256 he was granted permission to sue in the king's name to recover his rights in similar cases.[120] Did Roger therefore line up with those 'selfish and conservative' (but sadly nameless) councillors who were already standing in the way of progress?[121]

If the earl's position looks ambiguous in the autumn of 1258, it appears at first glance to have been acutely compromised during the Candlemas parliament of the following year. It was at this juncture that Gloucester, the most powerful but least convincing among the reformers, seems to have demurred at the prospect of having his extensive network of private courts investigated by the panels of four knights. At precisely the same moment, Roger and Hugh Bigod gave their backing to an alliance between Gloucester and Edward, whose antipathy to the Provisions was well known. It all looked highly suspicious. Treharne concluded that the pact was *not* a covert attempt to undermine the reform movement, but only on the basis that it was backed by the Bigods. However, his confidence in the brothers' reformist credentials is never substantiated.[122]

As it happens, Treharne was probably right: far from moving towards Gloucester's position, Roger and Hugh were still highly credible reformers. The Bigods, confronted with Gloucester's backsliding, may not have reacted as furiously as the earl of Leicester (who, protesting loudly, left the parliament for France); but it was the rest of the magnates, not Montfort, who succeeded in persuading Gloucester to submit.[123] In Roger

---

[118] *DBM*, pp. 108-9.

[119] *Baronial Plan*, p. 136.

[120] *CRR*, xix, 1249-50, pp. 77, 86; KB26/142, mm. 7, 28; JUST/1/561, m. 5d; *CPR*, 1247-58, p. 506. The drive to revivify Earsham seems to have been part of the earl's expansion of his interests along the Waveney valley. In 1228, within a few weeks/months of acquiring his estate, Roger was granted the right to hold a fair at Harleston; in 1260 he further expanded his commercial operations in the same vill (*CChR*, 1226-57, p. 84; *CChR*, 1257-1300, p. 26; *CIPM*, i, 241). His attempts to obtain the manor of Redenhall are discussed in Carpenter, 'Justice and Jurisdiction', pp. 30-32; In 1274, Roger was among those accused of appropriating the Waveney for their private use. *Rot. Hund.*, i, 540.

[121] *Baronial Plan*, p. 136.

[122] Ibid., pp. 139-40; Powicke, *Thirteenth Century*, p. 152. For the agreement, see *Report on the Manuscripts of Lord Middleton*, ed. W.H. Stevenson (Historical Manuscripts Comm., 1911), pp. 67-9 (transl. in M.A. Hennings, *England under Henry III* (London, 1924), pp. 93-5).

[123] *Baronial Plan*, p. 140; Maddicott, *Montfort*, p. 180.

Bigod's case, there is clear and compelling evidence to show where he stood on the issue. As well as the half-hundred of Earsham, the earl also held the Suffolk hundred of Loes. Uniquely, a return from the 1258 knightly inquiry has survived for this hundred.[124] Merely by virtue of its existence, the document proves that Roger had been prepared to let a panel of four knights delve deep into his private administration – a stark contrast to the obstructive position adopted by Gloucester on precisely this matter.[125] It was, moreover, an investigation into the very heart of the Bigod franchise, for Loes is the hundred in which Framlingham lies.

Predictably, the return does not give Roger a clean bill of health. A handful of officials are named and charged with minor offences; the chief complaint was that Robert de Doinges, a Bigod bailiff, had exacted a novel charge of two shillings each year when he took pledges from vills in the hundred.[126] It is possible, with some searching, to uncover other complaints about Roger as a landlord. In 1257, his bailiff in the half-hundred of Earsham, one Valentine de Shotford, was charged with taking the horses of two summoners.[127] In 1240, the men of the Halvergate in Norfolk protested when Roger pulled down their houses as part of an ongoing effort to compel the performance of villein services.[128] In 1275, five years after the earl's death, numerous individuals lined up before the hundred rolls inquisitors to complain about transgressions committed by his bailiffs. Robert de Hales was accused of illegally taking a horse; Hugh fitz Adam was alleged to have prevented the holding of a hundred court.[129] The worst offender, Robert Ster, stood accused of unjustly distraining beasts, accepting a bribe for releasing a prisoner, and ejecting the king's sub-escheator from the manor of Fishley.[130] There were also complaints that the earl's justice had on occasion been excessively rough; jurors remembered how a captured female thief had been detained at Roger's manor of Hollesley until she died; and how another thief, apprehended in the earl's park at Staverton, had perished in prison at Framlingham.[131] Alongside these specific accusations, there were also complaints of a more general nature: tolls and tallages had been introduced without warrant at the market of Hanworth; the earl had taken fines for making purprestures and then failed to amend them.[132]

---

[124] For a transcript, see Jacob, *Studies*, pp. 337-44.
[125] It is clear that Roger administered the hundred court (at his manor of Hoo), as opposed to simply receiving the profits. *Rot. Hund.*, ii, 188.
[126] Jacob, *Studies*, pp. 341-2.
[127] JUST/1/568, m. 10. Valentine was a close relative of affinity member Thomas de Shotford. *Sibton*, i, 100.
[128] *CRR*, xvi, 1237-42, pp. 224-5, 250, 271, 349-50, 514.
[129] *Rot. Hund.*, i, 440, 496.
[130] *Rot. Hund.*, i, 497, 504, 506, 537
[131] *Rot. Hund.*, ii, 189, 191.
[132] *Rot. Hund.*, i, 496-7.

It is, however, important to set these complaints in context. The offence committed by Valentine de Shotford in Earsham is the only misdemeanour by a Bigod official recorded in the rolls of the 1257 East Anglian eyre. The men of Halvergate complained, but ultimately Roger won the case.[133] The complaints of the hundred roll jurors can seem to amount to a tide of protest, but they are allegations only, untried and unanswered.[134] Everyone who held land was accused of malpractices in 1275, even Hugh Bigod, the popular hero of 1258, a man praised above all others for his moral fibre.[135] Quite incidentally, the hundred rolls reveal Bigod bailiffs on two separate occasions correcting the wrongs committed by others.[136] In the one instance where we have both plaint *and* procedure – the 1258 return for Loes – Bigod's bailiffs were acquitted of all charges.[137] Even with regard to the issue of suit of court, which has been used in the past to condemn Roger, it is possible to view his actions in a more sympathetic light than has previously been allowed. The writ 'of grace' which allowed the earl to recover lost suits at Earsham hardly proves he was an overbearing landlord in the mould of Richard de Clare, William de Valence, or even Simon de Montfort.[138] Like Henry III, Roger may well have lost rights during his minority and struggled to recover them. In the one recorded case Roger brought to recover customs and services to Earsham, the defendant, Stephen de Brockdish, freely admitted to having withdrawn them.[139] Even then, there was seemingly little resultant rancour. Unable to beat Bigod, Brockdish appears to have joined him.[140]

Behind every acquittal, of course, we can imagine foul play: juries suborned and judges bribed. Against our worst suspicions, however, we have to set the contemporary voices assuring us of the Bigod brothers' good credentials. The chroniclers were united in their opinion that Hugh Bigod was a good thing – a *vir fidelissimus* and a true-born Englishman.[141] His elder brother also received good press, both before 1258 and after. From a comparative analysis of Matthew Paris's comments on English

[133] *CRR*, xvi, 1237-42, pp. 369-70. Their descendants did no better against Roger IV Bigod. *Rot. Hund.*, i, 537; *CCR, 1272-79*, p. 424; *PA*, pp. 195, 231, 270.
[134] H. Cam, *Studies in the Hundred Rolls* (Oxford, 1921), pp. 142, 190.
[135] e.g. *Rot. Hund.*, i, 286, 319, 389, 393.
[136] *Rot. Hund.*, i, 474, 476.
[137] Jacob, *Studies*, pp. 34, 341-2.
[138] Carpenter, 'King, Magnates and Society', p. 104n. The other evidence cited by Carpenter to show that Roger kept company with such men – the earl's recovery of his rights at the exchequer – amounts to nothing. This was not an attempt by Roger to expand his jurisdiction at the Crown's expense, but rather a demand that an ancient entitlement ignored by the king should be respected. Above, p. 29n.
[139] JUST/1/561, m. 5d.
[140] Stephen, or perhaps a namesake descendant, is later found as a bailiff in the service of Roger IV Bigod. SC6/932/11 (Caistor, 1270); SC6/837/12 (Chesterford, 1272, where he received 63s 2d for his robes); SC6/768/7 (Kennett, 1274). In 1275, in his capacity as Bigod's bailiff, he was accused of attacking a king's sergeant. *Rot. Hund.*, i, 532.
[141] *Flores*, ii, 426; Paris, v, 698; Hershey, 'Success or Failure', pp. 68-70.

earls, none emerges so spotless as Roger Bigod. The opinionated monk, who detested foreign interference in English affairs, found much in Roger's political stance worthy of praise.[142] His comments, and those of other chroniclers on Hugh Bigod, were probably the inspiration behind the sympathetic opinions ventured (but not explained) by Treharne and Jacob.[143] As the above analysis shows, their somewhat unwarranted assumptions were in fact substantially correct.

It would be disingenuous to argue that, having gained a voice in government, the Bigod brothers did not exact some private advantages for themselves. In 1258, Hugh lost a considerable amount of revenue when his stepson and ward, Baldwin Wake, came of age.[144] The following year, therefore, the justiciar's colleagues on the council made good his losses with the grant of a new wardship (the heirs of William de Kyme).[145] In the same year, Hugh was granted permission to improve the disused quay at Brokenwharf in London, where he had acquired a new riverside residence.[146] Similarly, Roger Bigod was able to secure a number of favours from the king and his new council. Most of these did not amount to very much: some gifts of deer and timber, a pardon of homicide for an East Anglian man.[147] Like his brother, the earl was able to obtain a wardship; on 4 August 1258 he received the lands of Richard de Dover (once in the custody of William de St Ermine, but recovered after the latter took flight with the Lusignans).[148] Roger was also granted the Suffolk manor of Brandeston, but the grant does not appear to have stood for very long.[149]

By far the greatest advantage that Roger obtained after 1258 was the right to the profits of his brother's special eyre, a perquisite he demanded in his capacity as earl marshal. It was, however, far from being an incontrovertible claim; in ordinary circumstances, the profits from an eyre

---

[142] For positive or sympathetic comments on Roger, see Paris, v, 85-6, 269, 382-3, 423. Cf. the chronicler's opinions of Richard de Clare and Roger de Quincy (Paris, iv, 653; v, 83, 363-4). For Paris's world view, see A. Gransden, *Historical Writing in England, c. 550–c. 1307* (London, 1974), pp. 367-72.

[143] *Baronial Plan*, p. 140; Jacob, *Studies*, p. 35.

[144] *CPR, 1247-58*, pp. 654-5.

[145] *CPR, 1258-66*, p. 60. The wardship cost Hugh £3,000.

[146] *CChR, 1257-1300*, pp. 16-17; *CIM*, i, 86-7.

[147] *CR, 1256-59*, pp. 237, 251, 413, 416, 454; *CPR, 1258-66*, p. 61.

[148] *CR, 1256-59*, p. 254.

[149] Brandeston, part of the *terra Normannorum*, was previously held by John Weyland, a royal clerk. When John died in 1259, it was granted to Roger (*CChR, 1257-1300*, pp. 20-22). However, the manor was never subsequently recorded as being held by the earl, either in demesne or through a tenant. When Brandeston next occurs, it is held by John Weyland's younger brothers, William and Thomas, both of whom were employed by the earls of Norfolk (P. Brand, 'Chief Justice and Felon: The Career of Thomas Weyland', *The Making of the Common Law* (London, 1992), pp. 115-18; *CCR, 1272-79*, pp. 96, 300).

went to the ushers of the exchequer.[150] In 1258, however, the Bigods were in a strong position to assert that Hugh's visitation was special in every sense, and that its emoluments belonged to the marshalship. The archbishop of Canterbury, for example, was convinced that it fell to him to dispose of his bailiffs if they were convicted before a justice in eyre; it took a personal appearance from the earl marshal in January 1259 to persuade him that on this occasion things were different.[151] Similarly, the monks of Dunstable, who also baulked at the eyre's novel aspects, were distrained until they overcame their objections; they too found that the profits of justice where diverted elsewhere.[152] The situation only changed when Hugh was removed from office in 1260. When the special eyre resumed under the direction of a new chief justice, Roger sent one of his sergeants to claim the profits as before. Hugh Despenser, however, was not satisfied of the earl's entitlement, and referred the matter back to parliament.[153] Nothing more was heard on the matter; in any case, the special eyre soon collapsed.[154]

There is no denying that Roger's vested interest in the progress of his brother's eyre gave both men a special incentive to back the reform movement. By the same token, there are no grounds for believing that either man was an enthusiastic reformer on this basis alone. If his somewhat dubious rights as marshal meant that Roger had more to gain from the reform process than others, the return from the hundred of Loes indicates that he probably had less to fear. Whatever personal benefits he might have enjoyed after 1258, it is highly unlikely that the earl's decision to confront the king that year was based on a cynical calculation of profit and loss. The balance of the evidence suggests that, like his brother, Roger was a committed reformer. Throughout 1259, the earl's witnessing of royal charters was exceptionally high; Hugh's was second to none.[155] Their work on the council reached its high point in the Michaelmas parliament of 1259, with the publication of the Provisions of Westminster.[156]

---

[150] Cam, 'Marshalsy of the Eyre', pp. 126-37.
[151] Jacob, *Studies*, p. 58n.
[152] *Baronial Plan*, p. 148.
[153] H.G. Richardson, 'Year Books and Plea Rolls as Source of Historical Information', *TRHS*, 4th ser., 5 (1922) p. 61 (transl. in G. O. Sayles, *Functions of the Medieval Parliament of England* (London, 1988), p. 96). This source makes it clear that Roger was in receipt of the fees from the eyre until Hugh's dismissal.
[154] Maddicott, *Montfort*, p. 203.
[155] Appendix A; *RCWL*, ii, 122-7; *CLR, 1251-60*, pp. 446, 448, 454, 457, 460, 463, 469, 490-93; *CPR, 1258-66*, pp. 10-13, 15, 21-2, 30, 36-7, 39-41, 44-5, 48, 57, 62-3; *CR, 1256-59*, pp. 357, 366, 406-7, 411-14, 434, 466-8, 452, 454, 489, 495.
[156] *DBM*, pp. 136-57; *Baronial Plan*, pp. 157-212.

THE REVOLUTION UNDONE

It was at this point, however, that Simon de Montfort returned to England and rejoined the debate. Having occupied the high moral ground in February, Montfort had nevertheless devoted the rest of the year to pursuing his private grievances with Henry III. His principal complaint was the inadequacy of his wife's Irish dower, and the king's failure to provide redress. (Eleanor de Montfort, sister of Henry III, had first been married to William II Marshal, earl of Pembroke.) In his capacity as chief negotiator of the French peace in 1258, Montfort had linked the treaty's ratification to a satisfactory dower settlement, and had thus been able to obtain arbitration on the issue the following year. In the late summer of 1259, a panel of three men sat in judgement on this crucial point of contention.[157]

Chief among the arbitrators was Roger Bigod. In many ways he was an unsurprising, even an ideal choice; the earl's pivotal role in the creation of the council in 1258 indicates the faith others had in his judgement. In one crucial respect, however, his inclusion on the arbitration panel was astonishing. Montfort's demands for land in Ireland threatened the interests of the several heirs to the Marshal estate – chief among them the earls of Norfolk and Gloucester. Expecting Roger to endorse 'self-denying' aspects of reform was one thing; believing he would disinherit himself and his family was quite another. The award agreed by the panel is not known, but it clearly did not meet Montfort's immodest expectations. Henry III would later accuse the earl of suppressing the outcome.[158]

Thus, in spite of their triumph in Michaelmas 1259, the barons simultaneously faced two points of danger – the unratified French peace and an unpacified earl of Leicester. In the course of the October parliament, Montfort had allied himself with the Lord Edward and, although their pact achieved nothing in the short term, it revealed that the earl was now ready to wage war in pursuit of his private aims.[159] No less alarming, in order to finalise the French peace, the reformers were obliged to let Henry III cross the Channel, with all the attendant risks that loosening their control would entail. In mid-November, the king set sail, taking with him the most obviously royalist members of the baronial council – most notably the earl of Gloucester. With Montfort also in France to fight his corner, the splits in the baronial council had never been more apparent. When the peace was eventually sealed, Montfort's carefully contrived leverage evaporated. The earl sought another means to attack

---

[157] Maddicott, *Montfort*, pp. 155-6, 178-87; *Treaty Rolls*, i, 1234-1325 (HMSO, 1955), pp. 41-8.
[158] Maddicott, *Montfort*, pp. 186-7. On the 'modesty' of Montfort's demands, cf. pp. 52-3, 183.
[159] D.A. Carpenter, 'The Lord Edward's Oath to Aid and Counsel Simon de Montfort, 15 October 1259', *Reign of Henry III*, pp. 241-52.

the king, and thereby rediscovered his enthusiasm for the reform programme. Returning to England at the start of the new year, Montfort seized on the requirement in the Provisions for regular parliaments.[160]

Since Henry had crossed to France, the government of England had been in the hands of the remaining baronial councillors – principally Roger Bigod, Hugh Bigod and Philip Basset. These men were now caught between Montfort, who attempted to hold the Candlemas parliament in spite of the king's absence, and Henry, who, having prohibited the assembly from meeting without him, deliberately lingered on the Continent, relishing the divisions that had arisen among his unwanted council. Both sides began raising troops in the expectation of war.[161] For the Bigods, however, there was little doubt as to which party they would support. The king was merely provocative; Montfort was exasperating. For the past year he had wilfully ignored the reform programme, pursuing his personal grievances to the extent of threatening war. Now dressed in the robes of a reformer once more, and with Edward by his side, the earl was ready to make good his threat. His garb, however, was unconvincing – not least (for men like Roger Bigod) because he seemed ready to accept the return of the Lusignans as a means of ensuring victory.[162] Henry's summons of tenants-in-chief to London, directed to Hugh Bigod at the end of March, reveals the extent of the king's support and, by implication, the weakness of Montfort's position.[163] To his fellow councillors, the earl's actions not only appeared deeply cynical; they were also highly dangerous. Up until this point, the reform process had been going well; a real measure of success had been achieved on several fronts (and exemplified recently by the Provisions of Westminster). To go in arms against the king because of his failure to hold a parliament was to risk everything that had been achieved to date.[164]

The crisis was averted through the intervention of Richard of Cornwall, the offices of Hugh Bigod, and – crucially – the defection of Edward to his father's camp. The stand-off left the king considerably stronger, but the council nevertheless continued to have a large measure of control over royal government.[165] The Bigods, having been instrumental in ensuring the kingdom's peace, rode high in Henry's esteem; favours flowed from the king to both brothers (including, importantly, Hugh's appointment as constable of Scarborough Castle).[166] At the same time, their attestation of

---

[160] Maddicott, *Montfort*, pp. 187, 192-3.
[161] *DBM*, pp. 156-7, 170-73; Maddicott, *Montfort*, pp. 193-4.
[162] Maddicott, *Montfort*, pp. 195-6
[163] *CR, 1259-61*, pp. 157-8. For Henry's other orders involving the Bigods at this time, see *DBM*, pp. 176-7, 190-91; *CR, 1259-61*, pp. 278, 283-4.
[164] Maddicott, *Montfort*, p. 197.
[165] *Baronial Plan*, pp. 230-35.
[166] *CChR, 1257-1300*, p. 26; *CPR, 1258-66*, p. 74; *CR, 1259-61*, p. 56; *CIM*, i, 89. For the state of Scarborough when Hugh took custody, see *Yorks. Inq.*, i, 72-3.

royal writs and witnessing of royal charters indicate the Bigods' continued importance to the work of the council.[167]

In the summer of 1260, however, the council broke up. It was a planned diaspora rather than a permanent fracture, leaving the kind of reduced 'working' council that had been envisaged between parliaments in the Provisions.[168] In July, Builth Castle in Wales fell to the Welsh, and it is possible that those councillors with lands in the Marches, such as Roger Bigod and Humphrey de Bohun, left the king's side to safeguard their own interests.[169] Others stayed close by the king; Hugh Bigod remained in attendance until mid-August, and Gloucester was still at court at the start of the following month.[170] Nevertheless, the temporary loosening of the council's control allowed others to regain the initiative. By the autumn, Montfort, who had been left out in the cold since his unsuccessful Easter rising, had worked out a way of intruding himself into government. When a parliament assembled in October, the earl reappeared and struck an astonishing deal with his former opponents. In return for a role in government, he bowed to the wishes of Richard de Clare, and agreed that the investigation into seigniorial abuses would be abandoned. The two earls, together with the Lord Edward, forged an extraordinary alliance, and forced a new set of officials on a reluctant Henry III. The chancellor and treasurer were removed and replaced with Montfortian appointees. In came Hugh Despenser as the regime's new justiciar. Out went Hugh Bigod.[171]

Hugh Bigod's reaction to being deprived of power was to move closer to the king; along with a number of other councillors, including Basset and Audley, he was recruited into the *familia regis*.[172] As for Roger Bigod, there is no sign that he attended the Michaelmas parliament (although, to judge from a writ sent on 8 October, he was probably expected).[173] The most likely scenario is that, as his brother was ousted from office, the earl also quit the council. He appears to have retired from government altogether, probably to his own estates.[174]

---

[167] Appendix A; *RCWL*, ii, 128-30; *CLR, 1251-60*, p. 501-3, 508, 511-13, 519, 521, 524; *CPR, 1258-66*, pp. 72, 75-6, 79, 85; *CR, 1259-61*, pp. 38-40, 48-50, 66-7, 70, 72, 75, 82, 94, 170.
[168] *Baronial Plan*, p. 244.
[169] Maddicott, *Montfort*, p. 199; *CR, 1259-61*, p. 198.
[170] *CLR, 1251-60*, p. 524; *RCWL HIII*, ii, 130.
[171] Maddicott, *Montfort*, pp. 200-202; H. Ridgeway, 'King Henry III's Grievances against the Council in 1261', *Historical Research*, 61 (1988), pp. 230, 241.
[172] *CR, 1259-61*, p. 317.
[173] *CPR, 1258-66*, p. 96.
[174] He was certainly absent on 16 November (*CDS, 1108-1272*, p. 438). His absence, and the removal of Hugh Bigod, somewhat undermines the suggestion that the earl of Leicester modified the Provisions 'with the sanction of the other councillors'. Maddicott, *Montfort*, p. 203.

Despite their different reactions to being eclipsed, the brothers soon found themselves in the same position as before, caught between the king and his implacable opponents. Early in 1261, Henry retreated into the Tower and launched a damning attack on the changes that had been forced on him in October by Montfort and Clare.[175] Roger Bigod's attitude is impossible to read: the earl is entirely absent from the record during the first half of 1261. Hugh, however, appears to have inclined towards the king.[176] From a purely personal point of view, he can have had little sympathy for the militant faction that had demoted him. More important, perhaps, was the fact that the Montfort/Clare junta had displayed a selective attitude to the reform programme, discarding those elements which conflicted with its own interests. Thus Henry and his advisers, like their opponents on the council, were able to claim that they were still backing the Provisions.[177]

That Henry was acting in extreme bad faith, professing his adherence to the Provisions while secretly negotiating with the pope for their annulment, is now well appreciated.[178] This was not, however, immediately clear to Hugh Bigod. Having probably sided with Henry over Easter, Hugh rendered the king inestimable good service at the start of May by agreeing to hand over Dover Castle to a new constable, the royalist Robert Walerand.[179] Prima facie, it might be assumed that, by agreeing to this transfer, Hugh exposed himself as a converted royalist. He offered no apparent opposition to the king's order and, when Henry was back in London, Hugh figures among the king's charter witnesses.[180] Yet, conversely, if the former justiciar really had abandoned his principles, there would have been no need for Henry to replace him. The decision to swap constables at Dover suggests that the king realized that, as soon as he went against the Provisions, Hugh would turn against him.

For this was exactly what happened. At the start of June, while celebrating Whitsun at Winchester, Henry threw off his disguise; possessed of his papal absolution, the king declared he would rule as of old, as he alone saw fit, recognizing neither the baronial council nor the Provisions. Predictably, this roused the already militant malcontents – Clare and Montfort – to new levels of opposition; immediately they denounced the papal bulls, and prepared for war.[181] More surprising was the reaction from the wider constituency of more moderate magnates – in particular the two Bigod brothers. Now that the scale of Henry's

[175] Ridgeway, 'King Henry III's Grievances', pp. 227, 229, 239-42.
[176] *RCWL HIII*, ii, 133; *CPR, 1258-66*, p. 141.
[177] Maddicott, *Montfort*, p. 208.
[178] Ibid.
[179] *CPR, 1258-66*, p. 151; Gervase, ii, 212; *AM*, iv, 127. Hugh had held the castle since 9 September 1259. *CR, 1264-68*, p. 408.
[180] *RCWL HIII*, ii, 134.
[181] Maddicott, *Montfort*, p. 209.

deception was finally exposed, Hugh Bigod must have bitterly regretted his decision to surrender Dover. By way of atonement, he made a principled stand over the two other, far less important royal castles that remained in his charge. Ignoring threats of excommunication, Hugh refused to relinquish Scarborough or Pickering, declaring pointedly (in view of Henry's recidivism) that only the king *and the council* had the authority to remove him.[182]

At the same time, Hugh's elder brother, having lain low since the autumn of 1261, now re-entered the debate with customary vigour. In spite of the probable existence of deep differences of principle between him and the Montfort/Clare party, Roger elected to join them in order to make a stand in defence of the Provisions. On the one hand this took the form of trying to induce outside powers to arbitrate on the issue.[183] But the magnates also mounted organized resistance to the king's government in the provinces. Public opinion was behind them, not least because Henry, as well as repudiating the reform programme, had also dismissed all twenty-two of the baronial sheriffs appointed in 1258, nominating his own supporters in their place.[184] In Norfolk, for example, local man Hervey de Stanhoe was obliged to make way for the curialist Philip Marmion, while in Essex Richard de Tani was replaced by the royalist Matthew de Mara. The king anticipated that these new appointees would also take custody of his castles; their baronial keepers, however, refused to comply. Just as Hugh Bigod had rejected Henry's demands to surrender his castles in Yorkshire, so Roger defied the king by retaining Colchester and Orford.[185] Magnate resistance also extended to creating rival sheriffs, or 'keepers of the counties'; Norfolk was committed to William Bardolf, a local baron of some standing, already closely identified with the reform movement. Suffolk was placed under the charge of the somewhat less imposing William de Bovile.[186] These men had tenurial links with Roger and, in Bovile's case, social ones too (he had hunted with the earl in 1255).[187] It seems very likely that in both cases Roger was their sponsor.[188] Unable to take control of the king's castles, and constantly impeded in his work by the baronial keepers, the new sheriff of Norfolk and Suffolk faced an

---

[182] *Foedera*, I, i, 408; *Baronial Plan*, pp. 265-6.
[183] Maddicott, *Montfort*, pp. 209-10.
[184] Ibid., p. 212.
[185] *CPR, 1258-66*, pp. 163-4. Cf. *Baronial Plan*, p. 263. The castles were not surrendered until the summer of 1262. Below, p. 88.
[186] Maddicott, *Montfort*, p. 212; *CR, 1268-72*, pp. 342-3.
[187] Bardolf was one of the baronial twelve in 1258, and a member of Montfort's party in 1264 (*DBM*, pp. 100-101, 284-5). He and his descendants held two fees in Narborough (Norfolk) from the Bigods (*Feudal Aids, 1284-1431* (6 vols., HMSO, 1899-1920), iii, 446; *CIPM*, ii, 115-16; iv, 303; see SC6/935/12 for Roger IV Bigod's distraint of a later William Bardolf for his £10 relief on these two fees). For Bovile, see *CR, 1254-56*, p. 415; *Feudal Aids*, iii, 397; *CIPM*, iv, 303. His namesake ancestor witnesses RBII 9.
[188] Bardolf was a witness to RBII 6, and was part of a Bigod gang that disseized Hugh fitz John of 4 acres in Tacolneston in 1257. JUST/1/567, m. 48d.

almost impossible task in enforcing the king's will in his counties.[189] From the summer of 1261, it looks very much as if East Anglia was being run by Roger Bigod rather than Henry III.

The king, however, could still count on one advantage, namely, the extreme reluctance of his opponents to wage war against him.[190] Despite a long history of disagreements with Henry, and notwithstanding the threat of force in 1258, Roger had not taken up arms in rebellion since 1233. The king may have sensed that, despite the show of unity presented by the magnates in the summer of 1261, men like the earl of Norfolk and his brother, although they might resist in their own parts, were unlikely to back the call to arms taken up by Montfort. In the event, the issue was never put to the test. In the autumn, the alliance between Montfort and Clare, an improbable marriage of convenience from its inception, cracked under the strain. Gloucester, a natural conservative, reverted to type and rejoined the king.[191] At the same time, Humphrey de Bohun, earl of Hereford, also made his peace with Henry.[192] While Montfort rehearsed his reproaches from the previous year and once again prepared to quit England for France, the remaining magnates sought terms. On 9 December, at Kingston in Surrey, a peace was concluded.[193]

Roger Bigod may well have participated in the negotiations for this peace, which had taken place throughout the month of November. Under the terms of the Treaty of Kingston, it was agreed that the points at issue between the king and his opponents would be decided by a panel of six arbitrators – three chosen by the king, and three by the barons – and one source, the Osney annalist, names Roger as a member of the baronial contingent.[194] The earl would certainly have been an obvious choice to take on such a role. As well as being one of the original and most senior reformers, a number of precedents indicate that he was possessed of the requisite negotiating skills.[195] Furthermore, as one of the most powerful English magnates, with great influence in what was proving an especially restless region, it would have been desirable for all parties to achieve a peace which carried the earl's endorsement.

If, however, the earl participated in the process of negotiating the Treaty of Kingston, it seems clear that he did not consent to its terms as published in December; the final version of the treaty named six different arbitrators.[196] Along with a much-diminished rump of rebel magnates,

---

[189] *CR, 1268-72*, pp. 342-3. See also Henry's decision to send a special messenger into East Anglia at this time. *CPR, 1258-66*, p. 174.
[190] Maddicott, *Montfort*, p. 214.
[191] Ibid.; *Baronial Plan*, p. 271.
[192] *Baronial Plan*, p. 269; *RCWL HIII*, ii, 135.
[193] *Baronial Plan*, pp. 271-2; Maddicott, *Montfort*, pp. 214-15.
[194] *AM*, iv, 128-9; Maddicott, *Montfort*, p. 214; *Baronial Plan*, pp. 272, 279n.
[195] For example, 1245 (Council of Lyon), 1258 (selecting Council of Fifteen and French embassy), 1259 (Montfort's dower claim).
[196] *Foedera*, I, i, 415.

Roger remained recalcitrant.[197] A week after the peace was concluded, the earl was informed that, if he wished to be included in the treaty's terms, he should send someone to seal it by Epiphany at the latest.[198] There is no indication that he ever did so, and the suspicion is that he continued to brood defiantly in East Anglia.[199] He was not seen at court in the first half of 1262, and during this time he appears to have retained possession of the royal castles at Colchester and Orford.[200]

Ultimately, however, such resistance to the king's will was useless. Nothing was left of the unity that had characterized the reformers in 1258. Gloucester, whose wealth and power made him essential to the success of any challenge to royal authority, had repeatedly shown himself to be untrustworthy and infinitely biddable. Leicester, whose charisma and connections made him equally indispensable, had demonstrated an intense but selective attitude towards reform; quick and loud in his support when the programme worked to his own advantage, he was also happy to abandon, compromise and frustrate the process when it suited his own ends. Among the other magnates, the earl of Hereford had acted erratically, backing Montfort in the spring of 1260, but returning to the king's camp in October the following year.[201] John de Warenne, for all his recent support, remained a flighty and unstable young man who had previously been bitterly opposed to the reform programme.[202] Peter of Savoy had long since returned to the king's side, and John fitz Geoffrey was long since dead.[203] In such circumstances, the Bigod brothers were bound to come back on board sooner or later. Hugh was the first to make his peace with Henry. In February 1262, he makes his first definite appearance at court since his defiant stand over Scarborough and Pickering.[204] Roger, meanwhile, held out until the end of May, at which point the protections that Henry had issued to his opponents the previous

---

[197] The others are named in *Baronial Plan*, p. 273. The number of men with East Anglian interests is striking. Of the fourteen men mentioned, six (Bigod, Warenne, Bardolf, de Burgh, Hastings and Munchensi) were major landholders in the region.

[198] *CR, 1261-64*, p. 95

[199] The only reference to Roger before June 1262 comes in a letter sent from the pope, dated 23 January that year. This was a request to receive favourably Master Leonard, precentor of Messina, who was coming to England to collect money for the Roman Church. Knowing something of the earl's attitude towards both foreigners in general and papal interference in particular, one can only assume his name was included optimistically by someone with a distant knowledge of affairs in England. *CPL, 1198-1304*, p. 383.

[200] Above, p. 85; below, p. 88.

[201] Maddicott, *Montfort*, p. 195; above, p. 86. Hereford was rewarded with the wardship of the earldom of Gloucester in the summer of 1262. *CPR, 1258-66*, pp. 226-7.

[202] *Baronial Plan*, pp. 76-7, 264, 269, 273. As a character note, see *inter alia* his murder of Alan la Zouche in 1269. *Peerage*, xii (part 1), 505.

[203] Maddicott, *Montfort*, pp. 178, 193, 197.

[204] *RCWL HIII*, ii, 136. The king's decision to include Hugh in a list of summons the previous autumn was probably an act of optimism. Cf. *Baronial Plan*, p. 269.

December expired.[205] The first indication of the earl's weakening came on 4 June, when the king felt sufficiently confident to repeat his demand for the surrender of Colchester and Orford.[206] Two weeks later, Roger appeared in person at Westminster – his only appearance at court that year, and his first recorded appearance in Henry's company for well over eighteen months.[207] A gift of deer, promised but not delivered in 1260, was soon dispatched as a sign of royal gratitude.[208] And thus, confident that his kingdom was finally pacified, and anxious to deal with Simon de Montfort, Henry set sail for France.[209]

DIFFERENT PATHS

The king's victory in 1262 was a hollow one. As the Kentish chronicler commented, many did not consent to the Treaty of Kingston, but were unable to resist.[210] With little support at home, Henry's government was left dangerously exposed while he and his court were abroad. In the autumn of 1262, a series of crises in England left the regency government reeling. Firstly, having taken the decision to purge Edward's household of its more unruly elements, the king and queen faced a backlash from the disgruntled knights formerly in their son's service. At the same time, Henry had managed to alienate Gilbert de Clare, heir to the earldom of Gloucester. Finally, at the end of the year, there was a general rising in Wales.[211]

These misfortunes compelled the king to return home; Henry was back in England by 20 December.[212] They also contrived to bring the earl of Norfolk back to the heart of government. Having maintained a low profile since the autumn of 1260, it seems fairly certain that Roger was once again involved in the direction of the kingdom's affairs.[213] What caused this turn-around? Possibly the earl was prompted to act out of self-interest; as the owner of a Welsh lordship, his own lands and finances would be damaged if Llywelyn's advances remained unchecked. On the other hand, Chepstow was the least valuable part of Roger's estate, worth only 10 per cent of the whole, and there is no evidence which can place the earl in or near the Marches during the early part of the year.[214] Even when, in March, the Welsh advance did appear to threaten Netherwent, a letter

---

[205] *Baronial Plan*, p. 272.
[206] *CPR, 1258-66*, p. 214.
[207] *RCWL HIII*, ii, 138.
[208] *CR, 1261-64*, p. 66.
[209] Maddicott, *Montfort*, p. 218.
[210] Gervase, ii, 213. Maddicott, *Montfort*, p. 216.
[211] Maddicott, *Montfort*, p. 220-21
[212] Ibid., p. 221.
[213] Unfortunately, there is no charter roll for the regnal year 47 HIII. Roger's involvement is adduced from the scattered references discussed below.
[214] For the value of the estates, see above, pp. 37-8.

from Peter de Montfort makes it clear that Roger was still directing the king's affairs in London, rather than safeguarding his own interests on the border.[215]

The more likely cause of the earl's return as a royal councillor at the start of 1263 was Henry's sudden decision to reverse his policies and renew his commitment to reform. On 22 January, with maximum publicity, the king reissued the Provisions of Westminster. A seemingly desperate effort to placate a country which was slipping out of control, this move was accompanied, according to the London chronicler, by a promise from Henry to observe 'other things to be provided' by Roger Bigod, Simon de Montfort, Philip Basset and Hugh Bigod.[216] Isolated although this reference is, other evidence bears out the suggestion that the king succeeded in drawing Roger back into his counsels at this time.[217] This suggests two things. Firstly, it indicates that, desperate and unsubtle as the king's actions might now seem, they must have been presented at the time with a considerable degree of sincerity, and perhaps even genuine repentance. Roger had quit the council when the reforms were diluted in 1260, and resisted staunchly when the Provisions had been overthrown in 1261. Only after months of subsequent defiance had he made his peace with the king. Given this past record, it seems unlikely that his sudden reinvolvement in the king's government was lightly undertaken, or bought by Henry with half-baked promises. Secondly, Henry's declaration that he would follow the counsels of the Bigod brothers, and also those of Basset and Montfort, is a telling indication that each of these men continued to be held in high popular esteem. Montfort's reputation as a force for good is, of course, well known; cultivated by the earl himself as well as his wide network of friends and supporters, it was a resource on which Henry clearly felt compelled to draw, in spite of the fact that the rift between the two men was wider than ever before.[218] In like manner, the king's pronouncement also reveals that the names of Roger and Hugh Bigod could be used to conjure widespread popular support. Whether it was as architects of the reform programme, as righters of injustices, as the heirs to the Marshal tradition, or as true-born men of the realm of England, the Bigods were still perceived as a remedy for the ill-effects of Henry's misgovernment.

Yet while Roger and Hugh were united in backing the Provisions at the start of 1263, there were nevertheless indications that the brothers now differed in the extent to which they were prepared to back the king. Up until this point, they had largely operated in tandem. Having participated in the launch of the reform programme in 1258, both had subsequently

---

[215] Maddicott, *Montfort*, p. 222; *CACWales*, pp. 52-3.
[216] Maddicott, *Montfort*, p. 221; *Cron. Maior.*, pp. 52-3.
[217] *CACWales*, pp. 52-3; Appendix A.
[218] Maddicott, *Montfort*, pp. 221-2, 248-54.

recoiled from Montfort's attempt to wage war, ostensibly in the programme's defence, in 1260. Similarly, when Henry overthrew the Provisions in the summer of 1261, both brothers resisted the king's orders and refused to hand over the royal castles in their custody. Since the start of 1262, however, Hugh Bigod had been arguably less discriminating. After his return to the royal fold in February that year, Hugh had stuck close by Henry's side and, in fact, would never again see fit cause to leave it. Roger, as has been seen, was more circumspect, waiting until the last possible moment to make his peace in 1262, and subsequently shunning the court until the king's remarkable volte-face at the start of the following year.

It is likely – though no more than that given the limited evidence – that these tendencies found further expression as the dramatic events of 1263 unfolded. In April Montfort returned to England to take command of another improbable coalition of malcontents, a party which included the new, disaffected earl of Gloucester, and also the young and disenchanted men who had been expelled from Edward's household. Under Leicester's leadership, this militant group began to bang loudly on the drum of the Provisions, and started to attack the property of aliens and royalists, particularly along the Severn valley and in the Welsh marches. Henry, for his part, also looked for a military solution to his problems, placing his trust in the large mercenary army that Edward had brought into England in February, and relying on his ability to bring over yet more troops from the Continent. On 25 May the king issued a feudal summons, requiring his tenants-in-chief to assemble at Oxford in August on the pretext of checking the Welsh threat. Both Roger and Hugh Bigod were included in the list.[219]

Given his record since February 1262, and in view of his subsequent behaviour, we may suspect that Hugh complied with the king's order. He was certainly in Henry's company on 4 April, and again in June, on the eve of the king's retreat into the Tower.[220] Of Roger, however, there is no word throughout the turbulent summer of 1263. It is possible, given the attacks that were taking place under Montfort's direction along the Severn, that the earl headed west to protect his marcher lordship from opportunistic plunder.[221] Equally, with the perpetual threat of armed intervention from the Continent, he may have gone east to safeguard his more valuable ancestral estates. At this point in time, neither side in the conflict was liable to have commanded his respect; as a marcher lord, he was unlikely to have approved of Montfort's decision to ally with the

---

[219] Maddicott, *Montfort*, pp. 222-9. *CR, 1261-64*, pp. 302-4.

[220] *CR, 1261-64*, p. 223; *CPR, 1258-66*, p. 263.

[221] The suggestion that the earl spent at least part of the summer of 1263 at Chepstow is supported by a royal gift of deer in October, given to Roger's countess in the forest of Dean. *CPR, 1258-66*, p. 292.

Welsh.[222] As a backer of the Provisions, he must have been less than impressed by the willingness of Henry and his son to introduce foreign troops into England. Just as he seems to have ignored the king's call to arms, so too Roger probably failed to respond to the appeal launched by Montfort in the wake of his bloodless coup in July.[223]

By October, however, Roger had joined with his brother, and the majority of other magnates, to throw his weight behind Henry and Edward.[224] The royalist party, thanks to the popular indignation encouraged by Montfort's regime, had by this date been rendered less objectionable by the removal of its army of foreign mercenaries.[225] More crucially, as Leicester's regime began to collapse (as before, largely under the weight of its own contradictions), the king and his son were perceived to be the only viable means of guaranteeing security of tenure and re-establishing the kingdom's peace.[226] Having joined the king at Windsor, Roger stayed with the court as it moved into Kent.[227] When both sides agreed to put their case to Louis IX of France, the earl and his brother were listed among the king's party.[228]

Had the Bigods finally abandoned their attachment to the reform programme? In Hugh's case, almost certainly. Throughout the previous months he had been assiduous in assisting Henry to regain power, travelling with him to France in September, and loaning the king money in order to advance his cause.[229] At the very end of the year, Hugh accompanied the king to Amiens, there to hear the French king deliver a verdict which quashed the Provisions completely.[230]

But what of Roger? His support was by no means so wholehearted, his sympathies by no means so clear. The earl, as has been shown several times already, was a man who believed in arbitration rather than armed conflict. It is therefore unsurprising that, having joined the king in October 1263, he participated in the royal request for Louis's mediation, drawn up at Windsor on 16 December.[231] If the earl was indeed present when this letter was sealed (i.e. if it was not sealed for him by proxy), this was his last appearance in Henry's presence until after the battle of Evesham. (His last certain appearance by the king's side took place on 5 December.)[232] On

[222] Maddicott, *Montfort*, p. 228.
[223] *CR, 1261-64*, pp. 308-9.
[224] Gervase, ii, 226; *AM*, iv, 137; Appendix A.
[225] D.A. Carpenter, 'King Henry III's "Statute" against Aliens: July 1263', *Reign of Henry III*, pp. 261-80.
[226] Maddicott, *Montfort*, p. 237.
[227] Gervase, ii, 229; Appendix A.
[228] *DBM*, pp. 282-3.
[229] *CPR, 1258-66*, pp. 263, 281, 283.
[230] *CPR, 1258-66*, p. 377; Gervase, ii, 233; *DBM*, pp. 286-91.
[231] *DBM*, pp. 284-5.
[232] Appendix A.

both these dates, and even as late as 20 December, the king was still letting it be known that he intended to keep the oath he had sworn at Oxford. Only in the last days of 1263 did Henry draw up his short submission, in which he made it clear that he desired to have the Provisions quashed and annulled.[233]

Unlike his brother, Roger did not cross to France with the king to hear Louis's damning verdict. Nor did he rally, as Hugh did, to the royalist flag at Oxford in March 1264, despite being summoned there by Henry at the start of the month.[234] While his younger brother fought in the king's name at Northampton in April, the earl himself stayed away.[235] And, whereas Hugh was highly conspicuous at the critical encounter at Lewes on 11 May, both in fighting for the king's cause, and in fleeing the field when that cause seemed lost, Roger was again notable only by his absence.[236] As an enthusiastic advocate of reform, he was probably among the wide range of people who sympathized with Montfort's party after the overthrow of the Provisions, and was unwilling to take up arms against them.[237]

At the same time, Roger showed little enthusiasm for the administration established by Montfort after his inconclusive victory at Lewes.[238] In June, he appeared at the regime's first parliament, and endorsed the Montfortian constitution.[239] In return, the earl of Leicester accepted the need to recognize Roger's dominant position in East Anglia. At the start of July, a series of writs confirmed Bigod as keeper of the peace for Norfolk and Suffolk, and committed to his custody the royal castle at Orford.[240] Thereafter, however, Roger took no part in the direction of the kingdom's affairs. Everything suggests that, from that point onwards, he looked exclusively to protecting his own interests. With the bulk of his lands concentrated in the eastern counties, many within a few miles of the coast, the earl was particularly vulnerable to the royalist invasion which threatened England in the autumn of 1264.[241] But while Roger would no doubt have defended his own property against spoliation, he was unlikely to go out of his way to oppose an invading army. In a letter of 9 July addressed to 'the whole commonalty' of Norfolk

---

[233] Maddicott, *Montfort*, pp. 256, 260. *DBM*, pp. 252-7.

[234] *CR, 1261-64*, pp. 337, 377; *CPR, 1258-66*, pp. 306, 308-9; *RCWL HIII*, ii, 143.

[235] Gervase, ii, 234. For Hugh's rewards after the battle, see below, pp. 97, 103-4.

[236] *AM*, iii, 232; iv, 452; *Flores*, ii, 495; Rishanger, *De Bellis*, p. 35; Gervase, ii, 237.

[237] Maddicott, *Montfort*, pp. 263-4.

[238] For the battle, see D.A. Carpenter, *The Battles of Lewes and Evesham, 1264/65* (Keele, 1987), pp. 19-36. For the subsequent negotiations, see J.R. Maddicott, 'The Mise of Lewes, 1264', *EHR*, 98 (1983), pp. 588-603; D.A. Carpenter, 'Simon de Montfort and the Mise of Lewes', *Reign of Henry III*, pp. 281-91; Maddicott, *Montfort*, pp. 272-8.

[239] *DBM*, pp. 298-9.

[240] *CPR, 1258-66*, pp. 331-2; *CR, 1261-64*, p. 349.

[241] Maddicott, *Montfort*, pp. 290-91. Cf. the attitude of Walter of Bronescombe, bishop of Exeter. Ibid., p. 302.

and Suffolk, Montfort at first ordered the men in the region to look to Bigod for direction. After the letter had been enrolled, however, Roger's name was struck out and replaced with that of Hugh Despenser.[242]

After the invasion threat had receded, Roger continued to maintain his distance. Tellingly, the business of exchequer at Michaelmas 1264 was disrupted because his deputy marshal failed to turn up.[243] He appears not to have taken part in the peace negotiations at Canterbury in the latter half of the year, nor to have joined in the appeals for arbitration directed towards the French king and the papal legate.[244] Similarly, although he was summoned to attend Montfort's last and most celebrated parliament, there is nothing to indicate that the earl was actually present when the assembly met in January 1265.[245] Nevertheless, in spite of his apparent lack of commitment to the earl of Leicester's government, Roger's tacit support of the new order was enough for him to be included in the bull of excommunication delivered against the king's enemies.[246] His stance, like that of Walter of Bronescombe, bishop of Exeter, appears to have been entirely pragmatic.[247] What options were left to men of moderation? Whatever censures the Church might throw upon him, Roger was unlikely to quit England in order to join the royalists in exile, abandoning his earldom, and leaving his lands liable to confiscation or depredation. At the same time, he can have had little enthusiasm for Montfort's increasingly radical schemes, which by 1265 may even have included plans for removing the Plantagenet dynasty and elevating his own family in its place.[248]

It was not until the summer of 1265, when Montfort's star was clearly in the descendant, that the silence between the two earls was broken. On 9 June, Leicester wrote to Norfolk, noting his great power in East Anglia, and requesting that he should put down a rebellion there.[249] The letter reveals a number of important points. In Montfort's case, it underlines the desperateness of his situation. Events in the provinces were already starting to slip away from his control, obliging him to appeal for the support of a man whose recent conduct suggests a studied neutrality and indifference. The letter is also testimony to the strength of the earl of Norfolk's position in East Anglia. Behind the obvious flattery, there is also perhaps a hint of envy when Montfort refers to Roger's 'great power' in Norfolk and Suffolk. At precisely this critical moment, the steward of

[242] *CPR, 1258-66*, pp. 360-61.

[243] E368/39, m. 1.

[244] Maddicott, *Montfort*, pp. 293-300.

[245] *CR, 1264-68*, p. 86; Maddicott, *Montfort*, p. 309.

[246] J. Heidemann, *Papst Clemens IV: Das Vorleben des Papstes und sein Legationregister* (Munster, 1903), p. 244.

[247] Maddicott, *Montfort*, p. 302.

[248] Ibid., p. 322.

[249] *CR, 1264-68*, p. 125.

England's recently constructed networks and alliances were failing him; the earl marshal's ancient and established networks appear to have remained intact.[250]

At Evesham, Roger took no part in the fighting.[251] His reasons were probably the same ones that explained his absence at Lewes; namely, a general indifference to the causes and personalities on both sides. Other possible motives are once again suggested by Leicester's letter of early June. Although drafted two months before the decisive encounter on 11 August, the writ nevertheless suggests that, as the theatre of conflict was opening in the west, along the Severn valley and close to his own lordship of Chepstow, Roger was content to stay in the east. His lands in Norfolk and Suffolk were the bulwark of his power, ten times more valuable than his Welsh estates. East Anglia was in a state of considerable unrest, divided between Montfortians and royalists, and at the same time still vulnerable to an invasion from overseas. Even if the earl had been able to muster any enthusiasm for either cause in 1265, self-interest alone would have recommended a policy of stay-at-home and wait-and-see.

Nevertheless, after Montfort's defeat and death at Evesham, Roger moved quickly to rejoin the king. His movements are for the most part uncertain, but it is possible that the earl may have appeared in the royalist camp within days of the decisive battle. A list of men who came into the king's peace at Gloucester suggests that Roger was an agent through which defeated rebels had sought terms of surrender.[252] By itself, this goes some way to proving that the earl suffered no reprisals for his conduct since Henry's capture the previous year, and reinforces the belief that his support for Montfort's regime was never more than tacit. Better evidence that Roger was well received by the royalists is his appearance in London in mid-October, and also the sum of 500 marks which the king deducted from the earl's Crown debts at Michaelmas.[253] If there were any hard feelings about the way things had gone since Lewes, for the moment neither Roger nor Henry was acknowledging their existence.

Disagreement, however, soon broke out, not over the earl of Norfolk's own fate, but over the treatment of those who stood accused of rebellion. In the days and weeks after Evesham, the estates of former Montfortians had been seized; Roger himself confiscated at least four East Anglian manors from their owners for this reason.[254] The expectation of moderate

[250] Maddicott, *Montfort*, p. 327-37; below, pp. 97-8.
[251] See O. de Laborderie, J.R. Maddicott and D.A. Carpenter, 'The Last Hours of Simon de Montfort: A New Account', *EHR*, 115 (2000), pp. 378-412.
[252] Jacob, *Studies*, pp. 151-2.
[253] E368/40, m. 3d. The pardon of 500m never found its way onto the pipe rolls.
[254] The earl seized rent from Sproughton in Suffolk, formerly held by Montfort. He also seized Martlesham (Suffolk) from Simon fitz Simon, Surlingham (Norfolk) from Thomas

men on both sides was that, given time, and once appropriate financial compensation had been made, these lands would eventually be restored.[255] By mid-October, however, the king and his hard-line advisers had decided that, on this occasion, there was no room for mercy; those who had rebelled would be treated as traitors, and their lands would be regarded as forfeit. This drew protests from the moderates, most notably from Roger himself, and also from Richard, earl of Cornwall. The two earls, along with Philip Basset, condemned the king's policy of total disinheritance, and withdrew from the court.[256]

The argument over 'the Disinherited' was in itself probably not enough to threaten the repaired relations between Roger and the king. Nevertheless, their public rift at Westminster was violent and visible enough to fuel rumours of continuing bad blood between the two men. Some fifty years later, William Rishanger reported Henry's activities in 1265 in considerable detail. In mid-December, the chronicler explained, the king and his army were assembled at Northampton, preparing for a strike on the Isle of Axholme, where Simon de Montfort junior had retreated with the remnant of his father's forces. The greater part of the royal host, said Rishanger, were foreign knights, and Henry proceeded to reward them with the confiscated estates of his rebel opponents. In particular, the chronicler alleged, the earldom of Norfolk was bestowed on the count of St Pol. He added, however, that the count had not actually taken seisin of any land in East Anglia, nor had he presumed to approach the region in person, because the present incumbent, 'a warlike man, was eager to meet him'.[257]

It would be tempting to dismiss this as pure invention on Rishanger's part, were it not for the exacting detail of the chronicler's account, and also the fact that, at the start of 1266, Henry III was moved to deny exactly the same story. Writing to the sheriffs of three south-western counties, and also to the sheriff of Kent, the king urged all his agents to take action against 'sowers of discord' who were spreading certain malicious rumours: that Edward had been mortally wounded; that Edward had fallen out with the earl of Gloucester; and that, contrary to justice, the king had conferred the lands of Roger Bigod on aliens. All these stories, Henry asserted, were false.[258]

Fortunately, this is one of those rare occasions when we can afford to take Henry entirely at his word; Roger, or at the very least one of his representatives, was in actual fact with the king at Northampton, carrying

---

de Moulton, and 'Wyleghby' from William de Evereux. E159/67, m. 19; *CIM*, i, 250; *Rotuli Selecti*, ed. J. Hunter (Record Comm., 1834), p. 226.
[255] Powicke, *Thirteenth Century*, pp. 203-4.
[256] *AM*, ii, 367; Rishanger, *De Bellis*, p. 65.
[257] Rishanger, *De Bellis*, pp. 49-50.
[258] *CPR, 1258-66*, p. 653.

out his role as marshal of the king's army.[259] If Henry had ever entertained ideas of disinheriting the earl, they had quickly and quietly been dropped after Evesham. Most likely the story was, as the king maintained, a malicious falsehood, spread by the large numbers of disaffected people who lamented Leicester's defeat. It is testimony to the strength of the propaganda networks established by Montfort that, in spite of the king's denials, the story of Roger's disinheritance could still command credence half a century later.[260] It also suggests that, in 1265, Roger continued to be regarded as a popular (as well as a warlike) figure – what better to excite the anger of genuine patriots than a rumour that the earl of Norfolk, a true-born Englishman famed for his anti-alien sentiments, had been replaced by a foreign count?

In fact, despite his disapproval of the treatment of former Montfortians, Roger continued to help in bringing them into the king's peace. In July 1266, he was empowered to receive those East Anglian rebels who wished to surrender.[261] In October, the men who had been holding out on the Isle of Ely were granted safe-conduct to come with the earl to the king at Kenilworth.[262] Roger was at the castle by the end of the month and, although he was not part of the committee which decided on the Dictum, he was a member of Henry's council at the time, and would have approved of the new and better terms that were offered to the die-hard rebels.[263] Still with the king at Kenilworth at the start of December, Roger may have remained there until the middle of the month, when the castle was finally surrendered.[264] In the new year, his involvement in the kingdom's pacification continued. In February 1267 the earl attended the parliament at Bury St Edmunds which attempted to resolve the ongoing problem posed by the unpacficied rebels. After the situation was given fresh urgency by the earl of Gloucester's seizure of London in April, Roger joined the king at Windsor before moving on towards the capital. Negotiations for a settlement, begun at the abbey of Stratford Langthorne in May, were concluded by 18 June, at which point Henry entered London unopposed. When a peace was proclaimed a few days later, it was an achievement ascribed by one chronicler to the counsels of Richard of Cornwall, Philip Basset and Roger Bigod; the same moderate

---

[259] Ibid., pp. 535, 539. The representative in question, John de Vaux of Keswick, was a late-comer to Roger's affinity – this is his first appearance. He also appears in the 1268 list, and was one of the earl's executors. *CR, 1264-68*, p. 500; E368/44, m. 4d. For evidence of further co-operation between Roger and Henry in February, see *CLR, 1260-67*, p. 200.

[260] Cf. Maddicott, *Montfort*, pp. 346-7.

[261] *CPR, 1258-66*, p. 618. Cf. *Rot. Hund.*, i, 506.

[262] *CPR, 1258-66*, p. 648.

[263] Only a few fragments of the charter roll for 50 HIII survive (*RCWL HIII*, ii, 151). For Roger's presence at Kenilworth on 29 October, see Jacob, *Studies*, pp. 199-200. For the terms of the Dictum (given on 31 October), see *DBM*, pp. 316-37.

[264] *CR, 1264-68*, p. 257.

men whose prudent advice had been rejected in the days immediately after Evesham.[265]

The summer of 1267 not only marks the end of the turbulent period which began when Roger Bigod confronted the king in April 1258; it also signals the conclusion of the earl's own political career. Thereafter he appears to have retired from Henry III's court, forgiven but perhaps never fully rehabilitated, and perhaps not too bothered on this score.[266] He had helped in the restoration of royal power, but mostly operating from a distance, concerned first to pacify the rebels in his own region, and only occasionally found at the heart of royal counsels.

By contrast, his younger brother Hugh was intimately involved in the king's affairs, during and after the battle of Evesham.[267] He also reaped more of the rewards, receiving estates confiscated from rebels in Essex, Lincolnshire, Northamptonshire, Nottinghamshire, Derbyshire and Yorkshire. Clearly, the former justiciar had fewer qualms about the legitimacy of the redistribution process than his elder brother.[268] Little time, however, was left for him to enjoy these spoils. Before 7 May 1266, Hugh was dead.[269]

The politics of the two brothers since 1263, which undoubtedly explain their different relationships with the king after his restoration, may also explain the different fates of their affinities. As far as can be judged, Roger's entourage weathered the storm of 1258-67 and remained intact. Information about the earl's household at the very end of his career is somewhat lacking, but in the few glimpses we are afforded of the earl and his men at this time, we find the same names that occurred on the eve of the revolution in 1258. Richard de Holbrook, Robert Hovel, Thomas Lenebaud, Henry de Rushall and Robert de Vaux were all still in Roger's service in 1268.[270] So too was Philip de Buckland, and quite possibly Hubert de Bavent and William Malherbe.[271] During the period of reform and rebellion, several of the more important of these men received grants at times which reflect the earl's own pattern of allegiance. In the autumn of 1263, for example, after Roger had thrown his weight behind the king,

[265] Powicke, *Thirteenth Century*, pp. 213-14; Appendix A; Gervase, ii, 246.
[266] The final reference to him comes in relation to the collection of the aid of 1268. *CR, 1264-68*, p. 559.
[267] *AM*, iv, 165; *RCWL HIII*, ii, 149-51; *CPR, 1258-66*, pp. 470, 524, 580.
[268] *CRsup*, p. 47. Hugh had likewise received lands from the king's opponents after the battle of Northampton in 1264. *CPR, 1258-66*, p. 314.
[269] *CR, 1264-68*, p. 192.
[270] Ibid., p. 500. For Lenebaud, see above, n. 65. For Hovel, see below, pp. 142-3, 145, 149, 151. Rushall and Holbrook were executors of Roger's will (E368/44, m. 4d; *Select Cases in the Exchequer of Pleas*, ed. Jenkinson, p. 89) and charged expenses to one of his manors in 1268 (SC6/997/1), as did Robert de Vaux (SC6/998/18).
[271] For Buckland, see below, pp. 121, 137, 142-3, 145-6, 149-51. For Bavent, see above, n. 69. Malherbe was still alive in 1270 (*CIPM*, i, 239).

Robert Hovel received a grant of free warren. The following year, after the earl had given his backing to the Montfortian constitution, similar grants were made to Hubert de Bavent and Henry de Rushall.[272]

By contrast, the affinity of Hugh Bigod appears to have sustained several fractures during the 1260s. We are, admittedly, very poorly informed about Hugh's entourage: only one of his charters has survived. Nevertheless, a close study of this grant (an exchange of land with church of St Mary in Malton, Yorkshire) suggests that the eight knights named in the witness list were in all probability Hugh's leading *familiares* in or shortly before the period that he was the baronial justiciar; it dates from a time, in other words, when his reformist credentials were still impeccable.[273] Ralph Bigod, the first witness, was Hugh's younger brother; Nicholas de Ewyas, who witnesses fourth, was one of his household knights.[274] Two further witnesses, William de Stonegrave and Nicholas de Hastings, belonged to families with close connections to the justiciar.[275] Later in his career, however, after Hugh had thrown his lot in with the royalists, there are signs of strain between him and his men. In November 1263, Hugh had occasion to complain to Henry III that Peter de Percy, the second witness to the above charter, was disregarding royal orders.[276] Peter de Stonegrave, younger brother of the witness William, gave his backing to Simon de Montfort in 1264; so too, moreover, did Hugh's own stepson, Baldwin Wake. The lands of both men were among those assigned to Hugh after the royalist victory at Evesham.[277]

There is even the tempting possibility that, as a result of his increasingly royalist stance, the former justiciar was deserted by his own son. Roger Bigod, eldest son of Hugh (and hereafter known as Roger IV) is found among the earl of Norfolk's men in 1268.[278] Another reference locates him at his uncle's coastal manor of Hollesley in 1267.[279] Both these references, of course, post-date Hugh Bigod's death; neither is sufficient to prove that the son had broken with his father in the years beforehand. At some point during the 1260s, perhaps even earlier, Roger III Bigod must have recognized that his namesake nephew would be his successor; welcoming the young man into the comital household would have been an obvious preparatory measure for this eventuality. In the spring of 1270, Roger IV appeared at the king's court with a letter from his uncle, seeking

---

[272] *CChR, 1257-1300*, pp. 46, 49, 50.
[273] Ibid., p. 31. The charter was confirmed by Henry III on 25 October 1260, but the first witness, Hugh's brother Ralph, died before 28 July that year. *Excerpta*, ii, 333.
[274] *CChR, 1257-1300*, p. 17; *Reg. Giffard*, p. 140.
[275] Stephen de Hastings was his seneschal of Kyme in Lincolnshire in 1259 (*Rot. Hund.*, i, 319); John de Stonegrave, younger brother to William, was one of Hugh's executors. *Reg. Giffard*, pp. 43-4; E159/49, m. 18.
[276] *CLR, 1260-67*, p. 128.
[277] *CRsup*, p. 47.
[278] *CR, 1264-68*, p. 500.
[279] Appendix B.

permission to assume the role of marshal. Henry, having taken counsel with Edward, agreed to the request. Royal assent was not, however, given as a favour to the old earl marshal, or for that matter to his new deputy. The king approved the transfer in memory of 'the good and faithful service that [Roger's] father Hugh did for the king'.[280] It may perhaps be going too far to regard this as a loaded statement; to suggest, on this basis alone, that young Roger had indeed been a part of his uncle's household during the period of reform and rebellion, and that perhaps this was a conscious political choice. In 1270, Roger IV was around twenty-four years old, and was therefore only a teenager during the time of the disturbances. Nevertheless, the implication of the king and his son seems clear: the new earl marshal, when his time came, would do well to emulate the ways of his father, rather than those of his uncle.

That time was close to hand. Roger III's decision in May 1270 to delegate his responsibilities as marshal can probably be taken as an indication that his considerable physical powers were finally starting to fade. Now in his early sixties, he had, according to one chronicler, given 'all he had' to his nephew the previous year, and thereafter lived off an annuity.[281] If this was the case, his retirement was a short one, for he did not live to see out the summer. According to the most accurate report, the earl died at Cowhaugh, near Ipswich, on 4 July 1270.[282] Another, much later source ventured a cause of death; Roger apparently met his end 'from a bruise, running at tilt'.[283] Given his reputation for skill in arms, and his fondness for hunting and tourneying, it is a picture that, if not wholly reliable, is at least entirely credible. It certainly makes for a fitting end to this earl's story.

From Cowhaugh, Roger's body was taken to Thetford. There, on 10 July, in accordance with the terms of his will, the earl was interred in St Mary's Priory.[284] Founded in 1106 by his great-great-grandfather, Thetford was the traditional resting place of the Bigod family, and successive generations had sought to provide for their immortal souls by enlarging its fortunes.[285] In Roger's own case, however, there is no evidence to indicate that he left the monks anything beyond his mortal remains.[286] Likewise, there is nothing to suggest that the earl had made any grants to the great Cistercian abbey at Tintern, the favourite house of his Marshal

---

[280] *CR, 1268-72*, p. 264.

[281] *CSM*, ii, 143-4.

[282] *Bury*, p. 47. Cf. *AM*, iv, 235 and *Flores*, iii, 23. Cowhaugh, now Broke Hall, was held from the earl by the Burnavilles and the Bucklands. *CIPM*, iv, 300.

[283] J. Weever, *Ancient Funerall Monuments* (London, 1631), p. 829. The antiquarian took his information from a matryrology in the Blackfriars, Ipswich.

[284] *Bury*, p. 47; *Flores*, iii, 23.

[285] Raby and Reynolds, *Thetford Priory*, p. 16.

[286] RBIII 14. He did, however, confirm the grants of his ancestors. RBIII 5. For comparative purposes, see M.M. Sheehan, 'A List of 13th-century English Wills', *Genealogists' Magazine*, vol. 13 (1961), pp. 259-65 and *idem, The Will in Medieval England* (Toronto, 1963).

ancestors, and the burial place of his mother and uncles. Yet it would be unreasonable to assume from this that Roger was an impious man; there are large gaps in our knowledge, not least because no cartularies covering the thirteenth century have survived from either Thetford or Tintern.[287] While the overall number of his extant charters is pitifully small, those which have come down to us are sufficient to indicate that the earl was possessed of a conventional degree of piety for a man of his time. He made gifts of land to the hospital of St Giles in Norwich, and also to the priory that his father had founded at Weybridge.[288] To the nuns of the Holy Cross in Bungay he gave a mill, and a chance reference on a close roll reveals that the earl built a chapel at Hamstead Marshall, presumably for his own use.[289]

By way of conclusion, we might also note that, having tried to have his marriage annulled in 1245, Roger accepted the Church's ruling on its legitimacy with apparent equanimity.[290] He and Isabella were still together in February 1270, and the earl can therefore have outlived his countess by only a few months at most.[291] She was not interred at Thetford, but at the Blackfriars in London.[292] Their hearts, however, were buried together, in the parish church at Framlingham.[293]

---

[287] G.R.C. Davis, *Medieval Cartularies of Great Britain* (London, 1958), pp. 110-11.

[288] RBIII 7, 8, 12 and 13.

[289] RBIII 6; *CR, 1256-59*, pp. 99-100 (cf. *CR, 1254-56*, p. 297).

[290] Above, pp. 43-4.

[291] Denholm-Young, *SAIE*, p. 165. Roger must have outlived Isabella, for there are no mentions of her after his death, or arrangements made for her dower.

[292] *Peerage*, ix, 593n, citing BL, Harley MS 544, f. 68.

[293] A couplet commemorating their heart burials is copied into the flyleaves of Arundel 30, f. 211, an early fourteenth-century volume in the College of Arms. This reference I owe to the kindness of Antonia Gransden.

CHAPTER 4

The Wider Picture: Roger IV Bigod, 1270-89

CHANGE AT THE TOP

At a very basic level, the lives of Roger III Bigod and Roger IV Bigod were similar to a remarkable degree. The old earl, invested in May 1233, enjoyed a comital career of some thirty-seven years; the new earl, who succeeded in 1270, would manage thirty-six. The uncle, if our calculations are correct, lived to be sixty-one; the nephew, with the same proviso, died at precisely the same age.[1] Once we move beyond the numbers, however, the differences quickly start to multiply – not least because Roger III's life (1209-70) coincided with that of Henry III (1206-72), whereas Roger IV (1245-1306) was a close contemporary of Edward I (1239-1307). While in general this is good news for the biographer, there is one disparity that serves only to frustrate: our image of Roger IV is far less rounded than the one we can obtain of his predecessor. The old Roger, contemporaries tell us, was a *vir praeclarus*, a *miles strenuus* and a *vir bellicosus*. When he went to war, or fought in tournaments, we are assured that his conduct was distinguished; when we catch up with him at court, his speech carries a convincingly authentic ring. By contrast, we have no such adjectives or anecdotes to characterize his nephew. Between his accession in 1270, and his second marriage in 1290 (the period covered in this chapter), Roger IV is not mentioned so much as once by any chronicler. When, later in his career, certain words are put into his mouth, they sound stagey and contrived. It has been observed that, without a Matthew Paris, Edward I proves a more elusive individual than his father.[2] For the same reason, the last Bigod earl is a more shadowy figure than his likeably robust uncle.

In one important respect, however, we are much better informed about Roger IV's career than that of his predecessor (and, for that matter, than the careers of most of his contemporaries). When the earl died in 1306, his entire estate escheated to the Crown. As a direct result, almost forty years-worth of administrative records were also seized into the king's hand. Remarkably, these records have survived, and are now kept in the class SC6 (Special Collections: Ministers' Accounts) in the National Archives. Together they form the largest non-royal, non-ecclesiastical corpus of such accounts for the thirteenth century: all told, there are some 670 rolls covering over fifty manors. As financial records, they are primarily concerned to justify expenditure and account for loss, and for this reason

---

[1] Above, p. 3; below, p. 102.
[2] Powicke, *Thirteenth Century*, p. 227. Cf. Prestwich, *Edward I*, p. 108; M.T. Clanchy, *England and Its Rulers, 1066-1272* (2nd edn, Oxford, 1998), pp. 208-12.

they have been used in the past to answer economic questions, or to explore the workings of the comital administration.[3] However, they also contain a great deal of incidental information about the earl himself, and about his friends, family and dependants. Roger IV, therefore, presents us with another, better contrast to his uncle: while he can disappear into darkness when at court, he is often brightly illuminated when attending to his own affairs. As a consequence, his story is at times closer to family history than political biography. This, however, is by no means a bad thing. It is a story rich in detail, and the role of the earl's family is one of crucial importance.

A MULTIPLE INHERITANCE

Roger was probably born in the second half of 1245.[4] He was the eldest son of Hugh III Bigod and Joanna de Stuteville – the first blossom on what proved to be a very fruitful branch of the Bigod family tree. Over the next few years, Roger was soon joined by three younger brothers (John, Ralph and Richard) and four little sisters (Roesia, Elizabeth, Joan and Maud).[5] Theirs was a large family, and also a wealthy one. Hugh worked hard in royal service to establish himself as a major baron, and Joanna was a rich heiress in her own right.

As far as the Bigod children were concerned, however, their mother's fortune was an impermanent one. Joanna had been married once before, to the Lincolnshire baron Hugh Wake, and this earlier match had produced an heir. Roger and his siblings had an older stepbrother in the shape of Baldwin Wake, who had been committed to Joanna's custody after his father's death in 1241.[6] When Baldwin turned twenty-one in 1258, he naturally acquired two-thirds of his father's fortune. But he could look forward to a bigger prize when his mother died; in addition to the remainder of his paternal estate, Baldwin would also receive the entirety of the de Stuteville inheritance.

Mindful of the temporary nature of his wife's fortune, Hugh Bigod built up a sizeable estate of his own. In 1259 he obtained some riverside

---

[3] e.g. J.E.T. Rogers, *History of Agriculture and Prices in England from 1259 to 1793* (7 vols., London, 1866-90), ii, *passim*; E.A. Kosminsky, *Studies in the Agrarian History of England in the Thirteenth Century* (Oxford, 1956), pp. 58-67, 164-7; B.M.S. Campbell, *English Seigniorial Agriculture, 1250-1450* (Cambridge, 2000), pp. 172, 232-3; Denholm-Young, *SAIE, passim*.

[4] His parents had married between May 1243 and February 1244 (above, p. 54), and in 1270 he was said to be 24, 25, 26 or more (*CIPM*, i, 239). However, he cannot have been born before May 1245, since he was seemingly under age at the time of his father's death in May 1266 (*CR, 1264-68*, pp. 200, 209). He was probably of age before 7 November that year, when he received seisin of Hugh's estates (*Excerpta*, ii, 448-9).

[5] For Richard, John and Ralph, see *The Register of John Pecham, Archbishop of Canterbury, 1279-1292*, ed. F.N. Davis et al. (2 vols., Canterbury and York Soc., lxiv, lxv, 1968-69), ii, 179. For Elizabeth and Roesia, see *Calendar of Ormond Deeds, 1172-1350*, pp. 71-2. For Joan, see Sanders, *English Baronies*, p. 80. For Maud, see SC6/995/4.

[6] Above, p. 54n.

property at Brokenwharf in London.[7] In Sussex, he received the very valuable Marshal manor of Bosham, probably as a gift from his mother in the period 1246 x 1248.[8] In the same area of Sussex, the former justiciar acquired other properties: Thorney and Stoke were held from the bishop of Exeter, and Stoughton was held from the earls of Arundel.[9] In Norfolk, he acquired Caistor St Edmund and Markshall,[10] and in Cambridgeshire he purchased the manor of Kennett.[11] In Yorkshire, Hugh held the manor of Settrington (in its entirety after the death of his younger brother Ralph around 1260), the dependent manor of Wilton, and also the manor of Levisham, acquired from Henry III.[12]

These lands formed the patrimony of Roger IV Bigod when his father died, probably not long after Easter 1266.[13] Only two-thirds of them would have passed to him at this point, for his mother was still living, and would survive for another decade.[14] There is no contemporary statement to indicate which manors Joanna retained as her widow's third; all we know for certain is that her dower included some tiny scraps of land which Hugh had acquired in Ireland.[15] However, surviving manorial accounts show that Roger IV had custody of his father's properties in southern and eastern England before his mother's death in 1276.[16] It seems likely that, since her ancestral lands lay in Yorkshire and Cumbria, Joanna's dower may have consisted of the northern parts of Hugh's estate.

Roger also inherited some of his father's less permanent acquisitions. Shortly after losing his major stake in the lands of Baldwin Wake, Hugh had been compensated with the grant of the wardship of Philip de Kyme.[17] This was a fairly valuable gift; the Kyme family were substantial

---

[7] Above, p. 79.

[8] Above, p. 38.

[9] *VCH Sussex*, iv, 193, 195-6; *CRR*, xviii, 1243-45, p. 247; cf. *CIPM*, iv, 292.

[10] It is not known when Hugh acquired these from the previous owner, Aline la Marshal. Roger IV took custody in 1266, and was sued for non-payment of a £5 rent in 1268 (*CR, 1264-68*, p. 200; CP25/1/158/93, no. 1500). Accounts from Caistor survive from 1270 (SC6/932/11-26). Roger IV bought more property there in 1286 and alienated the manor in 1303 (CP25/1/160/114, no. 419; CP25/1/161/119, no. 948).

[11] *PQW*, p. 102; CP25/1/26/52, no. 13.

[12] For Settrington and Wilton, see Appendix C. For Levisham, see above, p. 54.

[13] Hugh's last certain appearance is 6 December 1265, but he probably died shortly before 7 May 1266. *RCWL HIII*, ii, 151; *CR, 1264-68*, p. 192.

[14] For the equestrian seal she used during her widowhood, see P. Coss, *The Lady in Medieval England, 1000-1500* (Stroud, 1998), p. 46; *EYC*, ix, frontispiece.

[15] It is not known how or when Hugh acquired this Irish property, which he held of Theobald Butler. Nor is it clear why Joanna was permitted to transfer it to her daughters, who subsequently alienated it by selling it back to Butler. The purchase price for Elizabeth's share – 20m – suggests it was an insubstantial holding. *Calendar of Ormond Deeds, 1172-1350*, pp. 71-2.

[16] E.g. SC6/932/11 (Caistor, 1270); SC6/1020/11 (Bosham, 1274); SC6/1029/20 (Stoke, 1273); SC6/1030/23 (Thorney, 1274); SC6/768/5 (Kennett, 1271). Roger had seisin of Caistor, Markshall and Bosham in 1266 (*CR, 1264-68*, p. 200), and Kennett was seized from him by Edward I in 1275 (below, p. 115).

[17] Above, p. 79.

Lincolnshire landowners.[18] It is not known, however, how old Philip was, or precisely which of his lands Hugh ended up holding. Both the heir and his estate would have passed to Roger in 1266, but neither can have remained in his custody beyond the early 1270s.[19] Roger also acquired those properties which had been assigned to his father from the lands of the Disinherited. From his Montfortian stepson, Baldwin Wake, Hugh had received the manors of Bourne, Skeldingthorpe, Deeping St James and Kelleby (all Lincolnshire), as well as the manor of Blisworth and £6 of rent in Thrapston (both Northamptonshire). Elsewhere in Lincolnshire he had been granted the lands of Geoffrey de la Mare at Maxey, Thurlby and Northborough. In Essex, Hugh was given Easthorp, Birch, Garnons (in Wormingford) and Theydon Garnon, formerly the property of Ralph Gernun, while in Yorkshire he received Adam de Everingham's manor of Sherburn, Gerard de Furnival's manor of Swanland and Peter de Stonegrave's manors at Stonegrave, Nunnington and West Nesse.[20] In most cases, Roger Bigod returned these manors to their original owners within a couple of years, honouring the terms of the Dictum of Kenilworth. Ralph Gernun, for example, paid £250 to Roger at the start of 1268 for the return of his property in Essex,[21] and later in the year Gerard de la Mare was reseized of his Lincolnshire manors.[22] Around the same time, Adam de Everingham was complaining that, in spite of his willingness to pay the ransom on his lands, Roger was refusing to return them; there is nothing, however, to indicate that this argument persisted.[23]

To this paternal legacy, both permanent and impermanent, Roger, made a very substantial addition of his own by virtue of his marriage. At

[18] Hugh married Philip to his daughter, Joan. Sanders, *English Baronies*, p. 80.

[19] Philip's age is not stated in his father's inquisition post mortem (*CIPM*, i, 131; *Yorks. Inq.*, i, 85-7), but he was in possession of his lands by 1275 (*Rot. Hund.*, i, 242-5). From his own inquisition post mortem of 1323, the Kyme estate included property in Sotby, Coningsby, Thorganby and South Kyme (all Lincolnshire), as well as in Lincoln itself (*CIPM*, vi, 250). The family also had manors in Yorkshire, but in 1258 these formed the dower of Philip's mother (*CR, 1256-59*, pp. 454-5; *PQW*, p. 189). Hugh III Bigod demised Sotby to his half-brother and executor John de Warenne, and may have done the same with other parts of the Kyme estate. If so, this might explain why Roger IV contested payment of the fine for the wardship with his father's executors (*Rot. Hund.*, i, 364, and below, p. 115-16).

[20] *CRsup*, p. 47; *CPR, 1266-72*, p. 263.

[21] *CR, 1264-68*, pp. 518-19; *Rotuli Selecti*, ed. Hunter, pp. 130, 141. See *CR, 1264-68*, p. 532 for a possible connection.

[22] *CPR, 1266-72*, p. 263. For evidence of Roger's brief tenure of Stonegrave, see *Reg. Giffard*, pp. 43-4.

[23] *CPR, 1266-72*, pp. 286-7. Only in one instance did controversy over a Disinherited manor continue until later in Roger's career. In 1268, Walter de Grey protested that Roger had deforced him of four manors in Lincolnshire, at Somerton, Navenby, Coleby and Timberland (*PA*, p. 169). At some later date, Walter's successor, Robert de Grey, granted Somerton to Anthony Bek (*CPR, 1272-81*, p. 339). In 1281, Roger acknowledged he owed Robert 220m, presumably for the unjust detention of Somerton (*CCR, 1279-88*, p. 139). Four years later, the king's bailiff was distraining the earl at his manor of Hamstead Marshall for this money (*SC6/748/19*).

some point in the period 1265-71, he was wedded to Lady Aline la Despenser. Aline was the widow of Hugh Despenser, the loyal henchman of Simon de Montfort who had fought and fallen alongside his leader at Evesham. This might have affected her fortunes more adversely, had she not also been the daughter of the royalist Philip Basset; as it was, the two connections effectively cancelled each other out.[24] The relationship between the Basset and the Bigod families, although it varied between individuals, had on the whole been strong for several decades, and it may be that the marriage of Roger and Aline was brokered by their fathers, both staunch royalists, in the months after Evesham.[25] Whatever political or personal attractions recommended the match, it undoubtedly improved the fortunes of both parties. Aline gained a new husband and protector, set to become far wealthier than her previous partner. Roger, meanwhile, had instantly acquired four new Midland manors (Loughborough, Freeby and Hugglescote in Leicestershire, and Barnwell in Northamptonshire), and was also anticipating a far greater dividend, because his new wife was the sole heiress to the Basset fortune.[26] When her father died in 1271, Aline inherited the manors of Lamarsh, Tolleshunt Knights, Tolleshunt Guisnes, Wix, South Weald and Layer de la Haye (Essex), Berwick Bassett, Wootton Bassett and Vastern (Wiltshire), Woking and Sutton Green (Surrey), Elsfield and Cassington (Oxfordshire), Aston Clinton and High Wycombe (Buckinghamshire), Soham (Cambridgeshire) and Speen (Berkshire).[27] This extensive list, however, came with a crucial caveat. Aline had a son from her earlier marriage who stood to inherit everything in the event of her death. Of course, in an age of high infant mortality, it was quite possible that this boy (also called Hugh Despenser) might predecease his mother, thereby clearing the way clear for any future Bigods. As it was, Roger had to regard his wife's estate as yet another temporary possession, with his custody entirely contingent upon her good health.[28]

Fortunately, he was one of the few men in England who could have contemplated the possible loss of such a large amount of land with something approaching equanimity. Impressive as were his tenurial gains

---

[24] *Peerage*, iv, 261-2nn.

[25] Above, pp. 9-10, 13-14, 18-20, 25, 82, 89, 95-6. In this particular instance, cf. *CPR, 1266-72*, p. 265.

[26] The Leicestershire manors, the property of Hugh Despenser, were granted to Aline to hold for life in November 1265 (*CPR, 1258-66*, pp. 459-60). Barnwell was Aline's *maritagium*. *CIPM*, ii, 228.

[27] Philip Basset also held Compton Bassett, Broad Town, Upavon, 'Meredene', and a carucate of land in 'Burebache' (Wiltshire), Euston and Kersey (Suffolk), Kirtlington (Oxfordshire), Mapledurwell (Hampshire) and Oxcroft (Cambridgeshire), all of which formed the widow's third for his second wife, Ela (*CIPM*, i, 272-3; *A Calendar of the Feet of Fines relating to the County of Wiltshire*, ed. E.A. Fry (Devizes 1930), pp. 73-74). Ela lived until 1297 (*VCH Hampshire*, iv, 150), so her dower manors never reverted to Roger and Aline. Below, pp. 124-5.

[28] Note that Roger therefore faced exactly the same predicament as his father. Above, p. 54, 102-3; below, pp. 124-5.

down to 1271, they all paled in comparison with the prize Roger obtained the previous year, when he succeeded his uncle as earl of Norfolk and marshal of England. The entirety of the estate described in Chapter Two, including as it did a county in Ireland, a marcher lordship in Wales and the many rich manors in East Anglia, passed unbroken from Roger III to Roger IV. With the addition of the estates outlined above, it made the new earl of Norfolk by far the wealthiest of his line to date. After the death of his father-in-law in 1271, and to a lesser extent the passing of his mother in 1276, Roger IV's income was raised to the same level as that of the very greatest of English earls.

It is necessary at this point to make some brief, general observations about the way in which these lands were managed (individual sections of the estate are dealt with later in this chapter, and the earl's household is discussed in Chapter Five). Thanks to the survival of the Bigod ministers' accounts, we can apprehend the elaborate machinery that the family had developed to govern their estates and keep check on their servants.[29] From 1270, there were four separate regional centres, preserved from the constituent parts of Roger's inheritance. By far the most important was Framlingham, the *caput* of the earl's lands in eastern England (including the outlying manors of Chesterford and Weston). Bosham, a very large and rich manor in its own right, was the centre of a much smaller estate in Sussex (Hamstead Marshall in Berkshire also answered to it).[30] In Wales and Ireland the Bigod lordships were respectively focused on administrations in Chepstow and Carlow. Each of these regional centres was headed by two important officials. The receiver was the chief financial officer for his region, responsible for collecting money that came in from the surrounding manors. The seneschal or steward oversaw the estate's overall administration, regularly visiting each property in turn, collecting dues and holding courts.

Although these separate administrations operated with considerable independence, they all answered to the same higher authorities. The working of the entire Bigod estate was subjected to regular inspection by the earl's auditors. These men were seemingly quite independent of the regular administration, and drawn from a variety of different backgrounds – relatives, household members, friends and neighbours (the abbot of Tintern, for example, is frequently found acting as an auditor).[31] But the highest authority, of course, was the earl himself (indeed, occasionally a provost or reeve would appeal to him directly over the

---

[29] This system is described in Denholm-Young, *SAIE, passim.*
[30] In 1282-83, 1,004 acres were sown at Bosham, the largest sown area in any surviving thirteenth-century account (Campbell, *English Seigniorial Administration*, p. 67). For payments made to Bosham from Hamstead Marshall, see SC6/748/23, SC6/748/25, SC6/748/28. It is not known where Hamstead Marshall accounted before 1270.
[31] Denholm-Young, *SAIE*, pp. 131-51.

heads of the auditors).[32] The diverse parts of the estate all worked to the same end of supplying Roger and his entourage with cash. The workings and personnel of the comital household are examined in the next chapter; for now it will suffice to note that this body had its own financial office: a floating receipt which siphoned money from its regional counterparts. The accounts sometimes refer to this office as the earl's 'chamber', at other times 'the wardrobe'; in all probability the same institution is being described.[33] It was headed by a chief official (the 'wardrober' or 'receiver') who was assisted by several deputies. To do their job effectively, these men must have accompanied the earl wherever he travelled. It is not impossible, however, that there was some kind of fixed financial office at Roger's London townhouse.[34] In addition, individual wardrobers would depart on specific fund-raising missions (to Ireland, for example) when occasion demanded.[35]

RELATIONS WITH THE CROWN, 1270-77

At the time of Roger's accession in 1270, England had been nominally at peace for almost four years. But the reality was a deeply troubled kingdom, where the machinery of state had been left impotent by the recent disturbances. The judicial system had all but collapsed; royal finance was hand to mouth, and even then the body politic frequently went hungry. Henry III himself, never a strong king, was finishing his reign as he had started it: physically feeble, and reduced to little more than a cipher for his council. Hope that matters might improve after the old king's death had been checked by despair when his eldest son departed on crusade. Thus, when Henry died in November 1272, his authority devolved to a regency government which, despite the talents and energy of its members, struggled to maintain even the perilous status quo which had existed on the eve of Edward's departure. The regents faced escalating tension in the Welsh marches, a damaging trade dispute with Flanders and widespread disorder in the counties.[36]

---

[32] Denholm-Young, *SAIE*, pp. 165-6.
[33] Ibid., pp. 19-20, imagined a number of competing wardrobers and receivers on the basis of appellations given in the accounts. He missed the fact that manorial reeves working as far apart (in some cases) as East Anglia and Ireland would use different terms to describe the same official. A simpler, more credible picture can be obtained by looking at the names of the individuals who received payments *ad expensas comitis*. For a good description of a similar system, see Altschul, *Baronial Family*, pp. 222-32.
[34] Denholm-Young, *SAIE*, p. 20. This rests, however, on a single ambiguous entry, which records a clerk sent to London 'to look at the account rolls from northern parts' (i.e. the Yorkshire estates). For Roger's townhouse at Denburgh Lane in London, and especially the trouble with the toilets there, see *Rot. Hund.*, i, 428, 433; *The London Eyre of 1276*, ed. M. Weinbaum (London Record Soc., xii, 1976), 97.
[35] Below, p. 155.
[36] R. Huscroft, 'Robert Burnell and the Government of England, 1270-1274', *TCE*, viii (2001), 60-61; Maddicott, 'Lessons of Baronial Reform', pp. 1-9.

At first glance, the earl of Norfolk's activities during these years make him appear a substantial thorn in the government's side. His itinerary rarely locates him at court, even on important occasions (such as Henry III's funeral) when other earls were certainly present.[37] He was quite happy, it has been suggested, to ignore the embargo on the export of wool, the violation of which was a cause of much embarrassment to the government.[38] Above all, he appears to have contributed to the rising tide of lawlessness. Soon after his succession (probably, in fact, to mark the occasion), Roger organized an unlicensed tournament at Chepstow, which the king was forced to prohibit.[39] During the regency period, complaints reached the council from the men of Bristol. They had detained the earl's poultryman for disturbing the peace in their town; Roger, in response, had not only refused to do justice in the matter, but had retaliated by distraining the goods of Bristol merchants at his Irish port of New Ross.[40] Lastly, around the same time, the earl attacked the royal port of Dunwich. His assault amounted to a full-scale siege, with a combined land–sea offensive that lasted six days. Certain burgesses were arrested and carried off to the Bigod manor of Kelsale, while jewels and other chattels to the value of 200 marks were also seized. Most damning of all, when the king instructed him to make amends and restore the seized items, Roger contemptuously ignored the royal order.[41]

This may, however, be an unfair assessment. Above anything else, Edward's absence meant that no royal charters were issued between November 1272 to September 1274, so we have little information to indicate the involvement of great men in government during this period. The fact that Roger is not recorded as having been present at certain important junctures does not therefore mean he was absent. Quite by chance, a later *inspeximus* of a private charter reveals that the earl was at court in the spring of 1273.[42] During the last years of Henry III's reign, Roger's witnessing of royal charters was, admittedly, infrequent. However, royal gifts of deer in June 1270 and June 1271, and also the pardon of a homicide at the earl's instance on Christmas Day 1270, suggest that cordial relations were maintained throughout this period.[43]

As to Roger's apparent contribution to disorder, this seems to be a false impression, or, at the very least, only one side of the story. The earl's attack on Dunwich, for instance, was probably carried out at the request of

[37] Appendix B; Huscroft, 'Robert Burnell', p. 63.

[38] R.H. Bowers, 'English Merchants and the Anglo-Flemish Economic War of 1270-1274', *Seven Studies in Medieval History and other Historical Essays presented to Harold S. Snellgrove* (Jackson, Mississippi, 1983), pp. 42, 49-50; Huscroft, 'Robert Burnell', p. 68.

[39] *CPR, 1266-72*, p. 460. The earl's involvement is taken as read.

[40] SC1/8/35.

[41] *Rot. Hund.*, ii, 200.

[42] *CPR, 1313-17*, p. 125.

[43] The earl was also at court on 6 January 1271. Appendix B.

the regency government. At the start of 1273, Robert Burnell – fast emerging as the prime mover of the kingdom's affairs – wrote to the chancellor, Walter de Merton, explaining the need to deal firmly with 'the armed outlaws and enemies of the king' who were 'continually attacking and wishing to confound the king's bailiffs and well-wishers' in the town. The solution, said Burnell, was to get the sheriff of Norfolk to raise a *posse comitatus*; also, Merton should write to the steward and bailiffs of the earl marshal, urging them to assist in the attack.[44] There was little love lost between Bigod's men and the citizens of Dunwich,[45] and it sounds from the later complaints as if the earl's private army exceeded their peace-keeping mandate. However, the conclusion from Burnell's letter is inescapable: far from creating difficulties for the government, Roger and his servants were arrayed on the side of law and order.

This was also true with regard to the embargo on the export of wool. Later in 1273, the earl again appeared in the guise of a law-enforcer, when certain men from the Cinque Ports arrived in his own harbour at Harwich. They had come to claim a ship which they suspected was being used to ferry wool to Flanders. Roger, however, intervened on behalf of the Crown. 'It seemed to us', he wrote to Walter de Merton, 'that, if it was forfeit, it should be yielded to the king.' The earl therefore promised to keep the vessel in safe custody until he received further orders. In response, the council advised him to release the ship and its cargo to the original owners.[46] Again, Roger appears to have profited as a result of this intervention: a garbled entry on the hundred rolls suggests that he may well have kept the impounded ship for himself, much like the jewels he was alleged to have taken during the raid on Dunwich.[47] In both these cases, however, he had acted to uphold the government's authority rather than undermine it. With this in mind, it seems unlikely that the earl had wilfully breached the embargo on trade with Flanders. More noteworthy than the inconclusive evidence in the hundred rolls is a letter written by Roger's countess to Walter de Merton, seeking a royal licence to export thirty sacks of wool.[48] An application for the chancellor's permission hardly suggests contempt for the government's authority. In this case, moreover, there were extenuating circumstances for wishing to break the embargo. Aline needed to raise cash, she explained, to finance her husband's 'passage to meet the king'. Having returned from his crusade, the uncrowned Edward had made his way to France, and was busy

---

[44] SC1/7/61.

[45] Cf. *CIM*, i, 406.

[46] SC1/7/38; *CCR, 1272-79*, p. 33.

[47] The jurors also complained of unjust extortions in Ipswich and Orwell, and accused the earl of compelling their ships to land at Harwich. *Rot. Hund.*, ii, 200.

[48] SC1/7/84, transcribed in *Recueil de Lettres Anglo-Francaises (1265-1399)*, ed. F.J. Tanquerey (Paris, 1916), pp. 10-11, transl. in *Letters of Medieval Women*, ed. Crawford, pp. 191-2.

attending to the affairs of Gascony. Roger, it seems, was loyal and astute enough to join the numerous others who crossed the Channel from England in 1273 and 1274 to pledge their allegiance.[49] The two men may have discussed the impending festivities in London; when the king eventually returned to England in August 1274, Roger officiated as earl marshal at the coronation.[50]

Roger's behaviour between 1270 and 1274 reveals that he was more than willing to assist the government in achieving its broader objectives. Nevertheless, the impotence of the administration meant that he was able to act largely as he saw fit, with little fear of the consequences. This attitude is also apparent in the way the earl conducted his own affairs, and especially in the stance he adopted on the issue of his Crown debts.

Roger's debts to the Crown are an important, integral but exceedingly complex part of his life story. By far the greatest problem they present is their uncertain scale. It is almost impossible for the modern historian to say exactly how great the earl's liability was at any given point, largely because the exchequer at the time was unable to provide a satisfactory answer to the same question. Orders to back-search the rolls frequently produced new debts from past decades, as well as long-forgotten allowances.[51] As a result, what Roger said he owed, what the exchequer claimed he owed, and what was owed in actual fact were rarely if ever the same. The only occasion on which there was consensus was in October 1304, when a 'final account' was drawn up in the exchequer in the presence of two of the earl's attorneys.[52] Long, detailed and seemingly comprehensive, it is a mine of useful information. But it also contains several major fictions and fudges; for reasons explored in the next chapter, not everything it says can be taken as true.[53] There are also a host of other problems which complicate the discussion. For example, in addition to the sums he owed in England, Roger had a separate set of debts (some his own, some inherited) at the king's exchequer in Ireland. These debts, never before discussed, are examined later in this chapter.[54]

After his accession in 1270, Roger was held responsible for the money owed to the Crown by his uncle. As we have seen (in Chapter Two), the old earl had run up two large debts. The first, a sum of £576, had arisen over a longstanding dispute about his scutage assessments; the second, which amounted to 1,600 marks, had accumulated because he had failed to pay the annual eighty-mark contribution that was required of him, as a

[49] Powicke, *Henry III*, pp. 615-16.
[50] *Peerage*, ix, 593.
[51] Below, pp. 114-15, 132-3, 157-9, 180-81.
[52] E372/149, m. 2d.
[53] Below, pp. 180-81.
[54] Below, p. 132-3.

Marshal heir, for the dower of Eleanor de Montfort.[55] The earl's share in the Marshal inheritance also made him and his heirs responsible for a share of the Marshal debts, but this had long been overlooked by the exchequer, and was not mentioned in 1270.[56] At this stage, the clerks took into account only the two sums above, and a host of smaller debts for fines. Added together, these came to £1,686.[57]

This sizeable sum paled in comparison with that owed by Roger's father. As a result of purchasing the wardship of Philip de Kyme in 1259, Hugh Bigod had incurred a massive debt of £3,000. This was supposed to have been paid off in annual instalments, but the exchequer had never received so much as a penny.[58] Luckily for Hugh's heirs and executors, the fine had been considerably reduced in recognition of his loyal support for Henry III during the later stages of the Barons' War. The king had struck off £800, and credited Hugh's expenses from his time as keeper of Dover, Sandwich and the Cinque Ports. When all these factors were taken into account, the Kyme debt fell from £3,000 to £925.[59] There were, however, other sums to take into account, mostly unpaid arrears of royal farms. From 1255, Hugh had held the castle, manor and wapentake of Pickering at £140 a year and, when he died in 1266, the arrears amounted to £449. His arrears for Bosham, held at £42 a year, were probably around £200, and for the bailiwick of Hay and the forest of Scalby (charged together at 4m 10s a year), Hugh owed £22. Two further debts of £38 (for 'certain escheats in Lincolnshire'), and one gold mark ('for the abbot of Beverley') brought his total liability to around £1,641.[60]

---

[55] Above, p. 50.

[56] The earl's share of the Marshal debts, a sum of £219 7s, is first mentioned in 1282. E372/127, m. 18.

[57] The exact figures were 1,600m (£1066 13s 4d) and £575 11s 8d. £22 10s was owed for scutage arrears in Essex (for the 6⅛ fees that had once belonged to Richard de Reimes). Roger III had also owed 15m (£10) for a forest offence, 100s (£5) 'for the escape of Geoffrey le Rede', and 100s (£5) for an unspecified default. E372/114, mm. 14, 14d; E372/113, m. 6d.

[58] See Carpenter, 'King, Magnates and Society', p. 92n for Hugh's successful liquidation of some of his earlier debts.

[59] CR, 1264-68, pp. 198, 408; E368/42, m. 4. There is no direct evidence to indicate how the reduction was calculated. The fee for keeping Dover, Sandwich and the Cinque Ports was 1,000m a year, and Hugh held them from 9 September 1259 until 2 May 1261 – a period of 20 months, which would make for an allowance of around 1,667m (£1,111). This, with the pardon of £800, would have reduced the Kyme debt to £1,089 rather than £925. It is tempting to assume that further allowance was made for the farms of Scalby and Pickering, which had been occupied by the Montfortians in 1264, as Henry recognized in his writ. However, the exchequer continued to charge Hugh's executors for the arrears of these farms. Below, n. 60.

[60] E372/111, mm. 14, 15, 15d. The figures given on the roll are: £140 + £70 + £239 = £449 (Pickering); £22 3s 4d (Hay and Scalby); £36 18s 6d + 12s (escheats). One gold mark = £6 13s 4d (E372/112, m. 25d). The arrears for Bosham are first recorded in 1271, when Roger IV owed £403. Assuming the earl had not paid the £42 per annum since 1266 (which seems likely: he certainly paid nothing in 1271), his father must have died owing around £200. E372/115, m. 13d.

Between them, therefore, Roger's father and uncle had left him a legacy of debt somewhere in the region of £3,300.[61] The question was one of liability: like his predecessors, the earl would argue that a large proportion of the above debts were not 'clear' (that is, they were not his responsibility). This dispute, at times very bitter, would dog him for the rest of his days. In 1270, however, the debate began in friendly fashion. From the Crown's point of view, Roger's accession as earl of Norfolk was the perfect opportunity to set the record straight on the matter of his uncle's debts. Early in July, soon after the old earl's death, the entire Bigod estate was taken into the king's hand (normal procedure when a tenant-in-chief died). Within a matter or weeks, Roger was at Westminster, doing homage to Henry III; in return, he was granted custody of his uncle's lands, and also a gift of deer.[62] The new earl was not, however, able to lay his hands on the goods that the Crown had confiscated. These, for the meantime, were set to remain in the care of the king's escheator. Their restoration was linked to a satisfactory answer to the question of debt.[63]

This was an issue which concerned not only Roger, but also several leading members of his uncle's household. John de Vaux, Richard de Holbrook, Henry de Rushall and Thomas Lenebaud were all executors of their late master's will. So too was the prior of Thetford; and Roger himself, as well as being the beneficiary, was also an executor.[64] In mid-August, some or all of these men came before the king at Clarendon with a view to obtaining free administration of the impounded property. There they 'proposed certain things' – presumably some kind of repayment plan. Henry III temporized; he needed time, he said, to take 'more mature counsel'. A royal clerk was dispatched to collect, view and value the goods in company with the executors, and a decision was promised in October.[65] October came and went, however, and nothing was done. It seems likely (in view of their subsequent behaviour) that none of the executors turned up on the given day. On 8 November, Roger appeared at court, trying in person to obtain seisin. In the absence of the other parties, however, negotiations once again stalled. More discussion and further evaluation followed, and another meeting with the king was scheduled for January. Henry's resolve, however, had begun to weaken. The clerk who had custody of the confiscated chattels was instructed to retain them until both Roger and the executors had given security that they would repay the debts.[66] The requisite promises must subsequently have been made

---

[61] i.e. £1,685 + £1,641. Cf. below, p. 115n.

[62] *Excerpta*, ii, 519; *CR, 1268-72*, p. 212.

[63] *CPR, 1266-72*, p. 455.

[64] E368/44, m 4d; *Select Cases in the Exchequer of Pleas*, p. 89; *CPR, 1266-72*, p. 491.

[65] *CPR, 1266-72*, p. 455. The king was in undistinguished company at Clarendon. *RCWL HIII*, ii, 184.

[66] Appendix B; *CPR, 1266-72*, p. 491.

because, by the time the earl appeared at the exchequer on 26 January, he had obtained seisin of his uncle's goods.[67]

Having gained control of all his inheritance, both lands and chattels, Roger discovered that he was much less interested in the accompanying debts. His co-executors were likewise seized with indifference; only two of them (Richard de Holbrook and the prior of Thetford) presented themselves in January. Together with the earl they said the debts were 'not clear' (i.e. they refused to recognize certain sums), and explained they could not proceed without the absentees. An increasingly frustrated exchequer instructed all parties to return in a month's time, 'without further delay'. In the intervening period, Roger accepted liability for the back-payments for the Marshal dower, a sum of 1,600 marks.[68] However, on the day appointed for the next meeting, neither the earl nor any of the other executors appeared. Only the solitary figure of Thomas Weyland, seventy-two hours late and in no mood to apologize, presented himself before the barons. A leading Bigod retainer and soon-to-be royal justice, Weyland had come on his patron's behalf but, in view of the others' absence, was unable to declare on the debts. He soon withdrew without licence, freely offering the opinion that no-one else was going to show up.[69]

The barons' patience was exhausted. A writ was sent to the sheriff of Norfolk, ordering him to compel the appearance of Richard de Holbrook and the prior of Thetford on the morrow of Easter by distraining their goods. Both men were notified that they had been gravely amerced, and warned that subsequent penalties would be graver still.[70] To the earl himself, the barons sent a stiff letter, requiring him to attend on the same date.[71] But these distraints and threats – assuming they were ever imposed or delivered – had no discernible effect. There is nothing to indicate that any further meetings took place. Eventually, therefore, on 7 November 1271, the sheriff of Norfolk was issued with new orders. He was to visit every Bigod manor in East Anglia, accompanied by a gang of six men, and seize goods to the value of 1,600 marks – this much, after all, the earl had acknowledged. The writ was quite uncompromising: anyone who offered resistance was to be arrested and brought before the exchequer; the money was expected in a month.[72] It was also entirely unsuccessful: not a penny was collected or delivered. The king's money-men could talk as tough as they liked, but the uncomfortable reality was that royal authority was in steep decline at the end of Henry III's reign. Great men like Roger Bigod,

[67] E368/44, m. 4d.
[68] Ibid., m. 4d.
[69] Ibid., m. 6d. For more on Weyland, see below, pp. 139-41, 144.
[70] E368/44, m. 6
[71] Ibid., m. 6d.
[72] E368/45, m. 2.

while they could support the government when it suited them, were also able to defy it (or at least to prevaricate) with impunity.

This situation changed when Edward returned. The king started his reign determined to recover his rights and improve his financial affairs.[73] The seriousness of the situation, however, was not immediately apparent to Roger Bigod. In the autumn of 1274, the sheriff of Norfolk was again instructed to distrain the earl for the Marshal money, again to no effect.[74] Around the same time, the issue of the arrears for Bosham (£425) was raised, only to be respited until Hilary on the orders of the king and council.[75] In the new year, however, nothing was paid: at the close of Hilary term 1275, the earl's indifference was underlined by the non-appearance of his deputy marshal at the exchequer.[76] To Roger, it must have seemed business as usual: distraints might be ordered but were easily ignored; demand would be followed by endless respite.

Edward, however, was simply (and characteristically) taking time to prepare for his assault. In Hilary, while ordering a further respite, the king also told the exchequer clerks to search their rolls diligently for the Bigod debts.[77] At Easter, when Roger once again defaulted, the king still restrained his hand. A few weeks later, the earl attended a parliament, where he sanctioned the new customs duties on wool exports, unaware that the drive to restore the Crown's finances was about to hit him hard.[78] On 11 June, the order went out to seize his goods. Writs were sent to six different sheriffs, spreading the king's attack across the entire Bigod estate in England.[79] In East Anglia, at least, the order found its mark: the bailiff of Forncett sent letters to his master in London, 'announcing to the earl the great distraint by the king of his manors in Norfolk and Suffolk'.[80]

Dialogue resumed immediately. As far as we can judge, Roger may have attempted to justify his non-payment by reviving the old arguments about his uncle's scutage liability: on 20 June, Edward sent an extraordinary letter to the exchequer, ordering the clerks to acquit the earl of a non-existent debt from the Gascon campaign of 1242.[81] But if the king

---

[73] Prestwich, *Edward I*, pp. 99-103.
[74] E159/49, m. 16. The 1,600m has mysteriously shrunk to 1,560m here. Elsewhere on the roll (m. 30) it is still given as 1,600m, and this remained the accepted figure, e.g. E372/120, m. 9d (1276); E372/124, m. 16 (1280).
[75] E159/49, m. 2.
[76] Ibid., m. 9d.
[77] Ibid., mm. 5, 7d.
[78] *Parl. Writs*, i, 2; CFR, 1272-1307, p. 60.
[79] E159/49, m. 19.
[80] SC6/935/4.
[81] CCR, 1272-79, p. 197. Edward told the exchequer to pardon Roger IV a sum of £311 10s, allegedly charged to Roger III for the 'aid' of 1242. The old Roger served in this expedition and was not charged scutage (above, p. 21). I have not seen this sum charged to either earl in any of the exchequer rolls. The barons too must have discovered it was a fiction; the pardon was never allowed to Roger IV.

was prepared to make concessions, he was also ready to make demands. The barons of the exchequer, having completed their diligent researches, were able to inform Edward that Roger owed a grand total of £3,577. The earl himself, they noted, had declared for £2,637.[82] Armed with this information, the king was able to take the draconian step of forcing Roger to surrender four manors (Hanworth and Suffield in Norfolk, Kennett and Soham in Cambridgeshire), to be kept until they had raised a sum of £943 for the Crown.[83]

We might conclude that Roger had got his just comeuppance; there is certainly a lot in his behaviour which is difficult to excuse. Two important points, however, need to be noted. Firstly, the earl's attitude may have been shaped by the apparent incompetence of the exchequer in recent years, which failed to keep a proper account of his contributions, and overlooked several of his legitimate allowances. For example, as early as 1272, Roger had (as instructed) paid his £120 relief to Poncius de Mora, yet this was not credited to him until 1283.[84] Similarly, there is no sign whatsoever that a sum of 350 marks paid by his uncle was ever deducted from his account, nor that the pardon of 500 marks granted in 1265 was ever enrolled.[85] Secondly, and perhaps more importantly, the earl appears to have fallen out with both his uncle's and his father's executors.[86] In 1277 he was suing the former group for withholding goods and chattels from the old earl's estate and, six years later, when one of their number died, Roger intervened to have his goods seized.[87] Meanwhile, in 1282, Hugh Bigod's three younger sons petitioned the archbishop of Canterbury, claiming that their father's will had been improperly executed.[88] There is nothing to indicate that Roger supported them, or that he ever litigated independently on this matter. However, throughout his career the earl

---

[82] E159/49, m. 22. Sadly these totals are enrolled without any breakdown. However, the grand total coincides very well with the £3,300 above (p. 112). Adding in the money Roger owed in his own right for Bosham, or the Marshal debts, would take this total to around £3,577.

[83] E159/49, m. 26; *CFR, 1272-1307*, p. 50.

[84] Below, n. 193.

[85] Carpenter, 'King, Magnates and Society', p. 90; above, p. 94. For other amounts that were allowed in 1282, see below, n. 185.

[86] For Roger III's executors, see above, p. 112. Hugh III Bigod's executors were John de Warenne, earl of Surrey, John de Oketon, John de Stonegrave and William de Northborough (E159/49, m. 18). The appearance of Warenne, Hugh's half-brother, suggests that the will may have been drawn up during their exile in 1264-65.

[87] The man in question was Thomas Lenebaud, for whom see above, pp. 66-7, 69-70, 97, 112. He was archdeacon of Suffolk, and his goods were seized by the bishop of Norwich. His executors came to the exchequer and said that Thomas had received nothing from Roger III Bigod's estate after the earl's death. Roger IV repeatedly failed to appear at the exchequer to present his case, and eventually the bishop was ordered to return Lenebaud's goods to his executors. E159/57, m. 2.

[88] *Register of John Pecham*, ii, 179.

would claim that responsibility for certain debts fell not to him but to Hugh's executors.[89]

Humiliating though his climb-down in June 1275 was, the temporary losses which Roger sustained were partially offset by some permanent gains. That same summer, Eleanor de Montfort, widow of Earl Simon, died in exile in France.[90] Her dower from the lands of William Marshal, her first husband – the cause of so much tension in English politics for a generation – finally reverted to the Marshal heirs. The division of this widow's third between the heirs had been carried out when the rest of the estate was partitioned in 1249, and so, on 3 June 1275, the king simply instructed his escheator to give each of them seisin of their portion. As anticipated, Roger inherited the entire manor of Weston in Hertfordshire, and substantial parcels of land in Kemsing (Kent) and Newbury (Berkshire).[91]

Moreover, barely a year after Edward had imposed on Roger to clear his debts, the repayment scheme was abandoned. The reason behind the king's change of heart was simple: the earl of Norfolk may have acknowledged his mastery, but the prince of Wales required more convincing. Llywelyn ap Gruffudd had also profited from the recent weakness of the English Crown, and had likewise failed to detect the sea-change in attitude that accompanied Edward's succession. Frustrated on several scores with the regency government, the prince made a fatal diplomatic miscalculation when he attempted to coerce the king into action. By repeatedly refusing to do homage to Edward, Llywelyn provided the perfect pretext for his own reduction. On 12 November 1276, in a full council of magnates at Westminster, the prince was declared a rebel.[92] Roger Bigod was present at the meeting, making his first recorded appearance at court for over a year. A few days beforehand, the earl had been reassured that his confiscated property would be returned once his debts had been cleared. A week later, the king decided it would be more politic to abandon the scheme altogether, and the four manors were restored. Roger was henceforth to pay off his debts at the rate of £100 a year.[93] Finally, in February 1277, Edward called off the exchequer entirely. The earl was granted a five-year respite, after which the annual payments would resume.[94]

---

[89] Above, n. 19; below, pp. 131-2, 158-9, 180-81.
[90] Maddicott, *Montfort*, pp. 369-70.
[91] *CCR, 1272-79*, pp. 190-91. In 1249 Weston was valued at £50 8s 10d; the lands in Kemsing and Newbury were worth £26 2s 7d and 106s 2d. Roger also became lord of 10 knights' fees, the majority of which lay in Wiltshire, Somerset and Dorset. *CPR, 1364-67*, pp. 266-7.
[92] Davies, *Conquest, Coexistence and Change*, pp. 320-30.
[93] *Parl. Writs*, i, 5; *CPR, 1272-81*, pp. 166, 170; *CCR, 1272-79*, p. 360; *CFR, 1272-1307*, p. 75.
[94] *CCR, 1272-79*, p. 371.

At first glance it seems that Edward had relented, and that Roger's payments had been postponed in return for his political and military support. In actual fact, the king had taken the opportunity to negotiate a new deal with the earl, potentially more punitive than their previous arrangement. On the same day that he respited Roger's debts, Edward advanced the earl a loan of 1,000 marks. Superficially this appears very generous; a useful injection of cash to enable preparation for the coming campaign in Wales. However, the terms on which the grant was made were less than altruistic. When, one week later, Roger pledged to repay the above money, he also agreed that before Easter 1279 he would surrender certain properties to the king (Bosham and its dependent manors, and also the recently acquired manor of Weston). These lands would subsequently be restored, but on different terms. The earl would hold them as before, but they could only pass to the legitimate heirs of his own body. If, when he died, such heirs did not exist, the manors would revert to the Crown.[95]

This kind of deal, whereby the Crown obtained an interest in a subject's property at the expense of any collateral heirs, was made something of a speciality by Edward I.[96] The king showed considerable concern for the family life of his great magnates, but only to the extent that he was willing to speculate on it. In 1277, Roger had been married to his countess for at least five years, perhaps as many as ten, but their union had produced no children. Disappointing though this may have been for the couple themselves, it posed no immediate problems for the Bigods as a dynasty. The earl still had three younger brothers, perhaps as many as sisters, at least one cousin and other more distant relatives besides.[97] All were lined up and ready to step in if Roger himself failed to procreate. In 1277, however, Edward altered the expectations of this wider kin-group. Using the earl's apparent impecuniousness as his lever, the king was able to put a couple of valuable properties beyond their reach. As in other cases, there was no risk to Edward himself in this transaction. He had respited Roger's debts, not pardoned them; the 1,000 marks he dangled in front of the earl were being put up by the Riccardi of Lucca, the king's Italian bankers, rather than his own exchequer.[98] Of course, this is not to deny that Roger may

[95] RBIV 7 and 8; Powicke, *Henry III*, p. 705. Cf. Prestwich, *Edward I*, p. 413, who errs in calling this a 'surety' for the loan. This would imply that the king expected to keep the manors until the money was repaid, which was not the case. The earl's surety was the conventional allowance that the money could be raised directly from his lands and goods if it was not repaid.

[96] Powicke, *Henry III*, pp. 704-5; McFarlane, 'Policy', p. 259; Prestwich, *Edward I*, pp. 348-9, 538-9; *idem*, *War, Politics and Finance*, pp. 243-5.

[97] For his siblings, see above, p. 102; below, pp. 137, 163-4, 173-4, 176, 184. For his cousin, John Bigod of Stockton, see below, n. 197 and pp. 138-9, 143-4, 149, 151, 174, 178-9. Roger IV also had dealings with the Bigods of Great Bradley in Suffolk, a cadet line descended from Hugh Bigod, son of Earl Hugh I Bigod by his second marriage. SC6/1006/2.

[98] *CPR, 1272-81*, p. 195.

also have considered the deal to be a good one. A five-year respite on debts and a generous loan were tempting, perhaps irresistible inducements; the possibility that later generations of Bigods would be a few manors worse off was a risk worth running. What the earl could not have seen in 1277, however, was that this deal set a precedent. It was the model for the more celebrated bargain he would strike with the king twenty-five years later, by which time the risks and the stakes would have been raised out of all proportion.

WALES AND IRELAND

As earl marshal, Roger played an important role in the Welsh campaign of 1277. Precise details about his activities, however, are lacking.[99] He was not involved in the immediate deployment of troops and commanders in the first half of the year, but his charter witnessing indicates that he participated in royal counsels while the main campaign was being planned. Edward visited Framlingham in April, the earl was at Westminster in May, and in late June both men were at Woodstock, en route to Wales. By 1 July they had reached Worcester, where Roger, in his capacity as marshal, along with Humphrey de Bohun, earl of Hereford and constable, drew up the lists for the feudal muster.[100] At this point, however, the royal charters come to an end. Roger probably moved north with the host to Chester, and thence to Flint, Rhuddlan and Deganwy. It was only when the king retired to Rhuddlan in mid-September that the earl appears to have taken his leave.[101] In this respect he was probably not alone. When the flow of charters resumed on 1 October, the council had closed ranks. Lincoln and Warwick, the two royalist earls, remained in Wales with Edward, but Gloucester, Surrey and Norfolk were nowhere to be seen.[102] By this stage, the campaign was all but over. On 9 November 1277 Llywelyn agreed to surrender.[103]

In the eighteen months that followed the war, important initiatives were undertaken in English government: the *Quo Warranto* enquiry, for example, was launched in the parliament of August 1278. Roger's attendance during this period was fairly regular, but there is no evidence that he made any special contribution to proceedings. Indeed, his personal record is remarkably humdrum at this time. Present at court at the start of

---

[99] Cf. his role in war of 1282-83, for which there is evidence in his ministers' accounts. Below, pp. 125-7. We know some of the men who were in his retinue in 1277. Below, pp. 149-50.

[100] Appendix B. For the campaign, see J.E. Morris, *The Welsh Wars of Edward I* (Oxford, 1901), pp. 110-48, and specifically pp. 126, 133.

[101] On 15 September, the justiciar of Chester was ordered to permit Roger to take three deer in Delamere Forest. *CCR, 1272-79*, p. 402.

[102] *RCWL Ed I*, p. 11.

[103] Davies, *Conquest, Coexistence and Change*, p. 333.

1278, he also attended parliaments in May and August, and may well have been present at the assembly held in October.[104] At some point during the winter, probably in the second week of December, there was some brief excitement when the king decided to stay at the earl's manor of Lopham: the royal visit demanded extra wine from Framlingham, and at least £25 was spent on improving the buildings.[105] In the new year, however, it was business as usual. Roger was back at court in January 1279 and, while there is no sign of him at the Easter parliament that year, the conclusion of a minor dispute with William de Valence suggests his probable presence.[106] Easter was also the time by which Roger was required to honour his agreement with Edward over Bosham and Weston; accordingly, he surrendered the manors to the king in June, and they were restored to him at the end of the following month.[107]

At this point, the earl's career takes an unexpected and interesting turn. In early July, while attending a gathering of magnates at Westminster, Roger appointed attorneys to superintend his affairs in England, and three weeks later he was granted royal letters of protection. A gift of two deer in the forest of Dean implies he intended to visit his Welsh lordship, but Chepstow was only a point of departure. At some time in late autumn, we must picture Roger taking ship at the town's quayside, and setting sail for his estates in Ireland.[108]

---

[104] Appendix B. There are no royal charters for October 1278. Prestwich, *Edward I*, p. 259.

[105] SC6/997/3, SC6/1007/9. See also SC6/991/19 (Bungay, 1279), which has 'Geoffrey the fisherman, fishing for the king'. The obvious gap in Edward's itinerary is the ten-day period between 5 December, when the king was at Burgh, and 15 December, when he reached Newmarket. *Itinerary of Edward I*, ed. E.W. Safford (3 vols., List and Index Soc., 103, 132, 135, 1974-7), i, 103-4.

[106] The two men appear to have clashed initially over the division of Eleanor de Montfort's dower in 1275: by Easter term 1276 they had reached an agreement over Kemsing (*PA*, p. 190). Very soon, however, their disagreement spread to include other parts of the Marshal estate (e.g. *CCR, 1272-79*, p. 349). Valence was married to the Marshal heiress Joan de Munchensi, who in 1249 had been allocated an annual sum of £6 16s 6½d in the lordship of Chepstow. Valence maintained that this had never been paid by the Bigods, but Roger countered that his uncle had satisfied William and Joan with an equivalent annual amount from the manor of Chesterford. In February 1278 the king and council intervened, giving Roger the opportunity to prove his point by producing charters, and proposing that certain properties split between the two parties be consolidated. This scheme collapsed when the arbitrators appointed on both sides failed to agree and withdrew. An impatient Edward subsequently drafted in Anthony Bek, who proposed a new solution. In 1279 the earl was persuaded to drop his claim that William and Joan had already been compensated, and a final settlement was reached (*CCR, 1272-79*, pp. 475, 560-62). In view of the fact that this settlement appears to favour Valence more than Bigod, it is interesting to note that Roger was also involved in litigation against Bek at this time (*CPR, 1272-81*, p. 339; *CCR, 1279-88*, p. 139).

[107] *Feet of Fines relating to the County of Sussex*, ed. L.F. Salzmann (3 vols., Sussex Record Soc., ii, vii, xxiii, 1903-16), ii, 108; *CCR, 1272-79*, pp. 535-6, 569-70; SC1/63/26 (ii).

[108] *RCWL Ed I*, p. 16; *CPR, 1272-81*, pp. 319, 322; *CR, 1272-79*, p. 535. The earl was unlikely to have arrived in Ireland before Robert Cockerel rendered account at the Dublin exchequer in Michaelmas 1279. *DKPR Ireland*, 36th report, p. 40; below, p. 121.

The Bigod estate in Ireland, outlined in Chapter Two, was essentially a lordship organized around two major towns, linked by the River Barrow. At the river's southern end, close by its mouth, lay the thriving port of New Ross. This was the richest urban settlement in Ireland, its commercial success reflected by the unrivalled contributions it made to the Dublin exchequer,[109] its civic pride advertised by a new set of walls, the result of a remarkable communal endeavour by the townspeople during the Barons' Wars.[110] The town had entirely replaced Old Ross, some five miles to the east, as a centre for trade. Yet the new port continued to rely on its venerable inland ancestor. Old Ross, also part of the Bigod demesne, was the site of large granges for sheep and cattle.[111]

For all its success, however, this thriving commercial partnership at the southern end of the river still answered to the lordship's other major settlement thirty miles upstream. The town of Carlow was the focal point for a number of other Bigod properties, specifically the borough and manor of Fothered, and the manor of Ballysax in County Kildare.[112] More importantly, Carlow was the seat of the entire comital administration in Ireland.[113] From a great stone castle on the town's quayside, probably established by William Marshal senior, the earl's officials oversaw the activities of both demesne farmers and tenants alike.[114] The lordship operated somewhat differently to the rest of the Bigod estate, partly out of geographical necessity, and partly because of the historical circumstances that had led to its creation. Like the other Irish lordships established in the twelfth century, Carlow was a 'liberty': it enjoyed quasi-independent status in relation to the king's government in Dublin, and its lords had developed their own institutions in imitation of the royal model. The liberty had its own private sheriff to police its borders and to superintend

---

[109] *DKPR Ireland*, 36th report, pp. 28-9, 48; 37th report, pp. 24-5.

[110] H. Shields, 'The Walling of New Ross: A Thirteenth-century Poem in French', *Long Room*, 12-13 (1976), pp. 24-33.

[111] Below, pp. 126, 134.

[112] Fothered, which lay in the parish of Grangeford, no longer exists. Later known as Castlemore, all that now remains of the settlement is a motte on the road between Carlow and Tullow. See M.C. Lyons, 'Manorial Administration and the Manorial Economy of Ireland, c. 1200–c. 1377', (Ph.D. thesis, Dublin, 1984), p. 54.

[113] This administration has been described in W.F. Nugent, 'Carlow in the Middle Ages', *Journal of the Royal Soc. of Antiquaries of Ireland*, 4th ser., lxxxv (1955), 62-76. For the most part it is a sound appraisal, but nevertheless contains several mistakes and misapprehensions. Although based on a close reading of the Irish material in SC6, the article regrettably carries only the occasional footnote. Nugent was a doctoral student at Trinity College, Dublin, in the 1950s, but never finished his thesis. R. Frame, pers. comm. See also J. Mills, 'Accounts of the Earl of Norfolk's Estates in Ireland, 1279-1294', *Journal of the Royal Soc. of Antiquaries of Ireland*, 4th ser., xxii (1892), 50-62.

[114] For the castle, see R.A. Stalley, *Architecture and Sculpture in Ireland* (Dublin, 1971), pp. 47-50; D. Grose, *Antiquities of Ireland*, ed. R.A. Stalley (Dublin, 1991), pp. 166-7. For the earl's tenants, see E. St John Brooks, *Knights' Fees in Counties Wexford, Carlow and Kilkenny* (Dublin, 1950), pp. 1-91; B. Colfer, 'Anglo-Norman Settlement in County Wexford', *Wexford: History and Society*, ed. K. Whelan (Dublin, 1987), pp. 65-101.

its own private judicial system. The chief financial official gloried in the name of treasurer, and had his own 'exchequer' at Carlow Castle. Both these men, however, were answerable to the seneschal, who was a far more powerful figure than his counterparts at Framlingham, Bosham and Chepstow. In Ireland, the seneschal was, in effect, a kind of vicegerent for the earl himself, rewarded with a generous salary of £100 a year, and extended a wide degree of latitude to govern at his own discretion.[115]

It was the power of the seneschal, or rather its abuse, that persuaded Roger Bigod to come to Carlow in person. Sir Robert Cockerel, appointed to the position in 1276, must have appeared at the time to be a worthy candidate; a former royal servant, he had been recruited into Bigod circles by the previous earl.[116] Three years later, however, and the auditors were evidently sending back disturbing reports. Upon his arrival in Ireland, Roger removed Cockerel, imprisoned him and confiscated his goods.[117]

This neat decapitation, however, was just the beginning. In the weeks and months that followed, the earl appears to have instigated a process of root-and-branch reform throughout his Irish lordship. According to Nugent, the deposition of the seneschal was followed by 'a general reappraisal of the administrative organization'.[118] No evidence is cited in support of this statement, but several important steps were taken at this time, all of which must be attributed to Roger's personal initiative. Firstly, Cockerel's replacement was a figure of special distinction. Philip de Buckland was a Suffolk landowner of some standing, a member of the Bigod inner circle both under the present earl and during the time of his uncle. No previous or indeed subsequent seneschals could boast of such close connections. Having misplaced his faith in Cockerel, Roger appointed a successor in whom his trust was absolute.[119] Secondly, the earl took steps to invigorate the lordship's economy. To New Ross he granted a new town charter.[120] In the north, he was probably behind the decision to create a new manorial centre at Fennagh, some ten miles south-east of

---

[115] Cf. J. Otway-Ruthven, 'The Medieval County of Kildare', *Irish Historical Studies*, xi (1959), 181-99; Altschul, *Baronial Family*, pp. 281-95.
[116] *CDI, 1252-84*, p. 217; *CPR, 1272-81*, p. 135; *RCWL HIII*, ii, 155, 161, 163, 166, 168-9, 172-3, 176, 179, 182-5, 187-92; SC6/934/17, SC6/934/29 and SC6/934/30 (payments of 100s made to him 'by a charter of the late earl').
[117] This is known from a later agreement between the two men. In November 1281, the earl remitted his anger and all demand against his former seneschal, saving £14 of arrears. In return, Cockerel dropped a plea of 'unjust detention and robbery' that he had moved against the earl in Ireland. *CDI, 1252-84*, p. 405; *CCR, 1279-88*, p. 138.
[118] Nugent, 'Carlow in the Middle Ages', p. 73.
[119] Appendix D; above, pp. 67-72, 97; below, pp. 137, 142-3, 145-6, 149-51. Buckland had been one of the earl's auditors in Ireland in 1278-79, and may therefore have been responsible for exposing Cockerel's corruption. Nugent, 'Carlow in the Middle Ages', p. 68.
[120] RBIV 10.

Carlow.[121] Thirdly, there is the strong possibility that Roger decided in the course of his visit to construct a new castle.

Across his entire estate, throughout his entire career, the earl invested in expensive new buildings.[122] Indeed, such was the scale of his commitment that he found it prudent to retain the permanent services of Ralph Gugon, a master mason from London.[123] In 1280-81, Master Ralph followed his employer to Ireland, and during this time he was directed to view 'the works at Fennagh'.[124] In the same financial year, the treasurer at Carlow expended £84 'for the construction of the castle' in the same place.[125] Today, however, there is no trace of a castle in the village of Fennagh, nor is there any evidence of one on the detailed Ordnance Survey map of 1837. Possibly it was entirely dismantled. Alternatively, it might be the mysterious building some two miles to the west. The castle now known as Ballymoon is situated directly between Fennagh, a new Bigod manor established around 1280, and Dunleckny, where a similar experiment to expand the earl's demesne was begun some five years later.[126] Long thought to date from the mid-fourteenth century, it has recently been reassessed on stylistic grounds as a late thirteenth-century creation. Built on a scale which presupposes a patron in need of extensive accommodation and with considerable resources at his disposal, Ballymoon must surely be a strong contender for the castle built 'at Fennagh' from 1280, under the direction of Ralph Gugon, and on the orders of Roger Bigod.[127]

To judge from its present appearance, Ballymoon was never completed. From what was built, however, it seems clear that the castle was intended to function as a residence more than a fortress. No ditch surrounds the site, and there are no projecting towers (the only parts of the castle which 'flank' the outer walls are the latrines). Such a lack of concern with defence (along with the stylistic evidence) effectively rules out a fourteenth-century date. By the reign of Edward II, attacks from the native Irish were on the increase, and the English settlement in Ireland was on the retreat.[128] Ballymoon, by contrast, speaks of a colony in the ascendant, confident of a

---

[121] Lyons, 'Manorial Administration', p. 63. The first account roll for Fennagh is SC6/1237/32, dated to 1280-81. It is also worth noting that the earl took the trouble to visit the most outlying part of his demesne, the manor of Ballysax in Co. Kildare. SC6/1237/1.

[122] Above, p. 119; below, pp. 130, 134, 136-7, 182, 185-6, 190-91.

[123] SC6/1020/20 ('Delivered…for the use of Master Ralph the Mason of London to make the quay at Brokenwharf'); SC6/1020/15 ('Paid to Master Ralph Gugon, mason of the earl, in part of his fee which is in arrears').

[124] SC6/1237/42. For his other appearances in Ireland at this time, see SC6/1238/1, SC6/1239/10 and SC6/1237/43.

[125] SC6/1239/1.

[126] Below, p. 135.

[127] T. O'Keeffe, 'Ballyloughan, Ballymoon and Clonmore: Three Castles of c. 1300 in County Carlow', *ANS*, xxiii (Woodbridge, 2001), 185; D. Sweetman, *Medieval Castles of Ireland* (Woodbridge, 1999), pp. 116-18, 133.

[128] O'Keeffe, 'Ballyloughan, Ballymoon and Clonmore', p. 185.

secure future ahead. Again, this would seem to fit the circumstances of the 1280s. As well as encouraging the expansion of the lordship during his visit, Roger also took the opportunity to come to terms with the native Irish chieftains.

Although a century had elapsed since the first Anglo-Norman lords had crossed to Ireland, English control of the country was by no means complete. Settlers still had to contend with a native population whose desire for greater political freedom sat uneasily with the expansionist tendencies of the colony itself. In the 1270s, native aspirations were focused on the MacMurroughs, a family descended from the last Irish king of Leinster. Much like the leaders of native Wales, they and their supporters were prepared to offer both cash payments and armed resistance in pursuit of their liberties. Neither was acceptable to the settler community, and as a result the government in Dublin found itself caught between the two groups, one ready to wage war in pursuit of its objectives, the other determined not to give ground.[129]

This was the situation in Leinster which Roger Bigod encountered in the autumn of 1279, and into which he was quickly drawn. The justiciar of Ireland, Robert de Ufford, urged the earl to meet with Art MacMurrough and his brother Murchertach, at the same time warning him 'to deal with them tactfully' lest the king's peace be disturbed.[130] Surprisingly perhaps, the Irish leaders were well-disposed to negotiate, not least because they regarded Roger as one of their own: the Bigods, as a result of their Marshal ancestry, could claim descent from Dermot MacMurrough.[131] If the earl was privately incredulous ('our kinsmen – or so they say' was how he described the brothers in a letter to Edward I), he did his utmost to disguise it.[132] During his time in Ireland, Roger rewarded Art and Murchertach with generous money fees, and plied them with wine, furs and robes.[133] By the summer of 1280, he was even suggesting that the brothers might like to accompany him back to England. This, as he explained to the king, was a politically motivated move, intended to increase Ireland's security.[134] Yet to have reached a point where such a plan seemed feasible indicates that the earl must have worked hard on improving relations with his long-lost cousins. It assumes that, across a wide cultural divide, bridges had been built and crossed.

---

[129] E. Curtis, *A History of Medieval Ireland* (London, 1923), pp. 160-62.

[130] R. Frame, 'The Justiciar and the Murder of the MacMurroughs in 1282', *Irish Historical Studies*, xviii (1972-73), 224, 229; SC1/15/64.

[131] Cf. L. Griffith et al., 'The Alleged Descent of the Marshalls from Dermot MacMurrough', *Genealogist's Magazine*, 6 (1932-34), pp. 311-13, 362-6, 410, 460.

[132] SC1/15/64; J.R.S. Phillips, 'The Anglo-Norman Nobility', *The English in Medieval Ireland*, ed. J. Lydon (Dublin, 1984), p. 104.

[133] SC6/1239/1; SC6/1238/25; SC6/1239/10.

[134] SC1/15/64.

Roger probably returned to England in the autumn of 1280 (his first datable appearance is at Burgh on 28 December that year).[135] In spite of the safe-conducts issued in July, it seems unlikely that either of the MacMurroughs came with him.[136] In 1281 Murchertach was causing fresh problems for the Dublin government, and Art must have been in Ireland at the end of the year, when a new safe-conduct was issued for him and his dependants.[137] Perhaps at this point a crossing was made: it is tempting to identify one of these men, Cearbhaill Ó Foirchtern, with an individual who appears in Bigod circles in 1289.[138] But if Art did visit England, his stay there must have been very short; both MacMurroughs were in Ireland during the summer of 1282, by which time the Dublin government had decided on a more permanent solution to the problem they posed. The new justiciar, Stephen de Fulbourne, had no time for the inconclusive methods of his predecessor, or for that matter the diplomatic efforts of the earl of Norfolk. On 21 July, the brothers were murdered at Arklow, by an assassin operating on Fulbourne's orders.[139]

Quite how Roger felt about the murder of the MacMurroughs is unclear. He later protested to Edward I about Fulbourne's conduct, but his grievance was financial rather personal.[140] In any case the death of his Irish kinsmen was greatly overshadowed by other losses closer to home. Soon after the earl's return from Ireland, probably in early April 1281, his countess died.[141] Only recently she had taken on greater responsibility for the management of her husband's estate;[142] her sudden death now imperilled a significant part of it. Aline had been sole heiress to the lands of Philip Basset, her father, and since his death in 1271 Roger had enjoyed custody of seventeen extra manors in right of his wife.[143] Now, however,

---

[135] Appendix B.

[136] *CPR, 1272-81*, p. 392; *CDI, 1252-84*, p. 352.

[137] Frame, 'The Justiciar and the Murder of the MacMurroughs', p. 225; *CPR, 1272-81*, p. 460; *CDI, 1252-84*, p. 405. On the day the safe-conduct was enrolled, Roger was at court, so it may have been issued at his instance. See Appendix B.

[138] Below, p. 141.

[139] Frame, 'The Justiciar and the Murder of the MacMurroughs', pp. 223, 226-8.

[140] The earl objected that Fulbourne, having done the deed in secret, had retrospectively charged the English communities for the brothers' 'head money' (*capitagium*). *CDI, 1252-84*, p. 435.

[141] *CFR, 1272-1307*, p. 146.

[142] In particular she cleared up a long-running dispute with Hugh de Essex, who claimed to have a greater right than the Bigods to North Weald Basset in Essex. Hugh was persuaded to drop his claim in exchange for the manor of Tolleshunt in Essex. JUST/1/238, m. 20d; *CPR, 1272-81*, p. 358; *Catalogue of Ancient Deeds*, i, 89; E40/14552 (for another copy, see DL25/1087); *PQW*, p. 236-7. For her other transactions while Roger was in Ireland, see *Catalogue of Ancient Deeds*, i, 63; iii, 183-4. Cf. her evident involvement in running the estate during Roger's absence in 1273-74, above, p. 109.

[143] For these manors, see above, p. 105. However, cf. Aline's inquisition post mortem, which mysteriously includes Winterbourne Basset in Wiltshire, but makes no mention of Wootton Bassett, Elsfield, Cassington, Aston Clinton or South Weald. *CIPM*, ii, 227-9.

that right was set to pass to the countess's son by her first marriage, Hugh Despenser the younger. For the earl this was a major blow, especially in view of the substantial debts still hanging over his head. The only way he could retain Aline's estate was through an unusual legal twist known as 'courtesy of England', by which a second husband was allowed a life interest in his late wife's estate if they had produced a child together – even if that child was no longer living.[144] With literally nothing to lose, Roger claimed that this was indeed the case; that Aline had given birth to a child – his child – at Woking, and it had drawn breath, though only for a short time. Hugh Despenser responded vigorously, challenging his stepfather in the courts. A jury was appointed and asked to pronounce on such matters as whether the child had given voice, whether it was male or female, where it was born and where baptized. At the last minute, however, Roger relented and dropped his claim.[145] He may have realized that the verdict was going to go against him, and wanted to avoid amercement. Alternatively, he might simply have recognized that Despenser had the greater right. The earl was perhaps closer to his stepson than their litigation suggests. Hugh had seemingly been committed to his mother's custody in 1265, and during his teenage years he occasionally appears as a visitor at certain Bigod manors (on one occasion in the company of the earl's brother, Ralph).[146]

After these dramatic scenes at Easter, the remainder of 1281 passed quietly. Roger attended the parliaments of May and October, and was also at Westminster in early December. It was not until Easter the following year that events in Wales gave fresh momentum to the his political career. On Palm Sunday 1282, Dafydd ap Gruffudd, the disgruntled younger brother of Prince Llywelyn, stormed and seized the English castle at Hawarden, while similar attacks were mounted right across the principality.[147] When news of the uprising reached Edward I, he quickly decided on a policy of total conquest, and summoned his magnates to a council at Devizes, where Roger Bigod reappears on 8 April. In mid-May the earl oversaw an abortive muster of troops at Worcester, before heading north to Chester in June, and finally reaching Rhuddlan in late July, where he supervised a second muster at the start of August.[148] This, of course, was a responsibility (and a privilege) that fell to him as marshal, along with the obligation to maintain discipline in the army. With the royal host

---

[144] *Letters of Medieval Women*, ed. Crawford, p. 17.

[145] *Select Cases KB*, i, 81; *PA*, p. 272.

[146] SC6/1007/5; SC6/837/13; SC6/873/9. That Aline had the wardship of her son in 1265 is suggested by its re-grant immediately after her death. Although Hugh was only a few months under age in 1281, and notwithstanding that he was allowed free administration of his father's lands, his marriage was given to the earl of Warwick. *CCR, 1279-88*, p. 88; *CPR, 1272-81*, p. 439.

[147] Davies, *Conquest, Coexistence and Change*, pp. 348-9.

[148] Appendix B; *Parl. Writs*, i, 222, 225-6, 228, 235; Prestwich, *Edward I*, p. 189.

numbering some 750 cavalry and 8,000 foot, this by itself should have been sufficient to keep the earl occupied.[149] However, when, in the autumn, the English advance stalled, and a winter campaign seemed inevitable, Roger was charged with new duties. On 7 October, he was granted letters of protection and safe-conduct to come and go in order to keep the army supplied.[150]

Some of the necessary provisions the earl sourced from his own estates in England and Wales. From Chepstow in particular, large amounts of money were sent to Rhuddlan on several separate occasions: sums of £36 and £40 were paid to John Bigod (probably Roger's cousin) for the earl's own use; a further £40 from Chepstow was escorted northwards by five men and two horses around the same time.[151] Meanwhile, £90 was sent from Bosham to London, where Walter Scissor (a regular payee) was making tents for the campaign.[152] Much the greatest part of the material that Roger received, however, came from across the Irish Sea. In 1282-83, Thomas Wade, treasurer of Carlow, made several trips to Ross in order to prepare victuals for export, and also visited Dublin for the same purpose.[153] His annual account contains several interesting specifics, such as the two tuns of ale he sent to Rhuddlan, or the four iron head-pieces (cost ten shillings) that he also dispatched. Far more revealing, however, is a unique account kept by the Bigod wardrober, Philip de Ottington, enumerating the items he received from Ireland. Here the scope and scale of the operation stand revealed. From Old Ross and Ballysax, large herds and flocks were driven to Dublin: all told 77 head of cattle, 56 hogs and 120 sheep were earmarked for export. So too were 100 quarters of oats and 200 quarters of wheat from the same manors. Forty-two stone of cheese, 4,000 onions, 31 hogsheads of wine and 14 hogsheads of beer were likewise loaded onto ships and sent into Wales. Nor was it just food that Ireland supplied. Twenty-four ells of canvas were bought for the use of the earl's bakers, and coloured cloth (red, green and yellow, as per the Marshal coat of arms) was purchased to make pennons.[154]

---

[149] Prestwich, *Edward I*, p. 190.

[150] *CRV*, p. 226.

[151] SC6/921/23; SC6/921/24.

[152] SC6/1020/14. Walter is also styled 'Walter the Tailor'. Below, p. 152.

[153] SC6/1239/2. An English translation of this roll is given in Mills, 'Accounts of the Earl of Norfolk's Estates in Ireland', pp. 58-62. The work of Capt. Philip Hore, it is not very accurate. Similarly, the extracts from the Bigod accounts given in H.F. Hore, *History of the Town and County of Wexford* (6 vols., London, 1900-11), being poorly translated and seamlessly blended with the author's own musings, should be treated with caution.

[154] *CDI, 1252-84*, pp. 459-61; Prestwich, *Edward I*, p. 199, cites E101/4/3, seemingly the same document. It is interesting to note that while Old Ross sent two-thirds of the sheep, Ballysax contributed two-thirds of the wheat.

Having remained at Rhuddlan for most of the summer and autumn, Roger vanished from the king's side in mid-November.[155] His disappearance could easily be attributed to the ongoing need for purveyance; he was, after all, licensed to come and go for precisely this purpose. A chance reference, however, suggests the earl may have been sent in search of further funds. The minister's account for Framlingham in 1282-83 records payment for a messenger, 'taking a writ of the king to the earl at Northampton'.[156] The entry is undated, but the likeliest (not to say the only conceivable) explanation for Roger's presence in Northampton during this financial year would be the money-raising assembly that Edward summoned there for January 1283. According to the record of the proceedings, the earl himself was exempted from the tax the gathering granted, because he was 'in Wales with the king'. This, however, need not have been the literal truth at that precise moment. More probably, given the coincidence of his disappearance and the reference to Northampton, the earl had been sent to oversee the assembly, perhaps even to address the knights and burgesses.[157]

Whatever the true cause of his absence, the earl was re-summoned to Wales on 13 March, and was back by Edward's side by 16 April. The army had now reached Conway, where work on a new royal castle had already begun.[158] There Roger started to receive more foodstuffs and money from Ireland. Ralph Wade, the constable of Carlow Castle, accompanied by Richard the clerk, arrived with £200; in Dublin, £25 of cereals and £8 of beer were purchased for the earl's use and duly dispatched.[159] By this stage, the English victory was only a matter of time. Llywelyn had been killed in December, and the last Welsh stronghold, Castell-y-Bere, fell on 25 April. By the time Dafydd was captured on 21 June, the campaign was already winding down.[160] In the second week of July, Roger took his leave of the king and headed for home.[161]

In the course of the next year-and-a-half, there was only minimal contact between the earl and King Edward. The only occasion on which they can be placed together during this time is October 1283, when the political communities of England and Wales gathered in Shropshire to

[155] The royal witness lists continue over Christmas and the New Year, and show Edward in the company of other earls, such as Gloucester, Lancaster and Lincoln. *RCWL Ed I*, pp. 45-7.

[156] SC6/997/4.

[157] *Parl. Writs*, i, 12; Prestwich, *Edward I*, pp. 238, 454, 457.

[158] R.A. Brown, H.M. Colvin and A.J. Taylor, *The History of the King's Works*, i (HMSO, 1963), 337-54.

[159] SC6/1239/2; SC6/1239/3.

[160] Davies, *Conquest, Coexistence and Change*, pp. 353-4

[161] His last witnessing was on 9 July. On 12 July he was granted deer in the royal forest of Pamber, which lay close to his own manor of Hamstead Marshall (Appendix B; *CCR, 1279-88*, p. 212). While the earl had been in Wales, many of his own deer in Norfolk had been poached. His cousin, John Bigod, also suffered in this regard. *CPR, 1281-92*, pp. 73, 96.

participate in the trial and execution of Dafydd ap Gruffudd.[162] It would be a mistake, however, to read this separation as a sign of any ill-feeling. After his victory in Wales, Edward spent much of the following year touring his new dominion, unaccompanied for the most part by any of his earls.[163] The magnates whom the king encountered were those with lands in Wales, obliged to house and entertain the court when it arrived. In this respect, Roger Bigod was no different to William de Valence or Gilbert de Clare. At the end of 1284, just a few days before Christmas, Edward stopped in the marcher lordship of Chepstow, in full expectation of a hospitable reception from the earl marshal.

Chepstow was one of the smaller marcher lordships. It stretched some twelve miles east to west, between the rivers of Usk and Wye, and eight miles north to south, between the forest of Wentwood and the Severn estuary.[164] Within these narrow bounds, Roger's demesne holdings were fairly limited, amounting to the town and castle of Chepstow itself, the large manor of Tidenham in Gloucestershire, and a number of small hamlets, parks and granges.[165] The earl's tenants, meanwhile, held just seven knights' fees between them: a handful of small farms and castles dotted along the length of the old Roman road which ran between Chepstow and Caerleon.[166]

But if the lordship itself was little, the region it lay in was rich. Netherwent had long been one of the most prosperous areas of Wales. Precocious manorialization had made it an attractive area for Norman adventurers immediately after the Conquest, and in the twelfth century its fortunes had been further enhanced by the introduction of large-scale sheep-farming, a development spearheaded by the Cistercian monks at nearby Tintern Abbey. By the late thirteenth century, Chepstow was both wealthy and politically stable. Like their Norman forebears, the Bigods farmed rich arable land and, like their monastic neighbours, they built up large flocks.[167]

Moreover, as a marcher lordship, Chepstow had advantages and attractions out of proportion to its size. Its lords revelled in a far greater degree of independence than they could enjoy in either England or Ireland.[168] In the march, as Bigod bailiffs were wont to remind royal officials from time to time, the king's writ did not run; the earls themselves

---

[162] Appendix B; Prestwich, *Edward I*, pp. 202-3.

[163] *RCWL Ed I*, pp. 52-8; Prestwich, *Edward I*, p. 235.

[164] See, *inter alia*, W. Rees, *South Wales and the Border in the Fourteenth Century* (4 sheets, Ordnance Survey, 1932).

[165] *CIPM*, iv, 294-6; above, pp. 37-8.

[166] *CPR, 1364-7*, p. 263. For the Bigods' fees in Pembrokeshire, see above, p. 52.

[167] W. Rees, *South Wales and the March, 1284-1415* (Oxford, 1924), pp. 26-7, 195-6; R.R. Davies, *Lordship and Society in the March of Wales, 1282-1400* (Oxford, 1978), pp. 109, 117.

[168] Rees, *South Wales*, pp. 43-4; Davies, *Lordship and Society*, pp. 3-4, 120, 149-75, 217-21.

Chepstow Castle, c. 1306

were the ultimate arbiters of justice.[169] They could hunt with impunity in their own forests, and dine like kings on dishes normally reserved for royalty.[170] In Chepstow one could literally acquire a taste for independence, and this alone made it an attractive destination for both Roger IV Bigod and his predecessors.[171]

There is little doubt, however, that Roger spent more money (and thus possibly more time) at Chepstow than his immediate ancestors.[172] Over the course of his entire comital career, the earl lavished money on rebuilding the great castle that stood at the heart of his Welsh lordship. He and his master mason, Ralph Gugon, created a residence appropriate to the luxurious lifestyle of a late thirteenth-century aristocrat. Beginning in the castle's lower ward, they conceived an elaborate new suite of rooms, comprising a bedchamber, hall and kitchen. Stretched along the cliff top, high above the River Wye, the cellar and service rooms of this new complex were ingeniously arranged across a natural cleft in the rock, enabling them to be supplied from the river below. At the same time, Roger was busy transforming the area around the castle. A great arc of walls, 1,200 yards long and punctuated by ten round towers, was constructed to gird the town of Chepstow and guard it from attack.[173]

It appears from the earl's accounts that these building operations were largely complete before Edward I's visit at Christmas 1284.[174] Nevertheless, news that the king was coming prompted a flurry of last-minute improvements; over £3 was spent on felling and splitting trees in Wentwood and the earl's chase, and a further 35 shillings were expended transporting the timber to Chepstow. Inside the castle, various carpenters were awarded a total of £7 for their collective labours. Feeding the royal party also demanded extensive logistical preparations. John Baret, the steward of the Bigod household, travelled as far as the earl's Sussex manor of Bosham in order to find provisions for the Chepstow feast.[175]

---

[169] E32/30, m. 10: 'William de Glanville, constable of Chepstow, came before the justices and accepted that he received the order of the king, but he did not execute it, because he says that the king's writ does not run.'

[170] On one occasion we find Roger IV feasting on porpoise. SC6/922/7; Rees, *South Wales*, pp. 43-4.

[171] For evidence of Roger III at Chepstow, see above, pp. 43n, 55, 90n; below, p. 186.

[172] Cf. R. Turner, *Chepstow Castle* (Cardiff, 2002), p. 13. While 'there is no evidence that Roger [III Bigod] undertook much new building at the castle', it does not automatically follow that 'he preferred to concentrate on his East Anglian estates'.

[173] Turner, *Chepstow Castle*, pp. 16, 48. See also *Chepstow Castle: Its History and Buildings*, ed. R.C. Turner and R. Shoesmith (Almeley, forthcoming).

[174] Turner, *Chepstow Castle*, p. 16. The sections of the Chepstow accounts that describe building work at the castle have been transcribed and translated by Stephen Priestly. I am very grateful, both to him and to Rick Turner, for permitting me to consult these transcripts prior to their publication.

[175] SC6/921/28; SC6/1020/15. Baret is described as 'steward of the household' in SC6/1005/28.

To judge from the events of 1285, this was money well spent. After a short stay at Chepstow, Edward and Roger crossed the Severn to celebrate Christmas at Bristol.[176] There, on New Year's Day, the king presented the earl with a very substantial gift. In recognition of his services in Wales, and as recompense for his losses, Roger received 1,000 marks.[177] This cannot possibly have covered all of his wartime expenditure: in addition to the hundreds of pounds in money and goods the earl had raised from his own estate, he had also been obliged to borrow almost £500 during the campaign.[178] Nevertheless, the king's gift was a considerable one, with a symbolic importance perhaps greater than its monetary value. On the eve of the first Welsh war, Edward had instructed the Riccardi to grant Roger a loan of 1,000 marks, and exploited the situation to create an entail on several Bigod manors. Now, with Wales conquered, the king had ordered his bankers to compensate the earl with an identical sum. For a ruler notoriously reluctant to reward good service, this was a strong indication that latterly Edward had been impressed. In April 1282, following Roger's complaint about Stephen de Fulbourne, the king had reacted in a manner reminiscent of his father: the justiciar was ordered to 'deal more favourably' with the earl, who was 'bearing himself well and laudably on the king's service in Wales'.[179] Throughout 1285, the earl's witnessing of royal charters was notably high, and remained so until Edward's departure for Gascony in May 1286. It was over ten years since Roger had been compelled to surrender four of his manors to the king, and it showed: relations between the two men were markedly improved.

THE SEEDS OF DISCONTENT?

Nevertheless, the cause of that earlier breakdown still remained unresolved. Roger's five-year respite of debts, dated from the declaration of war in 1276, had expired in November 1281. Accordingly, there was an extended review of his liability at Michaelmas 1282,[180] which led the exchequer to conclude that the earl owed a grand total of £2,905.[181] Of this sum, £1,168 was attributed to three debts: £218 (for the Poitevin scutage of 1230), one gold mark (received by Hugh Bigod from the abbot of

---

[176] *RCWL Ed I*, pp. 58-9.
[177] *CPR, 1281-92*, p. 149.
[178] In October 1282 he borrowed £370 from the royal sergeant Matthew de Columbers and £129 from John de Vaux. *CCR, 1279-88*, pp. 175, 196.
[179] *CDI, 1252-84*, p. 435
[180] See E372/127, m. 18 for all the figures in this paragraph.
[181] Precisely, £2,904 14s 7d. At a later date (after 1 July 1285) this total was raised by 80m to £2,959 0s 3d. All the subtotals on the roll were revised by the same amount. This was probably on account of the Marshal money, for which Roger was variously said to owe ¹,600m and 1,680m.

Beverley), and £925 (the remainder of money for the Kyme wardship).[182]
Roger, however, only acknowledged the remaining £1,738, which was
made up from twelve other sums.[183] Against this figure, he was able claim
certain deductions. The short-lived 'four manors' scheme had raised £300
before its abandonment.[184] A further £385 was subtracted for allowances
granted to his uncle by Henry III but never enrolled.[185] The earl also paid
£152 of cash into the treasury. But even when all these sums were credited,
his 'clear' debt still stood at £1,053.

There was also the question of Roger's Crown debts in Ireland. Owing
to the destruction of the Irish exchequer rolls, these cannot be traced and
computed with the same precision as his English debts.[186] Their earliest
known value is £611, a total recorded in 1275.[187] A payment that year of
£145 and a further deposit of £20 in 1279 reduced this sum to £446.
However, every time the earl's seneschal came to render account, more
debts had been incurred or uncovered. Thus, while several substantial
payments were made between 1280 and 1283 (£64 in 1279, £60 and £21 in
1280, £198 in 1283), his overall liability remained at a fairly constant
level.[188] In 1285, with the debt once again standing in the region of £600,[189]
the Dublin government apparently tried to force the issue by seizing the
entire Bigod estate in Ireland.[190] In his account for 1285-86, the treasurer of
Carlow noted a payment of £147, 'for the old debts of the earl from the
time of his uncle...all by severe (*gravissimam*) distraint of the king'.[191]

This renewed activity in both exchequers, and in particular the seizure
of Carlow in 1285, might suggest that Edward I was preparing for another
showdown with Roger on the issue of his debts. In actual fact, however,
this does not appear to have been the case. After the English exchequer
had done its sums in 1282, the king granted several respites to the earl,

---

[182] Precisely, £1,167 19s ½d. This, however, was an incorrect total. The true total of the
figures given (all of which are vouched for by earlier rolls: see above, pp. 16, 111) is
£1,148 16s 2½d.
[183] Precisely, £1,737 15s 6½d. A breakdown is given on the roll, where the subtotal is
erroneously given as £1,837 15s 6½d (i.e. a £100 error).
[184] Cf. *CPR, 1272-81*, p. 215.
[185] These were: £100 which Roger III Bigod had paid to Luke de Lucca (cf. *CR, 1256-59*, pp.
202-3; *CPR, 1247-58*, p. 620); £38 12s 8d and £28 8d which the same earl had been owed by
Henry III (cf. *CPR, 1247-58*, p. 394 and E368/38, m. 2); 100m which were allowed in
connection with Aymer de Valence (cf. *CLR, 1251-60*, p. 292; above, p. 52).
[186] The Irish pipe rolls perished in the Four Courts fire of 1922. Some of their contents are
known from extracts published in *DKPR Ireland*. Information about Roger's debts is
recorded in the 36th report, pp. 26, 40, 46, 52, 72-3; 37th report, pp. 32-3, 50, 55; 38th
report, pp. 36-7, 71, 96.
[187] *DKPR Ireland*, 36th report, p. 26. At least £228 14s 9d of this sum was inherited.
[188] *DKPR Ireland*, 36th report, pp. 40, 46, 73.
[189] *DKPR Ireland*, 37th report, p. 32. Roger owed £583 17s 4½d 'for various debts noted in
roll 13 Ed I'.
[190] *CDI, 1285-92*, p. 38; *CCR, 1279-88*, p. 330.
[191] SC6/1239/5. Also preserved from 1286 is a detailed account of the earl's debts,
rendered at the Dublin exchequer by the seneschal of Carlow. SC6/1237/14.

probably on account of the second Welsh war.[192] When, in 1285, the exchequer certified that Roger owed £1,053, Edward once again allowed him to pay it off at terms of £100 a year.[193] Similarly, there is nothing to suggest that either man took much interest in the Irish debts. In 1278, the king had respited them 'until further notice', albeit to little apparent effect.[194] When Carlow was seized in 1285, it was probably on orders from the justiciar; Edward's personal reaction when he heard the news was to cause the liberty to be restored.[195]

Nor was it the case that Roger was unable to pay his debts through lack of funds. Because of events at the end of his career (and, in particular, the comments of a certain chronicler), the earl has acquired a posthumous reputation as a great debtor.[196] As further proof of this point, several authors have cited the large loans he obtained from Italian bankers.[197] £1,000 is the figure normally quoted, but in actual fact Roger borrowed at least £1,950, and possibly as much as £2,500.[198] However, as a comparative survey shows, the sums that he borrowed, while large, were not untypically so: other nobles, clerics and townsmen were loaned similar amounts.[199] What in actual fact distinguishes the earl from his contemporaries is not the scale of his borrowing; rather it is that, thanks to the survival of his own accounts, we can show how he dealt with this burden. Between 1278 and 1281, the rolls for Roger's English manors record payments to Italian merchants totalling £862.[200] Given that his

---

[192] E159/57, mm. 2d, 9d.

[193] E159/58, m. 11; *CPR, 1281-92*, p. 183; *CFR, 1272-1307*, p. 217. This was another mistake on the exchequer's part, for by this stage the £1,052 15s 6½d had been reduced to £803 10s 10½d, a drop of £249 4s 8d. In 1283 Roger had been allowed the £120 that he had given to Poncius de Mora in 1272 (cf. *CPR, 1266-72*, p. 639). The remaining reduction of £129 4s 8d is not explained. E372/128, m. 3d.

[194] *CDI, 1252-84*, p. 281.

[195] *CDI, 1285-92*, p. 38; *CCR, 1279-88*, p. 330.

[196] Below, pp. 173-4, 176-81.

[197] e.g. J.L. Bolton, *The Medieval English Economy, 1150-1500* (London, 1980), p. 176; T. O'Neill, *Merchants and Mariners in Medieval Ireland* (Dublin, 1987), p. 59. Prestwich, *War, Politics and Finance*, pp. 206, 237 follows Denholm-Young, *SAIE*, p. 64, in further asserting that the earl granted two manors to Florentine merchants. In actual fact the manors were leased by John Bigod of Stockton, the earl's cousin. Cf. *CDI, 1285-92*, pp. 110, 201.

[198] The earl acknowledged debts to Italians at the exchequer on six separate occasions between 1277 and 1284 (E368/50, m. 9d; E159/51, m. 19; E159/52, m. 11; E368/52, m. 14; E159/55, m. 10d; E159/57, m. 17: the figures are helpfully tabulated in R.W. Kaeuper, *Bankers to the Crown: the Riccardi of Lucca and Edward I* (Princeton, 1973), pp. 60, 68). It is not always clear, however, whether one recognizance supersedes another. The £1,000 10s 1d Roger acknowledged in 1278 and the £950 6s 6½d he admitted the following year were explicitly identified as separate debts, so his minimum total was £1,950. If the sums of £330 (1277) and £182 (1284) were neither superseded nor the result of revised calculations, the earl's total approached £2,500.

[199] Kaeuper, *Bankers to the Crown*, pp. 60-69.

[200] SC6/998/21 (£2); SC6/935/28 (£26); SC6/997/3 (£132 15s 5½d); SC6/929/6 (£130 16s 3d); SC6/936/24 (£53); SC66/998/22 (£22); SC6/929/7 (£12 16s 2d); SC6/933/29 (£67 8d, £33 17s 6d and £8 19s); SC6/935/29 (£184 2s); SC6/936/25 (£66 20d); SC6/938/2 (£89 4s 5d); SC6/837/15 (£33); SC6/837/16 (venison).

accounts do not form a complete run, this figure accords very well with the revised statement of his liability given at the end of this period: in 1281, the earl's total debt to the Riccardi had dropped from around £2,000 to £1,133.[201] This outstanding sum was paid out from 1284 by Roger's treasury in Ireland, which over the next four years contributed at least £1,008.[202] An entry on the memoranda rolls confirms that, by 29 April 1288, the earl's relationship with the Italians had been brought to a satisfactory conclusion.[203] He had indeed borrowed money on a large scale; but over a period of just ten years, he had paid his debts in full.

What Roger's dealings with the Riccardi reveal is not a man crippled by debt, but a great magnate who, like his king, had availed himself of perfectly normal credit mechanisms, probably to finance his (admittedly ambitious) building programmes. In addition to his castle-building operations in Ireland and at Chepstow, Roger was also backing the monks of Tintern in their effort to build a new abbey church.[204] As, however, his repayments prove, these construction projects were well within his means. East Anglia, where the bulk of the earl's estate lay, was perhaps the most prosperous area in the kingdom. Densely populated (by thirteenth-century standards) and in the van of agricultural development,[205] it was also perfectly positioned to capitalize on the lucrative wool trade with the Continent.[206] In 1282, Roger expanded his demesne in the region by purchasing the Norfolk manor of Loddon (as well as a string of tenements in the surrounding area).[207] In Ireland, meanwhile, the earl's affairs looked, if anything, even more sanguine. In the 1280s, thanks to the ongoing need to supply troops and construction workers in North Wales, Carlow's economy was booming. At Old Ross and Ballysax the size of the earl's flocks reached record levels.[208] Previously uncultivated outlying territory

---

[201] E159/55, m. 10d. (£1,133 is given as 1,700m)

[202] SC6/1239/4 (£413 2s 2d); SC6/1239/6 (£360 3s 4d); SC6/1239/7 (£8 6s 8d and £226).

[203] E159/61, m. 7.

[204] Roger could easily have been involved with the project since its inception in 1269, at which point he may have taken over the running of his uncle's estate (above, p. 99). Before 1276 the earl had granted the monks his church of Halvergate in Norfolk, as well as half an acre of marshland in the same vill. RBIV 4; cf. D.M. Robinson, *Tintern Abbey* (Cardiff, 2002), pp. 14, 32. For other early grants to Tintern, see RBIV 1 and 13.

[205] *The Agrarian History of England and Wales*, vol. 2, ed. E. Hallam (Cambridge, 1988), pp. 139-174; R. Britnell, *The Commercialisation of English Society, 1000-1500* (Manchester, 1996), p. 124. Campbell, *English Seigniorial Agriculture*, pp. 51-4, also endorses this view, but notes the variable quality of land in Norfolk.

[206] For example, the 'thirty or more' sacks of wool which Aline la Despenser sought licence to export in 1273-74 was probably worth around £250. Above, p. 109, and cf. Davies, *Lordship and Society*, p. 119.

[207] *CCR, 1279-88*, pp. 190, 195. See SC6/934/1; SC6/935/9; SC6/935/10; SC6/1005/26 for expenses involved in this transaction.

[208] Lyons, 'Manorial Administration', pp. 57, 67-75. See also M.C. Lyons, 'The Manor of Ballysax, 1280-86', *Retrospect*, new ser., 1 (1981), pp. 40-50, and *idem*, 'An Account of the Manor of Old Ross, September 1284–September 1285, parts I and II', *Decies*, xxviii–xix (1981-82), 33-40, 18-31, which contain transcripts of SC6/1237/5 and SC6/1238/48.

was brought under the plough for the first time, a policy which involved investing in out-granges such as that constructed at Ballyconnor.[209] In County Carlow itself, a second new manorial development was launched at Dunleckny, a few miles west of the successful experiment at Fennagh.[210] Unburdened (except on one occasion) by the demands of the comital household, the treasury at Carlow Castle quickly filled with cash, enough to satisfy the Riccardi, and even to consider paying the Dublin exchequer. While Roger took out large loans to invest in stone and mortar, he did so safe in the knowledge that his estates could generate such huge surpluses.

To put the issue of debt into its proper perspective, however, is not to argue that the late 1280s were entirely free from tension. The appearance of calm relations between Edward and Roger at this point is in part an illusion created by the king's absence abroad. Like many other magnates, the earl had been vexed since 1278 by the *Quo Warranto* proceedings, which obliged landowners everywhere to justify their liberties in the face of vigorous counter-claims by Crown prosecutors.[211] It was a deeply irritating and highly expensive business. Lawyers had to be hired to defend perfectly legitimate ancient rights; jurors had to be rewarded in cases where the entitlement was not quite as old and unimpeachable.[212] Roger found himself forced to respond for all his English properties and, despite much expenditure, he sustained several losses.[213] At Colby in Norfolk he lost the view of frankpledge, at his wife's manor of Woking he lost judicial rights, and at Stoke, Stoughton, Forncett and Sutton he lost the right to free warren.[214] Such losses, while small, may have engendered considerable resentment.[215]

There were other indications of unease during Edward's absence. When in the summer of 1287 the disgruntled Welsh lord Rhys ap Maredudd led a minor uprising in South Wales, Roger was quick to assist in its suppression.[216] In the course of the campaign, however, something was done in respect of his rights as marshal which appears to have given him cause for concern, perhaps even anger. On 17 September, soon after the fall of Rhys's castle at Dryslwyn, the king's regent (Edmund of Cornwall) promised the earl that 'nothing done by him or his men in the suppression

---

[209] B. Colfer, 'In Search of the Barricade and Ditch of Ballyconnor, Co. Wexford', *Archaeology Ireland*, 10 (1996), pp. 16-19.

[210] Lyons, 'Manorial Administration', p. 64.

[211] Prestwich, *Edward I*, pp. 258-64.

[212] For the money Roger spent 'preserving' his liberties, see Denholm-Young, *SAIE*, pp. 113-16; T.F.T. Plucknett, *Legislation of Edward I* (Oxford, 1949), pp. 44-5.

[213] *PQW*, pp. 12, 102, 192, 306, 350, 482-3, 491-5, 729-30, 735-6, 740, 746, 755-6.

[214] *PQW*, pp. 482-3, 740, 746, 755-6. No proceedings survive for Forncett, but the loss of warren there is evident from the re-grant, below, p. 136, and from *Rot. Hund.*, i, 472.

[215] Cf. Prestwich, *Edward I*, p. 262, where the extent of the earl's losses is underestimated.

[216] *CPR, 1281-92*, pp. 272-3; Davies, *Conquest, Coexistence and Change*, pp. 380-81.

of the rebellion...shall be to the prejudice of the marshalcy'.[217] It is the first recorded instance of controversy on an issue which would contribute to the strained relations between Roger and Edward in the coming decade. There was also trouble the following year, when insurrection again raised its head – this time in England. On 22 August, Cornwall wrote to a considerable number of magnates, warning them, on pain of forfeiture, against 'going with horses and arms, or otherwise with an armed band in the realm'. Roger was included in the list, as were the earls of Gloucester, Surrey and Warwick, Hugh Despenser, Richard fitz John and Reginald de Grey. Letters publicizing the prohibition were sent to all sheriffs; whatever the problem was, it was nationwide in its extent. The murmurs are mysterious; there is no indication that any dialogue took place in October (as the regents proposed), or that Edward, after his return, took any reprisals. All we can conclude from the episode is that Roger, and other great men like him, were harbouring unspecified grievances against the king's government.[218]

In spite of this, however, it is difficult to see the earl simmering with discontent during the 1280s. The demands being made on his pocket by the king were not unreasonable and, since they had been attermined, were far from excessive. The *Quo Warranto* campaign was perhaps more aggravating, a fact which Edward appears to have belatedly recognized when he restored to Roger two of his lost warrens.[219] Yet there is nothing to suggest that the earl was worse hit than any of his contemporaries; his comital status may, in fact, have enabled him to get away with more than most others.[220] Against these irritations, there were many other reasons for the earl to be cheerful. The Welsh war had gained him considerable credit, and the economy of his Irish estate was booming thanks to the new markets the conflict had created. The large loans he had negotiated, probably for his building projects, had been entirely paid off. The new abbey church at Tintern was looking more and more splendid; Roger was probably present in April 1287 and October 1288 to hear the first masses sung in its newly completed sections.[221] Downriver at Chepstow, work had begun on a giant new tower (Marten's Tower), possibly inspired by

[217] *CPR, 1281-92*, p. 277.
[218] *CCR, 1279-88*, p. 547.
[219] *Rôles Gascons*, ed. Francisque-Michel and C. Bémont (3 vols., Paris, 1885-1906), ii, 441. The warrens in question were at Stoke and Forncett. Roger was simultaneously granted a market and fair at his Suffolk manor of Walton. The movements of both these charters can be traced in some detail. In 1289 a crier (*criator*) was paid 6d for proclaiming the warren of Stoke, and the clerk of the sheriff of Sussex was paid 2s for reading the king's grant in the county court. 18d was paid to the boy who took the charter to Norfolk, so the same processes could be repeated for Forncett. In the same year, Sir Philip de Buckland and others received 8s ½d, their expenses for reading and declaring the Walton charter at Ipswich. SC6/1020/17; SC6/1007/14.
[220] D.W. Sutherland, *Quo Warranto Proceedings in the Reign of Edward I* (Oxford, 1963), p. 83.
[221] Robinson, *Tintern Abbey*, p. 32.

the king's visit to the castle, and perhaps intended as a royal guest suite. If so, it was a manifestation in stone of the new spirit of détente between the earl and his overlord.[222]

If Roger had reason to feel ill-favoured during these years, it was down to the series of personal misfortunes he had experienced. His wife had died in 1281 and, later in the decade, two of his younger brothers also appear to have perished. Ralph and Richard Bigod had undistinguished careers; neither features so much as once in the records of royal government. They do, however, appear from time to time in the Bigod estate accounts. Richard, the more obscure of the two, is mentioned five times between 1270 and 1283.[223] In all but one case little is recorded beyond the expense occasioned by his arrival. In 1283, however, it was noted that the prior of Dodnash had received a shilling a day for a whole year, 'for the care (*custod*) of Richard Bigod'.[224] Any number of explanations becomes imaginable: a simpleton from birth, in need of constant attention; a man seized with a sudden illness, forced into a lengthy convalescence; a bold knight, badly maimed in North Wales, hoping but failing to recover from his terrible injuries. All we can say for certain is that this was Richard's last appearance. Ralph Bigod is rather better documented, appearing in forty-nine rolls between 1271 and 1288.[225] For the most part these entries are as nondescript as those for his brother, but occasionally additional information is provided. In 1278-79 Ralph attended at least three separate tournaments, at Stamford, Blyth and Guildford.[226] Elsewhere he received money while in London, and for going to 'northern parts' – probably Settrington.[227] In 1288, however, his expenses suddenly cease. The same year, Philip de Buckland and Bartholomew the chaplain travelled from Framlingham to Lopham, 'to provide against the burial of Sir R. Bigod'.[228]

At the end of the decade, Roger realized his family was failing. He had no countess, no children, and only one remaining brother – the celibate clergyman John. It was high time, he must have reasoned, to find a new wife.

---

[222] Turner, *Chepstow Castle* (Cardiff, 2002), pp. 16-17, 42-4.
[223] SC6/932/11; SC6/1020/12; SC6/931/23; SC6/938/2; SC6/1007/11.
[224] SC6/1007/11.
[225] e.g. SC6/768/5 (1271); SC6/1005/28 (1288).
[226] SC6/873/7; SC6/837/13. Ralph has also been spotted hunting with his brothers Roger and John in the forest of Dean. J. Birrell, 'Aristocratic Poachers in the Forest of Dean: their methods, their quarry and their companions', *Transactions Bristol and Gloucestershire Archaeological Soc.*, 119 (2001), p. 148.
[227] SC6/837/16; SC6/837/14.
[228] SC6/997/6.

CHAPTER 5

Lordship, Leadership and Loss:
Roger IV Bigod, 1290-1306

CHANGES IN THE HOUSEHOLD

When Edward I returned to his kingdom on 12 August 1289, Roger Bigod was just on the verge of leaving it.[1] Barely two months later the earl appeared at Westminster and sought the king's licence to cross overseas.[2] The purpose of this trip is somewhat mysterious – the royal protection Roger received offers nothing in the way of further details; but, as ever, the earl's own accounts furnish the necessary clues. During the same year, three East Anglian bailiffs had noted the coming and going of certain strangers 'from Hainault'. At Chesterford in particular, foreign knights had arrived as recently as 3 October, and in the company of Sir Ranulf de Belgrave, a *familiaris* who was about to join Roger on his impending voyage.[3] All this suggests that Hainault, a small county in the Netherlands, was their intended destination a few weeks later. Count John de Avesnes would have been the earl's host, and Alice, the count's daughter, the mission's objective. In June the following year, at the royal manor of Havering in Essex, Roger and Alice were married.[4]

The arrival of a new countess of Norfolk meant major changes in the Bigod administration. In the first place, a series of elaborate steps were taken to guarantee Alice's dower. Shortly before his wedding, on 12 June 1290, Roger set aside twenty-two of his East Anglian manors for this purpose.[5] The following day, seemingly as part of the same arrangements, the earl was permitted to grant £300 of land to 'someone in whom he has confidence', who would in turn re-enfeoff him and his new wife jointly with the same properties. The transaction was supposed to be effected by means of a final concord, but unfortunately no such record has survived.[6] From other evidence, it seems that the manors involved were Caistor, Dovercourt, Kennett, Peasenhall, Suffield and Seething. The third party, initially at least, was either John Bigod, the earl's clerical brother, or John

---

[1] Prestwich, *Edward I*, p. 339.
[2] Appendix B; *CPR, 1281-92*, p. 325.
[3] SC6/768/14; SC6/932/22; SC6/837/18.
[4] *Chronica Johannis de Oxenedes*, ed. H. Ellis (Rolls Ser., 1859), p. 276; *Bury*, p. 95; *Records of the Wardrobe and Household*, ed. Byerly and Byerly, p. 268; J.C. Parsons, *Eleanor of Castile: Queen and Society in Thirteenth-Century England* (New York, 1995), p. 50.
[5] RBIV 18. Seething was acquired with Loddon in 1282 (above, p. 134). It is not clear how or when the earl obtained Woodton or Yaxham. There is one account roll for Woodton, dated 1283. SC6/945/8.
[6] *CPR, 1281-92*, pp. 363-4.

Bigod of Stockton, his cousin.[7] The following year, however, the whole process was repeated, this time with Edward I as middleman; Roger surrendered the manors to the king in April and received them back as a joint enfeoffment in August.[8] Again, the precise terms have not been preserved, and it is unclear why the transaction had to be carried out a second time. There is nothing, however, to indicate that Edward's involvement was in any way sinister.[9]

A more visible change was the establishment of a separate household to cater for the countess. Like the earl's own household, little is known about the internal workings of this new institution.[10] It was headed, financially at least, by Goscelin the chaplain, who occurs from the time of Alice's arrival up until 1299.[11] A surviving (and unique) household roll of February 1295 gives some idea of his daily expenditure, but little else besides.[12] Of the other personnel almost nothing is known. There are references to Baldwin of Hainault, the countess's chaplain, Adam 'of the countess's chamber', and Agnes, one of her damsels; in practice there was probably a considerable overlap between the senior figures in Alice's *familia* and those in the earl's own establishment.[13] Nevertheless, the creation of this new institution, and the increase in expenditure needed to sustain it, represented a major change to Roger's domestic arrangements.[14]

The year 1289-90 also witnessed major upheavals in the earl's household, culminating in the fall of his chief counsellor, Thomas Weyland. Born of fairly humble peasant stock, Weyland had prospered to become a knight of considerable wealth and learning, largely through his connection with the Bigod family. His career was anticipated to some extent by his elder brother, William, who had acted as seneschal of Ireland for the previous earl in the 1250s, and Thomas himself had become a Bigod tenant in 1259 when he purchased the Suffolk manor of Blaxhall. It was not, however, until the succession of the new earl in 1270 that Thomas

---

[7] Accounts for the year 1290-91 survive for Peasenhall and Kennett. SC6/768/15 (Kennett) contains expenses for 'Philip the clerk and others with him to reseize the manor from John Bigod', and also notes payments made to John's bailiff, Andrew, and his clerk, Richard. SC6/1003/15 (Peasenhall) records Andrew's expenses 'for keeping the seisin of John Bigod', and a court held by 'Sir Baldwin, knight of Hainault, chaplain of the countess and Richard the clerk, attorney of Sir J. Bigod'.

[8] RBIV 19; *CPR, 1281-92*, p. 441.

[9] It does not correspond, for example, to the surrender of four manors in 1275, or the entail created in 1277. Above, pp. 115, 117-8, and cf. Prestwich, *War, Politics and Finance*, p. 237.

[10] For an exploration of a comparable comitissal household, see M.W. Labarge, *A Baronial Household of the Thirteenth Century* (Brighton, 1965).

[11] e.g. from SC6/932/22 to SC6/873/20.

[12] E101/531/12. My thanks to Stephen Priestly for sharing his transcript of this document.

[13] SC6/1003/15; SC6/837/24; SC6/768/17.

[14] e.g. SC6/998/29 ('to Goscelin for the countess's expenses, £114 17s 10½d'); SC6/873/20 ('to Goscelin the chaplain for the countess, £122 8s 8½d'). See also SC6/991/24, which details repairs to the countess's lodgings and chapel at Bungay Castle in 1294.

emerged as prime mover of the Bigods' affairs.[15] Over the next decade, he acted as accountant and attorney for the family on numerous occasions, the closeness of his relationship with Roger underlined by the gifts of deer he took in the earl's parks, and the employment of Ralph Gugon, the Bigod master-mason, at Weyland's Gloucestershire manor of Chipping Sodbury.[16] During precisely the same period, Thomas was rising rapidly through the ranks of the judiciary; first selected as a royal justice in 1272, he was appointed chief justice of Common Pleas in 1278. Disgruntled former litigants would later allege that Weyland's involvement with Roger led to judgements biased in the earl's favour. In general, however, there was no objection to the existence of such close relationships between royal justices and great magnates.[17] Weyland's fall in 1289 was precipitated not by his apparent conflict of interests, which was wholly unexceptional, but by a murder committed by two of his servants in the summer of that year. The chief justice was found guilty of concealment; he had known about the killing and sheltered the killers. Arrest and imprisonment (and, briefly, escape) were soon followed by exile.[18]

Weyland's disgrace was not the only scandal to rock Roger's establishment at this time. In June 1288, two of the earl's officials had been accused of committing a similarly heinous crime. Robert de Benhall and Geoffrey Atwater were said to have abducted William le Rede from his house at Acle and carted him off to Bungay Castle, where they maltreated him until he died. Arrested on the appeal of the dead man's brother and widow, the pair were found guilty as charged and imprisoned. As it turned out, however, they had been framed: a subsequent investigation by a grand assize jury not only exposed inconsistencies in the appellants' testimony; the jurors went on to declare that the appeal against Benhall and Atwater had been maliciously engineered by eight other Bigod officials, acting with the cognizance of Roger himself.[19] Benhall, it later emerged, had crossed swords with these men during his time as the earl's seneschal in Norfolk. What followed was an extraordinary struggle as he and Atwater tried to gain redress against their persecutors and recover their confiscated property. The accused, for their part, denied any guilt, and used every means in their power to frustrate the judicial process (at one point they travelled to Norwich and seized the lists of jurors from the

---

[15] Brand, 'Chief Justice', pp. 115-19; above, p. 113.

[16] SC6/932/13 (as accountant, with his brother, William); *CPR, 1272-81*, p. 319; *CCR, 1272-79*, pp. 475, 560-62, (as attorney); SC6/991/17 (1275: 'Thomas Weyland, for his expenses in London at parliament, £6 13s 4d'); SC6/997/2 and SC6/933/25 (hunting); SC6/921/23 (Chipping Sodbury).

[17] Brand, 'Chief Justice', pp. 120, 128-9; J.R. Maddicott, *Law and Lordship: Royal Justices as Retainers in Thirteenth- and Fourteenth-Century England* (Past and Present Supplement, 1978), p. 16.

[18] Brand, 'Chief Justice', pp. 113, 131-2.

[19] *CIM*, i, 410-11, 614; KB27/114, mm. 35, 50d. William was provost of Acle in 1277-78 and 1278-79. SC6/944/25; SC6/929/6.

coroners). For Robert de Benhall, dogged determination eventually paid off; in July 1289 a court awarded him damages of £300. Geoffrey Atwater, however, was not so lucky. Earlier in the same year a jury declared that he was a villein, and therefore threw out his plea.[20]

It is extremely tempting to try to link the two scandals together. The murdered man in the Weyland affair was variously described as 'Carewel the Forester' and 'William Carwel of Ireland'. Could he have been Cearbhaill Ó Foirchtern, associate of Art MacMurrough, licensed to visit Earl Roger in 1281? If so, his murder could plausibly have been part of the wider feud revealed in the Benhall–Atwater case.[21] Did Thomas take the wrong side in this dispute, and end up crossing his master? The earl certainly did nothing to save the man who had served him loyally for two decades, and seized Weyland's escheated estates as eagerly as he had confiscated the property of Benhall and Atwater.[22] Might the chief justice's fall (and, by implication, the king's subsequent purge of the higher judiciary) have been caused by the wrath of Roger Bigod? Sadly, there is not evidence enough to support such wild imaginings;[23] the connection which links Weyland, Benhall and Atwater is impossibly slight.[24] The most we can say is that there were major ructions in the earl's household during the summer of 1289, and that by the end of the year that body had lost its most important and longest-serving member.

Who else was important in Roger's inner circle during the first two decades of his career? In trying to answer this question we find that, once again, the earl presents a number of interesting contrasts to his uncle. In the first place, we have considerably more charters for the younger Roger. His thirty-three surviving deeds, while still a small corpus by contemporary magnate standards, seem impressive against his uncle's paltry cache of thirteen. They are, however, less homogeneous. While few of Roger III's *acta* can be precisely dated or located, it seems likely that the

---

[20] KB27/116, mm. 15d, 23; KB27/118, mm. 22, 23d; KB27/123, m. 9; KB27/124, m. 23; KB27/125, mm. 2d, 46d; JUST/1/1282, m. 32d. Even then this was not the end of the matter. The earl continued his vendetta against Robert de Benhall, alleging in 1297 that as receiver of Framlingham the former seneschal had defrauded him of £600. Geoffrey Atwater, meanwhile, continued to press his case for compensation, later accusing the royal judge William de Brompton of rigging the jury that had pronounced him unfree. CP40/116, m. 42; *State Trials of the Reign of Edward the First, 1289-1293*, ed. T.F. Tout and H. Johnstone (Camden Soc., 3rd ser., ix, 1906), xlvi.

[21] Brand, 'Chief Justice', pp. 131-2; above, p. 124.

[22] *CCR, 1288-96*, p. 75; *Rot. Parl.*, i, 46.

[23] If only one could read the letters which Benhall and Atwater sent to one another the weeks between the inquiry into Rede's death and their arrest in June! SC6/1020/16 (Bosham, 1287-88) includes expenses for 'a boy going to London taking letters of G. de Aqua to Robert de Benhall' and 'Richard le Bukere going to Framlingham taking letters of Robert de Benhall to Geoffrey de Aqua, Sunday before St Dunstan [15 May 1288]'.

[24] Benhall mainperned for John Weyland, son of Thomas, after his father's arrest. *CCR, 1288-96*, p. 59. Cf. Brand, 'Chief Justice', p. 131.

majority were drawn up in East Anglia, and that, limited in number though they are, they give a true reflection of the earl's entourage at the peak of his career. By contrast, most of the deeds issued by Roger IV have dating clauses which indicate that they were issued in a variety of places; not only in East Anglia, but also in London, Wales, Yorkshire and Ireland. As a result, their usefulness as evidence for identifying the earl's *familiares* is reduced, for in certain contexts the witness lists are unlikely to give a true picture of the comital *familia*. When, for example, the earl was at Chepstow, his local tenants took precedence over his regular retainers. The same was true in Ireland; in Roger's charter to New Ross, tenants predominate to the extent of excluding the ordinary entourage altogether.[25] If a charter was drawn up at court, its witness list was especially prone to being 'contaminated' by individuals drawn from outside the comital household, and distinguishing between the king's servants and Roger's own men becomes almost impossible.[26] Even when a charter was drawn up in East Anglia, there is no guarantee that those who witnessed it were intimate members of the earl's circle.[27] Furthermore, whereas we are lucky to possess several lists of Roger III's *familiares* explicitly identifying them as such, there is no comparable evidence for his nephew's followers. Once again, however, the saving grace is the ministers' accounts, wherein the last earl's *familiares* are sometimes named as such, or revealed by the nature of their activities.

A good indication of Roger IV's circle at the start of his career is provided by the witness list to charter RBIV 4, which is datable to the period 1271 x 1276. Although the grant is to Tintern Abbey, the appearance of the earl's seneschal of Norfolk and the toponymic surnames of other witnesses suggest it was drawn up in East Anglia. The witness list is headed by four knights, including Thomas Weyland, and the otherwise undistinguished William de Valeynes.[28] Chief among their number, however, are two men who had served Roger's uncle. Robert Hovel, a member of the old earl's entourage since the mid-1240s, took precedence over Philip de Buckland, who first appears in 1257.[29] Hovel, indeed, may well have been senior in years; his last appearance in Bigod circles was 1277, and he was certainly dead by 1286.[30] Buckland, as we have already seen, played a more prominent role in the service of his new master, acting as both an auditor of Roger's accounts and seneschal of Carlow from 1280

---

[25] RBIV 10. The reference to 'a boy of Henry de Tuddenham, staying sick at Carlow' during Roger's visit shows that the earl was attended in Ireland by his regular followers. SC6/1239/1; below, p. 148.

[26] Cf. Ridgeway, 'William de Valence and his *Familiares*', p. 242.

[27] e.g. RBIV 16.

[28] Valeynes reappears in 1294. Ridgard, p. 49.

[29] *CPR, 1232-47*, p. 454; *CR, 1256-59*, pp. 151-2; above, pp. 64, 67.

[30] *PQW*, p. 735. His son, also Robert, died in 1288, and was succeeded by his under-age brother, Hugh. SC6/995/3; Muskett, *Suffolk Manorial Families*, ii, 62.

to 1282.[31] His duties as a *familiaris* continued throughout the 1280s and beyond,[32] until June 1293, when he took up residence at the Bigod manor of Hollesley. After several months convalescing by the Suffolk coast, his lifelong service came to an end on 3 February 1294, when sixteen shillings were spent on his funeral.[33]

Hovel and Buckland were the only prominent members of the old guard who continued to serve under the new regime; other individuals of the same generation, no less distinguished, elected not to do so. The importance of Thomas Lenebaud, John de Vaux, Richard de Holbrook and Henry de Rushall among the *familiares* of Roger III Bigod was underlined by their appointment as his executors. It was, however, on precisely the issue of executing the old earl's will that these men fell out with his successor. In 1277 they were forced to defend themselves in court against Roger IV, who accused them of illegally retaining goods and chattels from his uncle's estate. It may, of course, have been a regrettable misunderstanding that led to this litigation, and deprived the new earl of several distinguished old hands. It is also possible, however, that their argument was symptomatic of a wider trend of desertion. Hubert de Bavent, perhaps the only other veteran of equal weight, also survived until the mid-1280s; yet neither he nor his son Thomas ever feature in connection with Roger IV. The Bavents had been Bigod tenants for at least three generations, but in 1270 a tradition of service stretching back to 1166 and beyond came to a sudden end.[34]

New men appeared to fill the void. Roger's cousin, John Bigod of Stockton, witnesses comital charters on at least four and possibly six occasions.[35] These are concentrated in the latter part of the earl's career, but the ministers' accounts show John was a regular visitor to Bigod manors from 1271.[36] John ap Adam, who witnesses five charters (again, all after 1290, with the last being 1305) was a regular member of the affinity from at least 1277.[37] He appears frequently in the accounts between 1284 and 1304,[38] and was one of the men who crossed to Hainault with the earl in 1289.[39]

---

[31] Above, p. 121.
[32] Above, pp. 136n, 137; also SC6/748/18; SC6/768/8; SC6/873/7; SC6/935/28; SC6/991/19; SC6/997/3; SC6/1237/40; SC6/1239/1; SC6/1238/25; SC6/1239/10; SC6/1237/14.
[33] SC6/998/26; SC6/998/27.
[34] Above, pp. 64-6, 69, 72, 97-8; *CIPM*, iv, 301.
[35] RBIV 27, 28, 31, 32. RBIV 18 and 29 could be the earl's brother. As well as Stockton, John held Theberton in Suffolk, St Mullins in Co. Carlow, and Aghmacart in Co. Kilkenny. Above, p. 38n; below, p. 133n.
[36] SC6/937/29. For other certain references to him (as distinct from the earl's brother), see SC6/991/18; SC6/995/2; SC6/991/20; SC6/997/4; SC6/998/23; SC6/921/24; SC6/934/2; SC6/1000/14; SC6/938/4; SC6/938/5; SC6/921/27.
[37] RBIV 18, 19, 20, 21, 33; *CPR, 1272-81*, p. 217.
[38] SC6/997/5; SC6/921/26; SC6/991/21; SC6/991/22; SC6/997/6; SC6/922/5; SC6/748/24; SC6/768/18; SC6/1006/5.
[39] *CPR, 1281-92*, p. 325.

If the presence of John Bigod of Stockton shows that Roger recruited along traditional East Anglian lines, the appearance of John ap Adam reveals the earl's readiness to seek support from outside the eastern counties. In the 1290s ap Adam inherited substantial estates in Somerset, Wiltshire, Gloucestershire and Sussex in right of his wife. His ancestral lands, however, were the manors of Beachley and Gorste, which lay in Roger's lordship of Chepstow.[40] In general the Bigods had only intermittent contact with their tenants in this region. The families of Seymour, de Mora and Bluet would attend the earl when he appeared at Chepstow, and help administer the lordship in his absence.[41] Only from time to time – perhaps when military service was required – would they join the earl's retinue. John ap Adam, however, was an exception to this general rule. Fully absorbed into the inner circle, John attended Roger wherever he travelled, and until the very end of his career.

Perhaps the most important clerk in Roger's administration during his first decade as earl was Geoffrey de Aspall. Like Thomas Weyland (with whom he stood as co-attorney for the earl in 1279), Geoffrey was clearly comfortable serving a number of masters simultaneously.[42] In 1265 he had been in the employ of the earl of Gloucester, and from 1277 he was engaged to serve the queen.[43] If this renders ambiguous some of his charter witnessings, Aspall's appearances in SC6 leave no doubt that Roger was his principal backer during the 1270s, and at least three of the fifteen livings he had acquired by the end of the decade were gifts from the earl.[44] After 1280, however, the well-beneficed clerk disappears from the earl's circle.[45] His new job as the queen's wardrober, coupled with his career as a prolific writer, were probably sufficient to occupy him until his death in 1287.[46]

Men such as Aspall and Weyland were members of Roger's 'council', a select group of individuals whom the earl could assemble when required to advise him in the direction of his affairs. Sadly, the evidence for the activities of this body is exiguous, and proves little beyond its existence as

[40] *Peerage*, i, 179-80; *CIPM*, iv, 294. See also RBIV 23.
[41] Cf. Appendix D and Crouch, *William Marshal*, p. 149. Roger III Bigod hunted with Ralph Bluet in the forest of Dean in 1251. E32/28, m. 4.
[42] E159/49, m. 2; *CCR, 1272-79*, p. 319. When Roger surrendered four manors to the king in 1275, Aspall was their temporary custodian. *CFR, 1272-1307*, p. 50.
[43] A.B. Emden, *A Bibliographical Register of the University of Oxford to A.D. 1500* (3 vols., Oxford, 1957-59), i, 61.
[44] RBIV 5, 7, 9; SC6/932/12; SC6/937/30; SC6/991/17; SC6/997/2; SC6/991/18; SC6/937/33; SC6/936/21; SC6/748/18; SC6/936/23; SC6/1000/12; SC6/936/24; SC6/944/3; SC6/768/9; Emden, *Bibliographical Register*, i, 61; *CIPM*, iv, 302, 304 (for the advowsons of Forncett, Starston and Tunstall).
[45] Curiously, a Roger de Aspall, perhaps a relative of Master Geoffrey, makes his debut at this point, and occurs as a *familiaris* down to 1287. E.g. SC6/1007/10; SC6/837/16; SC6/873/11; SC6/997/4; SC6/997/5; *Register of John Pecham*, ii, 144.
[46] Emden, *Bibliographical Register*, i, 61. For Geoffrey's literary output, see R. Sharpe, *A Handlist of Latin Writers of Great Britain and Ireland before 1540* (Turnhout, 1997), pp. 120-21.

an institution. In 1287, following a heated dispute between the Bigod bailiffs at Kelsale and certain men from nearby Dunwich, Roger demanded satisfaction from the townsmen 'by some of his council'.[47] Four years later, William de Ormesby 'and others of the earl's council' were paid 'for the earl's business before the justices at Norwich'.[48] Lastly, in 1303, there was a meeting of the council at Bungay Castle, at which Roger and his advisers carried out what looks to have been an extraordinary audit of his accounts.[49] Limited though these references are, they indicate that the earl's council was typical in concerning itself primarily with judicial and financial matters. Aristocratic councils had originated around the middle of the thirteenth century, by which time the switch from leasing to direct farming, combined with the mounting challenge to franchises from an increasingly combative Crown, had made it desirable for great landowners to retain permanently men with legal and financial expertise.[50] Thomas Weyland, a knight with clerical training and a royal justice, is the one man in Roger's entourage who most clearly fits this profile, and indeed in 1289 he was described as the earl's 'chief councillor'.[51] Geoffrey de Aspall, clearly an intellectual heavyweight, is another obvious contender for council membership. It was not the case, however, that all councillors had to be judges or clerks. A comparison with the earl of Gloucester's working practices would suggest that many members of Roger's council – perhaps the majority – would have been drawn from the ranks of his household knights; thus most of the men discussed above, such as Robert Hovel and Philip de Buckland, John ap Adam and John Bigod of Stockton, would almost certainly have attended meetings of the council and added their voice to its debates.[52]

How large was the Bigod household? It is clear from the surviving accounts that hundreds of individuals were involved in running Roger's estate, from councillors, receivers and wardrobers, through reeves and bailiffs, right down to groundsmen, ferrymen and fishermen.[53] At the same time, it is hard to find evidence for important knights or 'bachelors' in the first two decades of the earl's career beyond the individuals discussed above.[54] All of which is to say, the question of the size of 'the

---

[47] *CIM*, i, 406.
[48] SC6/935/34. For more on Ormesby, see below, pp. 152, 179.
[49] SC6/995/24; SC6/1005/19; SC6/999/2; SC6/1000/21.
[50] Maddicott, *Law and Lordship*, pp. 9-11. Cf. Denholm-Young, *SAIE*, pp. 25-31.
[51] Brand, 'Chief Justice', p. 129.
[52] Altschul, *Baronial Family*, pp. 235-6.
[53] SC6/1238/33 (ferryman); SC6/1004/8 (fisherman); SC6/1238/28 (men cutting the meadows).
[54] For debate on the meaning of the word 'bachelor', see 'Private Indentures for Life Service in Peace and War, 1278-1476', ed. M. Jones and S. Walker, *Camden Miscellany XXXII* (Camden Soc., 5th ser., iii, 1994), 19-20, and J.M.W. Bean, *From Lord to Patron: Lordship in Late Medieval England* (Manchester, 1989), pp. 22-32.

household' depends entirely on how we decide to define its membership. Consider, for instance, the varying estimates on the size of the household of the greatest magnate of the early fourteenth century, Thomas of Lancaster. J.R. Maddicott bases his estimate on a prosopographical treatment of a particular year's wardrobe account, and postulates a household of fifty to fifty-five. J.M.W. Bean prefers to extrapolate from the amount of cloth used for liveries, and suggests a figure nearly three times as large. Both estimates are dwarfed by that of C.M. Woolgar, who works from levels of food consumption, and concludes that the household must have consisted of more than 700 people. All three authors, however, as well as using the evidence in different ways, are using different definitions of 'the household'. Maddicott (who speaks of 'the retinue') confines his count to knights; Bean (despite objecting to Maddicott's figures) includes in his count both knights and esquires; Woolgar, meanwhile, assumes a very wide definition indeed, including not only retainers and household servants, but also grooms, guests, and even the poor.[55]

Where should we draw the line with Roger Bigod? With no surviving household accounts, we have to rely on the documents drafted by receivers and bailiffs, which give only a worm's-eye view of the comital administration. Consequently the lesser, local staff feature more prominently than the members of the earl's *familia*. Correcting for this lowly perspective, we should certainly pass over the reeves and bailiffs on each manor, and probably also the receivers and constables; typically, all these posts were filled by men of low status.[56] The seneschals, by contrast, were important men, probably regular attendees of the comital council, and should therefore probably be considered as members of the household as well.[57] Nevertheless, it is necessary to issue a number of caveats. The importance of the seneschal had been declining in the thirteenth century, as a number of his administrative and financial tasks were transferred to other officials like the wardrober and the receiver.[58] Whereas at one time it had been common practice for lords to circulate the office among their closest *familiares* (who regarded the appointment as a desirable reward), this appears not to have been true by the time of Roger IV Bigod.[59] Exceedingly few of the earl's seneschals were drawn from the ranks of his household knights. Philip de Buckland, seneschal of Carlow

---

[55] Maddicott, *Thomas of Lancaster*, p. 45; Bean, *From Lord to Patron*, pp. 155-7; C.M. Woolgar, *The Great Household in Late Medieval England* (New Haven, 1999), p. 12. All three estimates have the virtue of being grounded on correctly attributed documentary evidence, which is not the case with the figures presented in K. Mertes, *The English Noble Household 1250-1600* (Oxford, 1988), pp. 11, 82, 214; cf. Crouch, *Image of Aristocracy*, pp. 293-4 and *Household Accounts from Medieval England*, ed. C.M. Woolgar (2 vols., Oxford, 1992), ii, 692.

[56] Denholm-Young, *SAIE*, pp. 32-4, 45.

[57] The same was also true of the wardrober. Altschul, *Baronial Family*, p. 236.

[58] Denholm-Young, *SAIE*, p. 69.

[59] Crouch, *William Marshal*, pp. 172-3.

from 1280 to 1282, was a clear exception, appointed as he was during conditions of crisis.[60] William de Glanville, who served first as seneschal of Chepstow and later as seneschal of Norfolk, also appears to have been a householder in his own right.[61] Beyond this, however, there is no evidence of overlap. We can produce quite full lists of names for all the Bigod seneschalcies, and the vast majority of postholders cannot be otherwise linked to the earl's inner circle. Mostly they served for short periods of time – one or two years – after which they presumably moved on to serve other masters.[62]

If seneschals were not necessarily drawn from the ranks of the earl's bachelors, they were often of equivalent status; that is to say, they too were knights, and as such they were well paid. The seneschal of Carlow, as we have already seen, received the very large annual salary of £100.[63] His counterparts in Chepstow and East Anglia received smaller but still substantial sums: around £30 a year if they were knights, around £10 a year if they were not.[64] The distribution of such monetary fees (and, to a lesser extent, of robes) provides another means of identifying important members of the earl's circle. In some instances, fees are paid to lesser members of staff such as constables and foresters.[65] In other cases, the fee in question is only a temporary retainer, such as the frequent payments made to lawyers for the duration of particular cases.[66] There are also some occasions when fees appear to have been paid for political reasons rather than as reward for specific services (for example, the fees, robes and gifts given to the MacMurrough brothers, and perhaps also the fee paid to John de Kirkby).[67] In a handful of cases, however, we find some quite large fees being paid to men with no clear administrative function. Walter de

---

[60] Above, p. 121; Appendix D.

[61] Appendix D. Glanville occurs frequently from 1271-72 (SC6/921/21) until 1290 (SC6/944/29). Not listed with the knights in RBIV 4, he looks to have been knighted subsequently (his fee as seneschal of Chepstow was equivalent to that of Walter de Redisham: SC6/921/23; below, n. 64). Glanville left Chepstow after the outbreak of the second Welsh war, probably to join the earl on campaign.

[62] Cf. Denholm-Young, *SAIE*, p. 70. In this context, note that none of the seven identifiable seneschals of Roger III Bigod appears in any of the lists of his *familiares*. Appendix D; above, p. 60.

[63] Above, p. 121.

[64] Ralph de Crepping, a knight, was paid £26 13s 4d (40m) as seneschal of East Anglia for 13 Edward I, but John de Stanes, presumably of non-knightly status, received only £8 6s 8d (12½m) for 9 Edward I. Dated payments to Sir Walter de Redisham at Chepstow suggest that he took c. £30 a year, and Sir Geoffrey de Wroxhall, 'seneschal for half a year', received £16. However, in 1283, John Baret, esquire, was paid only 32s 6d for keeping the castle for 45 days, equivalent to just over £13 per annum SC6/935/11; SC6/1007/10; SC6/921/24; SC6/921/28.

[65] e.g. SC6/1239/2 (Ralph de Lund, constable of Old Ross); SC6/922/3 (John de Newent, forester).

[66] e.g. SC6/768/9; SC6/837/14; SC6/938/3 (John de Livermere); SC6/936/10 (William de Gisleham); SC6/935/26 (Robert de Bosco); SC6/873/9; SC6/936/31 (John de Bocking).

[67] Above, p. 123; SC6/837/13.

Eversley, a Berkshire knight who witnesses three of Roger's charters, was also in receipt of a five-mark fee from the earl. Thus, although his attendance seems far from regular, he might well be regarded as a household knight.[68] Likewise, Fulk de Vaux, a witness to two comital charters, received a fee of £10 in return for acting as the earl's deputy marshal in the royal household.[69] Meanwhile, Henry de Tuddenham, a man with only one charter to his name, received £5 as 'his fee for Michaelmas term', which (presumably) equated to £20 a year.[70]

The size of Tuddenham's fee is all the more surprising because he was an esquire rather than a knight.[71] We can identify a number of men of this degree in the Bigod household from the late 1280s. John de Frating occurs between 1286 and 1296, while John de Shottesbrooke features from 1287 down to 1294.[72] Tuddenham himself had an especially long career in service, beginning in 1275 and lasting until 1296.[73] Their duties as recorded in the accounts seem comparatively menial; several references to Tuddenham show him arriving to catch deer (and, on one occasion, fish).[74] There is little doubt, however, that these men were closely attached to Roger; on several occasions they are explicitly identified as members of his *familia*.[75] Whereas knights like Eversley or Vaux probably served in only a part-time capacity, Henry and his fellows were apparently permanently on-call, ready to accompany the earl at all times.[76]

The evidence for payment of fees, scanty though it is, nevertheless permits some reflection on the scale of the earl's household. In general it was rare for a magnate to spend more than 10 per cent of his income on retaining.[77] After 1281 (when he lost his first wife and her inheritance), Roger had an income much the same as that enjoyed by his uncle – i.e. somewhere in the vicinity of £2,500.[78] If, therefore, the earl was typical in his spending habits, and his bachelors customarily received fees of £20 a year, his retinue cannot have exceeded twelve or thirteen men. Even if his

---

[68] RBIV 9, 20, 21; SC6/1020/14. The proximity of Eversley's own estates to Hamstead Marshall, and perhaps his position as keeper of Pamber Forest, may explain his entrée. *CCR, 1268-72*, p. 196; *CPR, 1292-1301*, pp. 303, 329. Cf. *CCR, 1279-88*, p. 212 (also C81/1687/19); *CCR, 1288-96*, p. 97.

[69] RBIV 19, 20; SC6/1000/18; below, pp. 157, 160.

[70] RBIV 18; SC6/1007/11. Henry's retainer was certainly greater than £5. Elsewhere he received £7 6s 8d 'in part of his annual fee'. SC6/997/9.

[71] Ridgard, p. 49.

[72] SC6/748/20; SC6/837/21; *CPR, 1281-92*, pp. 272-3; Ridgard, p. 49. Also RBIV 18 and 21.

[73] SC6/1000/11 to SC6/837/21.

[74] SC6/997/5; SC6/837/19; SC6/837/21; SC6/1000/17.

[75] SC6/1006/2 ('expenses of John de Frating, Henry de Tuddenham and others *armators* of the earl coming from Bradley to Framlingham'); SC6/997/5 ('John Bigod, Roger de Aspall, John ap Adam, Henry de Tuddenham and others of the earl's retinue [*retinencie*]'); SC6/837/15 ('Henry de Tuddenham and others of the earl's household').

[76] Tuddenham, for example, crossed to Ireland with Roger in 1280. Above, n. 25.

[77] Bean, *From Lord to Patron*, p. 171.

[78] Above, pp. 41, 124-5.

income was closer to the £4,000 suggested by the king's commissioners in 1306, the number would only rise to twenty.[79] Clearly there are too many variables here to be absolutely certain – the fees for the men discussed above ranged from 5 marks to £30 a year, depending, it seems, on the scale of their duties. All indications, however, are that Roger's household was fundamentally similar in scale to those maintained by magnates in the mid-thirteenth century.[80] In normal circumstances, the earl probably retained between fifteen and twenty men, around half of whom might have accompanied him at any one time.[81] Neither the very limited financial data nor an exhaustive prosopographical trawl through the ministers' accounts will permit the figure to be pushed any higher.

The crucial qualifier here is the phrase 'in normal circumstances'; on certain extraordinary occasions, magnate households were liable to expand in size. When, in 1290, Roger IV attended the wedding of the king's daughter, Margaret, he was reportedly accompanied by a party of forty-eight liveried knights.[82] Similarly, his uncle took a larger than usual knightly contingent on his trip to Lyon in 1245 – a time when his income was still comparatively small.[83] What really forced the expansion of aristocratic households, however, was not ceremony or diplomacy but war. Sadly, we have no evidence for this transformation in the case of Roger III; the old earl must have increased the size of his retinue for campaigns in Wales and Gascony, and probably during the period 1258-65, but we do not know by what means or by how much.[84] By contrast, we are quite well informed about how the household of Roger IV operated in wartime; indeed, his retinue is better illuminated on campaign than it is in ordinary circumstances.

When the earl went to war in 1277, he took with him the stalwart members of his ordinary household: Robert Hovel, Philip de Buckland, John ap Adam and John Bigod of Stockton. Also in his company was a Chepstow tenant, William de Dernford, raising the possibility that other men from the lordship (who certainly owed military service) were present in the earl's contingent.[85] William de Lambourn, who perhaps hailed from a part of Berkshire not far from Hamstead Marshall, may have been drawn

---

[79] *CPR, 1301-1307*, p. 460.
[80] Above, p. 70.
[81] Above, pp. 68-70. With the exception of RBIV 10, no charter is witnessed by more than seven knights.
[82] Cotton, p. 177.
[83] Above, p. 70.
[84] Some of his extraordinary recruits after 1257 may be indicated by the witness list to RBIII 13.
[85] *Parl. Writs*, i, 198; *CPR, 1272-81*, pp. 217, 220. Dernford held Crick from Roger for half a knight's fee. In 1293 and 1294 he was paid a money fee of 50s, and received a further 50s for his robes. *CIPM*, iv, 298; SC6/922/3; SC6/922/5.

in by ties of neighbourhood.[86] The remaining members of Roger's retinue, however, were neither his tenants nor his neighbours. Stephen de Penshurst, Henry de Cobham, Roger de Mereworth and Simon de Cray were knights from Kent, an area of England to which the Bigod family had no historic ties, and where the earl's own territorial interests were insignificant.[87] They have every appearance of a sub-contingent, probably recruited specifically for the purpose of the campaign, and very likely assembled under the auspices of Penshurst, who was both father-in-law to Cobham and an old associate of Cray.[88] Penshurst was the only man to have a connection with Roger pre-dating the outbreak of war, having acted on his behalf at the exchequer in 1274.[89] He was, however, an important man in his own right – a fact reflected by his probable appointment as deputy marshal during the campaign.[90] A long-time servant of the Crown, with administrative responsibilities in his native county, Penshurst was evidently not bound to the earl to the same degree as Philip de Buckland, John ap Adam or even Thomas Weyland.[91] He neither depended on Roger's patronage nor accompanied him on a regular basis (between his first connection with the earl and in 1274 and his last in 1283, there is only one reference to him in the comital accounts).[92] It seems, therefore, that he was only drawn into the household on exceptional occasions.

While there is no evidence to indicate what rewards Penshurst received in return for his service, it is fair to say that men of his calibre did not come cheap. Between the start of the first Welsh campaign and the conclusion of the second, Roger recruited two other distinguished individuals into his circle. William Mortimer, a younger son of the marcher lord Roger Mortimer, was first awarded £5 of land and rent in

---

[86] *CPR, 1272-81*, p. 220. In 1280-81 Lambourn stayed at Framingham Earl whilst sick. SC6/935/31.

[87] *CPR, 1272-81*, p. 209; *Parl. Writs*, i, 198. In 1275, Roger inherited land at Kemsing in Kent, and less than 1½ knights' fees. These acquisitions post-date his relationship with Penshurst (see below), and do not connect him to any of the Kentish knights above. Above, p. 37-40, 116, 119n.

[88] N. Saul, *Death, Art and Memory in Medieval England: The Cobham Family and their Monuments, 1300-1500* (Oxford, 2001), p. 33; *CPR, 1266-72*, p. 374. Cobham witnesses RBIV 5 and 12.

[89] E159/49, m. 2. He appeared with Geoffrey de Aspall to deliver a royal order respiting Roger's debts. In 1279, he carried out an extent on the earl's behalf. *CCR, 1272-79*, p. 561.

[90] *CACWales*, p. 114.

[91] He held lands in Kent at Allington, Aylesford, Boxley, Chiddingstone, Hever, Penshurst and Tonbridge, and was sheriff of the county from 1268 to 1271. From his first appearance in 1263 he received an annual fee of 20m from the king. Constable of Dover from 1267 and warden of the Cinque Ports from 1271, he held both posts until his death in 1298. *CChR, 1257-1300*, pp. 46, 177, 233; *CPR, 1258-66*, p. 264; *CPR, 1266-72*, pp. 171, 269, 508; *CPR, 1292-1301*, pp. 308, 344.

[92] SC6/934/19 (taking venison at Earsham in 1277). Penshurst witnesses RBIV 7, 11, and 12, but all three charters were given at court and include non-*familiares* among their witnesses.

return for his service, but in 1279 this figure was supplemented by an annual fee of £25. In 1283 the earl made an even larger grant to Otto de Grandson, close confidant of the king and soon-to-be justiciar of North Wales. Grandson received the manor of Kemsing, and also the hamlet of Seal, a gift worth at least £38 a year.[93] As in Penshurst's case, there is very little in the way of other evidence to place these men in Roger's company,[94] and it seems likely that they too were enlisted to meet the earl's military needs in the period 1277-83.[95] As such, they illustrate the very steep demands which extraordinary recruitment could place on his financial resources.

As to the overall extent of the household's expansion during this period, we have little idea. The evidence for both the second Welsh war and the 1287 revolt is worse than it is for the campaign of 1277. The participation of regular bachelors in 1282-83 is indicated by John Bigod, while extraordinary recruits (besides Mortimer and Grandson) included William de May and Nicholas de Stuteville.[96] Meanwhile, in 1287, we have information only for Roger's less-distinguished *familiares*; the list of protections granted to the earl names just one knight, five esquires, and a number of domestic staff.[97]

The first time we can obtain a full view of Roger's household is during the Welsh revolt of 1294. Not only are the enrolled protections for this campaign very extensive; there also survives a list of the men in the earl's contingent.[98] At this stage Roger's career was well into its second half, and consequently some major changes had taken place in the personnel of his household. By 1294, Buckland, Hovel and Geoffrey de Aspall were all dead, while Weyland was disgraced and living in exile. Grandson and Penshurst disappear from the affinity after 1283, and Mortimer, having secured the arrears of his fee, formally severed his ties with the earl in 1289.[99] There is even, it seems, the strong possibility that, for reasons unknown, John Bigod of Stockton sought alternative service with the earl of Gloucester from 1287 and did not return to the Bigod camp until

---

[93] Following complex litigation down to 1279, Roger held his original portion of Kemsing, valued at £26 2s 7d, and £12 surrendered by William de Valence. *CIPM*, ii, 90; *CPR, 1272-81*, p. 561; above, p. 119n.

[94] See SC6/936/6 and SC6/935/11 for Mortimer, and below, n. 95, for Grandson.

[95] The grant of Kemsing would therefore be for services already rendered. This idea finds support in an undated letter Grandson sent to the chancery, in which he described Roger as his 'dear lord and friend', and sought remedy for 'the great trespass' that the earl had suffered. This seems to be a reference to the widespread park-breaking on the Bigod estate in early 1283, for which remedy was granted on 30 July, two months before Grandson was enfeoffed. C81/1691/11; *CPR, 1281-92*, p. 73.

[96] *CACWales*, p. 43.

[97] *CPR, 1281-92*, pp. 272-3. Cf. Ridgard, pp. 49-50.

[98] C67/10; C47/2/10/8, printed in Ridgard, pp. 48-50. Some surviving chancery warrants for certain individuals in the retinue have also been preserved.

[99] Above, pp. 140, 142-3, 144; *CCR, 1272-79*, p. 552.

c. 1300.[100] Only in the case of John ap Adam do we have certain proof of continued service into the 1290s, his loyalty rewarded and encouraged by a grant of land.[101]

The departures, naturally, were balanced by new arrivals. The most distinguished newcomers were Hugh Despenser, Roger's stepson, and Thomas de Berkeley, whose ancestral seat in Gloucestershire stood on the opposite bank of the Severn to Chepstow; both men first appeared in the earl's circle when they accompanied him to Hainault in 1289. Also in that party was Geoffrey de Wroxhall, a knight with estates in Somerset and Wiltshire who subsequently served as seneschal of Chepstow in 1292-93.[102] Sir Thomas de Akeny, whose debut appearance with Roger comes in 1291, continued to serve regularly throughout the following decade, as did William de Beccles, marshal of the exchequer since at least 1282, who was promoted to the rank of 'chancellor' in the early 1290s.[103] Thomas de Siddington, a royal justice, also joined the ranks of Roger's clerical staff at this time, while another judge, Sir William de Ormesby, makes regular appearances in the comital accounts and charters from 1291. He in particular looks to have filled the position, recently vacated by Weyland, as the earl's leading man of business.[104]

With the exception of Ormesby, all these men went to war with Roger in 1294, appearing among the men granted protections for 'going with the earl' that year. Despenser, Berkeley, Wroxhall and Akeny were joined by fifteen other knights, some of whom had prior connections with the Bigod household, others of whom did not.[105] Beccles and Siddington were united with five other clerks, including the wardrober and the chaplain. Twenty-five esquires were named, ranging in status from quite high-ranking individuals (ap Adam, Frating, Tuddenham) to less-distinguished domestics (John the Butler, Robert the Butler, Walter the Tailor, Jolanus the Cook). Like their knightly betters, and the five *valetti* beneath them, the esquires were a mix of long-serving regulars and first-timers.[106]

---

[100] *CPR, 1281-92*, p. 272; *CPR, 1292-1301*, p. 9; RBIV 26.
[101] He was given half the manor of Monewden (Suffolk), formerly held by Thomas Weyland. *CIPM*, iii, 308; above, p. 141.
[102] *CCR, 1279-88*, p. 180; Appendix D.
[103] RBIV 19, 23, 30, 31; *CChW*, p. 71; *Documents 1297*, p. 157; E159/56 m. 1; C81/1676/59; *CPR 1292-1301*, p. 261; below, p. 161. Cf. Crouch, *William Marshal*, pp. 153-4.
[104] RBIV 19, 24, 29, 30, 31; *Documents 1297*, p. 157; *Scotland in 1298*, ed. H. Gough (Paisley, 1888), pp. 33, 53; above, p. 145.
[105] Thirteen are given in C47/2/10/8; two more (Peter Crok and Thomas de Berkeley Jr.) appear in C67/10, mm. 1, 7 and C81/1695/40. Fulk de Vaux, John Bluet, Arnold Mordaghe, Peter de Tadington and John de Eshton had pre-existing links to Roger (RBIV 18, 19 and 20; *Feudal Aids*, vi, 82; *Yorks. Inq.*, ii, 164). Thomas de Snetterton and Ivo de Kenton were seneschals of Norfolk in 1294-95 (Appendix D). Peter Crok, Hugh Poinz, Robert de Sturmy, Roger de Sotterley and Thomas de Ingoldsthorpe had no prior Bigod connections.
[106] Twenty-three esquires are given in C47/2/10/8. Isambert de St Blitmund and Nicholas Poinz are underlined, seemingly because they were members of a sub-retinue

The evidence from 1294 therefore provides a very full picture of Roger's household. It seems fair to assume that, being on a war footing, it was the household operating at its maximum strength. More than anything else, this is signalled by the fact that three of the leading knights in the earl's retinue were accompanied by their own sub-retinues. Hugh Despenser brought with him two bannerets and seven other knights, Thomas de Berkeley one banneret and three knights,[107] and Maurice de Berkeley brought an 'associate' in the form of his uncle, Robert. Thus a further fourteen knights were added to the household's fighting capacity, bringing the total number to thirty-three. With the seven clerks, twenty-five esquires and five valets, the earl went to war in 1294 with a grand total of seventy men. This is a useful benchmark for assessing the extent of his recruitment in 1297. First, however, we must examine the period leading up to the crisis.

RELATIONS WITH THE KING, 1290-97

As we left Roger Bigod at the end of the last chapter, he had reason to feel resentment with the king's government on a number of issues. The obligation placed on him to clear his debts to the Crown, his several losses as a result of the *Quo Warranto* inquiries, and (although the circumstances are obscure) the apparent infringement of his rights as marshal during the Welsh campaign of 1287; all these must have irked the earl and perhaps tempered his respect for Edward I. The crucial question, however, is to what degree? None of these stand out as major grievances, and to a large extent can be regarded as part of the ordinary cut and thrust of politics. In 1290, with the king returned from his lengthy sojourn in Gascony, and Roger back from his trip to Hainault, the relationship between the two men looks amicable enough. The earl attended parliaments that year in January, April, July and October, and (as we have seen) was one of the principal guests at the wedding of Edward's daughter, Margaret, to the duke of Brabant in July.[108] This match, brokered in 1278, provided the king with a useful ally in the Low Countries, and it may be that Roger's own

---

accompanying Hugh Poinz, as is clear from C67/10, m. 7 and C81/1736/109. The two other men in Poinz's company, Geoffrey de Sloo and Thomas de Mere, bring the total number of esquires to twenty-five. Ap Adam, Shottesbrooke, Tuddenham, Houton, Frating, Baret and Walter the Tailor all had prior connections (above, pp. 126, 147-50; Appendix D). Jolanus the Cook, John the Butler, Robert the Butler, Clyf, Gurnay, Mettingham and Denardstone occur in later household contexts (SC6/938/9; SC6/922/6; SC6/873/17; *Scotland in 1298*, ed. Gough, pp. 33-4, 37-8), but Boyton, Buckland, Winslade, Blunt, Howel, Duxford and St Laud feature only in 1294.

[107] C67/10, m. 4 reveals that these men were Walter de Pavely, Roger Perceval, John Roges, and Richard Tensy.

[108] Appendix B. Cf. *Handbook of British Chronology*, ed. Fryde et al., pp. 548-9; above, p. 149. At the January parliament, the earl acted as an arbitrator in a dispute between Yarmouth and the Cinque Ports. Cotton, p. 175.

marriage to Alice de Hainault, celebrated just two weeks beforehand, was also intended to bolster English interests in the same region. With this possibility in mind, we should probably not interpret Edward's decision to absent himself from the Bigod wedding banquet as an indication of royal disapproval (no more so than his equally impolite behaviour on the day of Margaret's marriage, when he assaulted a squire with a stick). Whatever his reasons for staying away, the king showed there were no hard feelings in August, when he spontaneously granted the earl a gift of ten deer in the royal forest of Pamber.[109]

This good relationship between Roger and Edward was maintained over the course of the next two years, when the itineraries of both men were largely dictated by events in Scotland. The tragic accident that carried off Alexander III, king of Scots, in 1286, and the subsequent death of Margaret, 'the maid of Norway', in 1290, had left the northern realm not only leaderless, but also without an obvious candidate to succeed the late king. Edward made it his business to act as judge between the various contenders for the Scottish throne, seizing with both hands the opportunity to strengthen his claim to overlordship. Negotiations began in May 1291 at Norham, where the competitors were persuaded to accept the king's jurisdiction, and the hearings commenced at Berwick in August.[110] Roger Bigod's role in all of this was an important one – he was one of the twenty-four auditors selected by Edward to hear the case, a distinction he shared with only one of his peers.[111] Beyond this the evidence does not permit any greater analysis of the earl's role in the proceedings,[112] but when the court adjourned for a final time in July 1292, the king was sufficiently well disposed to make him a gift of hunting rights in the forest of Dean. Since this privilege only lasted a year, Roger may have taken the opportunity to exercise it in August and September, while the court was in recess.[113] But he was back at Berwick in the autumn, where a final verdict was delivered in favour of John Balliol on 17 November.[114] Edward's decision to launch an inquisition *ad quod damnum* on the earl's behalf (regarding shipping rights at New Ross) may also be interpreted as a sign of continued good relations between the two men at this time.[115]

---

[109] Prestwich, *Edward I*, pp. 111, 317, 333; *Records of the Wardrobe and Household*, ed. Byerly, p. 268; *CCR, 1288-96*, p. 97.
[110] Prestwich, *Edward I*, pp. 358-66.
[111] *Great Cause*, ii, 81. The other English earl acting as an auditor was Henry de Lacy, earl of Lincoln. At the Bigod manor of Walton in 1291, £4 19s were spent on 'taking supplies to earl at Berwick, there with the king'. SC6/1007/15. See also SC6/768/15.
[112] *Great Cause*, ii, 198, 213, 216.
[113] *CPR, 1281-92*, p. 499. It is also possible that the earl spent this time visiting his Yorkshire lands, as he had done during the break in proceedings the previous year. The king visited the vale of Pickering in August 1292. Appendix B; *RCWL Ed I*, p. 112.
[114] Prestwich, *Edward I*, p. 367.
[115] *CDI, 1285-92*, pp. 483-5. The result of this inquisition, however, was less than favourable, owing to the opposition of the men of Waterford, who were supported by the justiciar, Stephen de Fulbourne. *CDI, 1285-92*, pp. 522-3; *CDI, 1302-1307*, pp. 46-7.

Edward's next foreign policy adventure, however, was far less popular. In June 1294 he formally renounced his homage to Philip IV of France as a prelude to making war on the French king. Although there was ample justification for this move (the English government had, in essence, been tricked into surrendering Gascony that year) there was little support for this new military adventure among the English baronage. Their reaction was in part based on historic precedent; ever since the loss of Normandy in 1204, Englishmen had become increasingly less enthusiastic about campaigning on the Continent. In addition, there was also the widespread feeling that Edward had been ill-advised in the months leading up to the war, and had followed no other counsel but his own.[116] Whereas the king's policies in Wales and Scotland had proved popular precisely because they had been carried through with the consent of his magnates in parliament, in this case Edward had negotiated in secret, through the agency of his cousin, the earl of Lancaster. Both the arena of conflict and the failure to consult stirred memories of the worst days of the previous reign. As he became increasingly committed to prosecuting the war in the face of popular objection, Edward grew to seem more and more like his father, and ultimately provoked a similar reaction from his subjects.[117]

In 1294, the probable resistance to the king's demands for military service has been inferred from the postponement of the initial muster, and the fact that, when the army finally set sail, none of its contingents had been raised by feudal methods.[118] Roger Bigod's reluctance, however, cannot be taken as read at this stage. The earl was at court in early June, several days before the parliament to deal with the crisis had even been summoned. Moreover, on 18 June he sent his wardrober, Reginald de Honington, to Ireland, with orders to buy up foodstuffs and send them on to him when he arrived in Gascony.[119] Of course, this was well before the muster was ordered, and Roger may well have objected to the form of summons as it was eventually delivered. The direct evidence, however, suggests that he was supporting the king and making ready to sail.

Whatever misgivings the earl may or may not have had about Gascony at this stage, they were rendered irrelevant in early October when news reached England of a fresh uprising in Wales. By the middle of the month the decision had been taken to reroute the army assembled on the south coast and send it westwards.[120] Roger, who was at Westminster throughout October, sent two of his *familiares* to Portsmouth at precisely

---

[116] W.M. Ormrod, 'Love and War in 1294', TCE, viii (Woodbridge, 2001), 143-52.
[117] Prestwich, *Edward I*, pp. 376-81. Cf. J.R. Maddicott, '"1258" and "1297": Some Comparisons and Contrasts', TCE, ix (Woodbridge, 2003), 1-14.
[118] Prestwich, *Edward I*, p. 406.
[119] CPR, 1292-1301, p. 74; CDI, 1293-1301, p. 73; Ridgard, p. 49; SC6/748/24 ('expenses of the earl around 1 August in the time of Reginald the clerk staying in Ireland').
[120] Morris, *Welsh Wars*, pp. 240-43.

this time, probably with instructions to redeploy.[121] As with the previous Welsh campaigns, Edward determined upon a three-pronged attack, with initial musters at Cardiff, Brecon and Chester. The earl, along with William de Valence, was placed in command of the southern army.[122] In the conflict that followed, both men appear to have acquitted themselves well. Although very little evidence survives of their activities, Roger's ministers' accounts reveal that he did much more than simply guard his own lordship.[123] As well as recording the earl's arrival in Chepstow around 6 December, the roll for Tidenham also notes the cost 'of carrying oats to Newport on his departure for Wales'. It further reveals that Roger was back at the castle on 22 February, by which time his countess and her household had been in residence for a number of weeks. Fresh letters of protection issued in April suggest that he returned to the frontline again before reappearing at Chepstow on 22 May, by which stage most of the fighting must have been over. Even then, however, there is the possibility that Roger set off for Wales for a third time; a final expense is recorded 'for making hurdles for boats going to Swansea following the earl's horses'.[124]

Roger's apparently diligent execution of his responsibilities in South Wales in 1294-95 seems all the more surprising in view of his clash with the king on the eve of the campaign. On 21 November, the earl attended a final council of war at Worcester, during which he evidently protested that his rights as marshal were being overlooked. Just three days later, Edward found it expedient to promise Roger that he intended him no prejudice, either by sending the earl away from his side, or by appointing Roger de Meules, a knight of the royal household, as marshal of the southern army.[125] On the one hand, Roger's indignation is understandable; as earl marshal, it fell to him to accompany the king and proceed at the front of the royal host.[126] At the same time, however, his protest came surprisingly late in the day. It must have been clear as early as mid-October that Edward expected him to fight in the south, and yet Roger, who was at court at that time and for several weeks afterwards, had apparently raised no objection.[127] It seems possible, therefore, that in late November the issue had less to do with the loss of honour involved in being sent south, and more to do with the loss of revenue that de Meules's appointment appeared to threaten. As marshal of the royal army, Roger was entitled to

[121] Appendix B; SC6/1020/21 ('Fulk de Vaux, Richard de Rudham and others coming from London to Portsmouth for the earl's business, and for staying five days there, and returning to Norfolk around Michaelmas').
[122] Morris, *Welsh Wars*, pp. 244, 248.
[123] Cf. *Book of Prests, 1294-5*, ed. E.B. Fryde (Oxford, 1962), xxxii.
[124] SC6/859/24; E101/531/12; *CChW*, p. 55; Morris, *Welsh Wars*, p. 264. See other expenses for the same events in SC6/920/7. My thanks to Stephen Priestly for sharing his transcripts of these rolls.
[125] *CPR, 1292-1301*, p. 126; Morris, *Welsh Wars*, pp. 250-51; Prestwich, *Edward I*, p. 413.
[126] Cf. *CM*, vi, 374; below, pp. 161, 163.
[127] *Parl. Writs*, i, 265; Appendix B.

a wide range of monetary fees, but these were seemingly being denied to him. As Prestwich has discovered, the king had already begun to levy these fees himself, but their collection by the wardrobe was soon abandoned. Officially this was an act of royal kindness, inspired by shortages among the troops. In reality, the change of policy was probably adopted as a result of Roger's protest.[128]

The argument over the marshal's rights in wartime may have had earlier precedents: in 1287, 1282 and 1254 there had been similar clashes, though none of them is as well documented as that of 1294.[129] There was, however, a parallel argument about the marshal's peacetime rights, with an equally long history, and which had reared its head as recently as 1293.[130] At the start of the unusually long Easter parliament that year, Roger complained that the rights of his deputy marshals in the royal household were being overlooked, to which end he presented a number of written articles to the king. Edward responded with a characteristic blend of conciliation and threat. The clerks of the wardrobe were ordered to search their rolls and compile a transcript of the marshal's rights, which would then be presented to the earl in the presence of the king's council. Thereafter, these rights would be upheld and maintained in every respect. However, should Roger or his deputies exceed them in any way, the office of marshal would be forfeit.[131]

By curious coincidence – so sudden that it is difficult not to imagine some contrivance – grounds for forfeiture were discovered just a few weeks later. As marshal of the household, it fell to Fulk de Vaux (a Bigod *familiaris* since 1291) to take custody of prisoners tried before the King's Bench. Among his charges in 1293 was a certain Alan Osmund, clerk, appealed at the start of the year for arranging a murder, a crime for which he was found guilty on 21 May in the county court of Kent. Fulk, however, made the mistake of committing this particular prisoner to his groom, who in turn allowed the criminous clerk rather more liberty than was customary for convicted felons. Alan was subsequently spotted (by his victim's widow, no less) rambling and wandering the streets of London, hearing mass in various churches, and generally acting 'as if he were someone accused of no crime'. Defending his actions, Fulk explained that his charge had been unable to walk properly in leg-irons, but this excuse cut no ice with the justices. The marshal himself was imprisoned, and his office taken into the king's hands.[132]

The same parliament in 1293 also witnessed a public dispute between Edward and Roger over another long-running cause of contention, namely the earl's Crown debts. For a number of years since 1285, this issue had

---

[128] Above, p. 30; Prestwich, *War, Politics and Finance*, p. 249, citing E372/144.
[129] Above, pp. 48, 135-6; Prestwich, *War, Politics and Finance*, p. 249.
[130] Above, pp. 29n, 31, 79-80; *SR*, i, 92.
[131] *Rot. Parl.*, i, 93.
[132] Above, p. 148; *Select Cases KB*, ii, 149-50; *PA*, p. 232.

proved uncontroversial; that year Roger had acknowledged a total debt of
£857, and the king had granted him permission to pay it off at terms of
£100 a year.[133] This the earl proceeded to do, paying sums of £50 twice a
year with regularity down to Michaelmas 1290.[134] At that point, however,
the exchequer upset the agreement (and the earl) by ordering a distraint
on the Bigod manor of Levisham in Yorkshire, a misguided attempt to
recover debts owed by the previous owner. Roger complained to the king,
probably in person, and Edward responded by relaxing the distraint and
granting a six-month respite.[135]

The wider outcome of the incident, however, was a thorough review of
the Bigod debts; between January 1291 and November 1292 the king
repeatedly ordered the exchequer to recalculate the earl's overall liability
(as well as ordering further respites). It seems quite possible that Edward
may have done this at the urging of Roger himself. The two men were in
close contact during this period because of the Great Cause proceedings,
and indeed the earl was at court on each of the occasions when the king
wrote to the exchequer on his behalf. Throughout his career Roger was
convinced he was being overcharged for his debts, and may well have
believed that a proper reassessment would work in his favour.[136]

It must therefore have come as a considerable shock when at Easter
1293 the exchequer, having finally carried out the king's instructions,
presented the earl with a demand for £4,060.[137] Since his last
acknowledged total was £857, against which he had already paid £671,
this represented a colossal increase. On seeing the exchequer's evidence,
the earl conceded that £547 of the newly discovered sums were indeed
legitimate, and accepted liability for a total of £733.[138] The remaining
£3,326, however, he refused to recognize – and with good reason: as well
as including several long-disputed debts, this new total contained an
unjustified demand for £651 of scutage for the Welsh wars, as well as
some basic errors in book-keeping and arithmetic (for example, the £218
claimed for the 1231 Poitevin scutage had been erroneously increased to

---

[133] Precisely, £856 17s 6½d. This figure had initially been £803 10s 10½d, but after 1 July
1285 it was revised upwards by 80m. Above, pp. 131n, 133n.

[134] This is assumed from his payment of £671 by thirteen tallies by Easter 1293 (E159/66,
m. 25).

[135] E159/64, m. 2d. Edward's order is dated 17 October; Roger was with the king two days
beforehand (Appendix B). Regime change at the exchequer early in 1290, and the drive to
restore royal finances, may explain the initial error. Prestwich, *Edward I*, pp. 342-3.

[136] E159/64, mm. 7, 13; E159/65, m. 25d; E159/66, m. 12d. Cf. Appendix B.

[137] £733 2s 2d + £3,326 8s 8½d. For all the figures in this paragraph, see E159/66, m. 25.

[138] The £547 was for 16 debts, the largest of which was 520m, this being Roger's share of
the money paid by the Crown to Eleanor de Montfort for her Marshal dower between
1265 and her death in 1275. The remaining debts were small: seven were for fines, six
were for scutages and aids charged on fees from other honours, and two were for reliefs
for fees held by his first wife.

£318, and the grand total of unclear debts was exactly £500 greater than the true total of the figures given).[139]

No doubt incensed by this inflated demand, Roger raised the matter in parliament a few weeks later and sought a fresh inquiry.[140] This Edward granted, instructing the exchequer to re-examine the debts on 15 July. The day itself evidently saw some hard bargaining. The earl for his part accepted liability for two of the debts presented to him at Easter, namely the 400 marks of extra Marshal money, and £219 for the Marshal debts.[141] He also agreed to pay £143 for the Poitevin scutage of 1230 – a figure which reveals the highly forensic nature of the reassessment that was taking place.[142] On the other hand, the exchequer reduced their demand for the debts of Hugh Bigod from £1,351 to £800 – a revision in Roger's favour that was apparently caused by a misinterpretation of Henry III's writ of pardon.[143] In addition, the barons said nothing about scutage for the Welsh wars, and took more care with their calculations. At the end of the day, the earl acknowledged a total debt of £2,232. While this was far more than he had been prepared to admit in 1285, it was a great deal less than the £4,060 the exchequer had demanded just three months beforehand. To this extent, the earl's protest in the Easter parliament of 1293 had been vindicated.

To what extent did this episode damage Roger's relationship with the king? Michael Prestwich sees the earl being hit with increasingly large demands for debt from the mid-1280s, and smarting at the humiliation of having to beg 'to be excused payment' in parliament. Seen in context, however, it is clear that Edward's behaviour at this point was far from threatening (in contrast to the stance the king adopted in 1275 and 1297).[144] The decision to reinvestigate the scale of the debts in 1291 was only taken after an initial complaint (and perhaps subsequent requests) from the earl himself. When Roger sought the king's grace in parliament, it was not because he was unable to meet his obligations, but rather because he

---

[139] The unclear debts were given as: £651 for the Welsh scutages of 5 and 10 Edward I; £317 16s 8d (*recte* £217 16s 8d) for the Poitevin scutage of 1230; a £20 relief for the fee-farm of High Wycombe; £219 7s for the Marshal debts; £1,351 11s 8½d for the debts of Hugh Bigod; 400m of additional money for the Marshal payments made to Eleanor de Montfort after the death of Margaret de Lacy, countess of Lincoln. Total: £2,826 8s 8½d.

[140] E159/67, m. 19 for all the figures in this paragraph.

[141] In addition, he accepted some small sums which appear here from the first time, including rents from manors seized by his uncle in 1265. Above, pp. 94-5n.

[142] This scutage had been set in 1230 at £2 per fee, and Roger III Bigod was charged £337 16s 8d (for 125½ 'old fees', 37½ 'new fees', and the 6⅙ fees formerly held by Richard de Reimes in Essex). The old earl had paid only £120 (based on his ancient quota of 60 fees), and refused to acknowledge the shortfall of £217 16s 8d. By agreeing to pay £142 16s 8d of this sum, Roger IV showed he was willing to except liability for everything except the 37½ 'new fees'. Above, pp. 14-16.

[143] Above, p. 111. Cf. below, pp. 180-81.

[144] Prestwich, *Edward I*, pp. 413-14; *idem, War, Politics and Finance*, p. 237. Above, p. 116; below, p. 164.

disagreed with the exchequer's assessment of their extent. Whether or not this caused the earl any humiliation is open to question; it was arguably as embarrassing for Edward to have one of his magnates querying in public the legitimacy of demands made by his exchequer.[145] In any case, the king's response was to order another hearing, which ultimately provided Roger with a more favourable outcome. After this (as Prestwich notes) the earl was allowed to pay at the same terms as before.[146]

The dispute over the rights of the marshal during the 1293 parliament may well have been more serious, ending as it did with the imprisonment of Fulk de Vaux. Yet even here Edward soon intervened to secure the release of the deputy marshal, and pardoned him his trespass.[147] If, therefore, the king had contrived this demonstration of his mastery, he was at least characteristically magnanimous once it had been acknowledged.[148] If, on the other hand, the case against the marshal was not a deliberately engineered royal riposte to Roger's complaints in parliament (which is, after all, perhaps the fairer assumption), the king's pardon can only be read as another example of the earl receiving lenient and favourable treatment. Certainly neither this nor the debate on his debts in the summer of 1293 provoked any visible rift between Roger and the king; the earl was back at court later in the same year, witnessing charters in September and November.[149] The following year, as we have seen, he seems to have been preparing to follow Edward to Gascony, and fought for the king in South Wales, despite the diminution of honour this entailed, and notwithstanding the appropriation of his fees by royal officials.

The extent to which good relations between the king and the earl were maintained right up to the eve of their confrontation in 1297 is amply demonstrated by Roger's involvement in the Scottish campaign of 1296. Having attended the 'model' parliament of 1295, at which the campaign was discussed, the earl joined the general muster at Newcastle the following March.[150] Men and money from his estates in East Anglia were sent north to meet him.[151] In the six months that followed, Roger accompanied Edward as he toured Scotland, carrying out a 'deceptively easy' conquest.[152] To judge from the earl's witnessing, he was closely

---

[145] Only the previous year, the magnates had complained *en masse* in parliament about the exchequer, and in particular its attempts to levy money for old scutages when satisfaction had already been made. *Rot. Parl.*, i, 80.

[146] E159/67, m. 26d. Prestwich, *Edward I*, p. 414.

[147] *Select Cases KB*, ii, 151.

[148] Cf. Davies, *Conquest, Coexistence and Change*, p. 341.

[149] Appendix B.

[150] W. Stubbs, *The Constitutional History of England* (3 vols., Oxford, 1880), ii, 245; Appendix B; *Parl. Writs*, i, 31, 33, 275; *CCR, 1288–96*, p. 501.

[151] SC6/873/17; SC6/938/9. For a list of men who went with the earl, see *CChW*, p. 71.

[152] Prestwich, *Edward I*, pp. 469–76.

involved in the king's counsels.[153] Moreover, on this occasion, there was no controversy over his role as marshal; Roger was accorded his rights in full. A surviving plea roll, drawn up by his chancellor, William de Beccles, reveals for the first time the impressive scale and scope of the earl's powers whilst on campaign. Responsible for all matters of discipline within the army, and for regulating relations between soldiers and non-combatants, the marshal could judge cases involving life and limb with as much authority as a justice in eyre. The seriousness with which he regarded his right to proceed the host is vividly brought out by the case of an unfortunate individual who, having 'had the temerity to presume' to ride ahead of the marshal's banner, found himself arrested and imprisoned.[154] As well as the fines that this judicial activity generated, Roger was also awarded the perquisites which fell to him by virtue of his office – the same fees that had apparently been denied to him in 1294-95. At the end of August, when the campaign was over, Beccles received £50 from the king's wardrobe in part payment of his master's emoluments.[155]

1297

There is, therefore, not much evidence of antagonism between Roger and Edward in the period from the start of 1290 to the end of 1296. Yet between February 1297 and January 1301 the earl became the king's principal opponent. What went wrong? Many of the grievances of 1297 can be attributed to the economic pressures created by a state of almost uninterrupted war since 1294. In order to raise and provision troops for the campaigns in Wales and Scotland, and to fund the subsequent garrisoning and building operations in both countries, Edward had resorted in the first instance to extraordinary taxation. Here, as elsewhere, the king was characteristically careful to gain consent for his actions in parliament, and in general there had been little opposition from the assembly's leading lay members. In 1294 and 1295 magnates like Roger had consented to levies on their English estates, just as they had approved taxes for Wales and Ireland earlier in the decade.[156] In part this was because the very rich were able to mitigate or even circumvent entirely the

---

[153] Between March and September 1296, Roger witnessed 10 royal charters, a total which placed him second only to John de Warenne, who witnessed 12. The remaining earls, Warwick, Arundel and Hereford, witnessed 9, 5 and 4 charters respectively. *RCWL Ed I*, pp. 127-9.

[154] E39/93/15, printed in 'A Plea Roll of Edward I's Army in Scotland, 1296', ed. C.J. Neville, *Miscellany of the Scottish Historical Society XI* (Scottish Historical Soc., 5th ser., iii, 1990), 13-15, 22, 113. The pleas themselves were heard by John Lovel, the deputy marshal for the campaign, and one of the earl's most important *familiares* during the last decade of his life. Below, p. 179; cf. RBIV 26, 30-33.

[155] *CDS, 1108-1516*, p. 152.

[156] *CPR, 1281-92*, pp. 449, 511; *CDI, 1285-92*, p. 441. There was, however, some bargaining over the size of the award made in 1294. Prestwich, *Edward I*, p. 404.

king's demands. Roger, for example, seems to have been exempted from
the tenth and sixth granted in 1294, and in 1295 he was able to reduce
substantially his contributions to the eleventh and seventh by bribing
those who assessed it.[157] Nevertheless, even for the wealthy these taxes
were beginning to bite. Although it has been calculated that Roger paid
no more than 4½ per cent of his income in tax during the period 1294-97,
this was a figure large enough to trouble a man who was accustomed to
enjoying all of his revenue and who lived close to his profit margins.[158]

Taxation alone, however, cannot explain the earl's opposition. In
November 1296, in a parliament at Bury St Edmunds, the first seeds of the
coming crisis were sown not by the baronage but by the Church. Smarting
from their earlier tax assessments (which had been higher than those of
lay landowners) and fortified by the arguments set out in the new bull
Clericis Laicos, the clergy refused the king's demand for a grant of a twelfth
and an eighth. The laity, however, apparently approved the award with
little opposition. If Roger and his associates shared any of the Church's
misgivings, they buried them over Christmas (which the earl and his
countess spent at Alnesbourne Priory in Suffolk), and disguised them in
the new year, when Edward summoned them at short notice to Ipswich to
celebrate the wedding of his daughter, Elizabeth.[159] The politics behind
this match, however, may have given the guests cause for further concern.
It was a hastily arranged affair, a product of the king's recent diplomatic
endeavours to woo the count of Flanders into an alliance with England.
The marriage of the princess to the count's son indicated that, with Wales
and Scotland now subdued, Edward's attentions were once again focused
firmly on war with France.

Just a few days after the wedding, Roger felt the first effects of the
king's preparations for a Continental campaign. In November Edward
had ordered a massive prise – a compulsory seizure of foodstuffs,
theoretically in return for payment at a later date.[160] On 13 January, the
earl received news from Bosham that fifty quarters of wheat had been
seized for the king's use.[161] He was staying at Weston, a property suffering
the effects of another non-consensual royal imposition. The new tariff on
wool, introduced in 1294 and dubbed 'the maltote' in recognition of its

---

[157] *Parl. Writs,* i, 391; E. Miller, 'War, Taxation and the English Economy in the Late-Thirteenth and Early-Fourteenth Centuries', *War and Economic Development: Essays in Memory of David Joslin,* ed. J.M. Winter (Cambridge, 1975), p. 19. In addition to his examples, see SC6/937/3 and SC6/937/26. There were fairly general exemptions for those doing military service in 1294, 1295 and 1296. F. Willard, *Parliamentary Taxes on Personal Property, 1290-1334* (Cambridge, Mass., 1934), pp. 111-14.

[158] Miller, 'War, Taxation and the English Economy', pp. 20, 27.

[159] *Parl. Writs,* i, 48; *CCR, 1296-1302,* p. 75; Prestwich, *Edward I,* pp. 405-6, 411-12; SC6/768/19 (Thomas de Akeny and certain esquires of the earl coming from Chesterford, at the earl's order, towards Hollesley, to lead the countess to Alnesbourne at Christmas).

[160] *Documents 1297,* p. 12.

[161] SC6/1020/23.

economic demerits, had reduced wool prices there by as much as 40 per cent. Weston, moreover, was one of the better-off Bigod manors. At Peasenhall in Suffolk, the drop in value was greater than 60 per cent, while at Stoughton in Sussex, the clip was simply accumulating unsold.[162] Three weeks later, Roger would have heard of Edward's decision to place the clergy outside his protection, retaliation against their stance in the November parliament. On 12 February, royal officials began the seizure of the lands, goods and chattels of churchmen, including those of John Bigod, the earl's younger brother.[163]

All these things would thus have weighed on the earl's mind as he made his way to the parliament that the king had summoned to Salisbury for 24 February. Like the royal wedding of the previous month, this was a somewhat impromptu gathering, and also limited in numbers; the clergy had not been invited, and there was a visible lack of earls. In the past fifteen months, death had carried off both Lancaster and Gloucester. Warenne, meanwhile, was occupied in holding down the Scots, and Cornwall, Lincoln, and Hereford were engaged overseas.[164] Those who remained in England, besides Norfolk, were less imposing figures – Arundel and Warwick, both newly created, and Oxford, always inconsequential. When the Salisbury parliament sat, Roger, perhaps for the first time, found he was the greatest man present besides the king himself.[165]

Edward had called the meeting with the intention of discussing the French war, and was therefore surprised to discover that the magnates were ready to oppose his plans. The Bury chronicler suggests that the king offered the option of service in Flanders or in Gascony, but the earls, including Roger, refused point blank to leave England, on the grounds that the country was surrounded by too many enemies. Walter of Guisborough, on the other hand, while he offers no general explanation for the opposition, is clear that it was a request from Edward to serve in Gascony which provoked the resistance, and that the king scandalized the parliament by threatening to disinherit those that refused. According to the same writer, Roger based his objection on a strict interpretation of his entitlement as earl marshal.

'Willingly I will go with you, O king,' he reportedly said, 'proceeding before your face in the first line of battle, as it belongs to me in hereditary right.'

Edward, however, insisted that the earl would have to go to Gascony, without him and 'with the others'. Roger countered by simply restating

---

[162] Mille·, 'War, Taxation and the English Economy', p. 14.
[163] Cf. below, pp. 164, 182.
[164] Prestwich, *Edward I*, pp. 385, 413; H. Rothwell, 'The Confirmation of the Charters, 1297', *EHR*, lx (1945), p. 25n.
[165] *Parl. Writs*, i, 51.

his refusal more emphatically, thereby provoking the following celebrated exchange:

'By God, O earl, either you will go, or you will hang!'
'By the same oath, O King, I will neither go nor hang!'[166]

Neither chronicler's account is without its problems. Bury's belief that Gascony was offered as an alternative to Flanders, Guisborough's laboured punning on Roger's surname, and the assertion by both writers that the earl of Hereford was present – all these detract to some extent from the credibility of their stories. Nevertheless, there is no question that the Salisbury parliament was the start of a major crisis. Guisborough tells us that Roger withdrew without licence, and that he (and Hereford) were soon joined by many other magnates. Their forces, he says, numbered 1,500 horsemen, which seems rather unlikely, and thirty bannerets, which seems perfectly plausible. Whatever the true numbers, the opposition was unquestionably large. Roger soon stood united not only with Hereford but also with Arundel, and even Warwick. 'The king began to fear them,' said Guisborough, 'though he did not show it.'[167]

Edward had been in this position before, even if the odds against him had not been so heavily stacked. In 1295, a much smaller group of magnates refused an order to serve in Gascony, and the king had broken their resistance by distraining them for debt. Arundel, in particular, had been notably obstructive, but had buckled swiftly when the king's men had seized his assets.[168] If, therefore, the earl marshal wanted to argue about rights and entitlements, let him be similarly reminded that the Crown was entitled to several thousand pounds from his estate. In mid-Lent (around 24 March) an estreat arrived at Bosham, demanding £450 of silver. Possibly it was sent as a result of the general levy of Crown debts ordered on 12 March; but the demand itself, sealed as it was with green wax, suggests that Roger was being deliberately and personally targeted by Edward himself.[169] Just days after their row at Salisbury, the king had sought to hurt the earl by lashing out at his brother. There was no way whatsoever ('*nul fin ou purchaz qi il porra faire*'), Edward told the exchequer, that the Revd John Bigod could redeem his confiscated lands. Even his royal grandfather would have been hard pressed to match such levels of vindictiveness.[170]

Roger and his allies, however, showed no signs of flinching. Guisborough says that from Salisbury the earls had 'set out for their own lands...and prepared to resist', and in Roger's case this seems to have

---

[166] *Bury*, pp. 138-9; Guisborough, pp. 289-90.
[167] Guisborough, p. 290.
[168] Prestwich, *Edward I*, pp. 384, 407.
[169] SC6/1020/23; *Documents 1297*, p. 24; Cf. P. Chaplais, *English Royal Documents, King John to Henry VI, 1199-1461* (Oxford, 1971), p. 15.
[170] *Documents 1297*, pp. 13, 46. Edward later softened his stance. *CPR, 1292-1301*, p. 273.

meant his eastern estates: the earl was at Weston in March and Chesterford in early April.[171] At some point, however – probably not long after Easter – he travelled north-west, to meet with his associates at Montgomery. Hereford, Arundel and Warwick were present, as too were John de Hastings and Edmund Mortimer. According to the Evesham chronicler, they reiterated their determination not to cross with the king, citing the financial hardships that they had suffered as a result of the recent wars and taxes. Edward, meanwhile, was pressing ahead with preparations for the campaign. On hearing the news of the meeting at Montgomery, he determined to confront his critics, and ordered a muster in London for 7 July.[172]

The earls came to the capital on the appointed day, but their behaviour was still extremely guarded. The king's summons had been suspiciously unconventional and imprecise. It contained no mention of homage or fealty, nor for that matter of wages, and moreover there was no clear indication of where the king intended to send the assembled troops.[173] Edward called the constable and the marshal before him, but Roger stayed away, pleading illness, and sending in his stead John de Seagrave, a recently recruited *familiaris*. When it transpired that the king expected them to draw up muster lists as if his summons had been normal, the earls refused (in writing, via a messenger). Edward responded by dismissing them from their hereditary offices and appointing Thomas de Berkeley and Geoffrey de Joinville in their place. At this point, Roger, Hereford and their allies withdrew from court.[174]

The situation was now explosive. According to three related chronicles, the king had been ready to arrest the earls before their withdrawal, and they in turn were now preparing themselves in expectation of an attack.[175] As far as Edward's military plans were concerned, this new confrontation was a disaster; but at the same time, as the political temperature rose, and opposition looked increasingly like rebellion, so the king's position began to strengthen. On 11 July, a reconciliation was effected between Edward and the archbishop of Canterbury. The earl of Warwick, an unlikely antagonist from the start, was back with the king before 13 July, and John de Hastings, despite his stance at Montgomery, reiterated his loyalty the

---

[171] Guisborough, p. 290; SC6/1020/23. Roger seems to have favoured both these manors during the crisis. He was at Chesterford in June (Denholm-Young, *SAIE*, p. 168), and the 1297 account roll for Weston has 'the earl's expenses for many visits from the feast of St Fabian [20 Jan] to feast of St Michael [30 Sept]'. SC6/873/18.

[172] J.H. Denton, 'The Crisis of 1297 from the Evesham Chronicle', *EHR*, xciii (1978), 575-6. The chronicle's dating of the Montgomery meeting is vague (*'circa idem tempus'*), but appears to place it after 20 April and before the issue of the king's summons on 15 May.

[173] *Parl. Writs*, i, 282.

[174] *Documents 1297*, pp. 126-7 (*EHD*, iii, 478). For Seagrave, see below, pp. 171, 177-8, 182.

[175] Langtoft, pp. 290-91; *Chronica Monasterii de Melsa*, ed. E.A. Bond (3 vols., Rolls Ser., 1866-69), ii, 266; *Chronicles of the Reigns of Edward I and Edward II*, ed. W. Stubbs, (2 vols., Rolls Ser., 1882-83), ii, 38-9.

following day. The king's masterstroke was to require his magnates to come to Westminster on 14 July, in order to swear fealty to his son and heir, Prince Edward – a demand no loyal subject could reasonably refuse. Norfolk and Hereford pledged their allegiance, but only two days later, and (it would appear), from the safe distance of the city of London. If they had come to the capital confident in their numbers, their party was now much reduced, and they were looking dangerously exposed.[176]

In the four weeks that followed, attempts by the higher clergy to effect a reconciliation between the two parties failed. This was, it seems, largely because Edward was not interested in listening to his opponents' grievances. In an extraordinary propaganda letter issued on 12 August, the king explained that, despite their being given several opportunities for an audience, the earls had failed to appear before him. His account, however, does not square with the version of events provided by the Evesham chronicler, who says that a meeting took place at Stratford, and that, far from offering safe-conducts, royal representatives had suggested to the opposition that they put themselves entirely in Edward's grace.[177] The earl of Hereford answered that he and his party had said or done the king no wrong, and went on to present their complaints and demands. The Remonstrances, as they are now known, sought for the most part to address the adverse economic effects of recent royal policies – prises, taxes and the maltote. They also set out the earls' objections to fighting in Flanders, which included the unprecedented demand for service, the irregular form of the recent summons, and the general inadvisability of quitting England when Scotland and Wales remained unsettled.[178] Edward's response was further denial: he had never seen these articles, he claimed in mid-August (even as he went on to answer some of the specific charges they contained).[179] By this stage the king was heading for the south coast, determined to avoid further delay and still refusing to negotiate.[180] It looks very much as if he was planning to settle things by force; on 20 August, 170 knights were ordered to assemble at Rochester.[181]

It was the earls, however, who struck the first blow. On 22 August, at nine in the morning, Norfolk, Hereford and their supporters stormed into the exchequer. They had come, they declared, to stop the collection of the

---

[176] *RCWL Ed I*, p. 131; *Documents 1297*, pp. 17, 106-7. Hastings may have been encouraged by Edward's letter of 11 July. Arundel, who features in neither camp, was certainly in contact with the king, and had abandoned his opposition by August. *Documents 1297*, pp. 105-6, 141-2; Cf. Prestwich, *War, Politics and Finance*, p. 237.

[177] Edward claimed to have issued safe-conducts at St Albans on 28 July, but we only have his word for this. The official record shows safe-conducts issued only on 13 August. *CPR, 1292-1301*, p. 302.

[178] *Documents 1297*, pp. 115-17, 125-9 (*EHD*, iii, 469, 472, 478-80); Denton, 'Crisis of 1297', p. 577.

[179] *Documents 1297*, pp. 127-9 (*EHD*, iii, 479-80).

[180] Guisborough, pp. 293-4.

[181] Prestwich, *Edward I*, p. 425.

eighth – a new tax that Edward had ordered three weeks beforehand. The award had outraged the opposition because, although only a handful of councillors had approved its collection, the king was claiming that it had been granted with full consent. Bigod, Bohun and their bannerets now begged to differ; they and the rest of the community of the realm, Hereford observed, would not stand to be tallaged like serfs. Having made their point, the earls withdrew, and the king's clerks sent hasty letters to their master. If Edward was alarmed, however, he still refused to show it. Collection of the eighth must proceed, he replied, and a new propaganda offensive was desirable. Already embarked and anchored off Dover, the king directed the exchequer to look to his regency council for future orders, and set sail for Flanders.[182]

Civil war seemed imminent and inevitable as both sides in England sought to rally support. The earls made common cause with the citizens of London, and forged closer links with the clergy (who had also rejected the recent tax demand). The regency council made overtures for peace but continued to prepare for conflict. More knights were ordered to Rochester in late August and, when a parliament was called for 30 September, royalists and troops were summoned in advance of the opposition. In the event, however, an armed struggle in England was avoided thanks to a military disaster in Scotland; on 11 September, Scottish forces inflicted a crushing defeat on Warenne's army at Stirling Bridge. The fears expressed at Salisbury and Stratford had proved justified, and the regency council was forced to come to terms. In a capital charged with suspicious tensions, the parliament met and negotiations began.[183]

Eventually, on 10 October, a settlement was reached. Within days the regency council was able to obtain a new tax grant (a ninth), and summon an army to go against the Scots. In order to secure these gains, however, they had been forced to concede a great deal. The *Confirmatio Cartarum*, as the settlement was known, upheld and addressed the principal complaints that the earls had expressed during the summer in the Remonstrances. Primarily, the new document promised to publish and enforce the laws and customs contained in Magna Carta and the Forest Charter; but it also contained additional clauses, restricting the imposition of prises and abolishing the maltote. In addition, the *Confirmatio* stipulated that in future taxation would require consent. This had been the most important of the new demands made by the opposition in their draft proposal of October, *De Tallagio Non Concedendo*, and was a clear response to the provocative claims made for the eighth in July. Of course, the concessions still depended on the approval of the king himself, as did the pardons that

[182] *Documents 1297*, pp. 137-9 (*EHD*, iii, 482-3); Prestwich, *Edward I*, pp. 422, 424-5.
[183] Prestwich, *Edward I*, pp. 414, 425-7, 478. J.H. Denton, *Robert Winchelsey and the Crown, 1294-1313* (Cambridge, 1980), pp. 158-61; Guisborough, pp. 294, 308; F. *Nicholai Triveti...Annales Sex Regum Angliae*, ed. T. Hog (London, 1845), pp. 366-8; *Parl. Writs*, i, 55-6.

the regency council had promised to obtain for the earls and their supporters. Edward, however, stuck in Flanders, had no more room for manoeuvre than his councillors in London; on 5 November, he ratified the *Confirmatio* and assented to the pardons. After eight months of determined opposition, Norfolk, Hereford and their supporters had won a considerable victory.[184]

In many respects, however, this victory was just the beginning of a much longer struggle. Bigod, Bohun and their clerical supporters – chief among whom was Archbishop Winchelsey – had cause to be concerned on three heads. Firstly, in negotiating the October agreement, the regency council had insisted on a much looser definition of 'consent' than that proposed by the earls in *De Tallagio*. Whereas the draft document had envisaged tallages and aids approved by 'archbishops, bishops, earls, barons, knights, burgesses and other free men', *Confirmatio Cartarum* required only 'the common assent of all the realm' for such grants. Secondly, whereas the earls had wanted to add new clauses to Magna Carta, the government had succeeded in keeping the *Confirmatio*'s provisions separate and distinct. As a result, the biannual publication of the charters guaranteed by the new document did not apply to its own additional chapters, nor could violations of these chapters be enforced – as in Magna Carta's case – with spiritual penalties. The lack of protection for the *Confirmatio*'s new sections gave rise to the opposition's third major concern: namely, that Edward would find ways and excuses to overturn the concessions that had been wrung from him. The king was not renowned for keeping his word – and the next three years did nothing to improve his reputation.[185]

The concern of the king's opponents to safeguard their victory was very evident at the start of 1298. Early in the new year Norfolk and Hereford called a meeting of magnates to York, with the clear intention of bolstering the charters and the recent concessions in advance of the Scottish expedition. As well as summoning the earls of Surrey, Arundel and Gloucester, they sent for the bishop of Carlisle, who on 21 January performed exactly the kind of public ceremony demanded in the *Confirmatio*. Standing in the pulpit of York Minster, with the constable and marshal stood to either side, the bishop pronounced solemn sentence of excommunication on those who violated the charters.[186]

Feeling perhaps somewhat more secure, the earls set out for Scotland. Having mustered in Newcastle towards the end of January, they came to the relief of Roxburgh around the middle of the following month, and

[184] *Documents 1297*, pp. 154-6, 158-60 (*EHD*, iii, 485-7); *Parl. Writs*, i, 61-2, 302-3; Prestwich, *Edward I*, pp. 427-9.

[185] In general, see Denton, *Robert Winchelsey*, pp. 183-8; Prestwich, *Edward I*, pp. 517-28; H. Rothwell, 'Edward I and the Struggle for the Charters, 1297-1305', *Studies in Medieval History presented to F.M. Powicke* (Oxford, 1947), pp. 319-32.

[186] Guisborough, p. 314; Langtoft, pp. 306-9.

went on to recapture Berwick before 23 February. At that point, however, a message arrived from Edward, still in Flanders, halting the campaign and instructing Warenne to delay the advance until his return. The order was to remain in Berwick, but we know that Roger departed for his own estates in Yorkshire – we catch him at Settrington on 10 April.[187] The same day, the king, who had arrived back in England in mid-March, summoned all the earls to meet in York for a parliament on 24 May.[188]

This gathering must have been anticipated with some apprehension by all involved; it was first occasion (as far as can be seen) that Edward and the earl marshal had faced each other since their public row at the Salisbury parliament fifteen months beforehand. According to some commentators, ancient and modern, the meeting was an entirely amicable one.[189] Other writers, however, make it clear that suspicion still hung heavy in the air. Norfolk and Hereford had heard rumours that the king intended to renounce the *Confirmatio* on the grounds that it had been granted on foreign soil. They would go no further, they insisted, unless he gave them greater reassurances, both over the charters and the perambulation of the Forest. To this end, Edward induced three other earls and the bishop of Durham to swear on his soul that these things would be carried out once the Scots had been defeated.[190]

The great victory at Falkirk on 22 July may therefore have resurrected these arguments, for the king showed no sign of being about to fulfil his pledge. There were also fresh tensions that arose as a result of the conduct of the campaign itself. Soon after the army had left Lochmaben, Edward offended Bigod and Bohun by giving the isle of Arran to Thomas Bisset; consequently, when they reached Carlisle, both earls complained that their men were exhausted and sought licence to withdraw. Guisborough suggests that the king, in favouring Bisset, had broken an earlier promise not to make such grants without the earls' counsel. It is possible, however, that Bigod and Bohun had objected on the grounds that their rights as marshal and constable had been ignored; later tracts on the subject stated that the marshal had the right to attend councils of war. There had almost certainly been conflict over the size of the fees both men could claim in respect of their offices. A month after the earls' departure, Edward ordered the exchequer to look into the validity of their claims.[191]

By 1299, the measure of goodwill that had been extended to the king since his return had all but evaporated. Faced with his evident apathy

---

[187] Guisborough, p. 315; Appendix B.
[188] *Parl. Writs*, i, 65; *CCR, 1296-1302*, p. 201.
[189] *Bury*, p. 148; Powicke, *Thirteenth Century*, p. 689. There is no evidence in the references Powicke cites for a 'kiss of peace' between Roger and Edward.
[190] Guisborough, p. 324. Writing in Yorkshire, Guisborough is likely to have been better informed than Bury.
[191] Guisborough, pp. 327-9; Prestwich, *Edward I*, pp. 481-2; *CCR, 1296-1302*, pp. 179-80 (also SC1/30/1).

towards the charters, the opposition became more vigorous and more vocal. Edward found it impossible to raise another army for Scotland and, when confronted by his critics at a parliament in March, he responded first by prevaricating and then simply by running away from the assembly. The strength of the opposition is all the more striking in view of Hereford's death at the end of 1298. Although the earl was succeeded by his namesake son, who adopted and maintained his father's political position, the weight of leadership must have fallen all the more heavily on Roger Bigod's shoulders. The earl marshal appears to have borne it well, however; when another parliament was summoned for May, he turned up in great force, determined to hold the king to account. Having caused astonishment in April by publishing the Forest Charter with five of its clauses removed, Edward was now obliged to make concessions on the same issue. Perambulations of the Forest, first promised in October 1297, were scheduled to begin at Michaelmas.[192]

The celebration of Edward's marriage to Margaret of France in September 1299 provided the king with only a brief respite from the demands of his opponents.[193] In the following year's Lenten parliament the pressure was resumed, with calls for a new confirmation of Magna Carta and the Charter of the Forest. 'We know you to be a good and prudent prince', Roger told Edward. 'Human and divine reason demand that you accept our just petitions.'[194] It was financial necessity, however, rather than the dictates of reason, that compelled the king to act. Denied both funds and military support, his victories in Scotland were being undone. With great reluctance therefore, he conceded the *Articuli super Cartas*, a series of detailed provisions intended to enforce the demands made since 1297. In return Edward was able to obtain permission to levy a twentieth, but in the event he appears to have deliberately chosen not to do so.[195] The campaign planned for the summer nevertheless went ahead, for the king had issued a feudal summons, which could hardly be refused. Few magnates, however, participated in person.[196] Roger, perhaps surprisingly, does seem to have intended to accompany Edward, and travelled as far north as York. But at some point thereafter, the earl fell

---

[192] Guisborough, pp. 329-30; *Bury*, p. 152; *Parl. Writs*, i, 79-80; Prestwich, *Edward I*, pp. 520-21. Cf. Denton, *Robert Winchelsey*, p. 185.

[193] For Roger's attendance, see *Bury*, p. 153; Gervase, p. 317.

[194] *Parl. Writs*, i, 82; Rishanger, *C&A*, p. 404.

[195] *SR*, i, 136-41 (*EHD*, iii, 496-501); Prestwich, *Edward I*, pp. 523-5. Certain clauses in the *Articuli* may have been a covert attack on the treasurer, Walter de Langton. Maddicott, '"1258" and "1297"', pp. 8-10.

[196] *Parl. Writs*, i, 327, 331; Prestwich, *Edward I*, p. 484.

sick, and substituted John de Seagrave to serve in his place.[197] Once again, there were negotiations over the fees due to the marshal and constable.[198]

Roger's opposition to the king culminated in the Lincoln parliament at the start of 1301.[199] Local man Robert Manning of Bourne, writing thirty years later, remembered the occasion well. The marshal, he tells us, stayed at the Gilbertine priory of St Katherine, which lay to the south of the city, while the king lodged at the bishop's manor of Nettleham, some miles to the north-east.[200] As for the assembly itself, little had changed since the previous year (indeed, by royal request, even the members returned from the shires were the same). The king was still seeking a grant of taxation, and his critics continued to insist that the charters be enforced and the perambulation be completed. From the chroniclers' descriptions and the official record the meeting seems less important and more sober than those held in the years beforehand. But in fact the Lincoln parliament was decisive, and decisive in favour of the opposition. All the frustration this time was on Edward's part; he was especially indignant when the magnates requested a say in the appointment of royal ministers. On that issue the king silenced his critics, but in many other areas – his rights to taxation and prise, the scope of the Forest – he was forced to concede a great deal. Edward's subsequent bitterness (he spoke of both the 'undoing' of the Crown and 'the surrender of his hereditary right') is a good measure of the scale of his opponents' success.[201]

THE END OF AN EARLDOM

The Lincoln parliament of 1301 effectively marks the end of Roger Bigod's political career; thereafter, he all but vanishes from the public stage. In 1302, however, he made a rare appearance in order to strike a celebrated deal with Edward I.[202] The official record of this agreement is extended and complicated, but its fundamental points can be summarized as follows: on 12 April that year, the earl came to St John's Abbey in Colchester and, in the presence of several high-ranking royal officials, sealed a charter by which he surrendered his entire landed estate, the

---

[197] Appendix B; *Bury*, p. 154; Langtoft, pp. 322-3. For Seagrave as Roger's lieutenant, see SC1/27/150; *CDS, 1272-1307*, p. 292; *CDS, 1108-1516*, p. 163. For the earl's illness, see below, p. 182.

[198] *CDS, 1272-1307*, p. 292. These continued the following year: see *CDS, 1272-1307*, pp. 338-9; Prestwich, *War, Politics and Finance*, p. 267.

[199] *Parl. Writs*, i, 90.

[200] *Robert Mannyng of Brunne: The Chronicle*, ed. I. Sullens (Binghamton, N.Y., 1996), p. 675; F. Hill, *Medieval Lincoln* (Cambridge, 1948), pp. 239, 345-52.

[201] Prestwich, *Edward I*, pp. 525-7; Maddicott, '"1258" and "1297"', p. 13.

[202] For modern comment and analysis, see T.F. Tout, 'The Earldoms under Edward I', *TRHS*, new ser., viii (1894), 139; Powicke, *Henry III*, pp. 705-6; McFarlane, 'Policy', p. 262; Prestwich, *Edward I*, pp. 537-8. What follows is based on ideas first advanced in Morris, 'Murder', pp. 89-99.

marshalship of England and the earldom of Norfolk to the king.[203] One month later, on 11 May, Edward returned Roger's property and in July he restored his titles – but on new terms. Should the earl now die without direct, legitimate heirs, his estate would revert to the Crown. Roger had, of course, fathered no children despite his two marriages, and at fifty-six he was quite old, so the likelihood of reversion was high. The good thing about the deal from his point of view was that it made him substantially richer; the day after the surrender, the king gave the earl lands, rents and farms from the royal demesne worth £1,000 a year. Roger was entitled to retain these assets, in addition to his own restored estates, for the rest of his life.[204]

There were two other major points about this agreement that it is important to note. First, a small number of properties were excepted from the process of surrender and re-grant. The Yorkshire manors of Levisham, Settrington, Thornton and Wilton were retained by the earl, as were the advowson of Geldeston and the manors of Acle and Caistor in Norfolk. Shortly before the deal was struck, Roger was granted permission to alienate these properties 'to whomever he wants'.[205] Second, the deal had a built-in 'insurance clause', intended to protect the Crown's interests in the unlikely event of Roger producing an heir. This clause permitted the heir to inherit the Bigod estate, but required him or her to first pay the king an entry fine of £20,000, and also to repay whatever monies the earl had received down to his death from the £1,000 a year of royal farms and rents.[206]

While tailored to fit specific circumstances, this deal was by no means unique. The king had struck similar bargains with a number of other magnates, including the earl of Gloucester (1290), William de Vescy (1297), and even Llywelyn ap Gruffudd (1277). Later in 1302 he performed the same kind of transaction with the earl of Hereford and, as we have seen, he had already come to an identical arrangement in 1277 with Roger

---

[203] *CCR, 1296-1302*, pp. 581-2. There were a few significant exceptions to the process, discussed below.

[204] *CPR, 1301-1307*, pp. 29-31, 36; *CChR, 1300-1326*, pp. 25-6; *CFR, 1272-1307*, p. 452. Note that in the period between the surrender and the re-grant Roger was given custody of the castles of Nottingham and Bristol, either as security, or simply as accommodation. Note also that the earl's Irish estates were restored in July, at the same time as his titles.

[205] *CCR, 1296-1302*, p. 581; *CPR, 1301-1307*, p. 30. Note also that the manors of Dovercourt, Kennett and Suffield were restored to Roger on different terms. In 1290 these manors had been assigned to his wife, Alice, as part of her dower. They were therefore re-granted as a joint entail to the earl and the countess. *CChR, 1300-1326*, p. 25; above, p. 138.

[206] *CPR, 1301-1307*, p. 31; *CChR, 1300-1326*, p. 25; Morris, 'Murder', p. 91. Cf. Prestwich, *Edward I*, p. 538, where a subsequent reference to this clause (*CPR, 1301-1307*, p. 317) is misinterpreted as part of a non-existent later deal. Documents were exchanged in 1305 because the earl's original copy of the agreement did not make mention of this clause. E159/78, mm. 35, 40d, 67d.

himself, albeit on a much smaller scale.[207] Edward's fondness for this type of bargain has long been recognized. K.B. McFarlane thought that by and large they showed him in a poor light, even going so far as say from time to time it suited the king to 'murder' an earldom for his own ends.[208]

Contemporary opinion on the motives behind the deal was more mixed. At one extreme, the author of the Westminster *Flores Historiarum* asserted that it was orchestrated by the king in revenge for the events of 1297. Edward, we are told, summoned Roger and accused the earl of plotting against him while he was in Flanders; Roger, not knowing how to answer, submitted to the king and made him his heir.[209] In another famous account, however, Edward is involved only as a disinterested third party; the real cause of the deal is said to be a bitter row within the Bigod family itself. According to Walter of Guisborough, the earl was being pressed by his brother, John, for the repayment of a loan, and their argument caused Roger to turn to the king for assistance. Thus the deal becomes a spiteful exercise on the earl's part, in which he obtained the wherewithal to pay his brother, but at the price of denying him the ability to inherit the earldom.[210]

Both of these accounts have major problems. The story in the Westminster *Flores* is the most clearly compromised, since it misdates the deal by a number of years; rather than occurring in the proper context of April 1302, it is presented as if brokered in October 1305. The chronicler's subsequent comments, moreover, being based solely on biblical and patristic texts, advertise his ignorance of any genuine details.[211] His account is not entirely without interest, for Roger was actually in Westminster at the later date, making his first appearance at court for a number of years; no doubt his arrival excited *Flores*'s curiosity, even though it did not satisfy it. The chronicler goes on to describe Edward's humiliation of Robert Winchelsey, which *was* taking place in the autumn of 1305, as was the king's attempt to undo his recent concessions. The earl's reappearance in Westminster may well have been connected with these manoeuvres. But they clearly had nothing whatsoever to do with the surrender of his estate three years beforehand.[212]

---

[207] Prestwich, *Edward I*, pp. 348-9, 538-9; Davies, *Conquest, Coexistence and Change*, p. 336; above, pp. 117-18.

[208] Powicke, *Henry III*, pp. 704-11; McFarlane, 'Policy', pp. 251-4.

[209] *Flores*, iii, 125 (for 'earl of Warwick' read 'earl of Norfolk'). This story is repeated in the discredited 'Chronicle of William Rishanger, monk of St Albans', a late fourteenth-century compilation of earlier sources. Rishanger, *C&A*, p. 227; *The St Albans Chronicle, 1406-1420*, ed. V.H. Galbraith (Oxford, 1937), xxxiii–xxxvi; Morris, 'Murder', pp. 91-2.

[210] Guisborough, p. 352. For a translation, see Morris, 'Murder', pp. 93-4.

[211] For the suggestion that Roger *mortem perdidit et vitam invenit*, cf. *Patrologia Latina*, ed. J.-P. Migne (Paris, 1844–), e.g. xvii, 735; cxxxviii, 1226B; clxviii, 860. For the king's speech, cf. Ezekiel 33:11.

[212] Cf. Denton, *Robert Winchelsey*, pp. 221-2; Prestwich, *Edward I*, pp. 547-8.

Guisborough's story, perhaps at first sight less convincing, in fact demonstrates a much better acquaintance with the facts. Not only does the chronicler in this instance get the date right; he is also well informed about the earl's brother, calling him by his first name and correctly identifying him as a pluralist cleric.[213] Being based in Yorkshire, where the Bigods held several manors, Guisborough might have been drawing on local sources. Where his story fails to convince, however, is on motive. It is very hard to believe that Roger surrendered his earldom in a fit of pique. As is the case with the earl's other brothers, the evidence we have on John Bigod is somewhat limited.[214] Nevertheless, what information we do have suggests that he and Roger got on well enough, both up to the point of the earl's land deal and beyond.[215] John was still running up expenses at his brother's manor of Lopham in 1306, and around the same time Roger wrote to the pope on John's behalf, seeking permission for him to continue to hold his several churches.[216] Even if, however, the two men did quarrel in 1302, John was a celibate man in his fifties, and thus (as McFarlane observed) only the heir to the earldom in a temporary sense.[217] The real losers were John Bigod of Stockton, the earl's cousin, and his sons, and it is even less likely that Roger was seeking deliberately to disinherit this side of the family. His cousin, as we have seen, was one of the earl's longest-serving affinity members. The strength of their relationship is certified in 1302 by Roger's gift to John of the manor of Settrington, one of the few manors exempted from the surrender. It was a grant the earl made, to quote the deed itself, 'for good service done'.[218]

---

[213] *CPL, 1305-42*, p. 13. John was rector of Acle and Earsham in Norfolk, Eyke, Framlingham and Theberton in Suffolk, and Cottingham in Yorkshire. He was also rector of 'Tetherington', which is far more likely to be Settrington than the editor's suggestion of Terrington, Norfolk (where the Bigods held neither land nor advowson). In addition, John was the advocate of Thetford Priory, much to the financial disadvantage of the monks there. *Visitations of English Cluniac Foundations*, ed. G.F. Duckett (London, 1890), pp. 34-5; S. Wood, *English Monasteries and their Patrons in the Thirteenth Century* (Oxford, 1955), p. 104.

[214] There are many references to 'John Bigod' in the ministers' accounts, but it is not always possible to distinguish the earl's brother from his cousin, John Bigod of Stockton. For certain references to the former, see SC6/937/29; SC6/932/18; SC6/837/16; SC6/1005/26; SC6/938/4; SC6/748/19; SC6/1005/27; SC6/938/10.

[215] Edward I clearly believed that the brothers were sufficiently close in 1297 that an attack on John would hurt Roger (above, p. 164). In 1301, John witnessed two of his brother's charters to Tintern Abbey, and was machinating with the earl over the appointment of a new prior at Thetford. RBIV 27; *CPL, 1198-1304*, pp. 594-5; *VCH Norfolk*, ii, 365; Wood, *English Monasteries*, pp. 18, 57-8.

[216] SC6/938/11 (the reference here can only be John the brother; John Bigod of Stockton died before 21 March 1305: *CIPM*, iv, 216); *CPL, 1305-42*, p. 13.

[217] McFarlane, 'Policy', p. 262. John cannot have been much younger than Roger; the earliest reference to him comes in 1271, and in 1272 he was appointed rector of Cottingham by his mother. SC6/937/29; *Reg. Giffard*, p. 58.

[218] RBIV 30; above, pp. 143-5, 149. Note he also received the advowson of Geldeston.

The deal was also discussed by several other chroniclers, contemporary or nearly so, among whom there is more consensus. 'John de Trokelowe' (who may well have been William Rishanger) believed that, once the old earl of Hereford had died in 1298, Roger was not strong enough to carry on the struggle against Edward alone, and was motivated by fear (*timore ductus*) to seek the king's goodwill and make him his heir. Thomas Grey of Heton wrote that the earl had disinherited himself 'partly because he feared that the king might accuse him of bad conduct the time he and others conspired against him at Lincoln'. Less specifically, the author of the *Vita Edwardi Secundi* linked Roger's fate with those of Simon de Montfort and Robert de Ferrers. 'Each of these had resisted the king,' the chronicler wrote, 'and each in the end succumbed.'[219] Most writers therefore believed that by 1302 Roger had recognized that his position was vulnerable, and had submitted to Edward as a pre-emptive security measure.

This may in part be true. After all, the arrangement that the two men reached was neither 'balanced' nor 'fair'. The king required the earl to give up a vast amount in return for comparatively little. There must, it seems, have been some degree of compulsion involved. The question is, however, was this compulsion supplied by Edward? Undoubtedly the king proposed the shape of the deal, for it bears all the hallmarks of his other, similar agreements. But he was certainly not disinheriting the earl simply for the sake of seeing a former opponent humbled. For Edward, the transaction was primarily about the solution of a novel and pressing problem. His marriage to Margaret of France in 1299 had been negotiated on the understanding that any male children that the match produced would each receive estates worth 10,000 marks, and by 1301 the king had fathered two baby boys. Whether or not Edward desired revenge is debatable. That he needed vast amounts of land is unquestionable.

Roger, of course, had no children, and so was in a position to oblige. He did not, however, do so without condition. The king had to purchase his submission with the temporary alienation of £1,000 of royal demesne – a fact often overlooked. It behoves us, therefore, to ask why the earl wanted this extra money. According to an estimate of 1304, he was already worth some £4,000 a year, so we might well wonder what benefit he saw in a 20 per cent increase in income.[220] The rich may always desire to be richer, but it is difficult to imagine circumstances in which an extra £1,000 a year could be viewed as an inducement when the price was total disinheritance.

[219] *Johannis de Trokelowe et Henrici de Blaneforde, Chronica et Annales*, ed. H.T. Riley (Rolls Ser., 1866), p. 74; *St Albans Chronicle*, ed. Galbraith, p xxx; *Scalacronica by Sir Thomas Grey of Heton, Knight*, ed. J. Stevenson (Maitland Club, Edinburgh, 1836), p. 133; *Vita Edwardi Secundi*, ed. N. Denholm-Young (London, 1957), p. 44.
[220] Above, p. 40.

Walter of Guisborough, however, suggests just such a scenario. The earl, he says, was unable to repay his brother in 1302 because he had 'spent a great deal when he supported the party against the king'.[221] In the period from 1297 to 1301, it seems clear that Roger had massively over-recruited. 'The earl marshal came to court with a thousand horse', noted the Bury chronicler in 1299, clearly impressed by the size of Roger's retinue at that year's Easter parliament. Similarly, Robert Manning of Bourne saw only two camps when he looked at Lincoln in 1301; one for the king, the other for the marshal.[222] When, in the autumn of 1297, a number of magnates agreed to serve in Scotland, Roger's contingent of 130 horsemen was by far the largest; Gloucester, who stood second in the list, brought a company of only 100, despite the fact that his landed resources were 50 per cent greater. Compared with the force of seventy men that the marshal took to Wales in 1294, his household of 1297 was almost twice the size.[223]

It may also have been the case that Roger needed to recruit more men that year in order to compensate for the desertion of existing *familiares*. The small degree of overlap between the two household lists cited above has been used in the past to argue for the volatility of contemporary magnate retinues.[224] This is undoubtedly part of the explanation; only six individuals named in the 1297 list appear in that of 1294.[225] The reasons behind the change, however, might owe as much to specific circumstances as to general trends. Roger, for example, appears to have enjoyed an amicable relationship with Thomas de Berkeley, staying at his castle in 1291 and playing 'griesche' with him at Chepstow the following year.[226] At a critical moment in July 1297, however, Berkeley placed himself firmly in the royalist camp by contracting to serve Aymer de Valence. (The decision

---

[221] Guisborough, p. 352.

[222] *Bury*, p. 152; above, p. 171.

[223] *CDS, 1272-1307*, p. 267; above, p. 153. As noted above, a list drawn up in 1294 suggests the earl's retinue that year was 70 horsemen, 33 of whom were knights. A similar list compiled in 1297 appears at first glance to show a smaller company, but in fact the number of bannerets has increased. In the case of one of these men – John de Seagrave – we know from other evidence that he provided Roger with a sub-retinue of fifteen knights (below, pp. 177-8). This alone brings the total number of knights in 1297 to 29. The other four bannerets would thus have to bring only one additional man each to match the 1294 figure of 33. They probably brought a good many more, pushing the earl's retinue up to the 130 men he agreed to supply for Scotland. C81/1698/130, 131 (printed in *Documents 1297*, pp. 157-8).

[224] *Documents 1297*, p. 158n; M. Prestwich, *Armies and Warfare in the Middle Ages: The English Experience* (London, 1996), p. 44.

[225] Thomas de Akeny, Peter de Tadington, Master Thomas de Siddington, John de Bosham, Jolanus the Cook and Walter de Mettingham. Only three other men (all knights) in the 1297 list can be linked to Roger before that date: John Lovel, Ralph de Munchensi and Nicholas de Wokindon served with the earl in 1296. Above, p. 161n; CChW, p. 71.

[226] Above, pp. 152-3; RBIV 19; SC6/922/3. *Griesche* was evidently some sort of gambling game (Roger was paid 30s, and Berkeley lent him 25s, in order to play). Cf. *Dictionnaire de l'Ancienne Langue Francaise*, ed. F. Godefroy (10 vols., Paris, 1881-1902), iv, 355-6.

soon paid off; a week later the king appointed Berkeley as constable in place of Hereford.)[227] No less interesting is the indenture drawn up the following month between two of Roger's tenants, John Bluet and William Martel, and witnessed by a third, John ap Adam.[228] Bluet had served the earl between 1290 and 1294, only to subsequently disappear from his circle;[229] Ap Adam, a long-time *familiaris*, had campaigned with him in 1277, 1287, 1294 and 1296, yet was conspicuously absent from his retinue in 1297-98.[230] Two other witnesses to the agreement, John de Knoville and John de Howel, featured in the Bigod household of 1294 but not that of 1297.[231] Frustratingly, we cannot say where this cabal of men, all of whom had previously been attached to Roger, were staying when the agreement was drawn up.[232] The document itself, however, with its clause obliging Martel to go to war with Bluet not only in France or Wales but also in England (*'que Deu deffende'*) reveals something of the enormous strain that politics was placing on loyalty at the time.[233]

To boost the numbers in his household, and perhaps to compensate for desertion, the earl had to spend.[234] The amount of money he disgorged in the period 1297-1301 cannot be recovered, but the scale of the demands which recruitment placed on his purse is suggested by the well-known indenture he made with John de Seagrave in June 1297.[235] This document is, in many respects, an extraordinary one; Seagrave, who subsequently deputized for Roger on several occasions, was clearly an exceptionally important addition to the earl's circle.[236] The sub-retinue he agreed to

---

[227] 'Private Indentures for Life Service', ed. Jones and Walker, pp. 37-9; above, p. 165. It is interesting to note that Thomas and his son Maurice subsequently deserted Valence in similar circumstances at a later date. J.R.S. Phillips, *Aymer de Valence, Earl of Pembroke* (Oxford, 1972), pp. 255, 261-7.

[228] 'Private Indentures for Life Service', ed. Jones and Walker, pp. 40-41; *CIPM*, iv, 294, 299.

[229] RBIV 18 and 23; Ridgard, p. 49; SC6/922/3 ('paid to John Bluet, £20').

[230] Above, pp. 143-5, 149-50, 152. Ap Adam reappears in the affinity in 1304, representing Roger at the exchequer that year, and witnessing a charter in 1305. Below, p. 180; RBIV 33.

[231] Ridgard, p. 49.

[232] It is given at 'Ellcestre', which has proved unidentifiable.

[233] 'Private Indentures for Life Service', ed. Jones and Walker, p. 41.

[234] Men who had deserted the retinue might still constitute a drain on resources. This is most obvious in the case of individuals such as Grandson or Mortimer, who received permanent grants of land and rent from the earl for what looks to have been limited service during the Welsh wars. It could, however, also apply to men who had been granted annuities. Even though Roger fell out violently with Robert Cockerel, he was nevertheless obliged to continue to pay the former seneschal the £5 a year granted to him for life 'by a charter of the previous earl'. The disadvantages of such unconditional grants was one factor which led to the increasing use of the more precise indenture of retinue. Above, pp. 121, 150-51. Cf. Bean, *Lord to Patron*, p. 17.

[235] Denholm-Young, *SAIE*, pp. 24, 167-8.

[236] Seagrave often deputized when the earl was ill. It may be that this was part of Roger's reason for making this bargain. Note in this regard that the indenture was intended to

provide – sixteen knights, himself included – was exceedingly large, and as such his reward – a whole manor (Loddon, in Norfolk) – was correspondingly substantial.[237] Nevertheless, his indenture reveals something of the ordinary demands that day-to-day maintenance of the household entailed. Seagreave's knights insisted on having what the permanent Bigod bachelors took for granted: food ('bouche of court') for themselves, provender for their horses, and wages for their grooms; Seagrave himself wanted robes 'like the foremost banneret' in Roger's household, and sought liveries for his bachelors as good as those given to the earl's own.[238] Such expenses were by far the greatest drain on a magnate's resources; in 1319, for example, Thomas of Lancaster spent over 40 per cent of his £11,000 a year income (£4,800) on feeding his household.[239] To raise arms against the king was thus an extremely dangerous undertaking, not just because of the obvious political risks involved, but because of the huge financial outlay required to raise the necessary force. After their successful opposition to Richard II in 1387-88, the Appellants were voted no less than £20,000 by the commons for 'their great expenses in saving the kingdom'.[240] It takes little imagining to see that Roger Bigod could have quickly exhausted his resources during his four years in opposition.

As a result of money pledged to retainers in this period, the earl must have incurred numerous debts. He may also have turned to creditors in order to make ends meet. By 1297, of course, he no longer had access to the Italian bankers who had helped him earlier in his career. Thus Guisborough's suggestion that Roger had borrowed from his well-beneficed brother is perfectly plausible, even if his story of deliberate disinheritance is not. By 1302 there must have been much agonizing in the higher echelons of the earl's household; arguments among his council about where the money was going to come from, and talk of impending financial ruin.

One way Roger may have sought to minimize or settle these debts was by granting away property; we have already noted that John de Seagrave received the manor of Loddon in 1297. There were other similar alienations in the five years prior to the deal with the king. In 1298 the earl granted a messuage in Earsham to John de Newent, a *familiaris* from Chepstow; in 1300, he gave land in Seething to John Bigod of Stockton; and in February 1302, Roger conferred some parcels of property in Suffolk

---

last for the earl's life rather than Seagrave's own. *Documents 1297*, p. 126; Langtoft, pp. 322-3; below, p. 182.

[237] Cf. Roger's willingness to alienate land with Arundel's refusal to countenance such a measure at the same point in time. *Documents 1297*, pp. 6, 141-2.

[238] These privileges did not apply if Seagrave and his company fought overseas; instead they received a lump sum of £80 plus 2s per knight per day.

[239] Maddicott, *Thomas of Lancaster*, p. 27.

[240] A. Tuck, *Richard II and the English Nobility* (London, 1973), p. 128.

on his chamberlain John de Uffeton.[241] Not all these grants, perhaps, should be read as remuneration for recent military support; the grant to Uffeton, made on the eve of the surrender, might be better interpreted as a gift for faithful service over a longer period. Other examples, however, show the earl rewarding individuals with whom he had no longstanding connection. At some point before 1302, he alienated the manor of Peasenhall in Suffolk to Nicholas de Seagrave, brother of John, and granted the Norfolk manor of Attleborough to Ralph de Munchensi, who occurs in the household during the years 1296-98.[242] Moreover, Roger clearly intended this process to continue after 1302 – hence the four Yorkshire manors exempted from the surrender. Wilton was granted to John Lovel, who had served the earl since 1296 and taken a visible stand with him at the exchequer in 1297; Levisham was given to William de Ormesby, a leading justice and Bigod councillor; Thornton went to Robert de Beverley, who served as Roger's wardrober between 1301 and 1304; Settrington, as we have already noted, was given to John Bigod of Stockton.[243]

If then, as Guisborough suggests, the earl had exhausted his financial resources during his period of opposition, and moreover had incurred large debts, it would explain why an extra £1,000 a year was a tempting prospect. The sum is more significant than it sounds, since much of the earl's ordinary estate income would have been absorbed by the day-to-day costs of running his household and administration. The £1,000 he received from the king, by contrast, was disposable cash with no prior claims on it. There is one clear example of Roger using this money to meet a pre-existing commitment to a member of his household. In September 1303 the earl wrote to the monks of Christchurch, Canterbury, who contributed £10 each year to the annual £1,000 payment, asking them in future to give this sum directly to William de Spanby, a Bigod clerk, as his annual fee.[244]

As well as meeting his obligations to private individuals, Roger also seems to have been anxious to clear his debts to the Crown. These had not been in any way affected by the land deal of 1302. After the surrender, Edward expected the earl to continue paying his debts at terms of £100 a

[241] RBIV 25, 26, 28 and 33.
[242] *CPR, 1301-1307*, pp. 64, 318; *CIM*, i, 511; *CChW*, p. 389; *Documents 1297*, p. 157; SC6/873/19.
[243] *Feudal Aids*, vi, 136; *CCR, 1302-1307*, p. 19; *CPR, 1301-1307*, p. 153; above, pp. 172, 174; *Documents 1297*, pp. 137, 157; SC6/997/13; SC6/991/26. The exempted manor of Caistor was sold for £100 in 1303 to Walter de Langton, a transaction perhaps connected with Roger's illegal alienation of the advowson of Thetford Priory to the treasurer. CP25/1/161/119, m. 948; A. Beardwood, 'The Trial of Walter Langton, Bishop of Lichfield, 1307-1312', *Transactions of the American Philosophical Soc.*, new ser., 54 (1964), p. 34; *Records of the Trial of Walter Langeton, Bishop of Coventry and Lichfield 1307-1312*, ed. A. Beardwood (Camden, 4th ser., vi, 1969), 274.
[244] *CPR, 1301-1307*, pp. 30, 262; Canterbury, Dean and Chapter Muniments, Register I, f. 141v.

year, just as he had done before. Having secured the rights to the earldom, it seems that the king did not see any need to press the earl for full repayment. Despite this, however, Roger appears to have insisted on revisiting the issue. Once again, the explanation may lie in his irritation at the exchequer's attempts to distrain him and his newly enfeoffed tenants on their Yorkshire manors for debts incurred by the previous owner.[245] It is certainly striking that, when Edward finally intervened on the earl's behalf, he was staying at Birdsall, just a couple of miles from Settrington. Writing to the exchequer on 11 October 1304, he instructed the clerks to listen to Roger's arguments concerning a number of contentious debts, and to discharge the earl if his reasons were valid. In particular, the king mentioned the sums being charged to Roger for his father's debts, for the Welsh campaigns, and for the relief of his first wife.[246] Accordingly, an extraordinary meeting took place at the exchequer a few weeks later, at which John ap Adam and William de Spanby, the earl's attorneys, painstakingly went through all of his debts with the king's accountants.[247]

In 1293, after the previous extraordinary audit at the king's command, Roger's total 'clear' debt had stood at £2,232.[248] Soon afterwards it had been discovered that the earl also owed £410 for wardrobe prests; thus, in 1296, although he had paid a further £190 into the treasury, his overall liability had crept up to £2,427.[249] Thereafter, however, this figure fell steadily as Roger paid off £100 a year. By 1300 it had dropped by £400 to stand at £2,027, and in 1302 it dropped a further £300 to stand at £1,727.[250] This was the starting point for the earl's attorneys and the exchequer clerks in 1304. At great length, they broke the total down into its constituent parts, which they then divided, along with any undeclared sums, into two groups: namely, Roger's own debts, and the debts owed by his ancestors. From the first group, the auditors proceeded, as per the king's writ, to deduct the negligible demand of £10 for the relief of Aline la Despenser, and the far more substantial sum of £784, the total scutage charged to the earl for both Welsh wars. This, of course, was entirely proper: as the clerks noted, 'Roger did full service to the king in the armies aforesaid'. The treatment of the ancestral debts, however, was ludicrous. The auditors, citing the authority of Edward's recent instructions, simply wrote off the whole amount: a total of £2,042. Edward had referred them

---

[245] In March 1303, Edward ordered the exchequer not to distrain William de Ormesby for debts at Thornton, but to distrain the earl instead. A year later, the king instructed the clerks to acquit both Roger and his tenants of debts owed by Osbert de Bolebeck, the previous owner. *CCR, 1302-1307*, pp. 19, 132, 140-41. Cf. above, p. 158.

[246] *CCR, 1302-1307*, pp. 177-8.

[247] E372/149, m. 2d, and for all the figures below unless noted otherwise.

[248] Above, p. 159.

[249] E159/67, m. 26d; E372/141, m. 6d.

[250] E372/145, m. 12d; E372/147, m. 1d. Note that he paid throughout the period 1297-1301. Only at Easter 1299 did he fail to keep his terms, which were subsequently re-granted at the parliament in May. E159/72, m. 27d (*CFR, 1272-1307*, p. 414).

to a writ of his father, granting a partial pardon of debt to Hugh Bigod (up to £800, with allowances for other expenses). The king was clearly unaware that this document had already been used to diminish Hugh's debts once before; the clerks, if they knew better, nevertheless played along. Not only did they scratch from the record everything once owed by Roger's father; they also wrote off the controversial unpaid scutages of his uncle. Henry III's writ had seemingly become a magic remedy for every Bigod debt incurred before 1270.

It was not, however, enough to wipe the slate clean. Creative accountancy may have reduced Roger's previously declared total to £710, but the extensive audit had revealed new debts (mostly prests of the wardrobe, hitherto overlooked). When the final reckoning was completed, the earl was declared to owe £1,812. A session that the earl had hoped would reduce his liability had actually managed to increase it.

Thus, in March 1305, Edward intervened on Roger's behalf for a final time, granting the earl an unconditional pardon of all his Crown debts. According to the writ he sent to the exchequer, the king did this 'out of the great affection which [he] has towards [the earl] for his laudable service...up to this point', and there is no reason to doubt that this was indeed the case.[251] In his previous order to the clerks on Roger's behalf, Edward had similarly explained that he 'did not want the earl to be unduly aggrieved'.[252] The pardon had followed as a natural consequence of the friendly relations that had been re-established in 1302. Many chroniclers commented on the amicability that resulted from the bargain of April that year. 'Trokelowe' said that Roger obtained 'the king's goodwill'. This was a judgement echoed by Nicholas Trivet, who summarized Guisborough's story, but supplied the notion that the earl was *'captans benevolentia regis'*.[253] The London annalist, a well informed if economical writer, reported that Roger and Edward 'became friends' in 1302, and even that less reliable Londoner, the Westminster *Flores*, affirms that this was the case. There is certainly no evidence of further hostility between the two men after April 1302, and some other indications of friendship besides. Edward, for example stayed at Roger's manor of Hamstead Marshall later in the same year; in 1303 he pardoned certain convicted outlaws at the earl's instance; and the following year the king politely requested the use of timber from some of Roger's woods.[254]

It only remains to answer one question: why was Roger so anxious to clear his debts, not only those he owed to men who had served him in 1297-

---

[251] E159/78, m. 14d. Cf. *CPR, 1301-1307*, p. 317, in which the king's reason is not given.

[252] In light of this, and also the peremptory tone adopted by the king throughout his first letter, it may be that the clerks understood that they were to oblige Roger by adjusting the figures in line with his arguments regardless of their validity.

[253] *Nicholai Triveti...Annales*, ed. Hog, p. 401.

[254] *Itinerary of Edward I*, ii, 201; *CPR, 1301-1307*, p. 156; *CCR, 1302-1307*, p. 144.

1301, but also the ones he owed to the Crown? Certainly, in the case of the latter, no pressure was being brought to bear, either before the land deal or after, yet the earl's aim appears to have been total liquidation. By way of a tentative answer, we may make two observations. Firstly, Roger appears to have been possessed of a more than conventional degree of piety (another contrast with his predecessor). The chief reason for believing this is his lifelong sponsorship of the rebuilding of the abbey church at Tintern. The new building was finished in 1301 and the earl was almost certainly present at its dedication ceremony in August. The following year, he presented the house with the manor of Acle in Norfolk, the last of the properties exempted from the surrender, and a huge boost to the monks' income (it later accounted for a quarter of their revenue).[255] It was not just Tintern, however; Roger was similarly generous throughout his career to the friars, bestowing gifts on them at Cambridge, Gloucester, London and Kilkenny.[256] The earl's refusal in 1297 to collect fines from the clergy in his Welsh lordship may likewise have had as much to do with his religious sensibilities as his political stance that year.[257] Secondly, from around 1300 onwards, Roger appears to have been unwell; as we have already seen, he abandoned the Scottish campaign that year out of illness. The belief that the earl was suffering from some form of permanent complaint is borne out in a writ of the following February, requiring him to attend a muster four months later, or to send a deputy 'if…prevented by bodily illness'. This ailment may have been manifesting itself earlier in his career; John de Seagrave, his deputy in later years, was standing in for an incapacitated Roger in 1297, and there are references to doctors treating the earl in 1292 and 1294.[258]

Taking these two observations side by side, it seems that for Roger, a man who took his religion seriously, the end was very much within sight by 1302. Bearing in mind the Church's attitude to debt and debtors, it seems quite plausible that such a man would not have wished to die with his debts unpaid, and for this reason was doing his utmost to clear them. His will has not survived, so the earl's attitude is impossible to divine precisely or directly. It may, however, have corresponded to that of Edmund of Lancaster who, when on the point of dying in 1296, requested that his bones should not be buried until his debts had been paid.[259]

[255] Robinson, *Tintern Abbey*, pp. 15, 32; RBIV 27, 31.

[256] SC6/837/12 ('to the Carmelite friars at Cambridge, 26s 8d of the earl's gift'); SC6/873/18 ('two quarters of grain carried to Ware for the use of the Friars Minor of London'); SC6/921/26, SC6/921/27 and SC6/922/22 (£30 given to the Franciscans of Gloucester to build a refectory, plus gifts of timber in Wentwood for their use); SC6/1239/3 and SC6/1239/9 (gifts of 40s and 100s to the Franciscans at Kilkenny).

[257] *Documents 1297*, pp. 105-6. See also his foundation of a chantry. CChW, pp. 346-7.

[258] Langtoft, pp. 322-3; CCR, 1296-1302, p. 482; *Documents 1297*, p. 126; SC6/922/3 ('20s to Henry Holmes for treating the earl's shin'); SC6/748/24 ('expenses of a man with a horse bringing the earl's doctor to Chepstow').

[259] Guisborough, p. 262.

When Roger died in early December 1306, his body was not interred immediately. Instead, according to the Tintern *Flores Historiarum*, it was led from Framlingham Castle to Thetford Priory, and there placed in a 'certain old chapel', where it remained unburied for the next six months. No reason is suggested for this delay, but an ongoing need to clear the earl's debts would be a plausible explanation. The Tintern chronicler only tells us that on 4 June 1307 Roger was finally laid to rest 'with sufficient honour', and stated for the record that his soul had been gathered to God.[260]

---

[260] *Flores*, iii, 328-9. The chronicler states that Roger died on 7 December 1306, but his death must have come earlier than 6 December (cf. *CIPM*, iv, 290). The printed version erroneously gives the date of the earl's burial as *Julii* rather than *Junii* (cf. BL Royal MS 14 C vi, f. 254).

Conclusion

The death of Roger IV Bigod in 1306 signalled the end of his family as a political force. His brother, the clergyman John, if ever he recouped the money he allegedly wanted so much, had little time to spend it; by 1311 he was also dead.[1] The earl's widow, Alice, having secured her dower in England,[2] spent much of the next ten years abroad, travelling to France and Spain, as well as returning to her homeland in the Low Countries.[3] Independence, however, brought the countess her own share of misfortune. During her absence from East Anglia, her parks were targeted by poachers, and a pilgrimage to Santiago in 1310 was blighted when a ship carrying her clothes and jewels was raided by Flemish pirates.[4] Increasingly drawn to religious devotions, she died in the autumn of 1317.[5] Only Roger's cousins, the Bigods of Stockton, now also of Settrington, had a story that extended further into the future; but since they were low to middling gentry, it was rarely an important or exciting one.[6] Having raised themselves from rude eleventh-century Continental origins to the highest echelons of English aristocracy, the Bigods were returned to obscurity once more.

What conclusions can we reach about Roger III and Roger IV Bigod? Biographers should be slow to pronounce on their subjects, especially when their subjects have been dead for seven centuries. As David Knowles has put it, 'the historian is not a judge, still less a hanging judge'.[7] Nevertheless, a lengthy examination of the evidence demands, if not a final verdict, at least a summing-up. What follows is a consideration of the character, abilities and achievement of both earls.

Thanks to Matthew Paris, we have some memorable images of Roger III Bigod: taking the laurels on the tournament field; threatening to decapitate Henry III's bailiffs; making ready to seize the count of Guisnes; 'swearing terrible oaths' before the pope.[8] Together they form a portrait of a man who was skilled in arms and quick to anger, and who resented royal and foreign interference in his private affairs. This last trait would have made

[1] The appointment of new rectors at Cottingham and Framlingham in January 1312 suggests that he died towards the end of the previous year. *CPR, 1307-13*, pp. 411-12, 414.
[2] Above, pp. 33-4; *Flores*, iii, 329; SC1/61/43; *CCR, 1302-1307*, pp. 478, 484, 508-9, 511-13; 523; *CFR, 1272-1307*, pp. 551-2.
[3] *CPR, 1301-1307*, p. 520; *CPR, 1307-13*, pp. 195, 201, 215, 283, 393-4, 591; *CPR, 1313-17*, pp. 279, 526; *CCR, 1307-13*, p. 357.
[4] *CPR, 1307-13*, p. 533; *CPR, 1313-17*, pp. 54, 72, *CCR, 1307-13*, pp. 267-8; *CCR, 1313-18*, p. 143; SC1/32/113; SC1/33/153; SC1/34/116; *Select Cases on the Law Merchant*, ed. Gross and Hall, i, 94-5.
[5] *CPL, 1305-42*, p. 146; *CPR, 1317-21*, p. 45.
[6] Moor, 'The Bygods', pp. 172-213.
[7] M.D. Knowles, *The Historian and Character* (Cambridge, 1963), p. 13.
[8] *CM*, iii, 404; iv, 478-9; v, 85-6, 530.

him an appealing figure to Paris, whose attitude towards any authority which emanated from outside St Albans was equally critical; we should not, therefore, be too quick to accept his rather flattering description of the earl as a *vir praeclarus*.[9] Nevertheless, much of what the chronicler says is supported by other sources. Roger was addressed in poetry as a *miles strenuus*, and remembered long after his death as a *vir bellicosus*. His passion when confronting Henry III in 1258 is brought out vividly by the Tewkesbury annalist. We even have legal records which state that the earl was prone to act *ex ira*.[10]

As we have already noted, our image of Roger IV is much less rounded. With an abundance of record evidence but a dearth of chronicle descriptions, he is far harder to characterize. In many respects his pursuits were similar to those of his predecessor. We know, for example, that the last earl staged tournaments, so it seems safe to assume he participated in them as well.[11] As a contemporary of Edward I, he also had his fair share of experience in war. What we do not know is how well he acquitted himself in such circumstances. If we cannot write him off as unexceptional (as historians of an earlier age have been inclined to do), we can at least say that, in contrast to his uncle, he was undistinguished.[12]

What did distinguish Roger IV from his uncle was his building work. Again, we have to guard against the bias of our sources: the earl's ministers' accounts allow us to peer into his private administration to a greater degree than is possible for any of his predecessors and almost all of his contemporaries. Nevertheless, even allowing for the fact that we are not comparing like with like, Roger stands out as an extraordinarily prolific builder. The extent of the earl's investment is revealed not only by its written record, but also from the quantity of masonry that still survives. His large-scale works at Chepstow and Tintern are well known and justly celebrated.[13] But we should also not overlook his rebuilding of Bungay Castle, where new walls and a twin-towered gatehouse were added perhaps as late as 1294.[14] At his coastal manor of Walton in Suffolk the earl built a new hall, parts of which remained standing into the nineteenth century.[15] We know he engaged in castle-building in Ireland, and

[9] Above, pp. 21, 78-9.

[10] Above, pp. 20-21, 57, 58n, 95.

[11] Above, p. 101; SC6/932/12 (Caistor, 1271), which records the following expenses consecutively: 'Sir Reginald de Grey and Sir Amaury de St Amand, staying for the tournament, £12 17s'. 'Sir R. de St Amand, from Thursday after St Bartholomew the Apostle [27 August 1271] until the Nativity of the Blessed Virgin Mary [8 September 1271], when his leg was broken, 64s 6½d'.

[12] Cf. Morris, *Welsh Wars*, p. 304; Stubbs, *Constitutional History*, ii, 158.

[13] Turner, *Chepstow Castle, passim*; Robinson, *Tintern Abbey, passim*.

[14] No accounts survive between 1294 and 1301, but see *CPR, 1292-1301*, p. 68. Braun, *Bungay Castle*, p. 20.

[15] J. Fairclough and S.J. Plunkett, 'Drawings of Walton Castle and other Monuments in Walton and Felixstowe', *Proceedings of the Suffolk Institute of Archaeology and History*, 39

Ballymoon seems very likely to have been the result.[16] On the western edge of Wentwood Forest, close to the ancient borders of the lordship of Chepstow, the ruins remain of a miniature fortress-cum-hunting-lodge called Cas Troggy, described in the earl's inquisition post mortem in 1306 as 'newly built'.[17] When we add to these the numerous other enterprises, the results of which are now vanished, it seems fair to regard Roger IV as a man who revelled in redesigning and reordering the world around him.[18]

Roger III, by contrast, appears to have built very little. Even allowing for the absence of documentary evidence, the older earl stands out as the member of his dynasty least interested in leaving an architectural legacy. Roger I founded Thetford, Hugh I built Bungay, and Roger II reconstructed Framlingham. Even Hugh II Bigod, in the limited amount of time allowed to him, established a religious house at Weybridge.[19] But over a long career of forty-five years, Roger III's only recorded achievements in this area are a new chapel at Hamstead Marshall and a new bridge at Chepstow (both long since destroyed).[20] This suggests that he might have been a rather parsimonious individual. Other evidence points in the same direction; it is rare to find the earl making gifts of land or money, either to the Church or to his own followers.[21] Both his successor and predecessors were visibly more profligate in both cases.[22] This was in spite of the fact that, of all his family, Roger III paid the least to the Crown; not just because England was lightly taxed during the reign of Henry III, but also because the king never managed to induce the earl to pay what little money he owed.[23] Financial prudence – one hesitates to use a word like stinginess – could well have been a habit formed in youth; for the first seven years of his career, much of the revenue from Roger's estate – probably more than half – had to be siphoned off to pay for his early accession. Until the death of his mother in 1248, the earl had to make do

---

(2000), pp. 426-59. Expenses for the 'stone chamber' and the 'stone house' at Walton be found in SC6/1007/13-19.

[16] Above, pp. 122-3.

[17] *CIPM*, iv, 296. Cf. SC6/922/8 (Chepstow, 1304): 'Roger de Seymour, constable of the New Castle, £13 6s 8d *per annum*'. For descriptions, see O. Morgan and T. Wakeman, *Notes on Wentwood, Castle Troggy and Llanvair Castle* (Monmouthshire and Caerleon Antiquarian Association, 1863), pp. 23-7; A. Pettifer, *Welsh Castles: A Guide by Counties* (Woodbridge, 2000), p. 125.

[18] e.g., at Bosham, the new hall at 'La Breche' cost £15 3s 5d, the new garden 78s 4d and the new pond £36 2s 9½d (SC6/1020/17; SC6/1020/22; SC6/1020/21). In 1304 almost £23 were spent on the new hall at Hanworth (SC6/936/16). There were new quays built at Brokenwharf in London (cost £10) and Ipswich (£7 7s) (SC6/1020/20; SC6/1006/6).

[19] Above, pp. 1-2; D. Knowles and R.N. Hadcock, *Medieval Religious Houses* (London, 1953), p. 179.

[20] *CR, 1256-59*, pp. 99-100, 454.

[21] For his gifts to the Church, see above, pp. 99-100. His only recorded grant to a follower is the one he made to John Algar – and this was only a grant for life. Above, pp. 65-6.

[22] See Appendix E.

[23] Powicke, *Thirteenth Century*, p. 36; above, pp. 16, 49-51, 110-11.

with only half the income he enjoyed thereafter. Roger IV, on the other hand, might have grown up expecting much less and then had his expectations massively exceeded. By 1271, he found himself in possession not only of his father's lands, but also of his wife's rich inheritance and his uncle's earldom. Small wonder he was soon tempted to start spending.[24]

Turning from these reflections on the earls' characters to their politics, one might start by speculating that, had the two men come in a different order, they might have enjoyed better relations with the Crown. Roger III, an expert warrior and perhaps a tight-fisted one, might have seen eye to eye with Edward I; Roger IV, a prodigious builder, possibly less careful with money, might have found much in common with Henry III. As it was, however, neither earl enjoyed close relations with his respective king. Both were outsiders, rarely involved in the direction of politics at the centre and, in both cases, their family background explains why they were not ranked among intimate royal advisers. Because of his closeness to his Marshal uncles in the early part of his career, Roger III was never likely to find a place in Henry III's affections. Although matters improved once the Marshals were gone, suspicion and distance still prevailed in their relationship.[25] In much the same way, Roger IV found himself part of a camp – in this case his uncle's household – which was probably never fully rehabilitated after its ambiguous stance during the crucial events of 1264-65. Although Edward I successfully reintroduced to court many of the Crown's former opponents, he never regarded the new earl of Norfolk as one of his trusted friends (such as Lincoln and Warwick, or the lesser magnates who accompanied the king on crusade); by default, Roger became part of that other group of more powerful magnates (which included Gloucester and Hereford), with whom Edward's relations were hardly ever more than cordial.[26]

The outsider status of both Roger III and Roger IV was almost certainly reinforced by their failure in both cases to produce heirs. While this was in some ways advantageous (sons had to be supported, and daughters required dowries), it ultimately meant that the earls lacked the basic materials required to build political alliances. The contrast with those two great patresfamilias at the start of this story, Roger II Bigod and William Marshal, each blessed with many children and therefore able to unite the fortunes of their houses, could hardly be drawn more sharply.[27]

This basic similarity apart, however, there were important differences between the lordship of Roger III and Roger IV. The older earl, although he appears to have parted with little land, nevertheless seems to have enjoyed a strong local following. Without exception, his affinity was

---

[24] Above, pp. 6-7, 41-2, 102-6.
[25] Above, pp. 10-12, 19, 23, 51-4.
[26] Above, pp. 91-4, 98-9. For a useful comparison of Edward's earls, see Tout, 'Earldoms under Edward I', pp. 129-55.
[27] Above, pp. 2-3.

drawn from the Bigod heartlands in East Anglia, and seems to have included a greater percentage of tenants than was usual by contemporary magnate standards. If his influence at the centre was thereby limited, his power in his own region was enhanced, and when tested during the years 1258-65 it proved resilient.[28] Roger IV, on the other hand, aspired to a different kind of lordship (a fact he signalled from the outset by dropping the Bigod coat of arms and adopting the livery of the Marshal family).[29] No less vigorous than his uncle's model, it was, at the same time, far more ambitious. This is perhaps best exemplified by the last earl's decision to visit his estate in Ireland. The trip in itself was commendably proactive – not all magnates went to such lengths – and with the Irish economy booming at the time of his arrival, Roger could well have felt confident in the colony's future.[30] But if his new residence at Ballymoon was begun in the expectation that his visit would be repeated, or that future generations, as yet unborn, would from time to time want to make the same voyage, it suggests an over-confidence merging into rash fantasy. The success of Ireland in the 1280s proved to be ephemeral; the boom created by the conquest of Wales turned to bust when the theatre of operations switched to Scotland at the century's close.[31] Not only was Ballymoon, like Beaumaris, never finished; by the time of Roger IV's death, Carlow Castle itself was falling into ruin.[32] According to B.M.S. Campbell, the earl's lordship was less than exacting; an economic analysis of the Bigod manors in Norfolk leads him to conclude that Roger 'was more interested in living off rather than building up his vast inheritance'.[33] Of course, whether in this respect he was much different to his predecessors or contemporaries is almost impossible to say. The last earl's real problem may have had less to do with his skills as a landlord, and more to do with his lordly skills in general. Successive arguments between Roger and the leading members of his own establishment – his uncle's executors, Robert Cockerel, Robert de Benhall, Geoffrey Atwater, and perhaps Thomas Weyland – suggest that he may have lacked the personal skills necessary to retain men in his service.[34] Other individuals, such as Otto de Grandson and William Mortimer, having obtained substantial gifts of land and money in return

---

[28] Above, pp. 71-3, 93-4, 97-8.

[29] The Bigod arms were a red cross on a gold ground, the Marshal arms a rampant red lion on green and gold. *Rolls of Arms Henry III*, ed. T.M. Tremlett, H.S. London and A. Wagner (London, 1967), pp. 20, 23, 27, 30, 38-9. Roger III appears on his equestrian seal as used in 1258 in the traditional Bigod livery (RBIII 14). For Roger IV's use of the Marshal coat of arms, see RBIV 14 and above, p. 126.

[30] Above, pp. 119-24; R. Frame, *English Lordship in Ireland, 1318-1361* (Oxford, 1982), p. 52. However, note that, *pace* Frame (who cites Nugent), there is only evidence for the earl making one trip.

[31] Lyons, 'Manorial Administration', pp. 11, 58, 65-6, 335-49.

[32] *CIPM*, iv, 304.

[33] Campbell, *English Seigniorial Agriculture*, p. 172.

[34] Above, p. 121, 139-41, 143. See also the possibility of desertion in 1297. Above, pp. 176-7.

for their service, are never seen again in the earl's company.[35] Whereas his uncle's affinity seems tight, loyal and regionally based, Roger's following appears loose and fluid, its members drawn from counties all over England.[36] Moreover, in Roger III, we see a man endeavouring to overcome his dynastic disadvantage: struggling to dissolve his childless marriage, and compensating in the meantime by associating with his brothers, uncles and brothers-in-law.[37] Roger IV, faced with the same dilemma, appears altogether less concerned. His brothers-in-law, Philip de Kyme and John fitz John, are only found in his company on one occasion in each case, and after the death of his first countess in 1281, it was almost a decade before the earl remarried.[38]

Their different characters, abilities and approaches to lordship may explain their different fates. Roger III was not just characterized by rampant militarism or easily provoked anger: he was also possessed of subtler skills. Time and again he is the man selected for negotiation or arbitration, and on more than one occasion employed for diplomacy: the French truce of 1240; the mission to Lyon in 1245; choosing the baronial council in 1258; arbitrating on Eleanor de Montfort's dower in 1259, and on the Treaty of Kingston in 1261.[39] His prudence was not just financial but also political; for all the risks he was prepared to take in the saddle, he comes across as a cautious operator. (Again, perhaps learned in youth, from his early experience of rebellion and civil war.) It is very noticeable that, in the period 1258-65, the *vir bellicosus* stayed away from all the battles. Ultimately the earl was successful: his affinity weathered the storm of '1258', and although he did not back the king until after Evesham, his dynasty – unlike those of Montfort and Ferrers – suffered no reprisals, even though popular rumour suggested that they were planned.

Roger IV, by contrast, does not seem to have been so astute. He was not used by Edward I as a diplomat or an envoy (his brief foray into Irish politics was undertaken at the behest of the justiciar in Dublin rather than the king). In fact, the earl showed no sign of political activity for the first twenty-seven years of his career, and does not seem to have struck contemporaries as an important or imposing figure in this regard (he was, for example, almost totally ignored by chroniclers).[40] Only in 1297, perhaps for want of other candidates, did he take centre stage, and even then it is noticeable that his associate Humphrey de Bohun did most of the

---

[35] Above, pp. 150-51.
[36] e.g. John Lovel 'of Titchmarsh', Robert de Beverley, John ap Adam, Thomas de Siddington, Walter de Eversley, Stephen de Penshurst.
[37] Above, pp. 10-11, 19-20, 43-4, 54-5, 63-4.
[38] RBIV 21; SC6/937/30. Philip de Kyme was married to Roger's sister, Joan. John fitz John was married to the sister of Roger's first countess. Above, p. 104n; *DNB: Missing Persons*, ed. Nicholls, p. 226.
[39] Above, pp. 18, 21, 24, 74, 81, 86.
[40] His only notices before 1297 occur in 1290. Above, pp. 138, 149, 153.

talking (he was spokesman at Stratford, when the Remonstrances were read out, and also at the exchequer the following month).[41] After Bohun's death, Roger became the figurehead for a movement that was extremely popular, and the effect of this must have been intoxicating.[42] With a thousand supporters urging him on, he continued to oppose Edward down to 1301, but on issues (such as the Forest) which must have meant less to him personally than the financial grievances that had driven him to resist the king in the first place. The prudence that held back his uncle was lacking; the more improvident streak that prompted him to build on a grand scale across his estate may have taken over. Without a strong regional affinity to support him, the earl over-recruited, and spent his way to disaster. The irony is that, while he began his opposition in protest at the cost of the king's policies, opposing these policies for years on end appears to have bankrupted him. Whether in 1302 he jumped or was pushed, by the time of his death a few years later Roger IV was popularly regarded as a victim of his stand against Edward. The author of the *Vita Edwardi Secundi* ranked him with those other unsuccessful opponents of the Crown, Montfort and Ferrers – contemporaries of his uncle whose fate his uncle had managed to avoid.[43]

It would be a shame to leave Roger IV by dwelling on his dynastic and political failure, so we end by shifting our focus to the Wye valley, and the plight in 1311 of the citizens of Chepstow. Asked to contribute a ship to the ongoing Scottish wars, 'the bailiffs, good men and the whole community' of the town sought to be excused on grounds of poverty. Times were hard, they explained, principally because of 'the death of their liege lord, Roger Bigod'.[44] Here there was hardly room for exaggeration. In the course of his lifetime, the earl had transformed the port, rebuilding its ancient castle and walls to match his exacting requirements.[45] Upstream at Tintern, the magnificent new abbey church had only recently been finished, its giant east window above the high altar decorated with Roger's arms.[46] The army of masons, glaziers and labourers necessary to achieve these feats must have invigorated the local economy in much the same way that Edward I's castle-building campaigns in North Wales briefly stimulated the economy of south-east Ireland. But as a report, also of 1311, into the deteriorating condition of the castle showed, those days were now very definitely over.[47]

---

[41] Above, pp. 163-4, 166-7.
[42] e.g. Prestwich, *Edward I*, p. 426. Popular ownership of the earls in 1297 is perhaps suggested by Guisborough's use of the phrase '*comites nostri*'. Guisborough, p. 308.
[43] Above, p. 175.
[44] *CACWales*, p. 72.
[45] Above, pp. 129-30, 136-7.
[46] Above, pp. 134, 136, 182; Worcestre, *Itineraries*, p. 60-61.
[47] C145/71/14 (abstracted in *CIM*, ii, 26).

In Gwent, therefore, there was much reason to mourn Roger's passing and to remember him fondly. Until their house was dissolved in the sixteenth century, the monks of Tintern distributed alms to the poor five times a year for the repose of the earl's soul.[48] It is also in Gwent, bizarrely enough, that we can get closest to the earls of Norfolk. The Bigods' East Anglian properties suffered greatly in later centuries. The priory at Thetford was dissolved with a special thoroughness, the tower at Bungay toppled. At Framlingham, the mighty ring of twelfth-century walls now protects only a seventeenth-century poorhouse. At Chepstow and Tintern, however, can we apprehend the environment of the last earl directly, and begin to picture the world as he and his ancestors must have experienced it. Of all his family, therefore, Roger IV left the grandest legacy, and that, perhaps, is his greatest achievement.

---

[48] Robinson, *Tintern Abbey*, p. 15.

APPENDIX A

Itinerary of Roger III Bigod

1233
10 September, Hereford (*RCWL HIII*, i, 137)

1234
26 June, Westminster (*CRR*, xv, *1233-7*, p. 226)
2 July, Westminster (*CChR, 1257-1300*, p. 434)
27 December, Kempton (*RCWL HIII*, i, 140)

1235
8 March, Ipswich (*RCWL HIII*, i, 143)
16 March, Thetford (*RCWL HIII*, ii, 96)[1]
19 March, Bury St Edmunds (*RCWL HIII*, i, 144)
30 April, Westminster (*RCWL HIII*, i, 146)
2 May, Westminster (*CPR, 1232-47*, p. 102)
7 May, Sandwich (*RCWL HIII*, i, 147)
8 July, Westminster (*RCWL HIII*, i, 149)
14 July, Westminster (*RCWL HIII*, i, 149)
16 July, Westminster (*RCWL HIII*, i, 149)
10 August, Edinburgh (Queen's College, Oxford, MS 166, f. 28)
2 December, Westminster (*RCWL HIII*, i, 153)

1236
20 January, Merton (*RCWL HIII*, i, 154)
24 January, Merton (*RCWL HIII*, i, 154)

1237
8 March, Blyth (*CM*, iii, 403-4)
8 June, Westminster (*RCWL HIII*, i, 163)
11 September, Nottingham (*CRR*, xvi, *1237-42*, pp. 21-2)

1241
14 April, Northampton (*CM*, iv, 88)
12 August, Shrewsbury (*RCWL HIII*, i, 182)
1 October, Westminster (*RCWL HIII*, i, 182)
5 October, Westminster (*RCWL HIII*, i, 182)
16 October, Westminster (*RCWL HIII*, i, 182)
24 October, London (*Littere Wallie*, pp. 10-12)

---

[1] Misdated to 1233 in *RCWL HIII*.

1242

25 February, Acle (RBIII 7)
20 April, Westminster (*RCWL HIII*, i, 186)[2]
26 April, Winchester (*RCWL HIII*, i, 187)
30 April, Winchester (*RCWL HIII*, i, 187)
6 May, Portsmouth (*RCWL HIII*, i, 187)
25 July, Pons (*CPR, 1232-47*, p. 313)
13 August, 'In camp on the Gironde' (*CPR, 1232-47*, p. 315)

1243

c. 26 December, Westminster (*RCWL HIII*, i, 189)

1244

12 August, Newcastle (*RCWL HIII*, i, 193)
11 November, Westminster (*RCWL HIII*, ii, 3)

1245

22 March, Norwich (*RCWL HIII*, ii, 4)
29 March, Norwich (*RCWL HIII*, ii, 4)
20 May, Woodstock (*RCWL HIII*, ii, 5)
7 June, Westminster (*RCWL HIII*, ii, 5)
20-21 October, Deganwy (*RCWL HIII*, ii, 8)
28 October, Chester (*RCWL HIII*, ii, 8-9)
25 December, Westminster (*RCWL HIII*, ii, 9)

1246

17 January, Westminster (*RCWL HIII*, ii, 9)
27 January, Westminster (*RCWL HIII*, ii, 9)
4 July, Winchester (*RCWL HIII*, ii, 14)
20 July, Oxford (*RCWL HIII*, ii, 14)
20 August, Woodstock (*RCWL HIII*, ii, 15)
25 August, Woodstock (*RCWL HIII*, ii, 14)
16 October, Westminster (*RCWL HIII*, ii, 16)
18 October, Westminster (*RCWL HIII*, ii, 16)
7-8 November, Reading (*RCWL HIII*, ii, 17)
8 December, Clarendon (*RCWL HIII*, ii, 18)
23 December, Winchester (*RCWL HIII*, ii, 19)
26 December, Winchester (*RCWL HIII*, ii, 19)

1247

6 January, Westminster (*RCWL HIII*, ii, 19)
2 February, Westminster (*RCWL HIII*, ii, 19)
8 February, Westminster (*RCWL HIII*, ii, 20)

[2] Mistakenly given as Winchester in *RCWL HIII*.

10 February, Windsor (*RCWL HIII*, ii, 20)
26 April, Woodstock (*RCWL HIII*, ii, 21)
28 April, Woodstock (*RCWL HIII*, ii, 22)
30 April, Woodstock (*RCWL HIII*, ii, 21)
5 May, Woodstock (*RCWL HIII*, ii, 22)
21 May, Westminster (*RCWL HIII*, ii, 22)
24 May, Westminster (*RCWL HIII*, ii, 23)
8 July, Clarendon (*RCWL HIII*, ii, 23)

1248
9 February, London (*CM*, v, 5)
8 March, Bury St Edmunds (*RCWL HIII*, ii, 27)
16-17 March, Coxford (*RCWL HIII*, ii, 27)
29 March, Blythburgh (*RCWL HIII*, ii, 28)
30 March, Framlingham (*RCWL HIII*, ii, 28)
1 April, Butley (*RCWL HIII*, ii, 28)
26 April, Windsor (*RCWL HIII*, ii, 28)
8 June, Winchester (*RCWL HIII*, ii, 29)
10 June, Winchester (*RCWL HIII*, ii, 30)
13 October, London (*CM*, v, 29)
20 October, Westminster (*RCWL HIII*, ii, 32)

1249
5 January, Westminster (*CM*, v, 48)
23 April, Westminster (*RCWL HIII*, ii, 35)
26 April, Westminster (*RCWL HIII*, ii, 35)
14 October, Westminster (*RCWL HIII*, ii, 38)
19 October, Westminster (*RCWL HIII*, ii, 38)

1250
19 October, Westminster (*CACWales*, p. 212).

1251
15 March, Bury St Edmunds (*RCWL HIII*, ii, 45)
3 May, Westminster (*RCWL HIII*, ii, 44)
14 May, Westminster (*RCWL HIII*, ii, 47)
16 May, Westminster (*RCWL HIII*, ii, 47)
13 August, Forest of Dean (E30/28, m. 4)
16 September, Guildford (*RCWL HIII*, ii, 51)
14 October, Westminster (*RCWL HIII*, ii, 52)
4 December, Nottingham (*RCWL HIII*, ii, 55)
29 December, York (*RCWL HIII*, ii, 56)

1252
4 January, Bishopsthorpe (*CPR, 1247-58*, p. 124)

21-2 April, Westminster (*RCWL HIII*, ii, 62)
26-8 April, Westminster (*RCWL HIII*, ii, 63)
1 May, Westminster (*RCWL HIII*, ii, 64)
3 May, Westminster (*RCWL HIII*, ii, 64)
5 May, Wesminster (*RCWL HIII*, ii, 63)
1 September, Bury St Edmunds (*RCWL HIII*, ii, 71)
3 September, Bury St Edmunds (*RCWL HIII*, ii, 71)
16 October, Westminster (*RCWL HIII*, ii, 72)
19-20 October, Westminster (*RCWL HIII*, ii, 72)

1253
10 May, Westminster (*RCWL HIII*, ii, 88)
15 May, Westminster (*RCWL HIII*, ii, 89)
22-3 July, Portsmouth (*CDI*, *1252-84*, p. 39)
22-3 October, 'in camp at Benauge' (*CPR*, *1247-58*, pp. 245-6)
28 October, 'in camp at Benauge' (*CPR*, *1247-58*, p. 254)
3 November, 'in camp at Benauge' (*CPR*, *1247-58*, p. 253)
8-9 November, St Macaire (*CPR*, *1247-58*, pp. 249, 252, 257)
28 November, Bazas (*CPR*, *1247-58*, p. 253)
9 December, Bazas (*CPR*, *1247-58*, pp. 256-7)
11 December, Bazas (*CPR*, *1247-58*, p. 262)
20 December, Bazas (*CPR*, *1247-58*, p. 258)

1254

1255
22-3 April, Westminster (*RCWL HIII*, ii, 95-6)
30 April, Westminster (*RCWL HIII*, ii, 96)
20 July, Nottingham (*RCWL HIII*, ii, 97)
7 September, Wark (*RCWL HIII*, ii, 97)
16 September, Wark (*RCWL HIII*, ii, 97-8)
14 October, Westminster (*RCWL HIII*, ii, 98)
18 October, Westminster (*RCWL HIII*, ii, 98)

1256
25 March 1256, Norwich (SC1/14/166, ii)
2 April, Framlingham (*Worcester Cartulary Charters*, ed. R.R. Darlington
    (Pipe Roll Soc., new ser., xxxviii, 1968), 237-8)
4 June 1256, Blyth (*CM*, v, 557, 609)
20 October, Westminster (*RCWL HIII*, ii, 103)

1257
17 April, Westminster (*CChR*, *1341-1417*, p. 343)
28 May, Westminster (*RCWL HIII*, ii, 107)
4 June, Westminster (*RCWL HIII*, ii, 108)

25 July, Coventry (*RCWL HIII*, ii, 109)
14 August, Chester (*RCWL HIII*, ii, 110)
16 August, Chester (*RCWL HIII*, ii, 110)
18 August, Chester (*RCWL HIII*, ii, 110)
3 September, Deganwy (*RCWL HIII*, ii, 113)
12-15 September, Chester (*RCWL HIII*, ii, 110-13)
18 October, Westminster (*RCWL HIII*, ii, 114)
27 October, Westminster (*RCWL HIII*, ii, 114)
1 November, Westminster (*RCWL HIII*, ii, 116)

1258
8 March, Westminster (*RCWL HIII*, ii, 119)
12 March, Westminster (*RCWL HIII*, ii, 118)
12 April, Westminster (*RCWL HIII*, ii, 117)
17 April, Westminster (*RCWL HIII*, ii, 117)
19 April, Westminster (*RCWL HIII*, ii, 117)
3 May, Westminster (*RCWL HIII*, ii, 119)
5 June, Great Chesterford (RBIII 14)
12 June, Oxford (*RCWL HIII*, ii, 120)
14-15 June, Oxford (*RCWL HIII*, ii, 120-21)
17 June, Oxford (*RCWL HIII*, ii, 120-21)
19-20 June, Oxford (*RCWL HIII*, ii, 121)
6 July, Winchester (*CPR, 1247-58*, p. 640)
23 July, London (*Cron. Maior.*, pp. 38-9)
3 August, Southwark (*Calendar of Ormond Deeds, 1172-1350*, p. 56)
4 August, Westminster (*CR, 1256-59*, p. 324)
18 October, London (*DBM*, pp. 118-19)
5-6 November, Westminster (*RCWL HIII*, ii, 122)
Mid-November, France (*CM*, v, 720-21)

1259
8 January, Westminster (*RCWL HIII*, ii, 122)
7 February, Westminster (*CPR, 1258-66*, p. 11)
10 February, Westminster (*RCWL HIII*, ii, 122)
12 February, Westminster (*RCWL HIII*, ii, 122)
28 February, Windsor (*RCWL HIII*, ii, 123)
6 May, Westminster (*RCWL HIII*, ii, 123)
8 May, Westminster (*RCWL HIII*, ii, 123)
12 May, Westminster (*RCWL HIII*, ii, 123)
14 May, Westminster (*RCWL HIII*, ii, 123)
20 May, Westminster (*RCWL HIII*, ii, 123)
18 July, Westminster (*RCWL HIII*, ii, 124)
20 July, Westminster (*RCWL HIII*, ii, 124)
27 July, Westminster (*RCWL HIII*, ii, 124)
1 August, Westminster (*RCWL HIII*, ii, 125)

6 August, Windsor (*RCWL HIII*, ii, 125)
7 September, Westminster (*RCWL HIII*, ii, 125)
24 October, Westminster (*RCWL HIII*, ii, 125-6)
27-8 October, Westminster (*RCWL HIII*, ii, 125)
2 November, Westminster (*RCWL HIII*, ii, 127)
4-7 November, Westminster (*RCWL HIII*, ii, 127)

1260
7 January, Westminster (*CR, 1259-61*, p. 23)
20 May, Westminster (*RCWL HIII*, ii, 128)
3 June, Westminster (*RCWL HIII*, ii, 128)
12 June, Westminster (*RCWL HIII*, ii, 128)
18 June, Westminster (*RCWL HIII*, ii, 128)
12 July, Westminster (*RCWL HIII*, ii, 128)
16 July, Westminster (*RCWL HIII*, ii, 128)
18 July, Westminster (*RCWL HIII*, ii, 128)
24 July, Westminster (*RCWL HIII*, ii, 129)
28-30 July, Westminster (*RCWL HIII*, ii, 129)
2-3 August, Westminster (*RCWL HIII*, ii, 129)

1261

1262
16 June, Westminster (*RCWL HIII*, ii, 138)

1263
10 March, Westminster (*The Whitby Cartulary*, ed. J.C. Atkinson (2 vols.,
    Surtees Soc., lxix, lxxii (1878-79), ii, 535)
18 October, Windsor (*CPR, 1258-66*, p. 291)
26 November, Windsor (*RCWL HIII*, ii, 142)
5 December, Dover (*RCWL HIII*, ii, 140)

1264
Late June, London (*Foedera*, I, i, 443; *DBM*, pp. 298-9)

1267
13 February, Bury St Edmunds (*RCWL HIII*, ii, 154)
20 February, Bury St Edmunds (*RCWL HIII*, ii, 155)
3 May, Windsor (*RCWL HIII*, ii, 156)
12 May, Stratford (*RCWL HIII*, ii, 156)
14 May, Stratford (*RCWL HIII*, ii, 157)
16 May, Stratford (*RCWL HIII*, ii, 157)
20 May, Stratford (*RCWL HIII*, ii, 157)

Itinerary of Roger IV Bigod

1267
9 June, Hollesley (*Reg. Giffard*, pp. 43-4)

1270
8 November, Reading (*RCWL HIII*, ii, 187)

1271
6 January, Westminster (*RCWL HIII*, ii, 188)
4 April, Hollesley (RBIV 3)
10 June, Westminster (*RCWL HIII*, ii, 192)

1272
7 September, Hollesley (SP46/183, f. 2)
20-21 September, Norwich (*RCWL HIII*, ii, 200)

1273
22 March, Westminster (*CPR, 1313-7*, p. 125)

1274
19 August, Westminster (*Peerage*, ix, 593)

1275
26 February, London (*CSM*, ii, 180)
19 May, Westminster (*Parl. Writs*, i, 2)
22 October, Westminster (*RCWL Ed I*, p. 4)

1276
17 November, Westminster (*CCR, 1272-79*, p. 360)
28 December, 'La Breche' (SC6/1030/13)

1277
14 February, London (RBIV 7, 8)
9 April, Framlingham (SC1/22/42)
14 May, Westminster (*RCWL Ed I*, p. 10)
25 June, Woodstock (*RCWL Ed I*, p. 11)
3 July, Worcester (*RCWL Ed I*, p. 11)

1278
2 January, Westminster (*CCR, 1272-79*, p. 491)
26 May, Westminster (*RCWL Ed I*, p. 13)

30 May, Westminster (*RCWL Ed I*, p. 13)
10 August, Gloucester (*RCWL Ed I*, p. 13)

1279
6 January, Windsor (*RCWL Ed I*, p. 15)
7 July, Westminster (*RCWL Ed I*, p. 16)
28 July, Protection issued for going to Ireland (*CPR, 1272-81*, p. 322)

1280
28 December, Burgh (*RCWL Ed I*, p. 32)

1281
18 May, Westminster (*RCWL Ed I*, p. 34)
20 May, Westminster (*RCWL Ed I*, p. 36)
23 May, Westminster (*RCWL Ed I*, p. 35)
25 May, Westminster (*RCWL Ed I*, p. 36)
28-9 May, Westminster (*RCWL Ed I*, p. 36)
27-8 October, Westminster (*RCWL Ed I*, p. 39)
1 November, Westminster (*RCWL Ed I*, p. 39)
4 November, Westminster (*RCWL Ed I*, p. 40)
6 November, Westminster (RBIV 11)
10 November, Westminster (*RCWL Ed I*, p. 40)
12 November, Westminster (*RCWL Ed I*, p. 41)
1 December, Westminster (*RCWL Ed I*, p. 43)

1282
8 April, Devizes (*RCWL Ed I*, p. 44)
20 May, Worcester (*RCWL Ed I*, p. 44)
11 June, Chester (*RCWL Ed I*, p. 45)
5 July, Chester (*RCWL Ed I*, p. 45)
24 July, Rhuddlan (*RCWL Ed I*, p. 45)
28 July, Rhuddlan (*CRV*, p. 233)
7 October, Rhuddlan (*CRV*, p. 240)
8 October, Rhuddlan (*RCWL Ed I*, p. 45)
16 October, Rhuddlan (*CRV*, p. 241)
23 October, Denbigh (*CRV*, p. 243)
15 November, Rhuddlan (*RCWL Ed I*, p. 45)

1283
22 April, Conway (*RCWL Ed I*, p. 47)
2 May, Conway (*RCWL Ed I*, p. 47)
9 May, Conway (*RCWL Ed I*, p. 47)
26 May, Dolwyddelan (*RCWL Ed I*, p. 47)
3 June, Conway (*RCWL Ed I*, p. 50)
5 June, Conway (*RCWL Ed I*, p. 47)

7 June, Conway (*RCWL Ed I*, p. 48)
9-10 June, Conway (*RCWL Ed I*, pp. 47-8)
14 June, Conway (*RCWL Ed I*, p. 48)
18 June, Rhuddlan (*RCWL Ed I*, p. 48)
25 June, Rhuddlan (*CRV*, p. 273)
27 June, Rhuddlan (*RCWL Ed I*, p. 48)
4 July, Conway (*RCWL Ed I*, p. 49)
9 July, Conway (*RCWL Ed I*, p. 49)
1 October, Acton Burnell (*RCWL Ed I*, p. 49)
6 October, Acton Burnell (*RCWL Ed I*, p. 50)

1284
3 May, London (RBIV 14)
27-8 December, Bristol (*RCWL Ed I*, pp. 57-8)

1285
1-2 January, Bristol (*RCWL Ed I*, pp. 58-60)
7 May, Westminster (*RCWL Ed I*, p. 60)
9 May, Westminster (*RCWL Ed I*, p. 61)
11-12 May, Westminster (*RCWL Ed I*, pp. 61-2)
14-15 May, Westminster (*RCWL Ed I*, pp. 62-4)
20 May, Westminster (*RCWL Ed I*, p. 62)
27-8 May, Westminster (*RCWL Ed I*, p. 63)
7 June, Westminster (*RCWL Ed I*, p. 64)
12 June, Westminster (*RCWL Ed I*, pp. 64-71)
25 June, Westminster (*RCWL Ed I*, p. 66)
27-8 June, Westminster (*RCWL Ed I*, pp. 68-9)
18 July, Westminster (*RCWL Ed I*, p. 67)
9-10 September, Winchester (*RCWL Ed I*, pp. 72-3)
7 October, Winchester (*RCWL Ed I*, p. 74)
11 November, London (RBIV 15)

1286
15 February, Westminster (*RCWL Ed I*, p. 76)
20 February, Westminster (*RCWL Ed I*, p. 76)
25-8 April, Westminster (*RCWL Ed I*, pp. 77-9)
18 June, Norwich (RBIV 16)
25 October, Westminster (E159/60, m. 1d)

1287

1288

1289
14 October, Westminster (RBIV 17)

1290

4 January, Westminster (*RCWL Ed I*, p. 83)
5-6 May, Westminster (*RCWL Ed I*, pp. 85-6)
15-16 May, Westminster (*RCWL Ed I*, p. 86)
20 May, Westminster (*RCWL Ed I*, p. 85)
6 June, Westminster (*RCWL Ed I*, p. 90)
8 June, Westminster (*RCWL Ed I*, p. 90)
12 June, Westminster (*CCR, 1288-96*, p. 134)
20 June, Westminster (*RCWL Ed I*, p. 91)
13-14 July, Westminster (*RCWL Ed I*, p. 94)
16 July, Westminster (*RCWL Ed I*, p. 94)
15 October, Clipstone (*RCWL Ed I*, p. 95)

1291

4 April, Berkeley (RBIV 19)
11 April, Hamstead Marshall (E159/64, m. 12)
10 May, Norham (*Great Cause*, ii, 22-3)
2 June, Holywell Haugh (*Great Cause*, ii, 44-5)
3 June, Norham (*Great Cause*, ii, 72)
5-8 June, Norham (*Great Cause*, ii, 78-9, 86; *RCWL Ed I*, pp. 99, 101)
28 July, Thirsk (RBIV 20)
3-4 August, Berwick (*Great Cause*, ii, 126, 147)
7 August, Berwick (*RCWL Ed I*, p. 102)
10 August, Berwick (*RCWL Ed I*, p. 103)

1292

24 January, Westminster (*RCWL Ed I*, p. 106)
4 February, Westminster (*RCWL Ed I*, p. 106)
6 February, Westminster (*RCWL Ed I*, p. 107)
4 June, Berwick (*RCWL Ed I*, p. 109)
28 June, Berwick (*RCWL Ed I*, p. 110)
30 June, Berwick (*RCWL Ed I*, p. 110)
14 October, Berwick (*Great Cause*, ii, 198-9, 211)
24 October, Berwick (*Great Cause*, ii, 213)
3 November, Berwick (*Great Cause*, ii, 216)
19 November, Berwick (*Great Cause*, ii, 253)

1293

31 March, Hollesley (SC6/991/23)
10 May, Westminster (*RCWL Ed I*, p. 113)
14 May, Westminster (*RCWL Ed I*, p. 113)
24 May, Westminster (*RCWL Ed I*, p. 113)
7-8 June, Westminster (*RCWL Ed I*, p. 114)
10 June, Westminster (*RCWL Ed I*, p. 114)
12 June, Westminster (*RCWL Ed I*, p. 114)

25 September, Bristol (*RCWL Ed I*, p. 116)
24 November, Westminster (*RCWL Ed I*, p. 117)

1294

9 February, London (RBIV 22)
13 May, London (RBIV 23)
3 June, Westminster (*RCWL Ed I*, p. 119)
8 October, Westminster (*RCWL Ed I*, p. 122)
22 October, Westminster (*Treaty Rolls*, i, 99)
28 October, Westminster (*RCWL Ed I*, p. 122)
9 November, London (*Treaty Rolls*, i, 102)

1295

9 May, Chepstow (C81/1695/40)
12 August, Westminster (*RCWL Ed I*, p. 124)
30 November, Westminster (*RCWL Ed I*, p. 126)
5-6 December, Westminster (see RBIV 24, note)

1296

8 March, Newcastle (E213/185)
23 March, Wark (C81/1696/14)
8 April, Berwick (*RCWL Ed I*, pp. 126-7)
4 June, Roxburgh (*RCWL Ed I*, p. 127)
9 June, Edinburgh (*RCWL Ed I*, p. 127)
8 July, Montrose (*RCWL Ed I*, p. 127)
12 July, Glenbervie (*RCWL Ed I*, p. 127)
23 August, Berwick (*RCWL Ed I*, p. 127)
25 August, Berwick (*RCWL Ed I*, p. 127)
1 September, Berwick (*RCWL Ed I*, p. 127)
12 November, Bury St Edmunds (*RCWL Ed I*, p. 128)
15 November, Bury St Edmunds (*RCWL Ed I*, p. 128)

1297

7 January, Ipswich (*RCWL Ed I*, p. 129)
27 February, Clarendon (*RCWL Ed I*, p. 129)
9 June, Chesterford (Denholm-Young, *SAIE*, p. 168)
22 August, Westminster (*DIC1297*, p. 137)

1298

21 January, York (Langtoft, pp. 306-9)
10 February, Kirkwhelpington (SC1/26/116)
10 April, Settrington (RBIV 25)
22 July, Falkirk (Guisborough, p. 327)
12 August, Abercorn (*RCWL Ed I*, p. 132)

1299

18 March, Westminster (*RCWL Ed I*, p. 134)
15 May, Stepney (*RCWL Ed I*, p. 135)
17 May, Stepney (*RCWL Ed I*, p. 135)
15 September, Canterbury (*RCWL Ed I*, p. 136)
18 September, Canterbury (*RCWL Ed I*, p. 136)
3 October, Modesgate, near Tintern (Denholm-Young, *SAIE*, p. 165)
22 October, Westminster (*RCWL Ed I*, pp. 136-7)
3 November, St Albans (*CCR, 1296-1302*, p. 324)

1300

16 March, Westminster (*RCWL Ed I*, p. 138)
18 March, Westminster (*RCWL Ed I*, p. 138)
20 March, Westminster (*RCWL Ed I*, p. 139)
28 March, Westminster (*RCWL Ed I*, pp. 139-40)
1 April, Westminster (*RCWL Ed I*, p. 139)
12-13 June, York (*RCWL Ed I*, p. 140)

1301

28 January, Nettleham (*RCWL Ed I*, p. 143)
2 February, Nettleham (*RCWL Ed I*, p. 143)
3 February, Lincoln (*RCWL Ed I*, p. 143)
3 February, Nettleham (*RCWL Ed I*, p. 144)
5 February, Nettleham (*RCWL Ed I*, p. 143)
7 February, Nettleham (*RCWL Ed I*, p. 145)
10 February, Nettleham (*RCWL Ed I*, pp. 144-5)
12 February, Lincoln (*RCWL Ed I*, p. 144)
14 February, Lincoln (*RCWL Ed I*, p. 144)
25 February, Lincoln (*RCWL Ed I*, p. 145)
4 August, Modesgate, near Tintern (RBIV 27)

1302

18 February, Walton (RBIV 28)
16 March, Halvergate (DL25/1822)
12 April, St John's Abbey, Colchester (RBIV 29)
25 April, Caistor-by-Norwich (RBIV 30)
15 May, Fulham (*CCR, 1296-1302*, p. 582)
18 May, Fulham (RBIV 31)
18 July, Westminster (*RCWL Ed I*, p. 152)
13 August, Westminster (*RCWL Ed I*, p. 153)
20 October, Westminster (*RCWL Ed I*, p. 152)
28 October, Stepney (RBIV 32)
12-14 November, Westminster (*RCWL Ed I*, pp. 153-4)

1303

10 February, Bungay (SC6/999/17)
14 February, Bungay (Denholm-Young, *SAIE*, p. 166)
25 March, Caistor St Edmund (Denholm-Young, *SAIE*, p. 165)
8 May, Chesterford (SC1/28/48)
2 September, Walton (Canterbury Dean and Chapter, Register I, f. 141v)
23 October, Causton (SC6/991/26)
1 November, Kelsale (Denholm-Young, *SAIE*, p. 166)
8 November, Walton (Denholm-Young, *SAIE*, p. 166)

1304

5 January, Lopham (Denholm-Young, *SAIE*, p. 165)
14 January, Chesterford (Denholm-Young, *SAIE*, p. 166)

1305

11 October, Chelsea (RBIV 33)
20 October, Westminster (*RCWL Ed I*, p. 182)

APPENDIX C

Settrington, Yorkshire

Settrington was acquired by Hugh I Bigod in the early twelfth century as part of the inheritance of Aubrey de Lisle.[1] It was one of the properties seized by Henry II in 1177, and it remained with the Crown, farmed at £40 a year, until Michaelmas 1189.[2] At this point Richard I restored the manor to Roger II Bigod, who subsequently divided it between two of his sons.[3] Two carucates went to the earl's second son, Roger, and an unknown quantity of land went to his youngest son, Ralph.[4]

In 1231, a dispute arose between the two brothers when Roger tried to compel customs and services in Settrington from Ralph's tenants. In the face of objections from one of these men (William de Buckton), Roger argued that his brother had only been enfeoffed with land; the services which went with the manor, he claimed, belonged exclusively to him. The issue came to court, but the case was suspended until Ralph could come to Westminster and produce his charter of enfeoffment for inspection.[5] Almost immediately afterwards, however, Roger died; later in the same assize roll he is described as 'deceased', and we find his lands in Settrington being contested between Roger III Bigod (his nephew) and John Bigod (another son of Roger II, presumably the late man's immediate junior). The case was decided in favour of the young earl, who subsequently found himself in the same situation as the previous owner.[6] Like his namesake uncle, Roger III tried to claim customs and services from William de Buckton, who once again called Ralph Bigod in his defence. This time, however, the matter was resolved. Ralph recognised Roger's rights as overlord, and in return Roger granted his uncle half of the manor.[7]

---

[1] *EYC*, i, 466-7.
[2] *Pipe Roll 23 Henry II*, pp. 78-9; *Pipe Roll 1 Richard I*, p. 76.
[3] *Cartae Antiquae Rolls*, ii, 158-9.
[4] We know Roger son of Roger II held two carucates in Settrington from the court cases cited below. Probably born in the 1180s, he first appears in 1214, fighting in King John's campaign for Poitou. From 1222-30 he seems to have been a knight of the royal household; between these dates he received an annual fee of £20 from Henry III, while in 1229 he was granted the manor of 'Northon' in Suffolk 'to sustain him in the king's service'. Above, pp. 2, 8n; *RLC*, i, 206, 488, 529, 544, 575; *RLC*, ii, 7, 65; *CLR*, 1226-40, pp. 43, 58, 77, 106, 130, 149, 173; *CR, 1227-31*, p. 172. One of his charters is printed in *EYC*, i, 493-5, but c. 1205 x 1231 would be a more accurate date range than the one proposed.
[5] JUST/1/1042, m. 18 (cf. *EYC*, ii, 453).
[6] JUST/1/1042, m. 16d (cf. *EYC*, i, 494). John Bigod was a cleric, and godson of King John (*RLP*, p. 47). The principal justice on this eyre was Stephen de Seagrave, which may explain the charter RBIII 4. *Three Yorkshire Assize Rolls for the Reigns of King John and King Henry III*, ed. C.T. Clay (Yorkshire Archaeological Soc., Record Ser., xliv, 1911), 141.
[7] CP25/1/156/57, no. 578.

At some point before 1241, Hugh III Bigod acquired some property in Settrington.[8] The likeliest scenario is that that Roger III had granted his younger brother the remaining half of the manor. After 1234 there are no further indications that the earl had a demesne interest there, and at the time of his death in 1270 there was no mention of Settrington in his inquisition post mortem. A lawsuit over the dependant manor of Wilton in the 1280s reveals that Roger had remained chief lord of the fee during his lifetime, but also shows that Hugh Bigod had been the man in charge on the ground.[9]

In 1253 Ralph Bigod, uncle to Roger and Hugh and (following Roger's grant of 1234) owner of half of Settrington, died.[10] His moiety was split by agreement between Hugh and his younger brother, Ralph Bigod of Stockton. Under the terms of this concord, however, Ralph only enjoyed custody of this quarter share for life, and he predeceased both his elder brothers in 1260.[11] From that point, therefore, Hugh III Bigod must have held the whole manor, and after his death in 1266 it would have passed to his eldest son, Roger IV Bigod. Roger retained Settrington until 1302, when he permanently alienated it to his cousin, John Bigod of Stockton (son of Ralph, above).[12]

[8] *Yorks. Fines*, ii, 108.

[9] Cf. *CIPM*, i, 239-41; CP40/59, m. 81d (Cf. *Yorks. Inq.*, i, 20-21).

[10] Ralph's executors were distraining his debtors as early as Michaelmas 1253. E368/29, mm. 2d, 17 (cf. E368/30, mm. 3, 8d, 11d).

[11] *Yorks. Fines*, iii, 91; *Excerpta*, ii, 333.

[12] RBIV 30. For John Bigod of Stockton's descendants, see Moor, 'The Bygods', pp. 179-213.

APPENDIX D

Seneschals

Name	Dates	Reference
John Austin	1231	*Memoranda Roll 16-17 Henry III*, p. 52
William Lenveise	1233 x 1234	RBIII 1
William Russell	25 Feb 1242	RBIII 4
Gervase de Bradfield	1245, 1247, 1249	E368/16, m. 18; E368/19, m. 13; E368/21, m. 12d
Thomas de Shotford	1251	E368/24, m. 19
Robert Blund	1252, 1253	E368/26, m. 16; E368/27, m. 21; E368/28, m. 22d
Hugh fitz Adam	1268/69	SC6/998/18
John de Hastings	1269/70–1270/71	SC6/934/12–SC6/837/11
Walter de Pridington	1271/72–1275/76	SC6/937/30–SC6/995/15
John de Stanes	1274/75–1281/82	SC6/998/20–SC6/873/11
Walter Buckskin	1278/79–1284/85	SC6/933/27–SC6/934/27
Roger le Daneys	1280/81	SC6/768/11
Robert Baynard	1282/83–1285/86	SC6/995/2–SC6/935/11
Ralph de Crepping	1284/85	SC6/935/11
William Glanville	1287/88–1290	SC6/991/21–SC6/936/13
Robert de Benhall	1288	SC6/1005/28
Richard Davillers	1291	SC6/768/15
Adam de Schropham	1291/92	SC6/768/16
Roger de Coggeshall	1292/93	SC6/932/23
Daniel de Beccles and John de Cawston	1293/94	SC6/997/9
Thomas de Snetterton	1294/95	SC6/934/7
Ivo de Keneton	1293/94–1296/97	SC6/837/19–SC6/997/11
Robert Hereward	1296/97	SC6/997/11
Hamo le Parker	1298–1300	SC6/837/23–SC6/937/5
Richard de Stratford and William de Colney	1300/01–1301/02	SC6/1000/20–SC6/1007/19
Nicholas de Cressingham	1303	SC6/768/22
Peter de Wells	1303–1306	SC6/935/15–SC6/938/11
John Oliver	1306	SC6/991/28

CHEPSTOW

Name	Dates	Reference
William le Wasterne[1]	1270/71	SC6/921/21
Clement de Wyrwood[2]	1271/72	SC6/921/21
Adam de Creting	before 1278/79	SC6/921/22
William de Glanville	1279/80–1282	SC6/859/19–SC6/921/23
William Bluet	June 1282–Jan 1283	SC6/921/23–SC6/921/24
John Baret	Jan–March 1283	SC6/921/24
Walter de Redisham	1283–1286/87	SC6/921/24–SC6/921/28
Geoffrey de Wroxhall	1291/92	SC6/922/3
Geoffrey de Wroxhall	1292/93	SC6/922/5
Elias de Aylburton	1293	SC6/922/5
William de Valers	1298/99	SC6/922/6
Elias de Aylburton	July–Sept 1299	SC6/922/6

CARLOW

Name	Dates	Reference
Hugh de Alby	1261/62	DKPR Ireland, 35, p. 43
Robert de Raydon	1272	SP46/183, f. 2
William le Grasther	1275	DKPR, Ireland, 36, p. 26
Robert Cockerel	1276	CDI, 1252–84, p. 217
Philip de Buckland	1279/80–1282	SC6/1237/40–SC6/1237/43
William Cadel	1282 – 1287	SC6/1239/2–SC6/1239/6
John de Houton	1288–1292	SC6/1239/7; CDI, 1285–92, p. 471
Reginald Livet	1293/94	DKPR, Ireland, 37, p. 55
Robert Marchaunt	1297/98	CDI, 1293–1301, p. 222
William de Hawkswell	1299	CDI, 1293–1301, p. 285
Miles de Radburgh	1301–1305	DKPR, Ireland, 38, p. 71– CJRI, 1305–7, pp. 70, 155
John de Houton	1306	CJRI, 1305–7, pp. 328

[1] In SC6/921/21 William le Wasterne is paid '£4 16s 2d for the arrears of his fee'. William 'de Walston' is named as seneschal in a survey of Wentwood, dated to 1270/71. Morgan and Wakeman, *Notes on Wentwood, Castle Troggy*, pp. 40, 46.
[2] SC6/921/2 refers to 'the fee of Clemence for 23 weeks, £13 10s'. Clement de Wyrwood is named as seneschal in the undated but probably very early charter RBIV 2.

BOSHAM

Name	Dates	Reference
John de Hastings	1268	SC6/1030/9
Richard de Sanford	1287/8	SC6/1020/16
Geoffrey de Enepol	1288/9	SC6/1020/17

Calendar of Bigod Charters

CHARTERS OF ROGER II BIGOD (1177-1221)

RBII 1   **1177 x 1187**

Confirmation to Sibton Abbey of a grant by Walter son of William de Shadingfield.

Source: *Sibton*, iii, 116-17; *Book of Seals*, p. 231.

RBII 2   **1177 x 1189**

Grant to Reiner fitz Berengar and Richard his son of land in Friday Street, London.

Source: E40/2176; *Catalogue of Ancient Deeds*, ii, 47.

RBII 3   **1189 x 1193**

Grant to Reading Abbey of 3 marks of annual rent.

Source: *Reading Abbey Cartularies*, ed. B.R. Kemp (2 vols., Camden Soc., 4th ser., xxxi, xxxiii, 1986-87), i, 371.

RBII 4   **1189 x 1193**

Grant to West Dereham Abbey of the land of Geoffrey fitz Geoffrey.

Source: BL, Add. MS 46353, f. 10v.

RBII 5   **1189 x 1202**

Confirmation of a grant by Thetford Priory to Hickling Priory.

Source: Bodleian, Tanner MS 425, f. 44v.

RBII 6   **1189 x 1202**

Grant to William fitz Richard of a certain member of the manor of Notley (Essex).

Source: BL, Harleian Charter 46 D 42.

RBII 7   **1189 x 1202**

Confirmation to the nuns of St Mary's, Wix, of the alms that Roger de Glanville gave them in Middleton (Suffolk).

Source: E40/3464; *Catalogue of Ancient Deeds*, ii, 194.

RBII 8   **1189 x 1202**

Grant to Richard de Seething of 20 acres of land in Seething (Norfolk).

Source: C146/1169; *Catalogue of Ancient Deeds*, i, 502.

RBII 9 1189 x 1202
Grant to Roger de Reimes of the manor of Colne (Essex).
Source: BL, Cotton MS Julius C vii, f. 200v.

RBII 10 1189 x 1202
Grant to the men of Acle (Norfolk) that they shall have hereditarily their turbaries.
Source: *CPR, 1361-64*, p. 506; *CPR, 1461-67*, p. 309.

RBII 11 1189 x 1202
Grant to Hervey the Baker of 6 acres of land in Heveningham (Suffolk).
Source: *Sibton*, iii, 163; *Book of Seals*, pp. 232-3.

RBII 12 1189 x 1217
Grant to Sibton Abbey of land in Wrabton, in exchange for land of the abbey which the earl enclosed within his park at Kelsale.
Source: *Sibton*, iii, 22.

RBII 13 1189 x 1221
Grant to Barlings Abbey of all right in Holy Trinity, Bungay.
Source: BL, Cotton MS Faustina B i, f. 43v.

RBII 14 1189 x 1221
Grant to Anketil son of Anketil of Bungay of land in Halvergate (Norfolk).
Source: *The Cartulary of St Bartholomew's Hospital*, ed. N.J.M. Kerling (London, 1973), p. 131.

RBII 15 1189 x 1221
Grant to Dodnash Priory of his mill of Flatford in East Bergholt.
Source: *Dodnash Priory Charters*, ed. C. Harper-Bill (Suffolk Charters, xvi, Ipswich, 1998), 74-5.

RBII 16 1189 x 1221
Grant to Dodnash Priory of the homage and service of Adam Buris.
Source: *Dodnash Priory Charters*, ed. Harper-Bill, p. 73.

RBII 17 1193
Confirmation to Wymondham Abbey of the covenant between the abbey and Ralph de Melves, his knight.
Source: BL, Cotton MS Titus C viii, f. 67v.

RBII 18 1193 x 1198
Pledge to the monks of Reading to pay them 3 marks each year.
Source: *Reading Abbey Cartularies*, ed. Kemp, i, 222-3.

RBII 19   1193 x 1198
Grant to Reading Abbey of 3 marks of rent from the church of
Finchingfield.
Source: *Reading Abbey Cartularies*, ed. Kemp, i, 221.

RBII 20   1198
Confirmation to Felixstowe Priory of earlier grants.
Source: BL, Cotton MS Domitian A x, f. 197v.

RBII 21   1199 x 1202
Grant to Colne Priory of the church of Dovercourt and the chapel of
Harwich.
Source: *Monasticon Anglicanum*, iv, 102.

RBII 22   1199 x 1221
Grant to Hickling Priory of the chapel of All Saints, Hacheston.
Source: Bodleian, Tanner MS 425, ff. 44v–45.

RBII 23   1199 x 1221
Grant to Carrow Nunnery of two sheaves of the tithe of Halvergate.
Source: E40/14361.

RBII 24   1199 x 1221
Quitclaim to Ely Cathedral of all actions and plaints in the hundreds of
Carlford, Wilford and Loes.
Source: BL, Egerton MS 3047, ff. 233v–244.

RBII 25   1199 x 1221
Grant to Leiston Abbey of the church of St Mary, Middleton.
Source: *The Cartulary of Leiston Abbey and Butley Priory Charters*, ed. R.
Mortimer (Suffolk Charters, i, Ipswich, 1979), 84.

CHARTERS OF HUGH II BIGOD (1221-25)

HBII 1   1221 x 1225
Grant to Sibton Abbey of the homage and service of Hervey the Baker and
the tenement he holds in Heveningham.
Source: *Sibton*, ii, 284-5.

HBII 2   1221 x 1225
Grant to Hamo Lenveise of the manor of Stockton.
Source: BL, Lansdowne MS 229, f. 26.

HBII 3   1221 x 1225

Grant to John fitz Augustine of Framlingham of land in Mettingham in 'Boiscotes'.

Source: BL, Add. Ch. 37400.

CHARTERS OF MAUD MARSHAL (d.1248)

Maud 1   early May 1225

Grant to her son Ralph Bigod of land in Stockton (Norfolk).

Source: BL, Harleian Charter 46 D 38.

Maud 2   1240 x 1246

Grant to Richard de Otley, her chaplain, of a tenement in Thorne (Yorkshire).

Source: E40/315; *Catalogue of Ancient Deeds*, i, 35.

Maud 3   1241 x 1245

Grant to her son Ralph Bigod of land in Stockton (Norfolk).

Source: BL, Harleian Charter 46 D 41.

Maud 4   1246 x 1248

Confirmation of the union of the abbey of Killenny with the abbey of Duiske.

Source: 'The Charters of the Abbey of Duiske', ed. C.M. Butler and J.H. Bernard, *Proceedings of the Royal Irish Academy*, xxxv, section C, i (1918), 79.

Maud 5   1246 x 1248

Grant to St George's Nunnery, Thetford, of 3 silver marks of annual rent.

Source: *Monasticon Anglicanum*, iv, 478.

CHARTERS OF ROGER III BIGOD (1225-70)

RBIII 1   c. 22 April 1228

Roger Bigod, son of Hugh Bigod, is bound to lodge £1,000 of silver at the New Temple on behalf of Alexander, king of Scots, who was bound to deliver the said sum there by his letters patent. Roger is also bound to lodge at the New Temple 500 marks which Alexander has given to his sister Isabella, Roger's wife, out of the 1,300m which the king lent to pay the fine which Roger made with the executors of [William Longespee], earl of Salisbury, to have his lands. These sums are to be paid by Roger at a rate of 500 marks a year, half at Easter, half at Michaelmas, and used to purchase lands for Isabella's marriage portion. To this end Roger has assigned 500 marks worth of land and rents to Richard, prior of Thetford,

Oliver de Vaux, Roger fitz Osbert and Hamo Lenveise, who are sureties for this agreement.

Witnesses: Eustace de Fauconberg, bishop of London, Richard le Poore, bishop of Salisbury, Ralph de Neville, bishop of Chichester, Jocelin of Wells, bishop of Bath, Walter Mauclerc, bishop of Carlisle, Hubert de Burgh, earl of Kent, justiciar, William Marshal, earl of Pembroke, Gilbert de Clare, earl of Gloucester and Hertford, William de Warenne, earl of Surrey, John, earl of Huntingdon, Martin de Pattishall, Stephen de Seagrave, John Marshal.

Source: CChR, 1227-57, p. 72.

Notes: A royal *inspeximus* of this charter was made on 22 April 1228. The witnesses to the king's confirmation differ from those given on the charter. However, many of the men named in the original witness list were at court around this time (cf. *RCWL HIII*, i, 55-6).

RBIII 2   **c. 22 April 1228**

Roger Bigod, son of Hugh Bigod, is bound to Alexander, king of Scots, in 600 marks of silver; to be paid at the following terms [terms given, pledges as above]. Roger promises to Alexander that before his majority he will neither give, sell or assign any of his lands, holdings, advowsons or rents.

Witnesses: As for RBIII 1.

Source: CChR, 1227-57, p. 72.

Notes: As for RBIII 1.

RBIII 3   **c. 22 April 1228**

Roger Bigod, son of Hugh Bigod, conveys to [his four pledges, as above, various rents and farms in East Anglia, worth 500 marks a year], to be held from 1 May 1228 until Michaelmas 1234, in order to acquit Roger against Alexander, king of Scots, of 600 marks, and to acquit the king of England of 550m, and to lodge at the New Temple 2,000 marks to buy land to be the marriage portion of Isabella.

Witnesses: As for RBIII 1.

Source: CChR, 1227-57, pp. 72-3.

Notes: As for RBIII 1.

RBIII 4   **May 1233 x May 1234**

Roger Bigod, earl of Norfolk, son and heir of Hugh Bigod, onetime earl of Norfolk, has given, granted and confirmed to Stephen de Seagrave, justiciar of England, ten librates of land in Settrington; to be had and held, etc., for the service of a quarter of a knight's fee. And Roger will warrant, etc.

No date or place.

Witnesses: Oliver de Vaux, Herbert de Alencon, William Lenveise, then seneschal, Ralph de Wauncy, Roger de Vaux, Richard de Stratton, Roger de Thurkilby, Nicholas, parson of Framlingham, Thomas Bigod.

Source: BL, Add. Charter 17735; *Book of Seals*, pp. 209-10.

Notes: The date of this grant must lie between Roger's investiture as earl on 22 May 1233 and Seagrave's dismissal around 25 May 1234 (*Handbook of British Chronology*, p. 72). The justiciar received many similar gifts during his short time in office (Vincent, *des Roches*, p. 425). For the possible motivation behind this gift, see Appendix C.

RBIII 5   1233 x 1242

Roger Bigod, earl of Norfolk, to all faithful in Christ, etc., greeting. His father, Hugh Bigod, onetime earl of Norfolk, for the salvation of his soul and those of all his ancestors, gave with his body to the church of St Mary, Thetford, in return for ten librates of land, all the following in free alms; namely, twenty-six acres of land in Aslacton, which Roger II Bigod assarted, and twenty acres of land in the same vill which Countess Gundreda assarted, and all the alder grove and pasture which Hugh II Bigod had in the same vill. Roger has granted his father's gift to the church and accepted all the aforesaid.

No date or place.

Witnesses: Oliver de Vaux...

Source: BL, Lansdowne MS 229, f. 148.

Notes: Oliver de Vaux is the only witness given. The charter dates between Roger's investiture and de Vaux's death (Sanders, *English Baronies*, p. 47).

RBIII 6   1233 x 1246

Roger Bigod, earl of Norfolk, has granted and given his mill of Wangford to God and the Blessed Virgin Mary and the Church of the Holy Cross, Bungay, and the nuns serving God there.

No date or place.

Witnesses: Ralph Bigod, William de Hingham, William Bardolf, William de Verdun, Reginald de Pirnhow, William de Burnaville, Walter de Caen, William de Peasenhall.

Source: *Monasticon Anglicanum*, iv, 339-40.

Notes: Dated between Roger's investiture and his adoption of the title 'earl Marshal' in 1246.

RBIII 7   25 February 1242

Roger Bigod, earl of Norfolk, son of Hugh Bigod, patron and founder of the House of St Mary, Weybridge, grants to the warden and brothers of the same house the right in future to elect their own warden. He also grants that if the house prospers and becomes a priory or abbey, the brothers may elect their own prior or abbot; provided that no warden, prior or abbot shall be ordained except upon the presentation of the earl and his heirs.

Given at Acle, 25 February 1242.

Witnesses: Herbert de Alencon, Roger fitz Osbert, William Russell, then seneschal, Hugh de Vaux, Gervase de Bradfield, William de Sparham, Robert de

Stokesby, Adam de Burlingham, Thomas Bigod, parson of Framlingham, Master William de Ditchingham, John and William, chaplains, Thomas Lenebaud.
Source: *CCR, 1307-13*, p. 129.

Notes: Stokesby and Burlingham lie close to Acle. Cf. Knowles and Hadcock, *Medieval Religious Houses*, p. 179.

RBIII 8 1246 x 1260

Roger Bigod, earl of Norfolk and marshal of England, has granted, given and [confirmed to the priory of St Mary, Weybridge]... and Robert the prior and the brothers serving God there... all his marsh [in Acle]... ; to be had and held in free, pure, and perpetual arms forever. And Roger and his heirs will warrant.
No date or place.
Witnesses: Ralph Bigod, Herbert de Alencon, [Philip de Buckland, Henry de Rushall], Hubert de Bavent, knights, Robert Blund, Arnold de..., Richard..., John de Acle, Bartholomew de Southwood and others.
Source: Norfolk Record Office, KNY 28 (Knyvett-Wilson Deeds).

Notes: Blomefield, xi, 92 has a partial transcript of this charter, which supplies some of the portions now missing from the badly damaged original. It was given between Roger's adoption of the title 'marshal of England' in 1246, and the death of witness Ralph Bigod, either the earl's uncle (d.1253) or his younger brother (d. before 1260).

RBIII 9 1246 x 1251

Roger Bigod, earl of Norfolk and marshal of England, has given and quitclaimed Alan, son of Robert Thoke, with all his following (*sequela*) to Wakelin Visdelu; to be had and held to Wakelin and his heirs freely and quietly forever. In return for this gift and quitclaim Wakelin has given Roger twenty marks of silver.
No date or place.
Witnesses: Herbert de Alencon, Hugh de Vaux, Gervase de Bradfield, then seneschal, Hubert de Bavent, Robert de Blamd (Blund), Thomas de Shotford, William de Stuston, then bailiff of Walter (sic), John de Capel, Thomas de Langestun, Wakelin de Norton, Stephen Gunter, William his son, Thomas Lambert.
Source: BL, Add. Charter 19823.

Notes: Gervase de Bradfield was seneschal between 1245 and 1249, but by 1251 he had been replaced by Thomas de Shotford. See Appendix D.

RBIII 10 1246 x 15 May 1250

A covenant made and sworn between Earl Roger Bigod, marshal of England, and Roger de Carlton; the latter has sold to the earl all his manor of Carlton, including all the customs and services from its villeins, all the homages and services of the free men in Carlton, Kelsale, Monk Soham and Cransford, all the escheats, wardships and liberties when they fall in, and the advowson of the church of Carlton, for 250 marks (terms and

conditions for payment at Framlingham Castle follow). The earl will place Camilla, Roger de Carlton's daughter, in a nunnery until the age of thirteen, after which she can continue as a nun or have ten librates of land from the earl or his heirs. And if the manor of Carlton is obligated for any debt to the king, or anyone else, Christian or Jewish, Roger de Carlton will acquit the whole debt on the day of the first payment at Framlingham.
No date or place.
Witnesses: Herbert de Alencon, Ralph Bigod, Hugh de Vaux, Gervase de Bradfield, Bartholomew de Creake, Thomas Bigod, Thomas de Shotford, Robert Blund, Henry de Rushall, John Algar, Thomas Lenebaud, Richard de Cransford, Thomas... ...god... Roger... ...Scissore and others.
Source: Bodleian Library, MS Ch. Suffolk a. 12 (1261).

Notes: The agreement was made between Roger's adoption of the title 'marshal of England' in 1246, and the vigil of Pentecost 34 Henry III (15 May 1250), the date given in the charter for the first payment.

RBIII 11   January 1250 x September 1252

Roger Bigod, earl of Norfolk and marshal of England, has given, granted and confirmed to Walter [Suffield], bishop of Norwich, the messuage, land and tenement which John le Breton held from him in Hethel and Nayland; to be had and held by Walter, his heirs or assigns from the earl and his heirs, doing the service which John was accustomed to do for the same. And Roger and his heirs will warrant etc.
No date or place.
Witnesses: Hugh Bigod and Ralph [Bigod], my brothers, Matthew de Mautby, Hubert de Bavent, Thomas Bigod, Thomas Lenebaud, Thomas de Shotford, John Algar, Richard de Cransford, Roger le Gras and others.
Source: Norfolk Record Office, Great Hospital Deeds, 1271.

Notes: In January 1250 one messuage and sixty-seven acres of land in Hethel were restored to Roger, a year and a day after John le Breton, the former tenant, abjured the realm (*CR, 1247-51*, p. 259. For John's heinous crime, see *CRR, xix, 1249-50*, pp. 414-15). On 11 September 1252, Walter Suffield granted all the land he held in Hethel and Carlton 'of the fee of the earl of Norfolk' (Norfolk Record Office, Phillips MSS 600; Great Hospital Deeds, no. 1273).

RBIII 12   September x December 1252

Roger Bigod, earl of Norfolk and marshal of England, has granted, conceded and confirmed to God and St Giles's Hospital, Norwich, and the master and brothers of the same hospital, for the sustenance of the poor, all the land that Walter [Suffield], bishop of Norwich held from him in Hethel, in free alms forever, just as they had been given to the aforesaid bishop. However, the master of the hospital will pay Roger and his heirs 5s each year (half at Easter, half at Michaelmas) for reliefs, wards, suits of court, escheats, customs and demands, etc.
No date or place.

Witnesses: Ralph Bigod, Herbert de Alencon, Robert de Pirnhow, Matthew de Mautby, Hubert de Bavent, Bartholomew de Creake, William de Burgh, knights, Thomas Lenebaud, Henry de Rushall.
Source: BL, Add. Charter 7207.

Notes: Given after RBIII 11, and before the death of witness Bartholomew de Creake (above, p. 66).

RBIII 13   19 May 1257 x July 1270

Roger Bigod, earl of Norfolk and marshal of England, inspired by divine charity, has granted and confirmed to God, the Blessed Mary, St Giles and the St Giles's Hospital, Norwich, and to master Hamo and the brothers of the same hospital and their successors, all the tenement in Seething, and the advowson of Seething church, which the same master and brothers acquired of his fee from the abbot and convent of Langley for one portion, and from the prior and convent of Norwich by the ordination of Walter [Suffield], onetime bishop of Norwich of good memory for the other; the same abbot and convent of Langley acquired their portion from Sir Walter de Seething and the prior and convent of Norwich acquired their portion from Sir William de Seething; to be had and held to the same master and brothers, their successors and the said hospital in free, pure and perpetual alms. Roger remits all right and claim etc.
No date or place.
Witnesses: Ralph de Camoys, Fulk de Kerdiston, William de Burgh, Robert de Vaux, Henry de Rushall, William Malherbe, then our seneschal, William de Stalham, knights, Thomas Lenebaud, Hugh de Tuddenham, Hamo Blund, Edmund Tusseynz, John Algar and others.
Source: BL, Topham Charter 44.

Notes: Given between the death of Walter de Suffield, bishop of Norwich, and the earl's own death.

RBIII 14   5 June 1258

In the name of the Holy Trinity, Roger Bigod, earl of Norfolk and marshal of England, being in good health, makes his will thus: First he commends his soul to God and his body to be buried in the church of St Mary Thetford. Afterwards he bequeaths [from his goods movable and immovable, first and principally that all his debts be paid, in particular the 66 marks and 320 marks which he borrowed from the prior and monks of Thetford, which they borrowed from merchants for his use. Afterwards, £146 6s 4d to [Luke] de Lucca, and all his other debts that can be proved, should be paid according to the judgement of his executors. Also, he wills that those who continued in his service should be rewarded at the discretion of the same executors]. He has appointed as executors of this will Simon de Montfort, earl of Leicester, Richard de Clare, earl of

Gloucester and Hertford, William Malherbe, Thomas Lenebaud, and Hugh de Tuddenham.

Done at Chesterford, Wednesday after the feast of St Barnabus, A.D. 1258.

Source: BL, Harley MS 5019. Printed in *Testamenta Vetusta*, ed. N.H. Nicolas (2 vols., London, 1826), i, 48-9, but with the date given incorrectly as *ante* St Barnabus and William Malherbe omitted from the executors. Cf. Weever, *Ancient Funerall Monuments*, pp. 828-9 which gives the same document with slight variations. The section in square brackets is supplied from an English translation in T. Martin, *The History of the Town of Thetford in the Counties of Norfolk and Suffolk* (London, 1779), pp. 138-9.

Notes: Beneath the Harley transcript is a drawing of Roger's equestrian seal. This was not the earl's first will (*CPR, 1232-47*, p. 454), nor his last (above, p. 112).

CHARTERS OF ROGER IV BIGOD (1270-1306)

RBIV 1   **1270 x 1306**
Roger Bigod, earl of Norfolk, marshal of England, has granted, given and confirmed to the church of St Mary, Tintern, in perpetual alms, fifty-eight acres of land, of which twenty-eight are at 'Modesgate' and run from the valley called Halesowen towards the grange of the monks, and thirteen-and-a-half are at Penterry between the road which leads from the abbey to 'Platalanda' on the one side, and the land late of Wronoc Fot on the other, and sixteen-and-a-half are at 'Henfot', lying between the land which the said monks have from the earl and his wood by the brook between that wood and the wood of Roger fitz Peter; to be had and held by the monks and their successors, paying 9s 8d p.a. [terms given]. For this concession the monks have given the earl 25 marks, 9s 6d. And the earl will warrant.
No date or place.
Witnesses: William and Roger de Seymour, Robert fitz Payn, knights, Bartholomew de Mora, William de Lacu, Walter Sely, Robert de Gamages, William de Dernford.
Source: BL, Arundel MS 19, ff. 20-21v; *CChR, 1300-1326*, pp. 99-100.

Notes: Almost certainly given at Chepstow, and probably very early.

RBIV 2   **1270 x 1306**
Roger Bigod, earl of Norfolk and marshal of England, has inspected a charter which Bartholomew de Mora made to the church of St Mary, Tintern, and the monks there, in these words [recital of Bartholomew's charter, terminating with witnesses: Robert fitz Payn, Ralph Bluet, William Bluet, Roger de Seymour, Nicholas de Mora, William Dernford, knights, Clement de Wyrwood, then seneschal of Chepstow, John Martel, Robert Gamages, Matthew Denebaud, William de St Pierre, William de Lacu,

Adam Walensis de Dinham]. The earl, for the salvation of his soul and those of his ancestors and successors, ratifies and confirms this charter. No date or place.
Witnesses: None given to the earl's inspeximus.
Source: BL, Arundel MS 19, ff. 19v-20v.

Notes: Almost certainly given at Chepstow, and probably very early.

### RBIV 3								4 April 1271
Roger Bigod, earl of Norfolk and marshal of England has granted, remitted and quitclaimed to St Mary of Bec and St Neot's Priory and the monks there, all the right and claim he had in Cratfield church and its advowson. He has also granted and confirmed all the gifts, grants and confirmations which they have from Matilda de St Liz, William de Aubigny her son and Walter fitz Robert regarding the same church.
Given at Hollesley, Saturday after the feast of St Ambrose, 1271.
Witnesses: None given.
Source: BL, Cotton MS Faustina A iv, f. 141.

Notes: St Mary of Bec was the mother house of St Neot's. The first recorded donation was that of Matilda, daughter of Simon de St Liz, first earl of Huntingdon, who gave half her manor at Cratfield in Suffolk (cf. above, p. 36).

### RBIV 4								1271 x 1276
Roger Bigod, earl of Norfolk and marshal of England, has given, granted and confirmed the church of St Mary, Tintern, and the monks there, half an acre of his marsh in Halvergate, wherever in the marsh the monks want, and all the site on which the church of Halvergate is built, with the advowson of the church. And the earl will warrant.
No date or place.
Witnesses: Robert Hovel, Philip de Buckland, Thomas Weyland, William de Valeynes, knights, Walter de Priddington, then seneschal of Norfolk, William de Glanville, William de Halvergate, [John de Cretingham, Nicholas de Walsham, clerk, Robert Russel, clerk].
Source: BL, Arundel MS 19, f. 19-19v; CChR, 1300-1326, p. 99.

Notes: Almost certainly given in East Anglia. Walter de Priddington was seneschal of Norfolk between 1271 and 1276 (see Appendix D). Robert Russel was clerk of the earl's chapel in 1274/75 (SC6/935/4).

### RBIV 5								1275 x 1280
Roger Bigod, earl of Norfolk and marshal of England, has given, granted and confirmed to his dear cousin William Mortimer, for his homage and service, 106s 2d p.a. of land and rent in the town of Newbury, which falls to the earl as part of the inheritance of the marshalship; to be had and held from the earl and his heirs to William and his heirs forever, paying 1d p.a. at Easter at Hamstead [Marshal]. And the earl and his heirs will warrant.
No date or place.

Witnesses: John, abbot of Tintern, Bartholomew de Mora, William Bluet, Henry de Cobham, knights, Master Geoffrey de Aspall, Richard Preg' and others.
Source: BL, Harley MS 1240, f. 62v.

Notes: The earl inherited the 106s 2d of land and rent in Newbury on the death of Eleanor de Montfort in 1275.

RBIV 6   November 1276 x November 1277
Roger Bigod, earl of Norfolk, marshal of England, has granted to his dear wife (*consorti*) Aline la Despenser, for all his lifetime, all the manors which fall and descend to him and to her by the death of Philip Basset her father, from both her father's inheritance, and that of Helwise, her late mother. No date or place. Given in 5 Edward I.
Witnesses: None given.
Source: P. Morant, *The History and Antiquities of the County of Essex* (3 vols., London, 1768), ii, 269n.

RBIV 7   14 February 1277
Roger Bigod, earl of Norfolk and marshal of England, has granted for himself and his heirs to King Edward I, that he [Roger] will enfeoff the king and his heirs with the manor of Bosham in Sussex (which the earl holds by inheritance and acquisition) and the manor of Weston in Hertfordshire; which manors, because they are held of the king in chief, the earl quitclaims to the king and his heirs forever. However, if the earl should produce a legitimate heir or heirs of his own body, then those manors will remain to those heirs. Should the earl die without such heirs, the manors will remain to the king and his heirs forever. The earl also grants and promises in good faith that, within two years from next Easter, he will give the king full seisin of the said manors. The king or his heirs will then return the manors to the earl, to be had and held for life, and to revert to the king after the earl's death if, as aforesaid, the earl does not have a legitimate heir or heirs. A final concord will be made to this effect in the king's court. The earl obligates himself and his heirs to do all this within the said time; if he or they do not do so, they will be bound to pay £10,000 to the king and his heirs at Easter at the end of the above two-year period. This to be enrolled on the chancellor's roll.
Given [at the New Temple], London, the first Sunday of Lent 5 Edward I.
Witnesses: Robert Burnell, bishop of Bath and Wells and chancellor, Stephen de Penshurst, Master Geoffrey de Aspall, John de Kirkby and others.
Source: E159/66, m. 33; E132/3/40.

Notes: 'at the New Temple' is supplied by E132/3/40.

RBIV 8   14 February 1277
Roger Bigod, earl of Norfolk and marshal of England and his heirs is bound to King Edward I in 1,000 marks of sterling, which the king

delivered to the earl in prest, and which the earl will pay at the exchequer when the king wills. For this purpose the earl obligates himself and his heirs and all their goods movable and immovable wherever they may be found. And the earl will acknowledge to pay the money at the exchequer in the said form; if he does not, it will be levied from his lands and chattels by the sheriffs as the king pleases.

Given at London, the first Sunday of Lent 5 Edward I.

Witnesses: None given.

Source: E159/66, m. 33.

RBIV 9   c. 6 January 1279

Roger Bigod, earl of Norfolk and marshal of England, has granted to William Mortimer, son of Roger Mortimer, for his homage and service, twenty-five pounds p.a., to be paid on the close of Easter at the New Temple, London.

No date or place.

Witnesses: William de Middleton, bishop of Norwich, Roger de Clifford, Otto de Grandson, Adam de Gurdon, Grimbald Pauncefoot, Walter de Hopton, Master Geoffrey de Aspall, Walter de Eversley, John de Havering, Walter de Pedwardyn.

Source: *CCR, 1272-79*, p. 552.

Notes: The roll adds 'Memorandum: the earl came into the chancery and acknowledged the above, and granted that if he defaults it shall be levied on his goods in Norfolk... Afterwards, on 7 May 1289, William came into chancery and released the yearly sum and all arrears to the earl for 320 marks, and granted that the charter be annulled.'

RBIV 10   1280/81

Roger Bigod, earl of Norfolk and marshal of England, has given and granted to his burgesses of New Ross all the underwritten liberties, to have and to hold forever [long list of privileges and liberties follows].

No date or place.

Witnesses: Walter Porcell, William Grace, John de Vale, William Cadel, Richard de Rous, William de Canteton, Gilbert de Sutton, John de Vilers, knights, Reginald de Linet, Henry Tallon, Raymond de Neville and others.

Source: *Chartae, Privilegia et Immunitates; being Transcripts of Charters and Privileges to Cities, Towns, Abbeys, and other Bodies Corporate, 18 Henry III to 18 Richard II* (Dublin, 1889), pp. 84-6.

Notes: For a full transcript of this extremely long charter, see the above collection. Very probably given during the earl's visit of 1280-81.

RBIV 11   6 November 1281

An agreement made at Westminster on 6 November 1281 between Roger Bigod, earl of Norfolk and Marshal of England, and Sir Robert Cockerel, whereby the earl remits to Robert his anger and all exaction by reason of an account which Robert was bound to him for all the time when he was seneschal of the earl's lands in Ireland, saving to the earl fourteen pounds which are due to him from Robert for clear arrears. It is agreed that the earl will cause to be levied all arrears of all bailiffs and all debts in his demesne in Ireland for all the time when Robert was seneschal. It is also agreed that Robert will renounce all pleas or actions against the earl or any of his men by reason of any trespass committed upon him, and more especially the one moved by him against the earl and his men in the king's court of Dublin for unjust imprisonment and robbery.

Witnesses: Roger de Clifford Sr, John Ferre, Stephen de Penshurst, Thomas Weyland, John de Lovetot, Roger Loveday, Richard de Holbrook.

Source: *CCR, 1279-88*, p. 138.

RBIV 12 **c. 13 October 1283**

Roger Bigod, earl of Norfolk and marshal of England, has granted to Otto de Grandson, for his homage and service, the manors of Kemsing and Seal, in the county of Kent, with the advowson of Kemsing church, and all knights' fees etc., doing therefore the service of a quarter of a knight's fee.

No date or place.

Witnesses: John de Vescy, Reginald de Grey, Robert de Tibetot, Robert fitz John, Stephen de Penshurst, Guncelin de Badlesmere, John de Cobham, Henry de Cobham, his brother, John de Rokesle, William de Herre, Imbert de Monte Regali, Henry de Appelirfeud.

Source: *CCR, 1279-88*, p. 241.

Notes: Probably given at Acton Burnell, Shropshire, in the course of the parliament there in October 1283. Grandson, Vescy, Tibetot and fitz John all witnessed a royal charter there on 10 October (*RCWL Ed I*, p. 51).

RBIV 13 **1283 x 1287**

Roger Bigod, earl of Norfolk and marshal of England, sets forth that the abbot and convent of St Mary, Tintern, were wont to take all things they needed for building and burning in the forest of Wentwood under a charter of Walter fitz Richard, the [abbey's] founder, and under the confirmations thereof by the earl's other ancestors. It would be to the earl's advantage and the better preservation of the forest to assign to the abbot and convent a part of the said forest in compensation for the right of common. Therefore the earl has given them in free alms all the wood and soil [elaborate bounds given of the portion of the forest assigned to the monks]; to be held from the earl and his heirs by the monks in free alms, with the right to hunt in their woods and take venison, and to have all forfeitures, etc.

No date or place.

Witnesses: Thomas Weyland, Bartholomew de Mora, Ralph Bluet, Thomas de Honteleye, Walter de Redisham, seneschal of Chepstow, Robert de Gamages, John Martel, knights, Philip de Mora, Richard de Gardino.

Source: BL MS Arundel 19, ff. 26v-28v; *CChR, 1300-1326*, pp. 105-6.

Notes: Almost certainly given at Chepstow.

RBIV 14   **3 May 1284**
Roger Bigod, earl of Norfolk and marshal of England, sought from Edmund, the king's son, custody of the bailiwick which the earl held beneath the forest of Edmund in Pickering, and which was in Edmund's hand because of certain trespasses made by the earl and his ministers, both of venison and of vert, and of other things under the said bailiwick. However, the earl has made a fine of £100 sterling for damages to Edmund for the said transgressions, and for having custody once more, and has given Edmund security for this. And Edmund has returned the bailiwick to the earl, to be held as before, saving to Edmund and his heirs the usual services and customs. Moreover, Edmund remits to the said earl all the said trespasses pertaining to the said earl up to the present day, and the earl promises that he and his heirs keep the bailiwick properly etc.
Given at London, 3 May 1284.
Source: DL25/2178.

Notes: Original deed, with fine armorial seal attached.

RBIV 15   **11 November 1285**
An agreement between Roger Bigod, earl of Norfolk and marshal of England, and Richard Gladwyn and Alice his wife, concerning a certain solar and two shops which Richard and Alice acknowledged as pertaining to the earl in a plea between them in the hustings court in London. The said shops and solar are in the parish of St Mary Somerset, next to the earl's house in Denburgh Lane, and were once of William le Cooper. For this acknowledgement, the earl has demised, granted and confirmed to Richard and Alice for their lives, or to whichever of them lives longer, the said solar and shops; paying 8d at four terms for all secular demands. And the earl and his heirs will warrant etc. against all men and women, Christians and Jews, and especially against the abbot and convent of Missenden and their successors. Afterwards the shops and solar will revert to the earl or his heirs with no contradiction from the heirs of the Richard and Alice.
Given at London, Monday on the morrow of St Martin, 13 Edward I.
Witnesses: Gregory de Rokesley, Walter le Blunt and John Wade, then sheriffs of London, Richard de Chigwell, Roger Bruning, Richard de Hakeneye, Robert de Chalfont, Robert le Bret, Nicholas de Northampton, Edmund the clerk and others.
Source: Corporation of London Record Office, HR 16 (27).

Notes: Gregory de Rokesley was mayor of London until shortly before this charter was given (Prestwich, *Edward I*, pp. 245, 264-5). Richard de Chigwell was a merchant who bought wool from the earl (e.g. SC6/995/16, SC6/1007/9).

RBIV 16   **18 June 1286**
Roger Bigod, earl of Norfolk and marshal of England, has granted to Robert de la Sale of Aylsham three-and-a-half acres of land and half a rood, lying in two pieces in the field of Hanworth [bounds given]. This is

in exchange for three acres of pasture and marsh and half a rood lying in 'Heyhfen' in the vill of Hanworth. And the earl and his heirs will warrant. Given at Norwich before Solomon of Rochester and his fellows, justices.
Witnesses: Robert Baynard, Ralph de Crepping, Bartholomew de Intingham, Roger de Felbrigg, John de Barningham, Ralph de Curzon, Bartholomew de Castre, John de Melwode, Robert de Herward, Walter de Intingham clerk and others.
Source: BL, Add. Charter 46995.

Notes: For Robert Baynard and Ralph de Crepping, see Appendix D.

RBIV 17   14 October 1289

Roger Bigod, earl of Norfolk and marshal of England, has granted to King Edward I and Queen Eleanor the homages and services of William Martin, knight, Geoffrey son of Walter fitz Robert, Philip Bucher, Richard Harald and Adam de Angulo and their heirs, and of all the lands and tenements which the same William, Geoffrey, Philip, Richard and Adam previously held of the earl in Wales. And he remits and quitclaims these to Edward I and Eleanor and their heirs forever etc.
No place given.
Witnesses: John [Pecham], archbishop of Canterbury, John [de Pontoise], bishop of Winchester, Robert Burnell, bishop of Bath, John [de Kirkby], bishop of Ely, John de Warenne, earl of Surrey, Henry de Lacy, earl of Lincoln, John de St John, Robert Tibetot, William Latimer, Thomas de Rupe, Robert de Valle, Guy de Bryenn and others.
Source: KB27/122, m. 21.

Notes: Given at Westminster (cf. Prestwich, *Edward I*, pp. 339-40).

RBIV 18   c. 12 June 1290

Roger Bigod, earl of Norfolk and marshal of England, has assigned to his wife, Alice, daughter of John de Avesnes, count of Hainault, in dower, his manors of Chesterford and Dovercourt (Essex), Kennett, Earl Stonham, Walton, Hollesley, Staverton, Dunningworth, Kelsale, Peasenhall, Cratfield and Bungay (Suffolk), and [D]itching[ham], Earsham, Walsham, Acle, Halvergate, Seething, Woodton, Hanworth, Suffield and Yaxham (Norfolk), for the residue of all his other lands in England, Wales and Ireland.
No date or place.
Witnesses: Hugh Despenser, John Bigod, Arnold Murdach, Walter de Redisham, John Goubioun, John Bluet, John ap Adam, John de Shottesbrooke, John de Frating, Adam Roccaund, Henry de Tuddenham.
Source: CCR, 1288-96, p. 134.

Notes: Probably given at Westminster (cf. Appendix B).

RBIV 19   **4 April 1291**
Roger Bigod, earl of Norfolk and marshal of England, has granted to the
king the manors of Suffield, Caistor and Seething, Co. Norfolk; Peasenhall,
Co. Suffolk; Dovercourt, Co. Essex, Kennett, Cos. Cambridge and Suffolk.
Given at Berkeley, 4 April, 19 Edward I.
Witnesses: Thomas de Berkeley, Robert de Berkeley, his brother, Fulk de Vaux,
William de Ormesby, Maurice fitz Thomas, John ap Adam, Thomas de Akeny,
William de Capel, William de Cayly, John Visdelu, Robert de Stone, Robert
Wycher.
Source: *CR, 1288-96*, p. 201; *Ancient Kalendars and Inventories of the Treasury*
and of the Exchequer, ed. F. Palgrave (London, 1836), i, 43.

Notes: Enrolment adds 'this charter was delivered to Walter de Langton, keeper of the
king's wardrobe, on Saturday before the Assumption (31 May 1291), by the hands of
William de Warminster, clerk.'

RBIV 20   **28 July 1291**
Roger Bigod, earl of Norfolk and marshal of England, has granted to
Geoffrey Stulle and his wife Josiana and their heirs all the messuage and
land which William Tocke held from him in Settrington; to be had and
held to Geoffrey and Josiana and their heirs in fee and inheritance from
the earl and heirs, paying 16s 4d p.a. [terms given] for all secular
demands. And the earl will warrant etc, by the said service, and by suit of
the earl's court at Settrington.
Given at Thirsk, 28 July, 19 Edward I.
Witnesses: Thomas de Berkeley, Walter de Eversley, Fulk de Vaux, Peter de
Tadington, Roger de Grimet, knights, John ap Adam, John de Menethorpe,
William the Butler, John Parent, Robert de Buckton, Richard de Rudham, clerk,
and others.
Source: BL, Add Charter 5735.

RBIV 21   **c. July 1291**
Roger Bigod, earl of Norfolk and marshal of England, has granted to
Geoffrey Stulle one toft and croft in Settrington, which John Cuyst holds
of the earl; to be had and held to the earl and his heirs freely etc.,
paying therefore 1d at Michaelmas for all secular service. And the earl
will warrant.
No date or place.
Witnesses: Walter de Eversley, Ranulf de Belgrave, Philip de Kyme, knights, John
ap Adam, John de Frating, William the Butler, John the Clerk.
Source: BL, Add. Charter 5736.

Notes: Common witnesses suggest a date close to RBIV 20.

RBIV 22   **9 February 1294**
Roger Bigod, earl of Norfolk and marshal of England, has assigned to
Richard Gladwyn, citizen of London, and Amicia his wife for their lives to

pay the 8s of rent which the earl is accustomed to pay each year to the abbot of Missenden for a solar and two shops which Richard and Amicia have in the parish of St Mary Somerset next to Denburgh Lane in London, so that neither he nor his heirs will be able to exact or sell anything of the said rent against the said Richard and Amicia.
Given at London, Tuesday on the octave of the Purification, 22 Edward I.
Witnesses: None given.
Source: BL, Harley MS 3688, f. 153.

RBIV 23   13 May 1294

Roger Bigod, earl of Norfolk and marshal of England, has granted to his dear and faithful John ap Adam a weekly market on Wednesdays at his manor of Beachley, Gloucestershire, and an annual fair to last three days, namely the vigil, day and morrow of St Margaret the Virgin [12-14 July]; together with free warren in all his demesne lands of Beachley and 'La Gorste'.
Given at London, 13 May, 22 Edward I.
Witnesses: Ralph, abbot of Tintern, Thomas de Berkeley, Maurice de Berkeley, his son, John Bluet, knights, William de Beccles, then our chancellor, Philip le Waleys, Philip de Mora and others.
Source: *Descriptive Catalogue of the Charters and Muniments...at Berkeley Castle*, ed. I.H. Jeayes (Bristol, 1892), p. 148.

RBIV 24   early December 1295

Roger Bigod, earl of Norfolk and marshal of England, has quitclaimed to Nicholas, abbot of St Benet Hulme, forever, all right and claim which he had or might have in the marriage of the heirs of William de Stalham, knight, so that neither the earl nor his heirs nor anyone in his name may claim them in future.
No date or place.
Witnesses: William de Ormesby, knight, Master Thomas de Siddington...
Source: BL, Cotton MS Galba E ii, ff. 168v-169.

Notes: The earl sent two separate letters concerning this quitclaim to his officials, dated at Westminster, 5 and 6 December 1295 (BL, Cotton MS Galba, E ii, ff. 168v-169).

RBIV 25   10 April 1298

Roger Bigod, earl of Norfolk and marshal of England, has granted to John de Newent a messuage and all the land which William Kail held in Earsham, to be had and held from the earl and his heirs by John and his heirs etc forever; paying a barbed arrow annually at Michaelmas for all services and secular demands. And the earl and his heirs will warrant etc.
Given at Settrington, 10 April 26 Edward I.
Witnesses: None given.

Source: Cambridge University Library, Buxton Deeds, 7/30; *Report on Manuscripts in Various Collections* (8 vols., Historical Manuscripts Comm., 1901-13), ii, 228.

Notes: Original deed with well-preserved seal attached.

RBIV 26   **1300**
Roger Bigod, earl of Norfolk and marshal of England, has granted to Sir John Bigod a lordship in Seething. John will pay the earl a barbed arrow yearly for all services.
Given at Bungay.
Witnesses: John Lovel, Baldwin Picot, Peter Roscelyn, Edward Charles, John de Holbrook...
Source: Blomefield, x, 173; cf. *CIPM*, iv, 216.

RBIV 27   **4 August 1301**
Roger Bigod, earl of Norfolk and marshal of England, inspired by charity and for the salvation of his soul and those of his ancestors and heirs, has granted and confirmed to St Mary, Tintern, all the lands, possessions, liberties and customs underwritten which they have out of the gift of his ancestors and other founders or donors, or out of his gift. [very long list follows]
Given at Modesgate.
Witnesses: John Bigod, our brother, John Bigod of Stockton, Nicholas de Kingston, knights, Elias de Aylburton, then our seneschal of Chepstow, Philip de Mora, Roger de Seymour, William de Dinham, Andrew de Beauchamp and others.
Source: BL, Arundel MS 19, ff. 7v-12, 28v-29v; *CChR, 1300-1326*, p. 106.

Notes: Actually two separate charters confirming Tintern's possessions, but given on the same day with the same witnesses.

RBIV 28   **18 February 1302**
Roger Bigod, earl of Norfolk and marshal of England, has granted in fee simple with warranty to John de Uffeton, his yeoman, in consideration of his service, all the lands sometime of John de Glanvill and Joan de Grimilies his wife, of the inheritance of the said Joan in the towns of Saxmundham, Kelsale, Rendham and Sternfield, with the woods, meadows, pastures, ways, paths and rents and other appurtenances, together with the advowson of the church of Saxmundham; and also of Richard le Man and Robert le Coilleur, the earl's bondmen, with their issues, born or to be born, their goods, and their lands which they held of the earl in villeinage in Saxmundham, Sternfield, Friston, Kelsale, Snape and Benhall.
Given at Walton, 18 February, 30 Edward I.

Witnesses: John Bigod of Stockton, Nicholas de Falsham, Roger Sturmyn, knights, Richard de Moundevill, John de Bruisyard, John de Leiston, John de Rising, William Phelippe, Robert Swan.
Source: *CPR, 1301-1307,* pp. 125-6.

RBIV 29   **12 April 1302**
Roger Bigod, earl of Norfolk and marshal of England, has granted to King Edward I all the castles, towns, manors and lands that he holds in fee in England and Wales, except the manors of Settrington, Wilton, Thornton and Levisham, with the advowsons of their churches, in Yorkshire, and except the manors of Acle and Caistor, with the advowson of the church of Geldeston, in Norfolk.
Given at St John's Abbey, Colchester, 12 April, 30 Edward I.
Witnesses: John de Langton, archdeacon of Canterbury, chancellor, Roger de Brabazon, justice, John de Droxford, keeper of the king's wardrobe, John Bigod, William de Ormesby, justice, William de Carlton, baron of the exchequer, Walter de Gloucester, escheator this side of the Trent, Hugh Wake, John Filliol, Robert de Bardelby, clerk.
Source: *CCR, 1296-1302,* pp. 581-2.

RBIV 30   **25 April 1302**
Roger Bigod, earl of Norfolk and marshal of England, has granted to Sir John Bigod of Stockton, knight, and Isabel, his wife, for good service done to him, all the manor of Settrington in Yorkshire and the advowsons of the churches of Settrington and Geldeston, Norfolk; to be held by John and Isabel for their lives from the chief lords of the fee by the services due therefrom, with remainder to John, son of John and Isabel, and the lawful heirs of his body, and then to Roger, [second] son of John and Isabel and the lawful heirs of his body, and then to the earl.
Given at Caistor-by-Norwich, 25 April, 30 Edward I.
Witnesses: John Lovel, William de Ormesby, Hugh Wake, Thomas de Akeny, Roger de Hales, Richard de Brom, knights, William de Colneye, William de Curzon, John de Ingelose, John de Gernon, Roger de Fraxinis Jr., Robert de Martham.
Source: *CChR, 1300-1326,* p. 34

RBIV 31   **18 May 1302**
Roger Bigod, earl of Norfolk and marshal of England, inspired by charity and for the salvation of his soul and those of his ancestors and successors, has granted to the church of St Mary, Tintern, and the monks there all his manor of Acle [full description given] plus the advowson; to be had and held to them quit from all exaction and service. The earl and his heirs will warrant forever.
Given at Fulham, 18 May, 30 Edward I.

Witnesses: Robert fitz Roger, John Lovel, John Bigod, William de Ormesby, Thomas de Akeny, Thomas le Rous, knights, Master John Golafre, William de Overton, Robert de Beverley, Ralph de Minavilla, clerks.
Source: BL, Arundel MS 19, ff. 37v-38; *CChR, 1300-1326*, p. 31.

RBIV 32   **28 October 1302**
Roger Bigod, earl of Norfolk and marshal of England, has granted to the church of St Mary, Tintern, and all the monks there, all his manor of Alvington; to be held, from the donor, his heirs or assigns, in exchange for the manor of 'Platalanda', which the monks have given to the earl, his heirs and assigns.
Given at Stepney, 28 October, 30 Edward I.
Witnesses: John Lovel, John Bigod, Nicholas de Kingston, Thomas Lovel, knights, Master John Golafre, William de Spanby, Robert de Beverley, clerks, Roger de Seymour, Andrew de Beauchamp.
Source: *CChR, 1300-1326*, p. 31.

RBIV 33   **11 October 1305**
Roger Bigod, earl of Norfolk and marshal of England, has confirmed to John de Uffeton, his chamberlain, for life, the custody of all the earl's parks and woods of Framlingham, Kelsale and [Earl] Soham in Suffolk, with 4s a week for the custody, 20s a year for his robe, hay and oats for one horse (to wit, every night half a bushel), all trees blown down by the wind, and escheats of timber given or felled to the earl's use.
Given at Chelsea, 11 October, 33 Edward I.
Witnesses: John Lovel, John ap Adam, John Filliol, Robert de Raydon, knights, Peter de Welles, John Dauneys, William de Ludham, Walter de Bernham, John de Medefield, Edmund de Mikilfield, William Phelippe, Robert Bolle.
Source: *CPR, 1301-1307*, p. 382.

Bibliography

MANUSCRIPT SOURCES

London, National Archives

C47 (Chancery Miscellanea)
C53 (Charter Rolls)
C60 (Fine Rolls)
C66 (Patent Rolls)
C67 (Supplementary Patent Rolls)
C81 (Chancery Warrants)
C143 (Chancery Inquisitions *Ad Quod Damnum*)
C145 (Inquisitions Miscellaneous)
CP25 (Final Concords)
CP40 (Court of Common Pleas: Plea Rolls)
DL25 (Duchy of Lancaster, Ancient Deeds)
E32 (Forest Eyres)
E101 (King's Remembrancer, Accounts Various)
E132 (Transcripts of Deeds and Charters)
E159 (King's Remembrancer Memoranda Rolls)
E163 (King's Remembrancer Miscellanea)
E175 (King's Remembrancer, Parliament and Council Proceedings, Ser. II)
E213 (King's Remembrancer, Ancient Deeds, Ser. RS)
E368 (Lord Treasurer's Remembrancer Memoranda Rolls)
E372 (Pipe Rolls)
JUST 1 (Eyre Rolls)
KB26 (Curia Regis Rolls)
KB27 (Court of King's Bench, Plea and Crown Sides, Coram Rege Rolls)
SC1 (Ancient Correspondence)
SC6 (Special Collections: Ministers' Accounts)
SC12 (Special Collections: Rentals and Surveys)
SP46 (State Papers Domestic Supplementary)

London, British Library

Add. Charter 5735
Add. Charter 5736
Add. Charter 7207
Add. Charter 17735
Add. Charter 19823
Add. Charter 46995
Arundel MS 19
Cotton MS Faustina A iv
Cotton MS Galba E ii

Harley MS 544
Harley MS 1240
Harley MS 3688
Lansdowne MS 229
Royal MS 14 C vi
Topham Charter 44

London, College of Arms

Arundel 30

London, Corporation of London Record Office

HR 16 (27)

Cambridge, University Library

Buxton Deeds, 7/30

Canterbury Cathedral Library

Register I

Norfolk Record Office, Norwich

Great Hospital Deeds
KNY 28 (Knyvett-Wilson Deeds)
Phillips MSS 600

Oxford, Bodleian Library

MS Ch. Suffolk a. 12 (1261)

Oxford, Queen's College

MS 166

Suffolk Record Office, Ipswich

HD1047/1/20

PRINTED PRIMARY SOURCES

Anglo-Scottish Relations, 1174-1328, ed. E.L.G. Stones (London, 1965).

Annales Monastici, ed. H.R. Luard (5 vols., Rolls Ser., 1864-69).

Antient Kalendars and Inventories of the Treasury and of the Exchequer, ed. F. Palgrave (London, 1836).

Bartholomaei de Cotton, Historia Anglicana (A.D. 449-1298), ed. H.R. Luard (Rolls Ser., 1859).

Blythburgh Priory Cartulary, ed. C. Harper-Bill (2 vols., Suffolk Charters, ii–iii, 1980-81).

The Book of Fees, Commonly Called Testa de Nevill (3 vols., HMSO, 1920-31).

Book of Prests, 1294-5, ed. E.B. Fryde (Oxford, 1962).

Calendar of Ancient Correspondence Concerning Wales, ed. J.G. Edwards (Cardiff, 1935).

Calendar of Chancery Warrants, 1244-1326 (HMSO, 1927).

Calendar of Charter Rolls (HMSO, 1903-27).

Calendar of Close Rolls (HMSO, 1892–).

Calendar of Documents relating to Ireland, ed. H.S. Sweetman (5 vols., HMSO, 1875-86).

Calendar of Documents relating to Scotland, ed. J. Bain and others (5 vols., Edinburgh, 1881-1988).

Calendar of the Feet of Fines for Suffolk, ed. W. Rye (Ipswich, 1900).

A Calendar of the Feet of Fines relating to the county of Wiltshire, ed. E.A. Fry (Devizes, 1930).

Calendar of Fine Rolls (HMSO, 1911-62).

Calendar of Inquisitions Miscellaneous (HMSO, 1916-68).

Calendar of Inquisitions Post Mortem (HMSO, 1904–).

Calendar of Liberate Rolls (HMSO, 1916-64).

Calendar of Ormond Deeds, i, *1172-1350* (HMSO, 1932).

Calendar of Papal Registers: Papal Letters, 1198-1342, ed. W.H. Bliss (2 vols., HMSO, 1893-95).

Calendar of Patent Rolls (HMSO, 1906–).

Calendar of Plea Rolls of the Exchequer of the Jews, ed. J.M. Rigg and others (5 vols., Jewish Historical Soc. of England, 1905-72).

Calendar of Various Chancery Rolls, 1277-1326 (HMSO, 1912).

Cartae Antiquae Rolls (2 vols., Pipe Roll Soc., new ser., xvii, xxxiii, 1939-60).

The Cartulary of Leiston Abbey and Butley Priory Charters, ed. R. Mortimer (Suffolk Charters, i, Ipswich, 1979).

The Cartulary of St Bartholomew's Hospital, ed. N.J.M. Kerling (London, 1973).

Catalogue of Ancient Deeds (6 vols., HMSO, 1899-1915).

Chartae, Privilegia et Immunitates; being Transcripts of Charters and Privileges to Cities, Towns, Abbeys, and other Bodies Corporate, 18 Henry III to 18 Richard II (Dublin, 1889).

'The Charters of the Abbey of Duiske', ed. C.M. Butler and J.H. Bernard, *Proceedings of the Royal Irish Academy*, xxxv (1918).

Chartularies of St Mary's Abbey, Dublin with the register of its house at Dunbrody and Annals of Ireland, ed. J.T. Gilbert (2 vols., Rolls Ser., 1884).

Chronica Johannis de Oxenedes, ed. H. Ellis (Rolls Ser., 1859).

Chronica Monasterii de Melsa, ed. E.A. Bond (3 vols., Rolls Ser., 1866-69).

The Chronicle of Bury St Edmunds, 1212-1301, ed. A. Gransden (London, 1964).

The Chronicle of Pierre de Langtoft, ed. T. Wright, ii (Rolls Ser., 1868).

The Chronicle of Walter of Guisborough, ed. H. Rothwell (Camden Soc., lxxxix, 1957).

The Chronicle of William de Rishanger of the Barons' Wars, ed. J.O. Halliwell (Camden Soc., 1840).

Chronicles of the Reigns of Edward I and Edward II, ed. W. Stubbs, (2 vols., Rolls Ser., 1882-83).

Close Rolls, Henry III, (HMSO, 1902-38).

Close Rolls (Supplementary) of the Reign of Henry III, 1244-66 (HMSO, 1975).

Councils and Synods, II, 1205-1313, ed. F.M. Powicke and C.R. Cheney (Oxford, 1964).

Curia Regis Rolls (HMSO, 1922–).

De Antiquis Legibus Liber. Chronica Maiorum et Vicecomitum Londoniarum, ed. T. Stapleton (Camden Soc., 1846).

Descriptive Catalogue of the Charters and Muniments...at Berkeley Castle, ed. I.H. Jeayes (Bristol, 1892).

Dialogus de Scaccario, ed. C. Johnson, F.E.L. Carter and D. Greenway (Oxford, 1983).

Diplomatic Documents, 1101-1272, ed. P. Chaplais (HMSO, 1964).

Documents Illustrating the Crisis of 1297-98 in England, ed. M. Prestwich (Camden Soc., 4th ser., xxiv, 1980).

Documents of the Baronial Movement of Reform and Rebellion, 1258-1267, ed. R.F. Treharne and I.J. Sanders (Oxford, 1923).

Dodnash Priory Charters, ed. C. Harper-Bill (Suffolk Charters, xvi, Woodbridge, 1998).

Domesday Book, ed. J. Morris (35 vols. in 40, Chichester, 1975-86).

Early Yorkshire Charters, I–iii, ed. W. Farrer (3 vols., Edinburgh, 1914-16), iv–x, ed. C.T. Clay (7 vols., Yorkshire Archaeological Soc., Record Ser., extra ser., 1935-55).

Edward I and the Throne of Scotland, 1290-1296. An Edition of the Record Sources for the Great Cause, ed. E.L.G. Stones and G.G. Simpson (2 vols., Oxford, 1978).

English Historical Documents 1189-1327, ed. H. Rothwell (London, 1975).

Excerpta e Rotulis Finium in Turri Londinensi Asservatis...1216-1272, ed. C. Roberts (2 vols., Record Comm., 1835-36).

Eye Priory Cartulary and Charters, ed. V. Brown (2 vols., Suffolk Charters, xii–xiii, Woodbridge, 1992-94).

Feet of Fines 10 Richard I... and a Roll of the King's Court (Pipe Roll Soc., 24, 1900).

Feet of Fines for the County of Norfolk, ed. B. Dodwell (2 vols., Pipe Roll Soc., new ser., 27, 32, 1952-58).

Feet of Fines for the County of York, ed. W.P. Baildon, J. Parker, F.H. Slingsby and M. Roper (5 vols., Yorkshire Archaeological Soc. Record Ser., lxii, lxvii, lxxxii, cxxi, cxxvii, 1910-65).

Feet of Fines relating to the County of Sussex, ed. L.F. Salzmann (3 vols., Sussex Record Soc., ii, vii, xxiii, 1903-16).

Feudal Aids, 1284-1431 (6 vols., HMSO, 1899-1920)

Flores Historiarum, ed. H.R. Luard (3 vols., Rolls Ser., 1890).

Foedera, Conventiones, Litterae et Acta Publica, ed. T. Rymer, amended edn by A. Clarke and F. Holbrooke (4 vols. in 7, Record Comm., 1816-69).

Histoire de Guillaume le Maréchal, ed. P. Meyer (3 vols., Paris, 1891-1901).

Historical Manuscripts Commission Reports:
Manuscripts in Various Collections (8 vols., 1901-13).
Manuscripts of Lord Middleton, ed. W.H. Stevenson (1911).

Hastings Manuscripts, ed. F. Bickley and J. Harley (4 vols., 78, 1928-47).

The Historical Works of Gervase of Canterbury, ed. W. Stubbs (2 vols., Rolls Ser., 1879-80).

Household Accounts from Medieval England, ed. C.M. Woolgar (2 vols., Oxford, 1992).

Johannis de Trokelowe et Henrici de Blaneforde, Chronica et Annales, ed. H.T. Riley (Rolls Ser., 1866).

Letters of Medieval Women, ed. A. Crawford (Stroud, 2002).

Lincolnshire Records: Abstracts of Final Concords, vol. 1, ed. W.O. Massingberd (London, 1896).

Littere Wallie, ed. J.G. Edwards (Cardiff, 1940).

The London Eyre of 1276, ed. M. Weinbaum (London Rec. Soc., xii, 1976).

The Making of King's Lynn, ed. D.M. Owen (Records of Social and Economic History, new ser., 9, London, 1984).

Matthaei Parisiensis, Monachi Sancti Albani, Chronica Majora, ed. H.R. Luard (7 vols., Rolls Ser., 1872-83).

Medieval Framlingham, ed. J. Ridgard (Suffolk Records Soc., 1985).

Memoranda Roll 16-17 Henry III, ed. R.A. Brown (HMSO, 1991).

Nicholai Triveti...Annales Sex Regum Angliae, ed. T. Hog (London, 1845).

Parliamentary Writs and Writs of Military Summons, ed. F. Palgrave (2 vols. in 4, Record Comm., 1827-34).

Patent Rolls of the Reign of Henry III, 1216-32 (2 vols., HMSO, 1901-3).

Patrologia Latina, ed. J.-P. Migne (Paris, 1844–)

Pipe Roll 1 Richard I, ed. J. Hunter (London, 1844).

Pipe Rolls 5 Henry II to 14 Henry III (Pipe Roll Soc., 1884–)

Placita de Quo Warranto, ed. W. Illington (2 vols., Record Comm., 1818).

Placitorum in Domo Capitulari Westmonasteriensi Asservatorum Abbreviatio (Record Comm., 1811)

'A Plea Roll of Edward I's Army in Scotland, 1296', ed. C. J. Neville, *Miscellany of the Scottish Historical Society XI* (Scottish Historical Soc., 5th ser., iii, 1990), 7-133.

The Political Songs of England, ed. T. Wright (Camden Soc., vi, 1839).

'Private Indentures for Life Service in Peace and War, 1278-1476', ed. M. Jones and S. Walker, *Camden Miscellany XXXII* (Camden Soc., 5th ser., iii, 1994), 1-190.

Reading Abbey Cartularies, ed. B.R. Kemp (2 vols., Camden Soc., 4th ser., xxxi, xxxiii, 1986-87).

Records of the Trial of Walter Langeton, Bishop of Coventry and Lichfield 1307-1312, ed. A. Beardwood (Camden, 4th ser., vi, 1969).

Records of the Wardrobe and Household, 1285-1289, ed. B.F. and C.R. Byerly (2 vols., HMSO, 1977-86).

Recueil de Lettres Anglo-Francaises, 1265-1399, ed. F.J. Tanquerey (Paris, 1916).

Red Book of the Exchequer, ed. H. Hall (3 vols., Roll Ser., 1896).

The Register of John Pecham, Archbishop of Canterbury, 1279-1292, ed. F.N. Davis et al. (2 vols., Canterbury and York Soc., lxiv, 1969).

The Register of Walter Giffard, Lord Archbishop of York, 1266-1279, ed. W. Brown (Surtees Soc., cix, 1904).

Reports of the Deputy Keeper of the Public Records in Ireland (HMSO, Dublin, 1869-1922).

Robert Mannyng of Brunne: The Chronicle, ed. I. Sullens (Binghamton, N.Y., 1996).

Rôles Gascons, ed. F. Michel and C. Bémont (3 vols., Paris, 1885-1906).

Rolls of Arms Henry III, ed. T.M. Tremlett, H.S. London and A. Wagner (London, 1967).

Rotuli Chartarum in Turris Londinensi Asservati, ed. T.D. Hardy (Record Comm., 1837).

Rotuli de Liberate ac de Misis et Praestitis, ed. T.D. Hardy (Record Comm., 1844).

Rotuli Hundredorum (2 vols., Record Comm., 1812-18).

Rotuli Litterarum Clausarum in Turri Londonensi Asservati, ed. T.D. Hardy (2 vols., Record Comm., 1833-34).

Rotuli Litterarum Patentium in Turri Londonensi Asservati, ed. T.D. Hardy (Record Comm., 1835).

Rotuli Parliamentorum, i (Record Comm., 1783).

Rotuli Selecti, ed. J. Hunter (Record Comm., 1834).

Royal and Other Historical Letters Illustrative of the Reign of King Henry III, ed. W.W. Shirley (2 vols., Rolls Ser., 1862-66).

The Royal Charter Witness Lists of Edward I, ed. R. Huscroft (List and Index Soc., 2000).

The Royal Charter Witness Lists of Henry III, ed. M. Morris (2 vols., List and Index Soc., 2001).

The St Albans Chronicle, 1406-1420, ed. V.H. Galbraith (Oxford, 1937).

Scalacronica by Sir Thomas Grey of Heton, Knight, ed. J. Stevenson (Maitland Club, Edinburgh, 1836).

Scotland in 1298, ed. H. Gough (Paisley, 1888).

Select Cases in the Court of King's Bench, ed. G.O. Sayles (7 vols., Selden Soc., lv, lvii, lviii, lxxiv, lxxvi, lxxxii, lxxxviii, 1936-71).

Select Cases in the Exchequer of Pleas, ed. H. Jenkinson (Selden Soc., xlviii, 1932).

Select Cases on the Law Merchant, ed. C. Gross and H. Hall (3 vols., Selden Soc., xxiii, xlvi, xlix, 1908-32).

A Short Calendar of the Feet of Fines for Norfolk, ed. W. Rye (2 vols., Norwich, 1885-86).

Sibton Abbey Cartularies, ed. P. Brown (4 vols., Suffolk Charters, vii–x, Woodbridge, 1985-88).

Sir Christopher Hatton's Book of Seals, ed. L.C. Loyd and D.M. Stenton (Oxford, 1950).

State Trials of the Reign of Edward the First, 1289-1293, ed. T.F. Tout and H. Johnstone (Camden Soc., 3rd ser., ix, 1906).

The Statutes of the Realm, ed. A. Luders, T.E. Tomlins, J. France, W.E. Taunton and J. Raithby, i (Record Comm., 1810).

Testamenta Vetusta, ed. N.H. Nicolas (2 vols., London, 1826).

Three Yorkshire Assize Rolls for the Reigns of King John and King Henry III, ed. C.T. Clay (Yorkshire Archaeological Soc., Record Ser., xliv, 1911).

Treaty Rolls, i, *1234-1325* (HMSO, 1955).

Visitations of English Cluniac Foundations, ed. G.F. Duckett (London, 1890).

Vita Edwardi Secundi, ed. N. Denholm-Young (London, 1957).

The Whitby Cartulary, ed. J.C. Atkinson (2 vols., Surtees Soc., lxix, lxxii (1878-79).

Willelmi Rishanger, Chronica et Annales, ed. H.T. Riley (Rolls Ser., 1865).

William Worcestre, Itineraries, ed. J.H. Harvey (Oxford, 1969).

Worcester Cartulary Charters, ed. R.R. Darlington (Pipe Roll Soc., new ser., xxxviii, 1968).

Yorkshire Inquisitions, ed. W. Brown (4 vols., Yorkshire Archaeological Soc., Record Ser., xii, xxiii, xxxi, xxxvii, 1892-1906).

PRINTED SECONDARY WORKS

The Agrarian History of England and Wales, vol. 2, ed. E. Hallam (Cambridge, 1988).

Altschul, M., *A Baronial Family in England: The Clares, 1217-1314* (Baltimore, 1965).

Bean, J.M.W., *From Lord to Patron: Lordship in Late Medieval England* (Manchester, 1989).

Beardwood, A., 'The Trial of Walter Langton, Bishop of Lichfield, 1307-1312', *Transactions of the American Philosophical Soc.*, new ser., 54 (1964).

Bémont, C., *Simon de Montfort* (Paris, 1884).

Birrell, J., 'Aristocratic Poachers in the Forest of Dean: their methods, their quarry and their companions', *Transactions of the Bristol and Gloucestershire Archaeological Soc.*, 119 (2001), pp. 147-54.

Blomefield, F., *An Essay towards a Topographical History of the County of Norfolk* (11 vols., London, 1805-10).

Bolton, J.L., *The Medieval English Economy, 1150-1500* (London, 1980).

Bowers, R.H., 'English Merchants and the Anglo-Flemish Economic War of 1270-1274', *Seven Studies in Medieval History and other Historical Essays presented to Harold S. Snellgrove* (Jackson, Miss., 1983), pp. 21-54.

Brand, P., 'Chief Justice and Felon: The Career of Thomas Weyland', *The Making of the Common Law* (London, 1992), pp. 113-33.

Braun, H., *Bungay Castle: Historical Notes and an Account of the Excavations* (new edn, Bungay, 1991).

Britnell, R., *The Commercialisation of English Society, 1000-1500* (Manchester, 1996).

Brown, R.A., 'Framlingham Castle and Bigod, 1154-1216', *Castles, Conquest and Charters: Collected Papers* (Woodbridge, 1989), pp. 194-201.

Brown, R.A., Colvin, H.M., and Taylor, A.J., *The History of the King's Works*, i, (HMSO, 1963).

Cam, H., *Studies in the Hundred Rolls* (Oxford, 1921).

—— 'The Marshalsy of the Eyre', *Cambs. Hist. Journal*, Vol. 1, no. 2 (1924), pp. 126-137.

—— *The Hundred and the Hundred Rolls* (New York, 1930).

Campbell, B.M.S., *English Seigniorial Agriculture, 1250-1450* (Cambridge, 2000).

Carpenter, D.A., *The Battles of Lewes and Evesham, 1264/65* (Keele, 1987).

—— *The Minority of Henry III* (London, 1990).

—— *The Reign of Henry III* (London, 1996), which includes the nine essays listed immediately below. Original places of publication are noted, but my references follow the pagination in the book.

—— 'The Decline of the Curial Sheriff in England, 1194-1258', *EHR*, 101 (1976).

—— 'What Happened in 1258?', *War and Government in the Middle Ages*, ed. J. Gillingham and J.C. Holt (Woodbridge, 1984).

—— 'An Unknown Obituary of King Henry III from the Year 1263', *England in the Thirteenth Century: Proceedings of the 1984 Harlaxton Symposium*, ed. W.M. Ormrod (Harlaxton, 1985).

—— 'King, Magnates and Society: the Personal Rule of King Henry III, 1234-58', *Speculum*, 60 (1985).

—— 'The Lord Edward's Oath to Aid and Counsel Simon de Montfort, 15 October 1259', *BIHR*, 58 (1985).

—— 'Simon de Montfort and the Mise of Lewes', *BIHR*, 58 (1985).

—— 'Chancellor Ralph de Neville and Plans of Political Reform', *TCE*, ii (1988).

—— 'King Henry III's 'Statute' against Aliens: July 1263', *EHR*, 107 (1992).

—— 'Justice and Jurisdiction under King John and Henry III', previously unpublished.

—— 'The Second Century of English Feudalism', *Past and Present*, 168 (2000), pp. 30-71.

—— *The Struggle for Mastery: Britain 1066-1284* (London, 2003).

Chaplais, P., *English Royal Documents, King John to Henry VI, 1199-1461* (Oxford, 1971).

Chepstow Castle: Its History and Buildings, ed. R.C. Turner and R. Shoesmith (Almeley, forthcoming).

Clanchy, M.T., *England and Its Rulers, 1066-1272* (2nd edn, Oxford, 1998).

Cockayne, G.E., *Complete Peerage of England, Scotland, Ireland, Great Britain and the United Kingdom*, ed. V. Gibbs et al. (12 vols. in 13, 1912-59).

Colfer, B., 'Anglo-Norman Settlement in County Wexford', *Wexford: History and Society*, ed. K. Whelan (Dublin, 1987), pp. 65-101.

—— 'In Search of the Barricade and Ditch of Ballyconnor, Co. Wexford', *Archaeology Ireland*, vol. 10, no. 2 (Summer 1996), pp. 16-19.

Copinger, W.A., *The Manors of Suffolk* (7 vols., London, 1905-11).

Coss, P.R., 'Bastard Feudalism Revised', *Past and Present*, 125 (1989), pp. 27-64.

—— *The Lady in Medieval England, 1000-1500* (Stroud, 1998).

Crouch, D., 'The Last Adventure of Richard Siward', *Morgannwg*, 35 (1991), pp. 7-30.

—— *The Image of Aristocracy in Britain, 1000-1300* (London, 1992).

—— 'From Stenton to McFarlane: models of society of the twefth and thirteenth centuries', *TRHS*, 6th ser., 5 (1995), pp. 179-200.

—— *The Reign of King Stephen, 1135-1154* (Harlow, 2000).

—— *William Marshal: Knighthood, War and Chivalry, 1147-1219* (Harlow, 2002).

Curtis, E., *A History of Medieval Ireland* (London, 1923).

Davenport, F.G., *The Economic Development of a Norfolk Manor, 1086-1565* (London, 1906).

Davies, G.R.C., *Medieval Cartularies of Great Britain* (London, 1958).

Davies, R.R., 'Baronial Accounts, Incomes, and Arrears in the Later Middle Ages', *Economic History Review*, 2nd ser., 21 (1968), pp. 211-29.

—— *Lordship and Society in the March of Wales, 1282-1400* (Oxford, 1978).

—— *Conquest, Coexistence and Change: Wales, 1063-1415* (Oxford, 1987).

De Laborderie, O., Maddicott, J.R., and Carpenter, D.A., 'The Last Hours of Simon de Montfort: A New Account', *EHR*, 115 (2000), pp. 378-412.

Denholm-Young, N., *Seignorial Administration in England* (Oxford, 1937).

—— *Richard of Cornwall* (Oxford, 1947).

—— 'The Tournament in the Thirteenth Century', *Studies in Medieval History presented to F.M. Powicke*, ed. R.W. Hunt, W.A. Pantin and R.W. Southern (Oxford, 1948), pp. 240-68.

Denton, J.H., 'The Crisis of 1297 from the Evesham Chronicle', *EHR*, xciii (1978), 560-79.

—— *Robert Winchelsey and the Crown, 1294-1313* (Cambridge, 1980).

Dictionnaire de L'Ancienne Langue Francaise, ed. F. Godefroy (10 vols., Paris, 1880-1902).

The Dictionary of National Biography (63 vols., London, 1885-1900).

The Dictionary of National Biography: Missing Persons, ed. C.S. Nicholls (Oxford, 1993).

Dugdale, W., *Monasticon Anglicanum* (6 vols. in 8, London, 1817-30).

Duncan, A.A.M., *Scotland: The Making of the Kingdom* (Edinburgh, 1975).

Emden, A.B., *A Bibliographical Register of the University of Oxford to A.D. 1500* (3 vols., Oxford, 1957-59).

Fairclough, J. and Plunkett, S.J., 'Drawings of Walton Castle and other Monuments in Walton and Felixstowe', *Proceedings of the Suffolk Institute of Archaeology and History*, 39 (2000), pp. 419-59.

Farrer, W., *Honors and Knights' Fees* (3 vols., London and Manchester, 1923-25).

Frame, R., 'The Justiciar and the Murder of the MacMurroughs in 1282', *Irish Historical Studies*, xviii (1972), 223-30.

—— *English Lordship in Ireland, 1318-1361* (Oxford, 1982).

Gransden, A., *Historical Writing in England, c. 550 to c. 1307* (London, 1974).

Green, J.A., 'The Descent of Belvoir', *Prosopon*, 10 (1999).

Griffith, L., et al., 'The Alleged Descent of the Marshalls from Dermot MacMurrough', *Genealogist's Magazine*, vol. 6 (1932-34), pp. 311-13, 362-6, 410, 460.

Grose, D., *The Antiquities of Ireland*, ed. R. Stalley (Dublin, 1991).

Grose, F., *Military Antiquities Respecting a History of the English Army* (2 vols., London, 1801).

Hagger, M., *The Fortunes of a Norman Family: the de Verduns in England, Ireland and Wales, 1066-1316* (Dublin, 2001).

Handbook of British Chronology, ed. E.B. Fryde, D.E. Greenway, S. Porter and I. Roy, (3rd edn, London, 1986).

Harcourt, L.W.V., *His Grace the Steward* (London, 1907).

Heidemann, J., *Papst Clemens IV: Das Vorleben des Papstes und sein Legationregister* (Munster, 1903).

Hennings, M.A., *England under Henry III* (London, 1924).

Hershey, A.H., 'Success or Failure? Hugh Bigod and Judicial Reform during the Baronial Movement, June 1258–February 1259', *TCE*, v (1993), 65-87.

Hill, F., *Medieval Lincoln* (Cambridge, 1948).

Holt, J.C., *The Northerners* (Oxford, 1961).

—— 'The End of the Anglo-Norman Realm', in his *Magna Carta and Medieval Government* (London, 1985).

Hore, H.F., *History of the Town and County of Wexford* (6 vols., London, 1900-11).

Howell, M., *Eleanor of Provence* (Oxford, 1998).

Huscroft, R., 'Robert Burnell and the Government of England, 1270-1274', *TCE*, viii (2001), 59-70.

Itinerary of Edward I, ed. E.W. Safford (3 vols., List and Index Soc., 103, 132, 135, 1974-77).

Jacob, E.F., *Studies in the Period of Baronial Reform and Rebellion* (Oxford, 1925).

Kaeuper, R.W., *Bankers to the Crown: the Riccardi of Lucca and Edward I* (Princeton, 1973).

Keats-Rohan, K.S.B., 'Belvoir: The Heirs of Robert and Berengar de Tosny', *Prosopon*, 9 (1998).

Keefe, T.K., *Feudal Assessments and the Political Community under Henry II and His Sons* (Berkeley, 1983).

Knowles, D., and Hadcock, R.N., *Medieval Religious Houses* (London, 1953).

Knowles, M.D., *The Historian and Character* (Cambridge, 1963).

Kosminsky, E.A, *Studies in the Agrarian History of England in the Thirteenth Century* (Oxford, 1956).

Labarge, M.W., *A Baronial Household of the Thirteenth Century* (Brighton, 1965).

List of Sheriffs for England and Wales (HMSO, 1898).

Lloyd, J.E., *A History of Wales* (London, 1911).

Loyd, L.C., *The Origins of Some Anglo-Norman Families*, ed. C.T. Clay and D.C. Douglas (Harleian Soc., ciii, 1951).

Lyons, M.C., 'The Manor of Ballysax, 1280-86', *Retrospect*, new ser., i (1981), 40-50.

—— 'An Account of the Manor of Old Ross, September 1284–September 1285, parts I and II', *Decies*, xxviii–xix (1981-82), 33-40, 18-31.

McFarlane, K.B., 'Had Edward I a "Policy" towards the Earls?', *The Nobility of Later Medieval England* (Oxford, 1973), pp. 248-67.

Maddicott, J.R., *Thomas of Lancaster* (Oxford, 1970).

—— *Law and Lordship: Royal Justices as Retainers in Thirteenth- and Fourteenth-Century England* (Past and Present Supplement, 1978).

—— 'The Mise of Lewes, 1264', *EHR*, 98 (1983), pp. 588-603.

—— 'Magna Carta and the Local Community, 1215-1259', *Past and Present* (1984), pp. 25-65.

—— 'Edward I and the Lessons of Baronial Reform: Local Government, 1258-80', *TCE*, i (Woodbridge, 1986), 1-30.

—— *Simon de Montfort* (Cambridge, 1994).

—— '"An Infinite Multitude of Nobles": Quality, Quantity and Politics in the Pre-Reform Parliaments of Henry III', *TCE*, vii (1999), 17-46.

—— '"1258" and "1297": Some Comparisons and Contrasts', *TCE*, ix (Woodbridge, 2003), 1-14.

Madox, T., *The History and Antiquities of the Exchequer of England, 1066-1327* (2 vols., London, 1711).

Martin, T., *The History of the Town of Thetford in the Counties of Norfolk and Suffolk* (London, 1779).

Menuge, N.J., *Medieval English Wardship in Romance and Law* (Cambridge, 2002).

Mertes, K., *The English Noble Household 1250-1600* (Oxford, 1988).

Miller, E., 'War, Taxation and the English Economy in the Late-Thirteenth and Early-Fourteenth Centuries', *War and Economic Development: Essays in Memory of David Joslin*, ed. J.M. Winter (Cambridge, 1975), pp. 11-31.

Milles, T., *The Catalogue of Honor* (London, 1610).

Mills, J., 'Accounts of the Earl of Norfolk's Estates in Ireland, 1279-1294', *Journal of the Royal Soc. of Antiquaries of Ireland*, 4th ser., xxii (1892), 50-62.

Moor, C., *Knights of Edward I* (5 vols., Harleian Soc., 1929-32).

—— 'The Bygods, Earls of Norfolk', *Yorkshire Archaeological Journal*, 32 (1935), pp. 172-213.

Morant, P., *The History and Antiquities of the County of Essex* (3 vols., London, 1768).

Morgan, O. and Wakeman, T., *Notes on Wentwood, Castle Troggy and Llanvair Castle* (Monmouthshire and Caerleon Antiquarian Association, 1863).

Morris, J.E., *The Welsh Wars of Edward I* (Oxford, 1901).

Morris, M., 'The "Murder" of an English Earldom? Roger IV Bigod and Edward I', *TCE*, ix (2003), 89-99.

Muskett, J.J., *Suffolk Manorial Families* (3 vols., Exeter, 1902-8).

Nugent, W.F., 'Carlow in the Middle Ages', *Journal of the Royal Soc. of Antiquaries of Ireland.*, 4th ser., lxxxv, 62-76.

O'Keeffe, T., 'Ballyloughan, Ballymoon and Clonmore: Three Castles of c.1300 in County Carlow', *ANS*, xxiii (Woodbridge, 2001), 167-97.

O'Neill, T., *Merchants and Mariners in Medieval Ireland* (Dublin, 1987).

Ormrod, W.M., 'Love and War in 1294', *TCE*, viii (Woodbridge, 2001), 143-52.

Otway-Ruthven, J., 'The Medieval County of Kildare', *Irish Historical Studies*, vol. 11, no. 43 (1959), pp. 181-99.

The Oxford English Dictionary, ed. J.A. Simpson and E.S.C. Weiner (20 vols., 2nd edn, Oxford, 1989).

Painter, S., *William Marshal* (Baltimore, 1933).

—— *Studies in the History of the English Feudal Barony* (Baltimore, 1943).

Parsons, J.C., *Eleanor of Castile: Queen and Society in Thirteenth-Century England* (New York, 1995).

Pettifer, A., *Welsh Castles: A Guide by Counties* (Woodbridge, 2000).

Phillips, J.R.S., *Aymer de Valence, Earl of Pembroke* (Oxford, 1972).

—— 'The Anglo-Norman Nobility', *The English in Medieval Ireland*, ed. J. Lydon (Dublin, 1984), pp. 87-104.

Plucknett, T.F.T., *Legislation of Edward I* (Oxford, 1949).

Powicke, F.M., *King Henry III and the Lord Edward* (Oxford, 1947).

—— *The Loss of Normandy, 1189-1204* (2nd edn, Manchester, 1961).

—— *The Thirteenth Century, 1216-1307* (2nd edn, Oxford, 1962).

Prestwich, J.O., 'The Military Household of the Norman Kings', *EHR*, 96 (1981), pp. 1-35.

Prestwich, M.C., *War, Politics and Finance under Edward I* (London, 1972).

—— *Edward I* (London, 1988).

—— *Armies and Warfare in the Middle Ages: The English Experience* (New Haven, 1996).

Raby, F.J. and Reynolds, P.K.B, *Framlingham Castle* (London, 1959).

—— *Thetford Priory* (HMSO, 1979).

Ramsey, J.H., *The Dawn of the Constitution* (London, 1908).

Rees, W., *South Wales and the March, 1284-1415* (Oxford, 1924).

—— *South Wales and the Border in the Fourteenth Century* (4 sheets, Ordnance Survey, 1932).

Richardson, H.G., 'Year Books and Plea Rolls as Source of Historical Information', *TRHS*, 4th ser., v (1922), 28-70.

Ridgeway, H., 'The Lord Edward and the Provisions of Oxford (1258): A Study in Faction', *TCE*, i (1986), 89-99.

—— 'King Henry III and the "Aliens"', *TCE*, ii (1988), 81-92.

—— 'King Henry III's Grievances against the Council in 1261', *Historical Research*, 61 (1988), pp. 227-42

—— 'Foreign favourites and Henry III's problems of patronage, 1247-58', *EHR*, 104 (1989), pp. 590-610.

—— 'William de Valence and his *Familiares*, 1247-72', *Historical Research*, 65 (1992), pp. 239-57.

Robinson, D.M., *Tintern Abbey* (Cardiff, 2002).

Rogers, J.E.T., *History of Agriculture and Prices in England from 1259 to 1793* (7 vols., London, 1866-90).

Rothwell, H., 'The Confirmation of the Charters, 1297', *EHR*, lx, (1945), 16-35, 177-91, 300-15.

—— 'Edward I and the Struggle for the Charters, 1297-1305', *Studies in Medieval History presented to F.M. Powicke*, ed. R.W. Hunt, W.A. Pantin and R.W. Southern (Oxford, 1948), pp. 319-332.

Round, J.H., *The Commune of London and other Studies* (London, 1899).

—— *The King's Serjeants and Officers of State* (London, 1911).

St John Brooks, E., *Knights' Fees in Counties Wexford, Carlow and Kilkenny* (Dublin, 1950).

Sanders, I.J., *Feudal Military Service in England* (Oxford, 1956).

—— *English Baronies* (Oxford, 1960).

Saul, N., *Death, Art and Memory in Medieval England: The Cobham Family and their Monuments, 1300-1500* (Oxford, 2001).

Sayles, G.O., *Functions of the Medieval Parliament of England* (London, 1988).

Sharpe, R., *A Handlist of Latin Writers of Great Britain and Ireland before 1540* (Tournhout, 1997).

Sheehan, M.M., 'A List of 13th-century English Wills', *Genealogists' Magazine*, 13 (1961), pp. 259-65.

—— *The Will in Medieval England* (Toronto, 1963).

Shields, H., 'The Walling of New Ross: A Thirteenth-century Poem in French', *Long Room*, 12-13 (1976), pp. 24-33.

Simpson, G.G., 'The *Familia* of Roger de Quincy, Earl of Winchester and Constable of Scotland', *Essays on the Nobility of Medieval Scotland*, ed. K.J. Stringer (Edinburgh, 1985), pp. 102-30.

Stacey, R., *Politics, Policy and Finance under Henry III, 1216-1245* (Oxford, 1987).

Stalley, R., *Architecture and Sculpture in Ireland*, 1150-1350 (Dublin, 1971).

Stringer, K.J., *Earl David of Huntingdon 1152-1219 : A Study in Anglo-Scottish History* (Edinburgh, 1985).

Stubbs, W., *The Constitutional History of England* (3 vols., Oxford, 1880).

Sutherland, D.W., *Quo Warranto Proceedings in the Reign of Edward I* (Oxford, 1963).

Sweetman, D., *Medieval Castles of Ireland* (Woodbridge, 1999).

Tout, T.F., 'The Earldoms under Edward I', *TRHS*, 2nd ser., 8 (1894), pp. 129-55.

Treharne, R.F., *The Baronial Plan of Reform, 1258-63* (2nd edn, Manchester, 1971).

—— 'Why the Battle of Lewes Matters in English History', *Simon de Montfort and Baronial Reform* (London, 1986), pp. 77-170.

Tuck, A., *Richard II and the English Nobility* (London, 1973).

Turner, R., *Chepstow Castle* (Cardiff, 2002).

Victoria County History of England:

    Hampshire, iv, ed. W. Page (London, 1911).

    Norfolk, ii, ed. W. Page (London, 1906).

    Sussex, iv, ed. L.F. Salzman (London, 1953).

Vincent, N., *Peter des Roches: An alien in English politics, 1205-1238* (Cambridge, 1996).

Walker, R.F., 'The Supporters of Richard Marshal, Earl of Pembroke, in the Rebellion of 1233-1234', *Welsh History Review*, 17 (1994), pp. 41-65.

Wareham, A., 'The Motives and Politics of the Bigod Family, c. 1066-1177', *ANS*, xvii (Woodbridge, 1994), 223-42.

Waugh, S.L., 'From Tenure to Contract: lordship and clientage in thirteenth-century England', *EHR*, 111 (1986), pp. 811-39.

—— *The Lordship of England: Royal Wardships and Marriages in English Society and Politics, 1217-1327* (Princeton, 1988).

Weever, J., *Ancient Funerall Monuments* (London, 1631).

Willard, F., *Parliamentary Taxes on Personal Property, 1290-1334* (Cambridge, Mass., 1934).

Wood, S., *English Monasteries and their Patrons in the Thirteenth Century* (Oxford, 1955).

Woolgar, C.M., *The Great Household in Late Medieval England* (New Haven, 1999).

UNPUBLISHED THESES

Atkin, S.J., 'The Bigod Family and its Estates, 1066-1306' (Ph.D. thesis, Reading Univ., 1980).

Lyons, M.C., 'Manorial Administration and the Manorial Economy of Ireland, c. 1200–c. 1377' (Ph.D. thesis, Dublin, 1984).

Miller, R.G., 'The Bigod Brothers in Thirteenth-Century England, 1212-1270' (Ph.D. thesis, Mississippi State Univ., 1973).

Wade, M.M., 'The Personal Quarrels of Simon de Montfort and his Wife with Henry III of England' (B.Litt. thesis, Oxford Univ., 1939).

Wareham, A., 'The Aristocracy of East Anglia, c. 970–c. 1154' (Ph.D. thesis, Birmingham Univ., 1992).

Index

Printed and bound by CPI Group (UK) Ltd, Croydon, CR0 4YY

29/12/2024